Agriculture and the Great Depression

What role did the agricultural sector play in the economic crash of 1929? Taking evidence from country cases across Europe and the Americas, this edited volume explores short-, medium- and long-term perspectives on the primary sector.

The monograph brings together the voices of an international panel of contributors who examine issues such as falling prices, industrial production, unemployment and the stagnation of aggregate demand. Together, they frame the interwar period as a pivotal turning point in the decline of subsistence agriculture and the growth of agricultural subsidies, which remain a key policy tool in many economies today.

This illuminating book will be of interest to advanced students and researchers in economic history, agricultural history, globalization and economic development.

Gérard Béaur, CNRS & Ecole des Hautes Etudes en Sciences Sociales, Paris, France.

Francesco Chiapparino, Università Politecnica delle Marche, Dises (Dipartimento di scienze economiche e sociali), Ancona, Italy.

Perspectives in Economic and Social History
Series Editors: Andrew August and Jari Eloranta

Early Modern Overseas Trade and Entrepreneurship
Nordic Trading Companies in the Seventeenth Century
Kaarle Wirta

Credit and Debt in Eighteenth-Century England
An Economic History of Debtors' Prisons
Alexander Wakelam

Luxury, Fashion and the Early Modern Idea of Credit
Edited by Klas Nyberg and Håkan Jakobsson

The Nordic Economic, Social and Political Model
Challenges in the 21st Century
Edited by Anu Koivunen, Jari Ojala and Janne Holmén

North Eurasian Trade in World History, 1660–1860
The Economic and Political Importance of the Baltic Sea
Werner Scheltjens

A History of Cold War Industrialisation
Finnish Shipbuilding between East and West
Saara Matala

Social Cohesion and Welfare States
From Fragmentation to Social Peace
Edited by Christopher Lloyd and Matti Hannikainen

Agriculture and the Great Depression
The Rural Crisis of the 1930s in Europe and the Americas
Edited by Gérard Béaur and Francesco Chiapparino

For more information about this series, please visit www.routledge.com/series/PESH

Agriculture and the Great Depression

The Rural Crisis of the 1930s in Europe and the Americas

Edited by
Gérard Béaur and Francesco Chiapparino

Routledge
Taylor & Francis Group
LONDON AND NEW YORK

First published 2023
by Routledge
4 Park Square, Milton Park, Abingdon, Oxon OX14 4RN

and by Routledge
605 Third Avenue, New York, NY 10158

Routledge is an imprint of the Taylor & Francis Group, an informa business

British Library Cataloguing-in-Publication Data
A catalogue record for this book is available from the British Library

Library of Congress Cataloging-in-Publication Data
Names: Béaur, Gérard, editor. | Chiapparino, Francesco, editor.
Title: Agriculture and the Great Depression : the rural crisis of the 1930s in Europe and Americas / edited by Gérard Béaur and Francesco Chiapparino.
Description: Abingdon, Oxon ; New York, NY : Routledge, 2023. | Series: Perspectives in economic and social history | Includes bibliographical references and index.
Identifiers: LCCN 2022026433 (print) | LCCN 2022026434 (ebook) | ISBN 9780367615505 (hardback) | ISBN 9780367615529 (paperback) | ISBN 9781003105466 (ebook)
Subjects: LCSH: Agriculture—Economic aspects—Europe | Depressions—1929—Europe. | Agriculture—Economic aspects—America. | Depressions—1929—America.
Classification: LCC HD1917 .A375 2023 (print) | LCC HD1917 (ebook) | DDC 338.109409/042—dc23/eng/20220831
LC record available at https://lccn.loc.gov/2022026433
LC ebook record available at https://lccn.loc.gov/2022026434

ISBN: 978-0-367-61550-5 (hbk)
ISBN: 978-0-367-61552-9 (pbk)
ISBN: 978-1-003-10546-6 (ebk)

DOI: 10.4324/9781003105466

Typeset in Bembo
by codeMantra

Contents

List of figures ix
List of tables xi
List of contributors xiii

1 **Introduction – Agriculture and the Big Crash** 1
GÉRARD BÉAUR AND FRANCESCO CHIAPPARINO

PART I
The crisis in a long-term perspective 19

2 **The Great Depression as Great Transformation? Global food regime crisis and (inter-)national transition pathways, 1925–39** 21
ERNST LANGTHALER

3 **Agricultural crisis in Spain (Nineteenth and Twentieth centuries)** 39
VICENTE PINILLA

PART II
The mechanisms of the crisis 57

4 **The 1929 crisis from the perspective of a food-importing country – The United Kingdom, 1928–35** 59
PAUL BRASSLEY

5 **International markets, policy, and mobility. 'Rural Italies' in the 1930s recession** 77
FRANCESCO CHIAPPARINO AND GABRIELE MORETTINI

6 **From boom to burst – Argentine's primary sector and the 1930s Crisis** 97
JULIO DJENDEREDJIAN AND JUAN LUIS MARTIRÉN

7 **The effects of the Great Depression on the agricultural economy of the tobacco-exporting countries in South-eastern Europe** 115
SOCRATES D. PETMEZAS

8 **The 1929 crisis in Hungary's dual agriculture** 138
ZSUZSANNA VARGA

9 **The impact of the crisis on the Polish agriculture (1929–35)** 155
TADEUSZ JANICKI

PART III
The crisis and the policies 169

10 **Swedish agriculture and the crisis of the 1930s** 171
MATS MORELL

11 **Spanish agriculture and the Great Depression** 190
JUAN PAN-MONTOJO AND JAMES SIMPSON

12 **Mexican agriculture in view of the crisis of the first globalization – Between the revolutionary crisis and the Great Depression (1914–29)** 206
ALEJANDRO TORTOLERO VILLASEÑOR

13 **The problem of the wheat and the political answers to the agricultural crisis in France of the 1930s** 224
ALAIN CHATRIOT

14 **Agriculture in Switzerland and the crises of the 1920s and 1930s** 236
ANNE-LISE HEAD-KÖNIG

15 Conclusion – Agricultural crises and government responses during the interwar period in the Atlantic trading network 255
PRICE V. FISHBACK

Index 275

Figures

2.1	Agricultural world trade, 1929–37	23
2.2	World trade of wheat and wheat flour, 1929–37	25
2.3	Acreage, production, stocks and prices of wheat, 1923–32	27
2.4	Annual production volume and trade balance of wheat in the Soviet Union, 1924–38	31
2.5	Annual production volume and trade balance of wheat in the United States, 1924–38	32
2.6	Annual production volume and trade balance of wheat in Germany, 1924–38	34
5.1	GDP and added value in agriculture, Italy 1911–51	78
5.2	Workers per sector in Italy 1919–40	79
5.3	Wholesale price index 1928–38	79
5.4	Provincial clusters in Italian agriculture, 1929	82
5.5	National and international (import) wheat prices 1921–39	83
5.6	Wheat yields and cultivated areas 1929 and 1938	89
5.7	Variation in agricultural output of Afa (1929–36/7) and mobility (1931–6)	92
6.1	Total GDP and GDP per capita in Argentina (1890–1935)	99
6.2	Cultivated area and cereal production (main crops: wheat, corn, flax)	102
6.3	Labor productivity (LP) in agricultural and industrial sectors. Argentina, 1900–37	105
6.4	Agricultural GDP, compared to all other sectors. Argentina, 1890–1935	107
6.5	European immigration to Argentina (1900–30)	108
6.6	Construction GDP compared to all other sectors. Argentina, 1890–1935	109
7.1	Indexes of per capita GDP growth in the Interwar period	116
7.2	Aggregate export of oriental tobacco (in million US$) by country of origin and its aggregate share in the total exports of the three countries	118
7.3	Aggregated oriental tobacco exports (in thousand tons) and the share of exports in the aggregated volume of tobacco production of the preceding year	120

7.4 The price of imported unprocessed tobacco leaves in the US 121
7.5 The Foreign Trade of Greece, Bulgaria and Turkey 124
7.6 The price index in Greece, Bulgaria and Turkey 125
8.1a Population and the number of employees in agriculture 138
8.1b Share of agricultural employees 139
8.1c Population per 100 active agricultural employees 139
8.2 Land distribution in Hungary in 1935 140
8.3 Production of main cereals 143
8.4 Average yield of main cereals 143
8.5 The agricultural land area of Hungary by land use categories 144
8.6 The evolution of day labour wages in agriculture in Pengős 145
9.1 The borders of modern and interwar Poland and the areas of the former Prussian, Russian and Austrian partitions 156
9.2 Price indices of goods purchased and sold by the village ('price scissors'), 1928–37 161
9.3 Market consumption index in Poland for villages and cities (1929–36) 165
10.1 Value added of agriculture and manufacturing in Sweden 1900–1940 172
10.2 Sweden 1900–1940. Percentage share of employment and GDP of agriculture and manufacturing plus construction sectors 173
10.3 Index of agricultural prices 1918/19–1940/41 174
10.4 Index of agricultural prices 1923/24–1940/41 175
10.5 Profitability in the interwar years 176
10.6 Income development among Northern smallholders in Sweden 1923/24–1938/39, compared to wage development in agriculture 178
12.1 Bean production (1909–39) 211
12.2 Overall agriculture production, 1893–1944 212
14.1 Cereal for bread making 239
14.2 Changes in the milk uses 242
14.3 Condensed milk and cheese exports 245
14.4 Food prices 249

Tables

2.1 Composition of leading agricultural commodities, 1929–37 24
2.2 Exports of wheat and wheat flower by selected countries, 1924–38 26
2.3 Imports of wheat and wheat flour by selected countries, 1924–38 26
2.4 Import duties on wheat, 1926–36 28
4.1 UK imports as a percentage of total world exports 60
4.2 World and UK product price indices 61
4.3 UK import costs 62
4.4 Physical quantities of UK imports 63
4.5 Sources of imports 63
4.6 USA – production and exports 64
4.7 Crop areas and outputs in Great Britain 69
4.8 The grass area and livestock population in Great Britain 70
5.1 Gross salable agricultural product (Gsp) per hectare of Agrarian and forestry area (Afa) in the clusters of Italian agriculture, 1929 and 1936–37 84
5.2 Estimation of the Italian gross agricultural production per groups of crops and macro-areas 87
5.3 Population growth, mobility, and its 'efficiency' per cluster in Italy 1931–6 91
6.1 Investment and export growth (1900–39) 100
6.2 Annual growth rates (%) in the value of production factors, output, and TFP, Argentina, 1895–1937 103
6.3 Professions declared by adults aged 14 years and over, Argentina, 1914 108
7.1 The compound annual rate of change of the value of imports and exports of Greece, Bulgaria and Turkey, and their average trade surplus or deficit 123
7.2 Bulgaria: annual rates of change of main agricultural indexes 126
7.3 Turkey: the compound annual rates of change of basic indexes of agricultural production and acreage 128
7.4 Greece: the compound annual rates of change of basic indexes of agricultural acreage and production 129

7.5	Unprocessed tobacco imports in the US and German markets	131
7.6	Turkey: basic indexes of agricultural acreage and production	134
9.1	Agrarian structure in Poland in 1931	157
9.2	Income of agricultural farms in Poland 1929–36	159
9.3	The yield of the major field crops in Poland by regions (1926–30 and 1931–35)	163
9.4	Farm animals in Poland between 1929 and 1935	163
9.5	Market consumption index for villages and cities in Poland (1929–36)	165
10.1	Sweden 1933. Percentage of farms of different sizes with debts exceeding 75% and 100% of asset values	177
10.2	Sweden 1929–33. Bankrupt farmers, farm properties sold on executive auctions and total value of executively sold farm properties	177
11.1	The nature of Spanish regional farming in 1929/33	192
11.2	Regional occupational distribution of active male agricultural population, 1956	193
11.3	Spanish economic indicators for the early 1930s	193
11.4	Prices of agricultural products	194
11.5	Agricultural exports	195
12.1	Indices of agricultural production value, 1928–35	212
14.1	Butter production and butter imports	243
14.2	The quality of Swiss hard cheese	247
14.3	Comparisons of milk prices for cheese-making paid to the producers in three competing markets	248
14.4	Cheese exports	248
15.1	Real GDP per capita in the interwar era and farm shares of working population	258

Contributors

Gérard Béaur, CNRS & Ecole des Hautes Etudes en Sciences Sociales, Paris, France.

Paul Brassley, University of Exeter, UK.

Alain Chatriot, Sciences Po, Center for History at Sciences Po (CHSP), Paris, France.

Francesco Chiapparino, Università Politecnica delle Marche, Dises (Dipartimento di scienze economiche e sociali), Ancona, Italy.

Julio Djenderedjian, Universidad de Buenos Aires, Instituto Ravignani / Consejo Nacional de Investigaciones Científicas y Técnicas, Argentina.

Price V. Fishback, University of Arizona, USA and Stellenbosch University, South Africa.

Anne-Lise Head-König, Université de Genève, Switzerland.

Tadeusz Janicki, University of Adam Mickiewicz in Poznań, Poland.

Ernst Langthaler, Johannes Kepler University Linz, Austria.

Juan Luis Martirén, Universidad de Buenos Aires, Instituto Ravignani / Consejo Nacional de Investigaciones Científicas y Técnicas, Argentina.

Mats Morell, Uppsala University, Sweden.

Gabriele Morettini, Università Politecnica delle Marche, Dises (Dipartimento di scienze economiche e sociali), Ancona, Italy.

Juan Pan-Montojo, Universidad Autónoma de Madrid, Spain. Universidad de Zaragoza and Instituto Agroalimentario de Aragón (IA2), Spain.

Socrates D. Petmezas, University of Crete and Institute for Mediterranean Studies/FoRTH, Greece.

Vicente Pinilla, University of Zaragoza, Spain.

James Simpson, Universidad Carlos III de Madrid, Spain.

Alejandro Tortolero Villaseñor, UAM-Iztapalapa, Mexico.

Zsuzsanna Varga, Loránd Eötvös University, Hungary.

1 Introduction – Agriculture and the Big Crash[1]

Gérard Béaur and Francesco Chiapparino

The crisis of 1929 hit the stock market, banks, industry and society as a whole, but it was also indisputably an agricultural crisis. The fall in agricultural prices and the distress felt by farmers and the wider rural population has long been known. John Steinbeck's novel, *The Grapes of Wrath* (1939), shed abundant light on the shocking conditions in which American farmers and sharecroppers lived. There have been many studies devoted to this subject and the debate is still ongoing. Not everywhere, however: in France, for instance, the inter-war crisis and remedies proposed for it stimulated a considerable literature at the time, but since then, the study of rural societies in the inter-war period has drawn 'little interest… and this field was long left to Anglo-Saxon researchers' (Chatriot and Lynch, 2012: 11).

Yet since the 1980s that economic accident remains a much-debated topic. For that matter, was it even an accident, something that came out of a clear blue sky? Or had its path been prepared by worsening conditions in the preceding years? Did its origins lie earlier, in the shaky or poor health of the post-First World War agricultural sector? Had it developed over a long period of time, or was it a sudden, unpredictable and drastic event? And how, in broader terms, was it linked to the overall economic crisis? Was it responsible for the Great Depression in the years following 1929? Did it make that Depression worse? Or, on the contrary, were the two phenomena separate? Was the agricultural crisis a simple by-product of an economic crisis that struck at factories, businesses and banks, a marginal event with only tenuous links to that worldwide economic collapse?

To this first set of questions, historians and economists gave contrasting answers. Some had no doubts. From the outset, they insisted on the impact of local bank failures in the United States, caused by insolvent farmers, who found they could not pay off the immense debts they had incurred in previous years. The origins of the crisis were said to lie in the banking sector as a whole, where a cascade of bankruptcies led, by a process of osmosis, to general collapse (Lewis, 1949; Temin, 1976). Contributing to this primary factor, the farm income started to grow more slowly, and then fell, either before or during the crisis. Declining revenue, in turn, led to less consumption, particularly of industrial products, and shrinking rural investment. These two

DOI: 10.4324/9781003105466-1

combined phenomena had a knock-on negative effect that brought about the collapse of the economy (Madsen, 2001).

By contrast, other researchers have claimed that although agriculture was admittedly not in very good condition on the eve of the crisis, it was by no means responsible for setting off the recession (Federico, 2005a). There was no way in which the general gap between supply and demand had been created by an imbalance between agricultural overproduction and effective demand; nor could agriculture be blamed for bringing about the fall of the banking sector by capillary action. At the most, the state of agriculture may have made worse the stagnation of the 1930s, once the cataclysm got started.

With the crisis of 2008, the role of the timing and relative weight of the agricultural sector in the onset of the Depression came back unexpectedly to haunt historians (Delli Gatti et al., 2012). How can one contaminated sector of activity undermine an entire economy? Some American researchers, Joseph Stiglitz among them, have emphasised how hard it was in the 2008 crisis for people previously employed in industry to shift to the tertiary sector after losing their jobs (Stiglitz and Bilmes, 2012). Setting aside the shock produced by the 1929 stock market, which wreaked roughly as much damage as the collapse of the sub-prime mortgage market in 2008, they put the agricultural crisis at the heart of their analysis. The crisis of 2008, they explained, had 'freed' a flood of people who had previously held jobs in industry, who were now unemployed because of the decline of the secondary sector, but ill-suited for jobs in the service sector; this mismatch set off a seismic upheaval. Applied to the events of the 1930s, this analysis suggested that the crisis in agriculture was not an accidental aftershock to the Great Crisis but at least one of the conditions and perhaps ***the*** condition that had made it possible in the first place.

This was the academic context for a large international conference held at Ancona in 2015 with the aim of taking a new look at the problem of economic crises; its theme was *Large Scale Crises: 1929 vs 2008*. It demonstrated that the Great Depression of the 1930s was still worth studying, but it also displayed the reluctance or hesitation of historians, and particularly rural historians, to take a position on this question. Had they nothing to say on this crisis and on crises in general? We decided to take up the challenge and pulled together a group of historians to talk about the historiography of crises at two working sessions of the European Rural History Conference held in Leuven (Belgium) in 2017 and of the World Economic History Congress held in Boston (USA) in 2018. The present book emerged from the suggestions and discussions that cropped up in the course of this exploratory work.

1. A set of questions in a large set of countries

Putting the agricultural crisis at the heart, rather than on the fringes, of the 1929 crisis led us to take a fresh view of the problem. The idea was to make a sharp break with previous approaches, no matter how well-founded they might seem, by drawing on expertise from different countries with widely different historical experiences. This approach led us to make the choices seen here, and we accept responsibility for them.

Up to now, most work was based on the American case, which was taken as the starting point and model, but we did not want to make it the single focus of our analysis. Nor did we want to concentrate on any particular or favourite geographical zone. On the contrary, we wanted to widen the spectrum as much as possible by taking into account countries at different stages of development, particularly of agricultural development, with different methods of cultivation and different landholding structures, countries that went through indisputably different political events. In this way the spectrum was enlarged, as we anticipated, to include Great Britain, whose status as a habitual wheat importer makes it a special case, and also France and Italy, which are big, but far from self-sufficient, producers; Spain, and also Greece, Poland, Hungary, Sweden, and even Mexico and Argentina. We could have cast our net still further without exhausting all the possible models, but that would have run the risk of watering down the original set of questions.

Because of the wide range of contexts, some authors were asked to place the event in the longer term, and to recreate it within its peculiar economic or political setting, so as to avoid the trap of focussing so microscopically as to lose sight of any significance. Thus such highly significant historical 'accidents' as the Mexican Revolution, Fascism and the Battle of Wheat in Italy, the Popular Front in France and the Second Republic and Civil War in Spain, were brought into the discussion and there were many other such examples. It also became possible to emphasise the effects of the First World War on the belligerent countries and its possible disruptive effect on production and prices.

Starting from these specific cases and with this international perspective, several related questions arose that help define the scope of the enquiry.

The first is a need to understand how greatly the impact of the Depression varied from one country to another. Prices, we know, began to falter seriously from at least 1929 and sometimes before that point, as we shall see. Were all countries affected to the same extent? Did all agricultural products decline? Did the Depression hit both large and small holdings? What was the impact on production volume?

A few examples, to start with. Grain prices, we know, took a particularly hard hit; the United States became the textbook case: within two years the selling price of wheat fell by more than half. But did the same occur everywhere else? We also know that three years into the Depression, French grain prices were only a third of what they had been in 1929, but that in Great Britain the decline was less, around a quarter (Brassley, 2000)[2]. Clearly there was a difference between these three countries, even though they all faced the same difficult conditions. It matters therefore to look at these different reactions before trying to explain what happened in each case. Hidden behind the differences we find different timing. In two of these cases, the United

States and France, price movements had been bumpy; they peaked after the First World War before falling steeply in 1920–1, recovering and then starting to fall again in 1925–6[3]. By contrast, the United Kingdom once again proved an exception; it experienced a continual slippage only barely interrupted by a few upswings, bringing prices as low as those in other countries, but with a quite different timing (Brassley, 2000). It may be argued that each country thus managed to take the same path, or so it would seem, but at a different speed and with a different result.

Was grain simply an exception to a general rule? Once again, we have to look at the specific sequence of events for different products. Cotton dropped almost as much as wheat in the United States. Maize fell much less, remaining at a high price until the Depression began; beef prices, too, stayed high through the 1920s, not collapsing until after 1929[4]. We also have to examine different case studies within the context of overall collapse. In Italy, for example, we can find the same discrepancy between products[5]. Prices of olive oil and wine first showed signs of weakness in 1927 and sank to a third of their 1926 value in 1933. As for citrus fruits, only lemons held up until 1931, before falling in 1932 and 1933 (Mignemi, 2020). What products maintained their prices and for how long? Which ones escaped the general collapse?

Another question is the consequence of prices for production. Falling prices do not seem to have had much of an impact on grain harvests; rather the opposite: farmers, faced with declining prices, doggedly insisted on producing even more than before (Brassley, 2014). What about other products? Did not certain products flourish during the core years of the crisis and others decline? Finally, if we go beyond the macroeconomic view, how did producers' behaviour vary on different-sized holdings, with contrasting involvement in the market? How did the resulting impact differ from one region to another? American statistics show that the crisis was felt more severely in the Mid-West than in New England, to cite only one example. What were the different levels, and what readjustments to production systems followed in their wake? These are some of the points this book explores on the basis of available data.

The second big question is the relative importance of the agricultural sector and its ability to act as a macroeconomic lever on a global scale. By using our comparative approach, we were able to see clearly that its impact varied greatly. Once again, we can start with a few simple observations. Agriculture in England was relatively small, employing only 907,000 agricultural workers (not including farmers), or less than 10% of the British active population (Brassley, 2000)[6]. But in other countries between the wars many people were still employed in agriculture. France had 6 million permanent farm workers, or 40% of the workforce, without even counting temporary labour[7], and in Italy, they amounted to more than 50%[8]. It would be wrong to think that the United States was an exception to this rule. The American 'farm population' comprised 30 million people out of 120 million inhabitants, in other words a full quarter of the active population[9]. The collapse in the price of agricultural products notably grain, and particularly wheat, therefore had a devastating effect on farm income. More can be said about the American case, which is very well documented. Converted into dollars, the total 'cash income from farm marketings' fell in three years to half of its 1929 value and a third of what it had been in 1919[10]. There was an equally big gap between retail prices and farm sale prices[11]. Farm sales came to between 50 and 60% of the level of retail prices in the years after 1910, but only 33% in 1932. If we set the prices of all household consumer goods bought by farmers against all prices paid for agricultural products (using the table for 'Index numbers of prices paid by farmers. Commodities bought for family maintenance'[12]), the outcome is equally harsh (Federico, 2005a).

This 'price scissors' helps to understand not only how spending on consumer goods fell but how farm investments dried up. Thus in the United States, the value of agricultural machine and tractor purchases weakened in 1930 and collapsed in 1931. Overall, spending on equipment came first to a halt, and then fell rapidly[13]. Fertiliser usage also declined, by a quarter in 1931, and by half in 1932; it then began slowly to climb back but never again returned to its 1929 level[14]. Unquestionably, this precipitous loss of purchasing power affected the market for consumer products in general – and agricultural products in particular. The same was true of the engineering and chemical industries, where the shrinkage was inescapable. Another example of this could be seen in France in the consumption of nitrogen, phosphoric acid and potash, and mechanisation also marked time there (Sauvy, 1965). The real question is the magnitude of this negative impact, and whether it was similar everywhere else in the world.

The third question concerns the antecedents of the crisis, the abruptness of its onset and historians' reluctance to come to a verdict on the balance sheet of the 1920s. Consider the example of the United States again. Clearly, the price of American grain fell continually from 1925 onwards, just as it did in France and Italy. Then it finally collapsed: by the eve of the crisis prices had sunk to the very low levels of 1921-2. The fall in cotton prices in the United States was even more dire well before the crisis[15]. So the depression was already present, long before the actual crash; and its effects were already perceptible. On the basis of individual farms, in the United States the 'cash Income' 'from farm marketings' had already declined by over a third in the 1920s[16] and they never again reached the heights of 1918–20. To take a wider view, in the United Kingdom, things were worse still: in relation to their high point of 1920–2, net revenue per farm sank from 1924–9 onward, well before the Depression had begun (Brassley, 2014).

At the same time, however, outlays on equipment and operating expenses stayed very high through all of the 1920s. Here again, American statistics allow us to put figures on the levels of investment in both fertilisers and machinery (tractors, harvesters and the like). The expenses for tractors and other farming equipment kept going up through the same period[17]. Fertiliser purchases surged[18].

Obviously in these conditions, American farmers of the 1920s had no choice but to borrow massively[19]. Outstanding mortgage debt had been trending upward ever since 1910, when statistics first become available. It shot up during the war, reaching a peak in 1923–4: a tripling over a mere ten years. Other countries also experienced this euphoric post-war frenzy of investment and debt, in a period when prices were still surging impressively. When the tide turned it took the farmers by surprise, and the ebbing value of the property they had used to back their mortgages wreaked havoc. In the United States, the cost of land, which never stopped rising during the First World War, suddenly collapsed in 1920[20]. Though the decline stalled in subsequent years, land prices remained stuck at a third less than their earlier level. For instance the process was identical in the United Kingdom, as the price of land started to go down in 1926 and fell by a third by 1929 (Britton, 1949; Lloyd, 1992: Appendix A11, Table A5); and of course, rents followed (Rhee, 1949). The same was true in France although the fall came later (Caziot, 1952; Dumant, 1962).

The penalty came quickly, in the form of skyrocketing bankruptcies[21]. In the United States, in the decade after 1910, 1,000 to 2,000 failures a year had been the norm. They skyrocketed to more than 3,000 in 1922, then 6,000 in 1923 and 8,000 from 1924 to 1926, before falling back slowly to 5,000 from 1927, after the weakest farmers had been eliminated. These bankruptcies inevitably affected the banking system. Thousands of banks, particularly local banks, disappeared (Madsen 2001; Federico, 2005) in connection with the failures of their rural borrowers, swallowed up by mortgage debts (Thies and Gerlowski, 1993), which also made credit shortages worse.

On a first analysis, then, it appears that the agricultural crisis not only accompanied the general crisis of the economy, but also preceded it. Was this the case elsewhere or did the political and social context change the timeframe, accelerating or deviating the course of change? Should we agree with Federico, who seems to exonerate agriculture from all responsibility for setting off the crisis with this ambiguous judgement: 'the condition of American farmers was not terrible, although surely not very good' (Federico, 2005a)?

A fourth question concerns the impact of the American crisis on other countries. To what extent did the United States export their crisis? We should recall that American grain exports at the beginning of the 1920s made up no less than 30% of national production, sometimes more. However, this fell to 21.8% in 1927 and was still only at 15.6% in 1928[22]. From then onward the collapse accelerated. By 1934, wheat exports stood at virtually zero. No such extreme reversal had been seen in the course of the previous 50 years, if not longer.

There are four reasons why this pattern broke down. First, the successful efforts of the belligerents to increase production after the war. Second, the return of the Union of Soviet Socialist Republics to world markets after its retreat into wartime communism between 1918 and 1921[23]. Third, the redirection of British imports, to the extent that 'imperial preference' gradually became the rule after the mid-1920s[24]. And fourth, the spread of protectionism to other countries.

As an example of the serious impact of these changes we can take the fate of the Italian and French markets, respectively the third and fourth biggest importers of American grain from 1925 to 1929[25]. Now, producers in these countries had to put up with lower prices on their domestic markets, and the effect was aggravated by over-abundant harvests and their opening to world – essentially, American – production. This process continued and even worsened until the cereal imports to France were abruptly limited during the 1930s and a safety net provided for French producers by the Popular Front's *Office national interprofessionnel du blé* in 1936 (Chatriot, 2016). During the same period, the 'Battle of Wheat' waged by the Italian Fascist government from 1925 onward, was its own way of responding to the need to cut back on purchases of American grain (Mignemi, 2010 and 2020). Here is another theme of this book: the range of government policies and the reactions of all those who were affected by them.

Not surprisingly, an increasing share of US production remained on American soil; the resulting surplus certainly helped drive American prices even lower[26]. Grain was not the only crop affected in this way. American cotton suffered the same fate too, though the downward trend for this product was nothing new. The fall in cotton exports was a long-term trend, explainable by increased competition from 'new' countries, particularly India and Egypt[27], and from artificial textiles. Exports of American maize also fell off, but they had never amounted to much, only about 6% of national production in the 1920s; Argentina was a much more important supplier to the world market than the United States[28]. As American farmers produced less than 1% of world consumption, the impact of declining US exports was clearly less.

Here again, this collection provides an approach to comparing the changes that had an impact on producers. It does more than that, however. Though sinking US prices pushed down agricultural prices in other importing countries by a process of osmosis, the impact of their fall varied greatly, as a function of importers' dependence on American grain, and of the rate by which local supply expanded. Conversely, the sudden crash in the American economy, and the tariff and monetary policies adopted by all countries, inevitably had an impact on all the traditional exporters to the United States. Its gravity depended on the weight of each product in the exporting countries' GDP and on the size of their active population. In other words, we cannot understand the price fluctuations of a product widely integrated into the world market by myopically focussing only on its domestic market. Exploring twisted by-ways like these, by which the crisis penetrated the economy, is also a theme of this book.

The fifth and last question concerns the mobility of labour and the way the agricultural depression changed its spatial distribution. Here again, the United States provides a test case. We know that the flight from the countryside, which had been intense down to the 1920s, had already begun to slow down by 1929. This shows up clearly in the American statistics[29]. But they also show that chronic migration to the cities ceased with the upheaval of that year. In fact, the rural population began to grow once again, slowly to be sure, but definitely breaking the long-established pattern. Why? Naturally, increasing unemployment, as Giovanni Federico (2005a) explained, made industrial labour and urban living less attractive. But there is an alternative explanation. To return to Stiglitz's hypothesis: if migration to the towns were already slowing down and ultimately came to an eventual and ultimate standstill, might it have been because the jobs created in the 1920s did not match the profile of the potential migrants? And can this hypothesis be transplanted from the United States to other countries? More generally, what were the geographic trends in migration in other countries? Not only shifts towards the towns in search of jobs in the secondary or tertiary sectors, but inter-regional movements, and flows from one rural zone to another, in response to effects felt differently in different areas? Here is another avenue worth exploring.

2. A combination of different perspectives

This book is built on diverse timescales: the short-term with a focus on the crisis itself; the medium-term, which takes the reader into the pre-crisis years and then goes back to the beginning of the twentieth century; and finally, the long-term. These scales are sometimes focussed on separately by individual analyses, sometimes adopted together and blended on occasion to address specific issues.

The resulting chapters of the volume are divided up overall into three sections. The first consists of just two contributions and concerns the long-term perspectives in which the agricultural recession of the 1930s can be framed. In the first of these contributions, Ernest Langthaler focusses on a general comparison between the United States, the Union of Soviet Socialist Republics, and Germany, and echoes the Polanyi-inspired perspective and the more recent 'global food regimes' approach of Friedmann and McMichael (1989 and 2009); while in the second chapter, Vicente Pinilla analyses the rural crises in the Spain of the last two centuries from a point of view that is closely connected to neo-institutional sensitivity.

The second section presents the dynamics of the agricultural crisis of the 1930s in various national cases. In this sense, the evolution of the recession within what is substantially an importing country with a minor primary sector, such as Great Britain (analysed by Paul Brassley), is compared with the cases of a recently settled country and a large exporter, such as Argentina (by Julio Djenderedjian and Juan Luis Martirén), or with one, like Italy (by Francesco Chiapparino and Gabriele Morettini), which is still largely agricultural and rather, characterised by a mosaic of rural environments, with different productive vocations and different reactions to the crisis. A different point of view is that of Socrates Petmezas, who analyses the spread of the depression from a sectoral perspective, looking at the difficulties of a production segment strongly aimed at the international market such as that of tobacco in three countries between south-eastern Europe and the Near East, i.e., Greece, Bulgaria, and Turkey. Further chapters in this section concern two nations of the central east part of Europe. The first, presented by Zsuzsanna Varga, is that of Hungary, characterised by a composite agriculture, with a strong dualism between small peasant farming, largely of subsistence, and big properties, linked to the market and even industrial transformation. The second, by Tadeusz Janicki, regards a rather populous and still remarkably rural country, like Poland, where the crisis in general had a significant impact on the countryside.

While the contributions of the second section aim to provide a general reconstruction of the recession that also includes a discussion on the policies adopted during the crisis, in the third part of the volume, the ratio between these two types of analysis is reversed. Although an examination of the evolution of the primary sector is not lacking here, the focus is shifted to the policies implemented in the various national cases. The opposites from this point of view, in some ways, are represented respectively by the example of Sweden, analysed by Mats Morell, in which the convergence of socialists with peasant interests gave rise to almost half a century of stability and social-democratic hegemony, and the Spanish case, examined by Juan Pan and James Simpson, where instead, the conflicts generated by republican reforms – and in particular the clash with the rural property classes, including small farmers – paved the way to Civil War and fascism.

Not too far from this dialectic, the tormented history of agrarian reform in revolutionary Mexico oscillates between the intelligence with the large agrarian properties and the support for small and middle peasants in the interwar period. Up to the 1930s, as Alejandro Tortolero observes, the agreement of the Cárdenas government with the latter, laid the foundations for about 50 years of political and institutional continuity, although within the framework of a scarcely productive primary sector. On the other hand, the arrangements achieved in the 1930s are not significant only for the general social and political balance of the countries where they were adopted. Anne-Lise Head-König, for instance, also points out the composite phases and the technical sophistication of the regulatory policies implemented in a small country with specialised agriculture such as Switzerland. While Alain Chatriot presents all the complexity, even from a strictly economic perspective, of the wheat market regulation developed in the relatively short but nonetheless politically and socially decisive – season of the *Front Populaire* in France. Occasionally embedded in contexts of political and institutional continuity like in Sweden or Mexico, often in totally new regimes, the pivotal role played by agrarian policies and State intervention in the primary sector to face the recession of the 1930s will be largely confirmed after the Second World War. At least from the specific point of view of agriculture, it may well be the main legacy of the Big Crash to the following age.

3. The Great and the Long Depressions compared

These considerations are a good starting point to outline the long-term development hypothesis underlying many of the recent views on the agricultural crisis in the 1930s and the general evolution of the primary sector in the nineteenth and twentieth centuries. When we re-examine what used to be called the 'Long Depression', the one that spanned roughly the last three decades of the nineteenth century, we can see striking similarities with the Depression of the 1930s. Prices plunged everywhere in the same way, pulled down by the weight of the dominant cereal sector (Breton, Broder and Lutfalla, 1997), although there were some differences among the countries (O'Brien and Keyder, 1978). We know that England took a specific path. There was however the same crisis in agricultural revenues and it was all tied in a similar way to widespread economic Depression.

True, the impact was different and historians understood to be so. The Long Depression of 1873–96 was undoubtedly much less brutal: it was a slow-spreading crisis which rolled out over several decades. It was not tied to one resounding stock market crash but rather to specific and occasional failures in the financial system. It received maybe much less press coverage. The epicentre of the crisis, the United States, did not witness the crushing unemployment that so struck people's imagination in the 1930s. And because worldwide exchanges were less developed, it did not take on the same international dimension due to less successful globalisation of trade. There were also two other size differences which gave pace to a part of explanations.

First of all, though American industry was solidly into the process of expansion, the American financial system did not carry as much weight in the economy as it later did. Second, the agricultural crisis was less intense. On this last point, we should recall that among the major factors generating the crisis (leaving aside for the moment the long string of local bank failures), was an imbalance between supply and demand, but in 1929 this imbalance was aggravated by the collapse of American exports, specially wheat exports. Nothing like that happened in the last three decades of the nineteenth: American exports did not really decline[30], despite the protectionist measures being brought almost everywhere (Golob, 1944; Aldenhoff-Hübinger, 2002, 2005). La mécanisation de la production, l'efficacité des réseaux de transport et des procédés de transbordement des grains (les *elevators*) abaissèrent les coûts de telle façon qu'ils déprimèrent les prix des pays européens importateurs, déjà confrontés à une montée, certes irrégulière, mais une montée quand même de la productivité de leurs exploitations. C'est en cela qu'on peut parler du « Grand tournant de 1878–80 (Sigaut, 2004).

4. From one Depression to another

In this sense, and from the specific point of view of the primary sector, the Great Depression of the last 30 years of the nineteenth century and the Big Crash of 1929, despite their diversity and separateness, belong to, or at least can in any case be framed within an identical historical structural dynamic: the progressive – and sometimes spectacular – growth of agriculture productivity from the nineteenth century (or even from the agricultural revolution of the previous eighteenth century) onwards and the related trend to the fall of agricultural prices.

After the upheavals caused by the First World War and the difficulties of the early 1920s, the evolution of productivity reaches a point, with the recession of the 1930s, beyond which agricultural production can be carried out profitably only with the support of dedicated economic policies. To survive, the primary sector needs specific measures such as subsidies, custom protections, designation of origin quality assurance labels (such as indication of geographical typicality and controlled designation of origin) and other kinds of valorisation schemes, or, at a microeconomic level, peculiar marketing strategies, like, for instance, specific brand and promotion policies or strict integration with food productions that enhance rural productions. Such circumstances even involve the highly productive US agriculture sector, which, for many respects, is one of the main promoters of the productivity growth in the primary sector of the previous decades. As the perspective of food regimes stresses, the American mass production of cereals is one of the main beneficiaries of the system of humanitarian aids distribution and other stock management schemes aiming to absorb overproduction after the Second World War (Friedmann and McMichael 1989).

At the same time, from a very different viewpoint, Federico underlines the new relevance that agricultural policies take on, starting from the 1930s and the continuity of this centrality with the crucial role assumed by State intervention in post-war agriculture, firstly in the European Community context (Federico, 2005b and 2012). Although framing the agricultural depression of the 1930s in very different visions – the crisis of the previous global food regime centred on the British imperial interests for the former, a recession (probably) imported from the industrial sector in that of Federico (2005a) -, both perspectives converge on assessing the new centrality assumed by rural policies with the 1930s. Almost all the contributions of this book dedicate part, and sometimes the main part, of their analyses to these policies and the new role they assumed as a consequence of the crisis; as well as this, the conclusions of the book are centred on this aspect.

As already mentioned briefly, Stiglitz and his coauthors add some further elements to this shared picture of the general evolution of agriculture between the late nineteenth and the first half of the twentieth century. Considering it from the viewpoint of dual development mechanisms *à la* Lewis, they stress how agriculture was characterised by an outflow of employees in parallel with the growth of its productivity. During the Long Depression of the late nineteenth century, the first globalisation allowed for elevated labour mobility, reallocating rural manpower to developing manufacturing sectors or to the new, high yield agriculture outside Europe. However, when international migration stopped, during the mid-20s, the workforce often remained trapped in the primary sector, now a mature sector characterised by high productivity and stagnant returns. The low incomes resulting from this entrapment, as well as all the other difficulties due to the sharp drop in prices, and sometimes even the reverse migratory dynamics from market to subsistence rural economies, depressed aggregate demand and in this way, had a significant impact on the global recession of the 1930s.

It is important to underline at least three aspects of this hypothesis, which are discussed recurrently in the chapters of this book.

First, at least as regards agriculture, this vision allows us to link the long depression of the end of the nineteenth century and the crisis of the 1930s to part of a unique process of maturation of the primary sector, making them for many respects more intelligible.

Second, it has to be stressed that, among the possible roles played by agriculture in the 1929 recession, this reconstruction does not assign the primary sector the role of triggering the crisis, but mainly only that of enforcing, deepening and prolonging the depression.

Finally, it cannot be denied that this analysis is aimed at identifying common mechanisms with – and therefore drawing lessons for – the other great modern recession comparable to that of '29, the sub-prime crisis of 2007–8. The lack of outflow of labour from the mature primary sector towards the developing manufacturing sector delays and dramatically worsens the crisis, just as it did in the 1930s, so in 2008 the trapping of workers in the now mature manufacturing sectors (as opposed to the advanced tertiary sector and knowledge economy) hinders recovery.

From this point of view, too, a question arises about policies and specifically concerns the reallocation of the workforce from mature to new, developing sectors. In this regard, it should be added that the economic policy interventions were largely inadequate in this sense, and indeed, as we have said, they aimed at relaunching the primary sector rather than abandoning it. It is therefore comprehensible that from this specific, perspective of the entrapment of the workforce, the only way out of the recession at the end of the 1930s was the war and the massive redistribution of labour it produced, absorbing unemployment (and also maybe what can often be referred to, at least in the European countryside, as rural underemployment) and therefore providing a boost for manufacturing productions. The discussion of this hypothesis among economists and historians, with all its actualising implications, has played an important role in the origin of this book. Verified or not, it has in any case the merit of stimulating thought and suggesting original perspectives in an attempt to put together the puzzle of the great economic crises of the modern world and that of 1929 in particular.

Conclusion

As we have just noted, the parallel is easy to make between the two depressions since both hit agriculture as well as the other sectors of the economy, and this brings us back to the same problem *which may come back in force: was agriculture at the origin of the crises or was it only either an aggravating* factor or even a disjointed phenomenon? Can we broaden the question by enlarging the focus and examining the various stages by which previous crises occurred in the past?

If there is a debate that has agitated historians for years, it is indeed the responsibility of the agricultural crises in the industrial slump in the old economies. Let's recall that the famines (see Béaur, 2000, ch. VIII; Chevet, 2004; Béaur, Chevet, O'Grada and Pérez-Picazo, 2011; Alfani and O'Grada, 2017; Béaur and Chevet, 2017) and these 'agrarian crises' (Abel, 1974).have been for many years the hobbyhorse of a whole French historical school (see, for instance, Meuvret, 1946; Goubert, 1960 and many others), after the work of Ernest Labrousse published nearly a century ago (Labrousse, 1933, 1944). Theses crises became later a battleground for a lot of historians (Lemarchand, 1996; Morineau, 1996) and they gave rise to countless studies on the demographic and social consequences of food shortages all over Europe (Appleby, 1979; O'Grada, 1995, 2009; Jover-Avellá, 2011; Hoyle, 2013).

Following on Labrousse who put these *crises agraires* at the heart of his interpretation of economic crises, the existence of 'contrary trends' (*Contrariété tendancielle*) between agricultural prices and industrial activity, historians then fiercely disputed and intensely debated the existence of these causal links as well for the eighteenth century (Gould, 1962; Perrot 1984; Simonin, 1990, 1992 vs Landes, 1950; Weir, 1991), as for the nineteenth century (Vivier, 2011). We may argue that such a causal relationship was central to the interpretation of crises, even though it was again and again debated and sparked intense debate among historians.

There was however an enormous difference between those distant crises and the one that occurred in 1929. The old crises were crises of food supply, caused by price surges set off by insufficient harvests (Lachiver, 1991; Alfani, 2011; Morell, 2011). These dearths (*chertés*) were thought to have affected the demand for industrial goods, sending artisan and manufacturing activities into a slump and thereby creating unemployment. It was no longer the case afterwards. In the course of the nineteenth century (except in wartime) these old-style agricultural crises disappeared, at least in Europe and in industrialised countries, where they gave way to the new-style crises typified by those of 1880 and 1929 (Lhomme, 1970; Collins, 2000).

But it would be wrong to think that the older sort of crisis is a thing of the past and that we are dealing with two strictly chronologically dated sequences. We still come face to face on occasion with food shortages and famines, stark and unbearable. Conversely, former times also witnessed demand crises, when harvests waxed over-abundant. Recurring crises of oversupply, like those of 'the big ears' (les *gros épis*) that marked France between the 1660s and the 1680s (Le Roy Ladurie and Goy, 1972: 362) and came back again to haunt the country after the French Wars in the 1820s provide ample instances of this. Thus, these two forms of crisis are not just a thing of the past. They still continue to coexist, and have similar effects. The collapse of prices or their soaring generate the same catastrophes. They are more or less widespread depending on the time and on the place, on the greater or lesser weight of agriculture in the economy, and on the degree of development attained by the manufacturing sector.

Notes

1 Translation for the French part by Judith Le Goff with the support of the Centre de Recherches Historiques.

2 For France, INSEE, Direction de la statistique générale, *Annuaire Statistique, 1946, Résumé rétrospectif. Agriculture, Forêts, Pêche, Froment, seigle, avoine*, Imprimerie nationale, 1947, table II: 80; Statistics from Ministry of Agriculture, Fischeries and Food (MAFF), 1968: 85.

3 United States Department of Agriculture (USDA), Agricultural Statistics, 1941: 10, table 1; INSEE, *Annuaire Statistique... Résumé rétrospectif. Agriculture,...*, table II.

4 USDA, *Agricultural Statistics*, 1941: 10, Table 1 (wheat); 64, Table 49 (maize); 117, Table 151 (cotton); 409, Table 552 (beef).

5 Instituto Centrale di Statistica, *Sommario ... Prezzi. Prezzi al' ingrosso. Prodotti agricole e forestali:* 110-111, tavola 88.

6 Paul Bolton, Carl Baker, Matthew Keep, 2015, Social & General Statistics, Agriculture: Historical statistics Standard Note: SN/SG/3339. 857,000 in 1930.

7 *Statistique agricole de la France publiée par le Ministère de l'agriculture. Direction de l'agriculture. Résultats généraux de l'enquête de 1929,* Tableau récapitulatif de le main d'œuvre permanente utilisée dans les exploitations agricoles et viticoles, p. 566-567.

8 Istituto Centrale di Statistica, *Sommario ..., Populazione, Stato dela populazione. Populazione residente, attiva e non attiva ai censimenti, Populazione residente in condizione professionale per settore di arrività economica*, p.13, Table 4b.

9 USDA, 1941, p. 545, Table 678.

10 *Ibid.*, p. 554, Table 685.

11 Farm-to-retail price spreads for 58 foods combined. *Ibid.*, p. 582, Table 708.

12 USDA, 1941, p. 555, Table 687.

13 USDA, 1936, p. 338, Table 444.

14 UDSA, 1936, p. 397, Table 511 and 1941, p. 697, Table 814.

15 USDA, 1941, p. 117, Table 151 (market price per pound in New York and New Orleans).

16 *Ibid.* p. 554, Table 685.

17 *Ibid*, p. 566, Table 696.

18 USDA, 1936, p. 338, Table 444.

19 USDA, 1941, p. 594, Table 720.

20 *Ibid.*, p. 583, Table 710 (index numbers of estimated value per acre).

21 USDA, 1936, p. 354, Table 460.

22 USDA, 1941, p. 10, table 1.

23 *Ibid.*, p. 15, Table 5.

24 The redirection of this trade flow by the country that had long been by far the largest importer of American grain had a radical effect. Though American grain (and flour) made up 37.9% of British imports in 1922 it only comprised 20.6% in 1929 and 0.1% in 1933 (compared to 67.5% for the Dominions in that year). Once again, the commercial readjustment initiated by the United Kingdom took place mostly before the crisis and the rearrangements that it brought about.

25 USDA, 1941, p. 32, Table 26. True, the amounts were, respectively, four and three times less than the amount of American exports to the United Kingdom.

26 *Ibid.*, p. 117, Table 151.

27 *Ibid.*, p. 119, Table 153. The data for Egypt and India are also taken from the American statistics.
28 *Ibid.*, p. 48, Table 49 and p. 64, Table 71.
29 USDA, 1941, p. 545, Table 678.
30 USDA, 1941, p. 9, Table 1.

Bibliography

Abel, W., 1974, *Crises agraires en Europe (XIIIe–XXe siècles)*, Paris: Flammarion [*Agrarkrisen und Agrarkonjunktur in Mitteleuropa vom 13. bis zum 19. Jahrhundert*, Berlin–Hamburg: Habilitationsschrift, 1935].

Aldenhoff-Hübinger, R., 2002, *Agrarpolitik und Protektionismus: Deutschland und Frankreich im Vergleich 1879–1914*, Göttingen: Verlag Vandenhoeck & Ruprecht.

Aldenhoff-Hübinger, R., 2005, 'Deux pays, deux politiques agricoles? Le protectionnisme en France et Allemagne (1880–1914)', *Histoire & Sociétés Rurales*, 23/1, pp. 65–87.

Alfani, G., 2011, 'The Famine of the 1590s in Northern Italy. An Analysis of the Greatest 'System Shock' of Sixteenth Century', in G. Béaur and *al*, *Histoire et Mesure*, XXVI/1, pp. 17–50.

Alfani, G. and O'Grada, C. (eds), 2017, *Famine in European History*, Cambridge: Cambridge University Press.

Appleby, A., 1979, 'Grain Prices and Subsistence Crisis in England and France (1590–1740)', *Journal of Economic History*, 39/4, pp. 865–887.

Béaur, G., 2000, *Histoire agraire de la France au XVIIIe siècle. Inerties et changements dans les campagnes françaises à la fin de l'époque moderne (jusqu'en 1815)*, Paris: SEDES.

Béaur, G. and Chevet, J.-M., 2017, 'France', in G. Alfani and C. O'Grada (eds), *Famine in European History*, Cambridge: Cambridge University Press, pp. 73–100.

Béaur, G., Chevet, J.-M., O'Grada, C. and Perez-Picazo, M. T. (eds), 2011, *Revisiter les crises*, special issue of *Histoire et Mesure*, XXVI/1.

Brassley, P., 2000, 'Output and Technical Change in Twentieth-Century British Agriculture', *The Agricultural History Review*, 48/1, pp. 60–84.

Brassley, P., 2014, 'Agricultural Output, Costs and Incomes in the United Kingdom, 1919–1940', in J.-M. Chevet et G. Béaur (eds), *Measuring Agricultural Growth: Land and Labour Productivity in Western Europe from the Middle Ages to the Twentieth Century (England, France and Spain)*, Turnhout: Brepols, Corn series 15, pp. 181–191.

Breton, Y., Broder, A. and Lutfalla, M. (eds), 1997, *La Longue stagnation en France. L'autre grande dépression, 1873–1897*, Paris: Économica.

Britton, D. K., 1949, 'The Sale Value of Farm Land Between the Wars', *The Farm Economist*, VI/1, pp. 125–133.

Caziot, P., 1952, *La valeur de la terre en France. Expertises rurales et forestières*, Paris: Baillière.

Chatriot, A., 2016, *La politique du blé. Crises et régulations d'un marché dans la France de l'entre-deux-guerres*, Paris: IGPDE/CHEFF.

Chatriot, A. and Lynch, E., 2012, 'Introduction', in A. Chatriot, E. Leblanc, and E. Lynch (eds), *Organiser les marchés agricoles. Le Temps des fondateurs*, Paris: Armand Colin, pp. 9–26.

Chevet, J.-M., 2004, 'Revisiting Subsistence Crisis: The Characteristics of Demographic Crisis in France in the First Half of the 19th Century', *Food & Foodways*, 12/2–3, pp. 165–195.

Collins, J.T., (ed.), 2000, *Agrarian History of England and Wales*, VII, 1850–1914.

Delli Gatti, D., Gallegati, M., Greenwald, B.C., Russo, A. and Stiglitz, J. E., 2012, 'Mobility Constraints, Productivity Trends, and Extended Crisis', *Journal of Economic Behavior & Organization*, 83/3, pp. 375–93.

Dumant, M., 1962, *Ce que vaut la terre en France*, Paris: Hachette.

Federico, G., 2005a, 'Not Guilty? Agriculture in the 1920s and the Great Depression', *The Journal of Economic History*, 65/4, pp. 949–76.

Federico, G., 2005b, *Feeding the World. An Economic History of Agriculture, 1800–2000*, Princeton: University Press.

Federico, G., 2012, 'Natura Non Fecit Saltus: The 1930s as the Discontinuity in the History of European Agriculture', in P. Brassley, Y. Segers, L. Van Molle (eds), *War, Agriculture, and Food. Rural Europe from the 1930s to the 1950s*, New York: Routledge, pp. 15–32.

Friedmann, H. and McMichael, P., 1989, 'Agriculture and the State System. The Rise and Decline of National Agricultures, 1870 to the Present', *Sociologia Ruralis*, 29/2, pp. 93–117.

Golob, E.O., 1944, *The Méline Tariff: French Agriculture and Nationalist Economic Policy*, New York: Columbia University Press, Studies in History, Economics and Public Law, 506.

Goubert, P., 1960, Beauvais et le Beauvaisis de 1600 à 1730. Contribution à l'histoire sociale de la France au XVIIe siècle, Paris, Ecole pratique des Hautes-Etudes, VIe section, S.E.V.P.E.N.

Gould, J.D., 1962, 'Agricultural Fluctuations and the English Economy in the Eighteenth Century', *Journal of Economic History*, 22/3, pp. 313–333.

Hoyle, R. W., 2013, 'Why Was There No Crisis in England in the 1690s?' in R. W. Hoyle (ed.), *The Farmer in England, 1650–1980,* pp. 69–100.

Jover-Avellá, G., 2011, 'Population, Subsistence Crisis and Agrarian Change in the Island of Majorca, 1560–1650', *Histoire & Mesure*, XXVI-1, pp. 51–74.

Labrousse, E., 1933, *Esquisse du mouvement des prix et des revenus en France au XVIIIe siècle*, Paris: Librairie Dalloz.

Labrousse, E., 1944, *La crise de l'économie Française à la fin de l'Ancien Régime et au début de la Révolution*, Paris: PUF.

Lachiver, M., 1991, *Les Années De Misère. La Famine Au Temps Du Grand Roi, 1680–1720*, Paris: Fayard.

Landes, D., 1950, 'The Statistical Study of French Crises', *The Journal of Economic History*, 10/2, pp. 195–211.

Lemarchand, G., 1996, 'A propos de l'article de M. Morineau', *Annales historiques de la Révolution française*, 303, pp. 109–112.

Le Roy Ladurie, E. and Goy, J., 1972, 'Première esquisse d'une conjoncture du produit décimal et domanial. Fin du Moyen Age-XVIIIe siècle', in J. Goy and E. Le Roy Ladurie (eds.), *Les fluctuations du produit de la dîme. Conjoncture décimale et domaniale de la fin du Moyen Age au XVIIIe siècle*, Paris: EPHE et Mouton, pp. 334–374.

Lewis, W.A. 1949, *Economic Survey, 1919–1939*, London: George Allen & Unwin.

Lhomme, J., 1970, 'La crise agricole à la fin du XIXème siècle en France: essai d'interprétation économique et sociale', *Revue Economique*, 21/4, p. 521–553.

Lloyd, T., 1992, *Present Value Models of Agricultural Land Prices in England and Wales*, PhD thesis, University of Nottingham, UK.

Madsen, J. B., 2001, 'Agricultural Crises and the International Transmission of the Great Depression', *The Journal of Economic History*, 61/2, pp. 327–365.

McMichael, P., 2009, 'A Food Regime Genealogy', *The Journal of Peasant Studies*, 36/1, pp. 139–169.

Meuvret, J., 1946, 'Les crises de subsistances et la population de la France d'Ancien Régime', *Population*, I/4, pp. 643–650.

Mignemi, N., 2010, *Nel regno della fame. Il mondo contadino italiano fra gli anni Trenta e gli anni Cinquanta*, Roma: Aracne Editrice.

Mignemi, N., 2020, 'The Battle of Wheat and Other Fascist Battles in Italian Agriculture (1920s–1930s)', in G. Béaur (ed.), *Alternative Agriculture in Europe (Sixteenth-Twentieth Centuries)*, Turnhout: Brepols, Rural History in Europe, 16, pp. 167–191.

Morell, M., 2011, 'Subsistence Crises during the *Ancien* and *Nouveau Régime* in Sweden? An Interpretative Review', in G. Béaur et al. (eds), *Histoire & Mesure*, XXVI/1, pp. 105–134.

Morineau, M., 1996, 'Esquisse et crise. Une relecture nécessaire d'Ernest Labrousse', *Annales historiques de la Révolution française*, 303, pp. 77–107.

O'Brien, P.K. and Keyder, C, 1978, *Economic Growth in Britain and France (1870–1914): Two Paths to the Twentieth Century*, London: Allen & Unwin.

O'Grada, C., 1995, *The Great Irish Famine*, Cambridge: Cambridge University Press.

O'Grada, C., 2009, *Famine: A Short History*, Princeton: Princeton University Press.

Perrot, J.-C., 1984, 'L'analyse dynamique des crises au XVIIIe siècle', *in La France d'Ancien Régime. Études réunies en l'honneur de Pierre Goubert*, t. 2, Toulouse: Privat, pp. 543–551.

Rhee, H.A., 1949, *The Rent of Agricultural Land in England and Wales, 1870–1946*, London, Central Landowner Association.

Sauvy, A., 1965, *Histoire économique de la France entre les deux guerres*, Paris: Fayard.

Simonin, J.-P., 1990, 'Les fluctuations des marchés des grains à l'époque moderne', *Histoire & Mesure*, V/3–4, pp. 181–211.

Simonin, J.-P., 1992, 'La crise d'Ancien Régime: un essai de justification théorique', *Histoire & Mesure*, VIÍ-3/4, pp. 231–247.

Stiglitz, J. E. and Bilmes, L. J., 2012, 'The Economic Crisis. The Book of Jobs', Vanity Fair.

Temin, P., 1976, *Did Monetary Forces Cause the Great Depression?*, New York: Norton.

Thies, C. and Gerlowski, D., 1993, 'Bank Capital and Bank Failure, 1921–1932. Testing the White Hypothesis', *The Journal of Economic History*, 53/4, pp. 908–911.

Sigaut, F., 'Le grand tournant de 1878–1880', unpublished paper, http://www.francois-sigaut.com/index.php/publications-diverses/publications/12-articles-fond/286-2004c.

Vivier, N., 2011, 'Pour un réexamen des crises économiques du XIXe siècle en France', *Histoire & Mesure*, XXVI/1, pp. 135–156.

Weir, D.R., 1991, 'Les crises économiques et les origines de la Révolution Française', *Annales ESC*, 4, pp. 917–947.

Part I

The crisis in a long-term perspective

2 The Great Depression as Great Transformation? Global food regime crisis and (inter-)national transition pathways, 1925–39

Ernst Langthaler

1. Introduction

In his social-scientific classic *The Great Transformation*, Polanyi makes a strong argument about the development of global capitalism:

> In the early thirties, change set in with abruptness. Its landmarks were the abandonment of the gold standard by Great Britain; the Five-Year Plans in Russia; the launching of the New Deal; the National Socialist Revolution in Germany; the collapse of the League in favor of autarchist empires. While at the end of the Great War nineteenth-century ideals were paramount, and their influence dominated the following decade, by 1940 every vestige of the international system had disappeared and, apart from a few enclaves, the nations were living in an entirely new international setting'.
>
> (Polanyi, 2001: 24)

Accordingly, during the Great Depression, state-led counter-movements to the laissez-faire marketization of society – including Soviet Socialism, the US New Deal and German Fascism – emerged and fundamentally changed the direction of capitalist development. The self-regulating global market that had been dis-embedded from society in the nineteenth century was re-embedded by interventionist nation states as diverse as the Soviet Union under Stalin, the United States under Roosevelt and Germany under Hitler in the early twentieth century, so the story goes (Polanyi, 2001). Whereas Polanyi's grand narrative has been controversially discussed at length (Dale, 2010: 45–88), its agrarian implications have gained less attention. This chapter adopts a Polanyian perspective for investigating the impacts of the Great Depression on the crisis of the global food regime as well as international and national transition pathways with a focus on those countries that feature most prominently in *The Great Transformation*: the Soviet Union, the United States and Germany.

For this purpose, two complementary approaches – food regime theory and transition theory – are applied. Food regime theory combines world-systems

DOI: 10.4324/9781003105466-3

analysis and regulation theory with regard to agriculture and food. It comprises three interrelated elements: first, value extraction and accumulation along transnational commodity chains; second, the regulation of commodity chains by formal and informal institutions and their actors (nation states, transnational companies, social movements, etc.); third, the social and environmental relations of food production, distribution and consumption. Among the food regimes since the onset of globalization, two are most relevant here: the British-centered or 'extensive' food regime (1870–1929)was built upon grain and meat flows from farming families in overseas settler colonies to working-class households in industrialized Europe in the institutional framework of bilateral free-trade contracts and the international gold standard. The US-centered or 'intensive' food regime (1947–73) combined the deposition of US surplus feeding stuffs in Western Europe and Japan as well as US surplus grains in the 'Third World' in the institutional framework of the General Agreement of Tariffs and Trade and the Bretton Woods System (Friedmann, 2005; McMichael, 2013; Magnan, 2012; Krausmann and Langthaler, 2019; Tilzey, 2019).

As a complement to food regime theory, transition theory conceptualizes the transformation of one food regime into another as interaction of multiple levels: niche, regime and landscape. If exogenous trends and shocks from the landscape – in our case, the Great Depression – or endogenous tensions destabilize the old regime and plunge it into crisis, technical and social innovations may break out of the niche and enter a new regime. Since transitions are contested among actors, they may also be incomplete or fail (Geels and Schot, 2007). The empirical basis of this theoretical framework comprises contemporary publications related to the International Institute of Agriculture in Rome (Bacon and Schloemer, 1940; Taylor and Taylor, 1943) and other experts and organizations dealing with agriculture in the Great Depression (League of Nations, 1931; Timoshenko, 1933; Hevesy, 1940).

2. Commodity flows

2.1 Agricultural trade

The world market for agricultural commodities that had come under pressure from the mid-1920s onwards was strongly affected by the Great Depression and vice versa. Trade volumes decreased by 22% from 1929 to 1934. Even more dramatic was the post-1925 pressure on market prices, with values per unit continuing to fall by 63% from 1929 to 1934. Due to diminishing volumes and prices, trade values deteriorated by 67% until 1934 and reached minus 57% of the 1929 level until 1937 (see Figure 2.1). The contractions of agricultural and non-agricultural trade in the Great Depression were similarly dramatic with regard to trade values but differed in other ways: while values per unit of agricultural trade fell steeper after 1929 (minus 57%, compared to minus 45%, on average in 1931–7), non-agricultural trade volumes

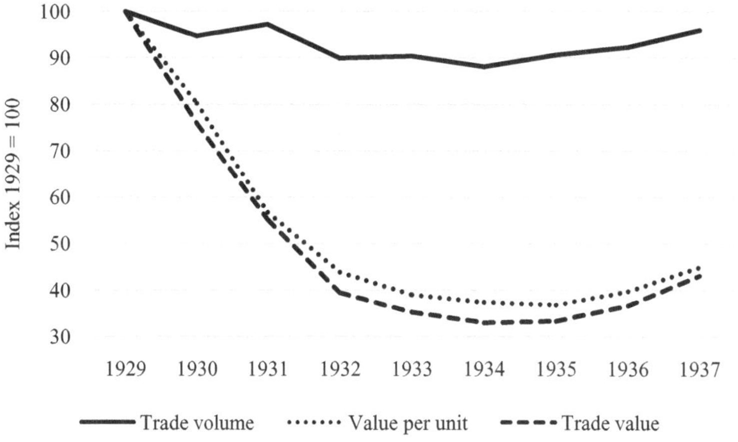

Figure 2.1 Agricultural world trade, 1929–37.
Source: Bacon and Schloemer, 1940: 510–13.

decreased stronger (minus 25%, compared to minus 8%, on average in 1931–7) (Taylor and Taylor, 1943: 6).

The Great Depression affected agricultural world trade not only quantitatively but also qualitatively, with regard to the composition of commodities. Each of the top-five commodities in 1929 – cotton, wheat, sugar, wool and coffee – summing up to 34% of total trade value, lost weight. While the value of agricultural trade generally decreased by 56% on average in 1930–7, the commodity-specific reductions amounted to 58% for coffee, 59% for cotton, sugar and wool and 60% for wheat (excluding wheat flour). Besides these losers, some winners – not in absolute but in relative terms – emerged among the leading commodities: tobacco (minus 46%), rice and corn (minus 50% respectively) and butter (minus 53%). While all of these commodities dramatically lost values per unit, some gained in trade volumes: coffee (plus 8%), butter (plus 12%), rice (plus 13%) and corn (plus 27%). All in all, the composition of commodities changed gradually, albeit not fundamentally, during the Great Depression (see Table 2.1).

2.2 *Wheat trade*

Among the globally traded agricultural commodities during the Great Depression, wheat played a leading role, as emphasized by the Economic Committee of the League of Nations in 1931:

> Of all agricultural products, wheat is the one with which the whole world is most seriously concerned. It is the most important of all for human food, and is the most international in character. In respect of both

Table 2.1 Composition of leading agricultural commodities, 1929–37

Commodity	*Share of total trade value 1929 (%)*	*Trade volume 1930–37 (index 1929 = 100)*	*Value per unit 1930–37 (index 1929 = 100)*	*Trade value 1930–37 (index 1929 = 100)*
Cotton	11.3	94	43	41
Wheat	6.6	80	49	40
Sugar	5.8	77	53	41
Wool	5.5	100	42	41
Coffee	4.5	108	39	42
Silk	4.4	79	33	27
Rubber	3.3	99	38	39
Rice	3.2	113	45	50
Butter	3.2	112	43	47
Tobacco	2.8	83	64	54
Corn	2.0	127	39	50
Total	100.0	92	47	44

Source: Bacon and Schloemer, 1940: 514.

> production and consumption, it concerns the greatest number of countries; it is consumed in large quantities in all countries of any importance. There is no country where production and consumption are so well balanced that wheat is not to some extent an import or export commodity; almost all countries take part in the international wheat trade. The wheat problem is therefore one of exceptional importance
>
> (League of Nations, 1931: 22)

Accordingly, contemporary experts regarded issues of wheat trade as key for the agricultural crisis in particular and the economic crisis in general. The brisance of the 'wheat problem' lay in the fact that this commodity was affected by the crisis more severely than agricultural trade as a whole. Post-1929 trade volumes of wheat and wheat flour fell by 36% until 1937, apart from interim recovery in 1931. Values per unit reached their low point in 1934 at minus 64% of the 1929 level. Consequently, post-1929 trade values deteriorated by 74% until 1934, before slightly improving to minus 60% until 1937 (see Figure 2.2).

The intercontinental and international division of tasks in the global network of wheat trade that had emerged in the pre-1914 Great Specialization became blurred during the post-1929 world economic crisis, sometimes labeled as 'Great Discontinuity' (Findlay and O'Rourke, 2007: 365–428; Federico, 2005: 191–96). Before the onset of the Great Depression, the global wheat web was divided into four major exporters outside of Europe – Canada, the United States, Argentina and Australia – that supplied 84% of total exports as well as six major European importers – the United Kingdom, Italy, Germany, France, Belgium and the Netherlands – that received 61% of total imports. During the Great Depression, the four major exporters cut down their

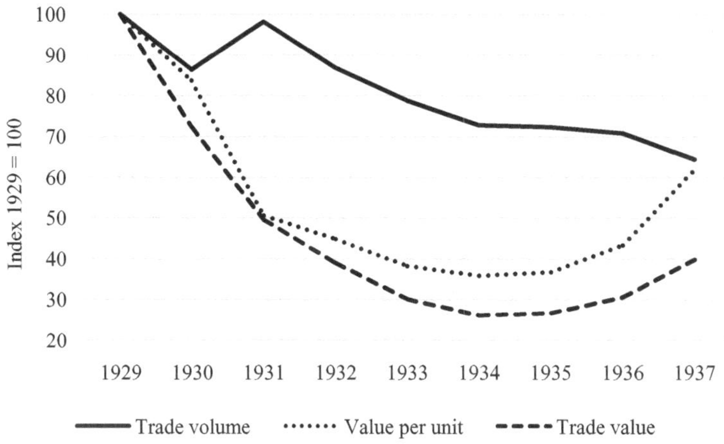

Figure 2.2 World trade of wheat and wheat flour, 1929–37.
Source: Bacon and Schloemer 1940: 56.

deliveries not only in absolute but also in relative terms, to 76% in 1929–33 and 70% in 1934–8. Besides these suppliers, other wheat exporters entered the scene and, at least periodically, raised their shares of total trade volume: the Danube countries – Bulgaria, Hungary, Romania and Yugoslavia – the Soviet Union as well as British and French colonies in Asia and Africa. The six major importers undertook a complementary movement by reducing purchases in the world market in both absolute and relative terms, to 57% in 1929–33 and 56% in 1934–8. Simultaneously, non-European countries such as Brazil, Japan and China raised their wheat imports. As a consequence, the Great Specialization of food-exporting and food-importing world regions became more diversified, but without vanishing completely (see Tables 2.2 and 2.3).

Among the drivers of the 'wheat problem' prior to and during the Great Depression, market forces and state regulation interacted in multiple ways. There is an ongoing debate to what extent the disequilibrium of the wheat market in particular and agricultural markets in general contributed to the Great Depression. According to conventional wisdom drawing on contemporary analyses (League of Nations, 1931; Timoshenko, 1933), rising food supply exceeded stagnating demand, therefore depressing world market prices from 1925 onwards and fueling 'structural deflation' (Kindleberger, 1974: 105–7). Rising wheat supply resulted from expanding acreage (extensive growth) due to application of labor-saving technology (e.g. large-scale machinery) in the Americas and Australia to meet extraordinary wartime and immediate postwar demand combined with rising yields (intensive growth) through application of land-saving technology (e.g. mineral fertilizers) in Europe after recovery from war-induced production shocks. Stagnating demand for wheat resulted from decelerated population growth in Europe as

Table 2.2 Exports of wheat and wheat flower by selected countries, 1924–38

	1924–28		*1929–33*		*1934–38*	
	Volume (1,000 bushels)	*Share %*	*Volume (1,000 bushels)*	*Share %*	*Volume (1,000 bushels)*	*Share %*
World	873,573	100	815,004	100	640,431	100
Canada	307,027	35	235,966	29	177,214	28
USA	189,338	22	107,401	13	49,054	8
Argentina	146,900	17	150,501	18	122,740	19
Australia	91,417	10	124,817	15	102,405	16
Major non-European exporters	734,682	84	618,685	76	451,413	70
Danube countries*	36,964	4	45,709	6	48,670	8
USSR	18,629	2	47,693	6	25,276	4
British India	18,739	2	5,254	1	10,078	2
French North Africa	9,517	1	20,209	2	17,844	3

*Bulgaria, Hungary, Romania and Yugoslavia.
Source: Taylor and Taylor, 1943: 126.

Table 2.3 Imports of wheat and wheat flour by selected countries, 1924–38

	1924–28		*1929–33*		*1934–38*	
	Volume (1,000 bushels)	*Share %*	*Volume (1,000 bushels)*	*Share %*	*Volume (1,000 bushels)*	*Share %*
World	832,641	100	815,298	100	625,676	100
United Kingdom	221,085	27	231,961	28	208,730	33
Italy	85,281	10	49,787	6	26,034	4
Germany	82,636	10	44,276	5	25,612	4
France	47,142	6	58,165	7	23,767	4
Belgium	43,688	5	46,921	6	42,854	7
Netherlands	29,762	4	31,342	4	22,590	4
Major European importers	509,594	61	462,452	57	349,587	56
Brazil	30,791	4	32,224	4	36,386	6
Japan	22,671	3	24,177	3	11,521	2
China	19,547	2	54,711	7	27,476	4

Source: Taylor and Taylor, 1943: 125.

well as diversifying diets, for the one part due to improved per-capita income and the associated shift of middle classes to animal-based food in industrializing countries, for the other part due to income losses of crisis-ridden working-class households relegated to plant-based food. Falling prices and mounting stocks of wheat did not prevent farmers from expanding production who

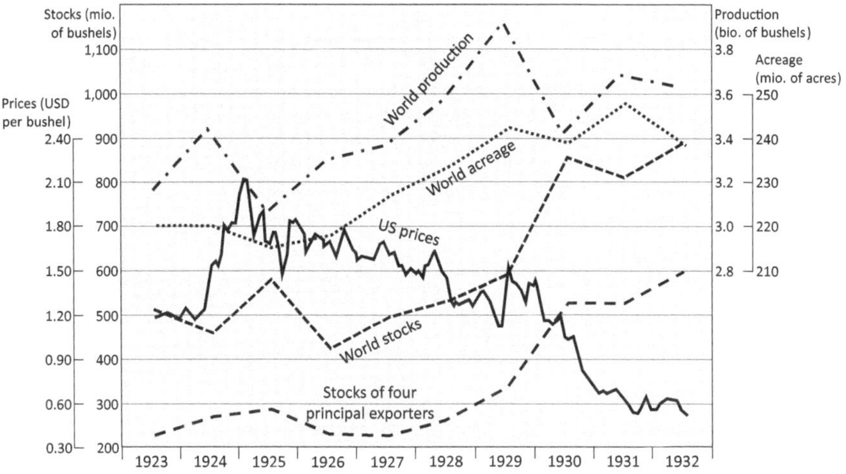

Figure 2.3 Acreage, production, stocks and prices of wheat, 1923–32.
Source: Timoshenko, 1933: 550.

aimed at exploiting previous technological investments and supplying their families (Kindleberger, 1974: 83–107; Aparicio and Pinilla, 2019: 49–61; see Figure 2.3). Revisionist accounts challenge this view by questioning the extent of over-production and market price deflation with regard to prewar levels (Federico, 2005: 192). However, both lines of argumentation emphasize the interconnectedness of economic and political drivers.

3. Regulatory institutions

3.1 International cooperation

The oversupply of wheat in relation to demand was accentuated by the implementation of protectionist measures in the late 1920s and their strengthening from 1929 onwards by large importers such as Germany, France and Italy, which stimulated national wheat production in order to raise self-sufficiency, as well as the abandonment of free-trade policies by the United Kingdom, the Netherlands and Denmark from 1931 onwards. Major importing countries raised tariffs with those on agricultural products doubling and those on cereals quintupling from 1927 to 1931 (see Table 2.4). Furthermore, several countries imposed quotas and other quantitative restrictions on agricultural imports. Finally, democratic and authoritarian governments intervened in the domestic market through production controls, minimum prices and subsidies, marketing boards and so on. While most export-oriented countries suffered from this protectionist wave, the British Dominions and Argentina were given 'imperial preference' for delivering surpluses free of duties to the

Table 2.4 Import duties on wheat, 1926–36
(gold francs per quintal)

	1926	*1927*	*1928*	*1929*	*1930*	*1931*	*1932*	*1933*	*1934*
France	2.68	7.11	10.15	16.24	16.24	16.24	16.24	16.24	16.24
Germany	4.32	6.17	8.03	3.89	13.81	13.89	13.89	4.32	4.32
Italy	7.50	7.50	14.00	16.50	19.65	19.95	20.47	19.78	18.40
UK	–	–	–	–	–	0.80	0.76	0.70	0.70
Netherlands	–	–	–	–	–	–	3.12	3.12	4.17
Belgium	–	–	–	–	–	–	–	1.45	1.04
Denmark	–	–	–	–	–	–	–	–	0.31
USA	5.71	5.71	5.71	8.00	8.00	8.00	5.03	4.76	4.72

Source: Hevesy, 1940: 762.

United Kingdom in 1932. To complicate matters, the Soviet Union reappeared as a wheat exporter and competitor in the world market in 1930–1 (Federico, 2005: 194–96; Aparicio and Pinilla, 2019: 56–61).

The shift from liberalist to protectionist trade policies did not terminate cooperation in crisis management across borders. On the contrary, though state intervention in domestic markets was implemented nationally, it was negotiated internationally. In the early 1930s, numerous conferences by public and private representatives from various countries across the globe debated solutions to the 'wheat problem', which oscillated between European and global approaches as well as exporters' and importers' interests. In terms of the share of wheat and wheat flower in total exports in 1926–30, Canada (31%), Argentina (27%) and Australia (17%) were more vulnerable to the fall in wheat prices than the Soviet Union (8%) and the United States (5%). Therefore, the latter could cope with export cuts more easily than the former that attempted to recover revenues through export increases. At the conference in Rome from 26 March to 2 April 1931, an approach privileging European exporters through a system of quotas gained dominance, thus provoking opposition from overseas exporters. Though the conference failed, it established the necessity of an international – and in fact global – commodity agreement as an alternative to free trade. At a follow-up conference in London from 18 to 23 May 1931, representatives of both European and overseas wheat exporters weighed up a system of quotas (as preferred by the European countries) against reductions of acreage (as preferred by the United States) without reaching consent (Aparicio and Pinilla, 2019: 61–2; Graevenitz, 2017: 299–306).

The turning point came at the Conference of Wheat Exporting and Importing Countries from 21 to 25 August 1933 in the wake of the London Monetary and Economic Conference that reached a 'gentlemen's agreement'. This was facilitated by the previous shift to the New Deal administration in the United States that eliminated legal barriers to production and export restrictions. The agreement was signed by Argentina, Australia, Austria, Belgium, Bulgaria, Canada, Czechoslovakia, France, Germany, Greece,

Hungary, Ireland, Italy, Poland, Romania, the Soviet Union, Spain, Sweden, Switzerland, the United Kingdom, the United States and Yugoslavia. Beyond dogmatic positions towards world trade, the conference arrived at a pragmatic combination of free-trade and interventionist measures, involving production and export restrictions and price-sensitive tariffs. The International Wheat Agreement's rationale was:

> to adjust the supply of wheat to effective demand, to eliminate the abnormal surpluses which have been depressing the wheat market, and to bring about a rise and stabilization of prices at a level remunerative to the farmers and fair to the consumers of bread-stuff.
>
> (Graevenitz, 2017: 311)

Since the Wheat Advisory Committee that was in charge of administering the agreement was lacking sanctioning power, the implementation of the measures soon clashed with national interests of major producers and exporters. However, the internationalization of crisis management and the associated convention of state-led market regulation contributed to ease the 'wheat problem': from 1934–5 onwards, wheat prices recovered and stocks shrank (Graevenitz, 2017: 306–14). Despite the attempts of international cooperation, the gravity center of trade policies shifted to the national domain, as shown by the Soviet, US and German cases.

3.2 The Soviet Great Break

As the Bolsheviks gained power in Russia in 1917, they inherited a largely agrarian economy that had been deeply integrated in the world market until World War I, the Russian Revolution and the Civil War severely hit foreign trade. The 1921 New Economic Policy aimed at reconnecting to the world economy through a mix of liberalized domestic markets and state-controlled foreign trade that fostered grain, timber and oil exports as well as technology imports for domestic industrialization under the international gold standard. This dual strategy increasingly came under pressure from the mid-1920s onwards through the decline of international grain prices as well as increasing domestic prices due to poor grain harvests and procurement, therefore melting down the state's hard-earned gold reserves to alarming levels. These exogenous and endogenous economic problems prompted the 'industrialization debate' in the Bolshevik leadership that shifted from integration in the liberal world economy ('right' position) to state-led collectivization of peasant agriculture ('left' position). Stalin, who emerged as the new leader after Lenin's death, undertook a shift from 'right' to 'left' that was driven by the progressing dissolution of the liberal order of the world economy rather than by peasant-hostile attitudes. On the contrary, his writings of the 1920s show sympathy with the peasantry, except for the wealthy and powerful 'kulaks' in the villages that were suspected of withholding marketable grain and fueling anti-government propaganda (Tauger, 2006a; Sanchez-Sibony, 2014; Allen, 2003: 65–87).

In view of the escalating disintegration of the world economy, the Soviet leadership under Stalin undertook a political shift – the Great Break – that appears as revolutionary as the Bolshevik revolution in 1917. The 1928 First Five-Year Plan aimed at boosting grain exports as a source of technology imports for accelerated industrialization. Periodic famines in the 1920s attributed to the backwardness of peasant farming and the boycott of grain procurement by the 'kulaks' persuaded the Stalin regime to transform Soviet agriculture through state action according to US-style industrial farming. As a first step before the great leap, technology-intensive state farms ('sovkhozy') were implemented from 1928 onwards, followed by forced conversion of peasant villages into collective farms ('kolkhozy') and displacement of 'kulaks' by military power from 1929 onwards. Collectivization and 'dekulakization' provoked many peasant rebellions that forced the regime to call off the campaign in 1930.

The Soviet Union exported much of the above-average grain harvest in order to finance imports of machinery for domestic industrialization in 1930–1. However, the regime again initiated collectivization and 'dekulakization' so that about 60% of the peasants were in 'kolkhozy' and 2 million 'kulaks' worked as forced laborers in factories and camps by 1931. Grain exports in combination with crop failures due to drought in 1931 and wet weather in 1932 caused a serious famine with millions of casualties in major grain-producing areas. Though the Soviet government, fearing attacks from German and Japanese imperialism, tried to conceal the Great Famine to the outside world, its internal relief effort in combination with a large harvest in 1933 ended the catastrophe. This involved the reorganization of the 'kolkhozy' through technology transfer, fixed delivery quotas and plots for family use. In comparison to the previous five years, in the period 1934–8 annual wheat production increased from 840 to 1,319 million bushels while annual net exports decreased from 48 to 25 million bushels (see Figure 2.4). By the end of the 1930s, the Great Break that aimed at industrializing the Soviet economy in general and agriculture in particular had been largely achieved, albeit at high costs borne by domestic peasant society (Tauger, 2006a, 2006b, 2011: 131–34; Sanchez-Sibony, 2014; Allen, 2003: 97–102).

3.3 The US New Deal

In the 1920s, US agricultural policy under Republican presidents exerted little direct influence on farmers' production decisions and commodity prices, which were largely shaped by market dynamics. After steep fall in 1920–1 and subsequent recovery, corn, cotton and wheat prices followed an accelerating downward trend after 1925. Repeated experiences with market volatility and rising indebtedness provoked claims by farmers, their organizations and politicians to control overproduction and stabilize commodity prices. In view of the depression of corn, cotton and wheat prices, members of Congress

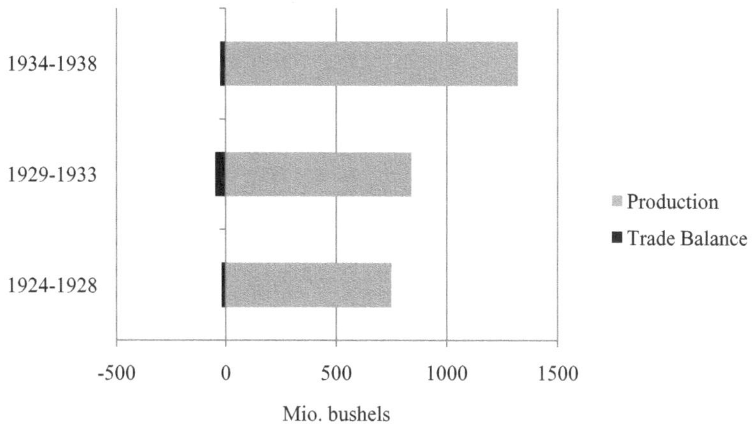

Figure 2.4 Annual production volume and trade balance of wheat in the Soviet Union, 1924–38.
Source: Mitchell, 1998: 301; Taylor and Taylor, 1943: 122.

from farming regions formed the Farm Bloc in 1921, which pushed for a bill raising prices by controlling surpluses. Though the McNary-Haugen bill supported by a comprehensive coalition of farming interests passed the Congress in 1927, it finally failed due to a veto by President Coolidge. Though his successor Hoover acknowledged the need to address agricultural surpluses, the government continued to define solutions to the farm problem in terms of market fundamentalism. Accordingly, the 1929 Agricultural Marketing Act provided financial and managerial support to agricultural cooperatives for marketing efforts, administered by the Federal Farm Board. However, this market-oriented initiative failed due to mounting surpluses, shrinking exports and deteriorating prices from 1929 onwards, pushing down gross farm income by 50%. Beyond the fragmentation of rural class and political party interests, claims for market intervention by the federal administration increasingly gained support (Winders, 2009: 31–50).

In the aftermath of the Democratic landslide over the Republicans in 1932, US agricultural policy shifted from market fundamentalism to state intervention under President Roosevelt's New Deal. The cornerstone of the New Deal for agriculture was the 1933 Agricultural Adjustment Act (AAA) that set up production control (through acreage allotments and marketing agreements) and price support (through loans) of basic commodities, with the aim of raising farm incomes in both absolute and relative terms by controlling supply. As a result, unsalable grain stocks coexisted with hungry people, forced to outmigration from rural devastated rural regions. Government subsidies under the AAA were funded by a tax on agribusiness firms. The implementation of the AAA resulted in shrinking acreages and supplies of basic crops as well as rising prices. From 1932 to 1936, for instance, wheat

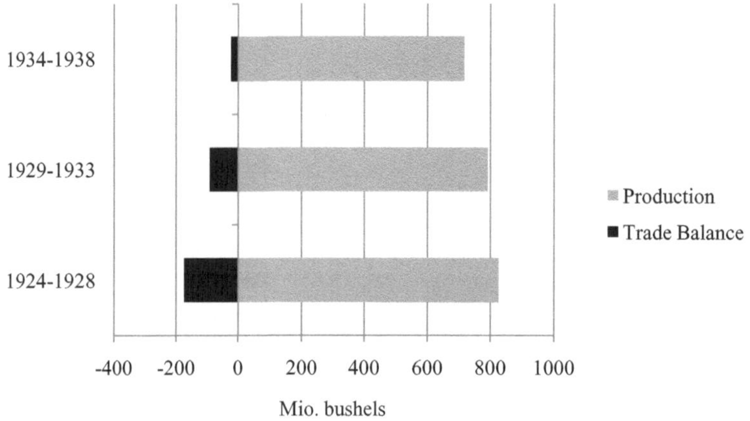

Figure 2.5 Annual production volume and trade balance of wheat in the United States, 1924–38.

Source: Taylor and Taylor, 1943: 123.

acreage fell from 57 to 49 million acres and production fell from 26 to 17 million metric tons; in the same period, wheat prices almost tripled. From the periods of 1929–33 to 1934–38, the cut in annual wheat production from 792 to 717 million bushels more than compensated for the shrinkage of annual net exports from 93 to 23 million bushels (see Figure 2.5).

Despite its obvious success, however, the AAA faced serious political challenges and provoked significant conflict within agriculture: Corn Belt farmers opposed the extent to which the federal government controlled their farming operations; Southern planters protested against the 'rural reform' softening their hierarchical ties with – mostly black – tenants and sharecroppers; agricultural processors and traders complained about the tax burden, which finally led to the AAA's repeal by the Supreme Court in 1936 (Winders, 2009: 51–67; Gilbert, 2015: 80–112).

To counter the opposition, the Democratic majority in the Congress passed the 1936 Soil Conservation and Domestic Allotment Act that enabled payments funded by the federal budget for limiting 'soil-depleting' (i.e. overproduced) crops as a means against the catastrophic droughts and wind erosions of 1934–6 ('dust bowl'). Moreover, it passed the second AAA that prevented the disputed processing taxes and instead funded the measures through the federal budget in 1938. Besides setting price-support levels between 52 and 75% of parity with non-agricultural income, the measures of production control comprised soil conservation allotments, acreage allotments and marketing quotas. With a more friendly Supreme Court, the Roosevelt administration and the Democratic majority in the Congress, the agricultural policy of supply management, representing the interests of the cotton-wheat-corn coalition, had been institutionalized for the decades to come (Winders, 2009: 68–9; Gilbert, 2015: 80–112).

3.4 The German New Order

The German Weimar Republic inherited the agrarian dual structure of large estates with wage laborers in the eastern provinces and small and medium family farms in the more industrialized West. While the former regained pre-war production levels of extensive grain farming not before the early 1930s, the latter intensified land use through shifting from arable to livestock farming already in the late 1920s. However, agricultural policy in general and credit policy in particular served the interests of large estates rather than peasant farms. Technology-driven productivity gains were mostly financed by credits of US origin, thereby raising indebtedness. Despite moderate tariffs, the downward tendency of international agricultural prices in the late 1920s put market-oriented farms under increasing pressure. Rural protest culminated in the foundation of the anti-democratic Green Front in 1929, which lobbied for external (e.g. tariff increase) and internal state intervention (e.g. price subsidies), but with uneven results: estate owners received state subsidies for debt relief in the framework of the 1929 East Aid (*Osthilfe*), whereas peasants were excluded from this aid. As the Great Depression increased pressure on indebted farms and actionist counter-measures by the conservative governments of Brüning and von Papen failed, the Nazi party successfully appropriated the rural protest movement through anti-capitalist propaganda, blaming the Jewish greed for profit for the misery of the 'German peasant' (Kluge, 2005: 19–26).

After the party's victory in the elections and Hitler's appointment as Reich Chancellor in 1933, the Nazi regime began to establish the New Order of German agriculture. The Reich Food Estate (*Reichsnährstand*), founded in 1933 with compulsory membership of producers, processors and traders, implemented a corporatist market order that channeled basic farm products from producers to consumers at fixed prices. As a result, agricultural prices improved in 1934–6 but afterwards stagnated in absolute terms and declined in relation to industrial prices. In order to raise national food autarky, the Reich Food Estate annually promoted a 'battle for production' (*Erzeugungsschlacht*) through application of farm technology from 1934 onwards, thereby emulating the 'battle for grain' *(battaglia del grano)* in Fascist Italy. The results were mixed, as exemplified by wheat production and trade in 1934–8 compared to 1929–33: although annual production slightly increased from 161 to 174 million bushels, the German Reich still depended on annual net imports that declined only from 29 to 22 million bushels. However, the degree of self-provision had considerably increased compared to the period 1924–8 (see Figure 2.6).

The Nazi ideology of 'blood and soil' idealized the medium-sized peasant farm that the 1933 Reich Hereditary Farm Law (*Reichserbhofgesetz*) protected from the seemingly destructive dynamics of the land and credit markets. The law distinguished the community-oriented – and ideally male – 'Peasant' (*Bauer*) as owner of a Hereditary Farm from the self-interested 'Farmer' (*Landwirt*) as owner of an ordinary farm. The 1936 Four-Year Plan incorporated agriculture

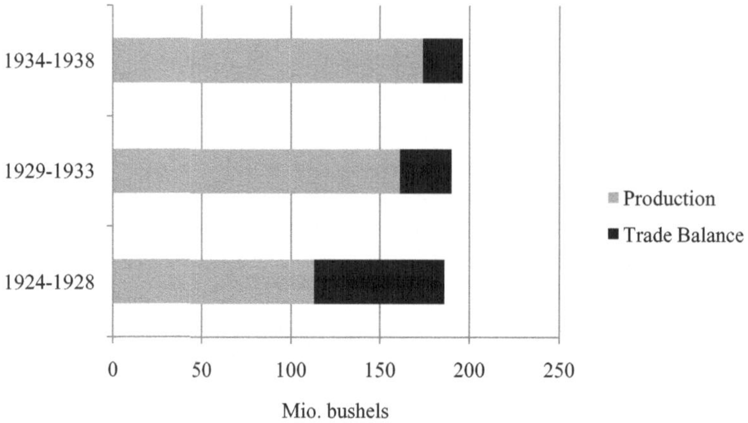

Figure 2.6 Annual production volume and trade balance of wheat in Germany, 1924–38.

Source: Taylor and Taylor, 1943: 121.

in the preparation of war for extending the German people's 'living space' (*Lebensraum*) to the East. By the end of the 1930s, German agriculture was linked to upstream and downstream industries in the regulatory framework of a comprehensive corporatist apparatus in service of the Nazi state. The large-scale development plan of Rural New Order (*Ländliche Neuordnung*) by the Reich Food Estate, which aimed at establishing well-equipped peasant farms throughout the Reich as well as resettling smallholders to East Europe to provide them with landed property at the expense of the indigenous population, was only partially realized during the war (Tooze, 2006: 166–199; Kluge, 2005: 27–32; Corni and Gies, 1997: 75–395; Mai, 2002).

4. Conclusion

The Great Depression had a decisive impact on the transition from the British-centered to the US-centered food regime, albeit in nationally different ways. Prior to the bubble burst at the New York Stock Exchange in 1929, the disequilibrium of the world market for agricultural commodities had already eroded the British-centered food regime from 1925 onwards. From then to the institutionalization of the US-centered food regime through the 1944 Bretton Woods System and the 1947 General Agreement on Tariffs and Trade, four phases of the transition can be distinguished (Geels and Schot, 2007). It must be emphasized that this food regime transition was by no means predetermined; alternative scenarios such as wheat exporters other than the United States emerged in the social struggles but failed to enter the regime (Friedmann, 2005: 237–40). In the first phase, the British-centered food regime slided into crisis due to the downward trend of commodity prices, reflecting the disequilibrium of supply and demand of basic grains, especially wheat. Therefore, agricultural producers in both exporting and importing countries came under pressure, thus putting the 'agrarian question' on the politico-economic agenda. Since the strategy of compensating falling prices through rising outputs did not solve but aggravate the crisis, agricultural producers withdrew from the market, as in the case of peasant villages in the Soviet Union, or mobilized for protection through state intervention, as in the cases of indebted commercial farmers in the United States and family-farm and estate owners in Germany.

In the second phase, innovations as solutions to the crisis emerged in niches of the politico-economic arena. These innovations were institutional rather than technical, altering the formal and informal 'rules of the game'. In the Soviet Union, the Bolshevik regime implemented large-scale state farms ('sovkozy') as a test project in its attempt overcome the 'backwardness' of peasant agriculture through US-style industrial farming from 1928 onwards. In the United States, a coalition calling for stronger state intervention in the imbalanced market successfully pushed through the McNary-Haugen Bill in Congress in 1927, but finally failed because of the President's veto. In Germany, the 1929-established Green Front lobbied for state protection against falling commodity prices and rising debt rates, but only obtained concessions for the estate owners to the disappointment of the peasants.

In the third phase, niche innovations were upgraded to enter the mainstream as solutions to the 'agrarian question' of the respective country, thereby downgrading alternative scenarios. The common feature of national transition pathways was the shift from international free-trade relations based on the gold standard to state-led regulation of the domestic market, comprising Soviet state socialism, US-organized capitalism and, as a 'third way' in between these extremes, German corporatism. Consequently, the pre-1914 Great Specialization of food-exporting and food-importing world regions became more diversified. In the Soviet Union, the Bolshevik leadership started the Great Break by transforming peasant agriculture through forced collectivization and 'dekulakization' according to US-style industrial farming. This decision was motivated by the disintegration of the liberal world-economic order and the lack of an international peace order. Peasant resistance could only delay the campaign for a short time, but was finally broken by military power. In the United States, the New Deal institutionalized an agricultural policy of supply management, accompanied by a peasant-friendly program of rural reform. The Roosevelt administration indulged to lobbying by the cotton-wheat-corn coalition as well as emulated measures of crisis management implemented by foreign, including Fascist, countries. In Germany, the Nazi regime integrated agriculture with upstream and downstream industries as well as subordinated the food, feed and fiber market to corporatist direction according to the ideal of the racially pure and economically efficient medium-sized peasant farm. The New Order of German agriculture was driven by the regime's tendency to expand the German people's 'living space' to East Europe through conquest, displacement and extermination of the Jewish and Slavic population.

Within the spectrum of agrarian modernities in the 1930s, the Soviet and US cases represented the extremes of high and low modernism: Soviet high modernism recklessly enforced the science-based industrialization of agriculture against resistance from peasant society. Conversely, US low modernism fostered rural reform through democratic participation with farming communities. The German pathway ambivalently combined low-modern actions, mostly directed towards the German medium-sized peasantry, and high-modern actions, mostly directed towards alien peoples and 'races' regarded as inferior by Nazi ideology (Scott, 1998; Gilbert, 2015; Langthaler, 2016).

The fourth phase already went beyond the era of Great Depression and coincided with World War II. The responses to the challenges of wartime economy in both Axis and Allied countries paved the development paths of postwar agriculture. For instance, the United Kingdom implemented a 'state-led agricultural revolution' through a shift from extensive pastoral farming to intensive arable farming that prevailed after the war (Short, Watkins and Martin, 2007). The Soviet Union and the United States emerged victorious from the 'total war', though their economies looked quite different: whereas the Soviet Union suffered from damages of cropland, capital stock and labor-force due to the perennial hostilities with Nazi Germany, the United States had mobilized its productive resources in the Allied war effort to full performance. Wartime plans to create a World Food Board, guided by the Food and Agriculture Organization of the United Nations, failed due to the bipolarization between West and East in the Cold War from 1947 onwards. Each superpower became the geopolitical hegemon and emerged as the center of the respective food regime that hierarchically incorporated sub-centers, semi-peripheries and peripheries. Nazi Germany was defeated in World War II and divided by the Allies in a western part under US dominance and an eastern part under Soviet dominance. Therefore, the shape of the US-centered food regime in the postwar era was largely determined by trends and shocks during World War II (McMichael, 2013: 21–40; Friedmann, 2005: 237–40). However, the Great Depression aggravated the crisis of the British-centered food regime and opened up national transition paths that contributed to what Polanyi has labeled the 'Great Transformation' of global capitalism (Polanyi, 2001).

Bibliography

Allen, R., 2003, *From Farm to Factory. A Reinterpretation of the Soviet Industrial Revolution*, Princeton/Oxford: Princeton University Press.

Aparicio, G. and Pinilla, V., 2019, 'International trade in wheat and other cereals and the collapse of the first wave of globalization, 1900–38', *Journal of Global History*, (14/1), pp. 44–67.

Bacon, L. B. and Schloemer, F. C., 1940, *World Trade in Agricultural Products: Its Growth, Its Crisis, and the New Trade Policies*, Rome: International Institute of Agriculture.

Corni, G. and Gies, H., 1997, *Brot – Butter – Kanonen. Die Ernährungswirtschaft in Deutschland unter der Diktatur Hitlers*, Berlin: Akademie Verlag.

Dale, G., 2010, *Karl Polanyi: the Limits of the Market*, Cambridge: Polity Press.

Federico, G., 2005, *Feeding the World. An Economic History of Agriculture, 1800–2000*, Princeton/Oxford: Princeton University Press.

Findlay, R. and O'Rourke, K. H., 2007, *Power and Plenty: Trade, War, and the World Economy in the Second Millennium*, New Jersey: Princeton University Press.

Friedmann, H., 2005, 'From Colonialism to Green Capitalism: Social Movements and Emergence of Food Regimes', in F. H. Buttel and Ph. McMichael (eds.), *New Directions in the Sociology of Global Development*, Amsterdam: Elsevier JAI, pp. 227–64.

Geels, F. W. and Schot, J., 2007, 'Typology of Sociotechnical Transition Pathways', *Research Policy* (36/3), pp. 399–417.

Gilbert, J., 2015, *Planning Democracy. Agrarian Intellectuals and the Intended New Deal*, New Haven/London: Yale University Press.

Graevenitz, F. G. von, 2017, *Argument Europa. Internationalismus in der globalen Agrarkrise der Zwischenkriegszeit (1927–1937)*, Frankfurt am Main/New York: Campus.

Hevesy, P. de, 1940, *World Wheat Planning and Economic Planning in General*, London: Oxford University Press.

Kindleberger, Ch. P., 1974, *The World in Depression 1929–1939*, Berkeley/Los Angeles: University of California Press.

Kluge, U., 2005, *Agrarwirtschaft und ländliche Gesellschaft im 20. Jahrhundert*, Munich: Oldenbourg.

Krausmann, F. and Langthaler, E., 2019, 'Food Regimes and their Trade Links. A Socio-Ecological Perspective', *Ecological Economics* (160), pp. 87—95.

Langthaler, E., 2016, *Schlachtfelder. Alltägliches Wirtschaften in der nationalsozialistischen Agrargesellschaft 1938–1945*, Vienna/Cologne/Weimar: Böhlau.

League of Nations, 1931, *The Agricultural Crisis*, vol. 1, Geneva: League of Nations.

Magnan, A., 2012, 'Food Regimes', in J. M. Pilcher (ed.), *The Oxford Handbook of Food History*, Oxford: Oxford University Press, pp. 370–88.

Mai, U., 2002, '*Rasse und Raum*'. *Agrarpolitik, Sozial- und Raumplanung im NS-Staat*, Paderborn et al.: Schöningh.

McMichael, Ph., 2013, *Food Regimes and Agrarian Questions*, Halifax/Winnipeg: Fernwood Publishing.

Mitchell, B. R., 1998, *International Historical Statistics: Europe, 1750–1993*, London/Basingstoke: Macmillan Reference.

Polanyi, K., 2001, *The Great Transformation. The Political and Economic Origins of our Time*, Boston: Beacon Press.

Sanchez-Sibony, O., 2014, 'Depression Stalinism: The Great Break Reconsidered', *Kritika: Explorations in Russian and Eurasian History*, (15/1), pp. 23–49.

Scott, J. C., 1998, *Seeing Like a State. How Certain Schemes to Improve the Human Condition Have Failed*, New Haven/London: Yale University Press.

Short, B., Watkins Ch. and Martin, J. (eds.), 2007, *The Front Line of Freedom. British Farming in the Second World War*, Exeter: British Agricultural History Society.

Tauger, M. B., 2006a, 'Stalin, Soviet Agriculture and Collectivization', in F. Trentmann and J. Flemming (eds.), *Food and Conflict in Europe in the Age of the Two World Wars*, Basingstoke/New York: Palgrave Macmillan, pp. 109–42.

Tauger, M. B., 2006b, 'Soviet Peasants and Collectivization, 1930–39: Resistance and Adaptation', *The Journal of Peasant Studies,* (31/3–4), pp. 427–56.

Tauger, M. B., 2011, *Agriculture in World History*, London/New York: Routledge.

Taylor, H. C. and Taylor, A. D., 1943, *World Trade in Agricultural Products*, New York: The Macmillan Company.

Tilzey, M., 2019, 'Food Regimes, Capital, State, and Class: Friedmann and McMichael Revisited', *Sociologia Ruralis,* (59/2), pp. 230–254.

Timoshenko, V. P., 1933, *World Agriculture and the Depression*, Ann Arbor: University of Michigan Business Studies, 5/5.

Tooze, A., 2006, *The Wages of Destruction. The Making and Breaking of the Nazi Economy*, London: Allen Lane.

Winders, B., 2009, *The Politics of Food Supply: U.S. Agricultural Policy in the World Economy*, New Haven/London: Yale University Press.

3 Agricultural crisis in Spain (Nineteenth and Twentieth centuries)[1]

Vicente Pinilla

1. Introduction

The nature of the agricultural crises in Spain fundamentally changed from the mid-nineteenth century. Although the food crises of the early decades of the nineteenth century still shared many similarities with those of the pre-industrial era, they disappeared during the second half of the century. The nature of the crises changed due to the profound transformation of the institutional framework which was shaping a capitalist market economy. Furthermore, the industrialisation and modern economic growth process that took place was fundamental for two reasons. First, because it represented a substantial increase in per capita income, which, in turn, gave rise to a significant improvement in calorie intake and a profound dietary diversification. On the other hand, agriculture lost substantial weight in the economy which meant that the sector's problems had a lower impact on other activities. A further change was Spain's increasing integration into the international economy also represented a noteworthy change. For these reasons, the agricultural crises during the last two centuries took a different form. Some of them, such as the depression at the end of the nineteenth century, the crisis of the 1930s or the one in the 1940s were highly conditioned by the international context, which to a great extent explains them. Others, such as the crisis of traditional agriculture from the mid-1950s until the 1970s, were mainly caused by the changes in other economic sectors and new technologies. Agricultural policy also helps to explain the difficulties encountered in the 1930s and 1940s. From the mid-nineteenth century, the problems of shortages started to disappear, with the unusual exception of Spain during the early years of the Franco regime. Meanwhile, overproduction and difficulties to sell crops at viable prices increased and from the beginning of the twentieth century the introduction of new technologies became necessary.

In order to understand the agricultural crises in a capitalist economy undergoing an industrialisation process, it is crucial to first take into account the profound change involved in transforming the sector from an agriculture that had difficulties in providing a regular and sufficient food source to the population to a hyperproductive sector which was even able to export a substantial

DOI: 10.4324/9781003105466-4

part of its output. The other side of this change is the shift from a highly energy efficient sector to an inefficient one, or from an activity which, while anthropising the natural environment, had a limited impact on it in terms of waste generation and pollution to one which was aggressive towards its environment with a high capacity to pollute it (González de Molina et al., 2020).

This double transformation was not unique to Spain, but was also the case for the other developed countries (Grigg, 1992; Federico, 2005). The causes that explain it are not unique either, although obviously each country has its own differentiating characteristics (Clar et al., 2018).

The very nature of the crises that are to be studied is not uniform. Institutional change, imbalances between demand and supply, competition with the output from other countries or different types of misalignments in production have played a crucial role, although highly varied, throughout the crises. Common elements to all of them reside in the imbalances or problems generated by a capitalist type of agriculture with a notable presence in the international economy.

From this perspective, the starting point should be the rupture caused by the disappearance or profound transformation of the agricultural institutions of the *Ancien Régime* which prevailed in most of Spain to a greater or lesser extent at the end of the eighteenth century. This rupture means that from approximately the mid-nineteenth century there was an agriculture with playing rules that were established within an institutional framework that was different and defined by what we consider to be a capitalist economy.

But this institutional framework has not remained unchanged since the nineteenth century. There was very little public intervention in agriculture throughout the nineteenth century which was mostly concentrated in trade policies and the early attempts to promote innovation in agriculture (Vivier, 2008; Moser and Varley, 2013). Thus, agriculture was basically a free-market activity with only modest State intervention as a consequence of the agricultural recession at the end of the nineteenth century (Koning, 1994). The central role of the market was limited considerably as in most developed countries the depression of the 1930s gave rise to a new era of governmental interventionism in the agricultural sector which significantly restricted the role of the market (Federico, 2012a). The passing of the 1933 Agricultural Adjustment Act by the Roosevelt administration marked the beginning of the end for laissez-faire in agriculture. The growth of intervention in Europe was much more limited in the interwar period than in the United States, but the imbalances between supply and demand or the attempt to achieve self-sufficiency in some products, gave rise to the widespread implementation of protectionist policies or production and price regulation policies (Gerhard, 2014; Grando and Volpi, 2014; Chatriot, 2016; Chevet et al., 2018; Aparicio and Pinilla, 2019).

After the war, in the most developed countries of Western Europe, this translated into an intense regulation of the agricultural sector and the implementation of policies to support agricultural income (Brassley et al., 2012;

Martiin et al., 2016). In Eastern Europe, public intervention in agriculture was much more radical as within the construction process of the centrally planned economies, it involved the collectivisation of the land and the abolition of the market as a mechanism for allocating resources.

In the case of Spain, the analysis of agricultural policies is crucial (Gallego et al., 2010). For example, the rigid and suffocating interventionism of the Franco regime constitutes a significant turning point with respect to the preceding decades; although this approach subsequently changed to become more aligned with the Western European policy of supporting agricultural incomes (Fernández, 2008). Spain's integration into the European Union finally meant the adoption of the common agricultural policy in 1986 which consolidated this line of action even further.

However, it is not only the institutional framework that is important for understanding the different crises experienced by Spanish agriculture over the last two centuries. The growing integration of the Spanish economy, together with its agriculture, into the international economy, is also a key element. Spanish agriculture participated in the economy of the first wave of globalisation, both as an exporter and as an importer of agricultural products. The exporting possibilities were determined by supply due to its competitiveness and the evolution and adaptation of the demand to it. The trade policies of these countries may have also affected the exporting possibilities. Similarly, agricultural imports into Spain were determined by the evolution of its income, the competitiveness of Spanish production and the trade policy developed (Gallego, 2001). Both imports and exports were facilitated by the reduction of the obstacles to trade, due to the fall in transport costs, the liberalisation of trade or other factors (Findlay and O'Rourke, 2007; Jacks et al., 2011). From 1914, a succession of serious phenomena on the international arena, such as the world wars and the depression of the 1930s, represented the end of the first wave of globalisation (Hynes et al., 2012). This seriously affected the international integration of Spanish agriculture in some types of products, while in others the effects were more limited.

After the Second World War, a second wave of globalisation began to emerge. In Spain, a reorganisation of the sector took place after the Civil War, however, within a context of strong isolation, partly sought by the dictatorship and partly forced by the political circumstances and international situation. The isolation from the outside was gradually corrected and mitigated, particularly after the beginning of the 1960s and ended completely upon Spain's entry into the European Union in 1986 (Clar et al., 2015).

Finally, technological change is another key variable to take into account. From the beginning of the nineteenth century, agricultural technology not only changed significantly with respect to the previous centuries but a profound technological rupture also took place. Unlike other sectors of economic activity, mainly industry, this technological rupture occurred several decades after the beginning of the industrial revolution, from a technological point of view. During a good part of the nineteenth century, the increase in agricultural productivity was determined by the adoption, in countries with the right environmental conditions, of innovations developed in the preceding centuries in Great Britain, the Netherlands or northern France. However, from the mid-nineteenth century, agricultural machines began to be developed which in the long term would completely change agriculture. Similarly, other innovations, such as the use of inorganic or chemical fertilisers, biological innovations in the seeds used or new livestock production methods, reinforced the idea that this technological rupture was to be much more profound from the first third of the twentieth century. The problems and crises faced by Spanish agriculture during the last two centuries are not unrelated to this technological change which has progressively accelerated over time. The competitiveness of the sector, the response options of producers to changes in demand, was largely determined by the successive technological innovation clusters that could be accessed by agriculture.

2. The agricultural crisis of the Ancien Régime

The principal objective of the liberal revolution consisted in establishing market economic institutions. Despite its institutionally rupturist nature, we should regard it as a continuance of a series of changes initiated in the last third of the eighteenth century. Its fundamental elements were the establishment and consolidation of new property rights and the transfer of rural estates from collective institutions, mainly the Church and local councils, to individuals.

These types of transformations were common throughout most of the European continent. Inevitably, friction arose between the interests of those who benefitted from the characteristic institutional framework of the society of the Old Regime, mainly the aristocracy and the Church, and those of the emerging groups, particularly the bourgeoisie, the peasants and the comfortable farmers. The opposition to the old institutional framework included very different interests and approaches. Therefore, while the bourgeoisie was inspired by a liberal paradigm, the peasants and the farmers, also interested in this type of reforms, were in favour of a more radical path of change. We are therefore contemplating a case in which there were clearly distributive disputes. The different social groups clashed over the definition of the economic institutions. That said, the nature of these disputes was also important so that economic growth could occur. In Europe, there is evidence that the countries which implemented the necessary changes decisively and early on benefitted from a faster economic growth a few years later (Acemoglou et al., 2011). Therefore, the so-called crisis of the Old Regime can be evaluated from this double perspective: on the one hand, in terms of the conflict between the old and new interests which gave rise to a fundamental change in agricultural society and the distribution of output; and, on the other hand, in terms of the consequences for economic growth.

Starting with the latter issue, in the Spanish case, the fluctuating nature of the liberal agrarian reform, which lasted for almost half a century until it became definitively consolidated, was not an element that favoured growth. It was a necessary condition for growth and the process was very slow, with too many setbacks and hesitations. The process began during the war with France it was not completed until mid-1850s.

On the other hand, from a distributive perspective, it can be said that the crisis and reforms were varied and enabled both the restructuring of stately old haciendas and forms of management and the extension of peasant properties and the access to ownership by a new bourgeoisie. This spatial heterogeneity in the results could be highly conditioned by the characteristics of the different rural societies at the end of the Old Regime. On the other hand, we should not forget that there was a common regulatory framework which these groups were not able to modify. Therefore, there would have been coordination between general policies and local interests. The crisis could have consolidated sizeable assets at the end of the eighteenth century, but the liberal agrarian reform was also an operation that could not be easily controlled. The outbreak of the war and the French invasion facilitated the sometimes-subversive nature of the revolution, creating space for the people's grievances, which enabled the agrarian model to be modified, particularly with respect to the access to irrigation or communal assets. In short, it could be concluded that the crisis did not necessarily mean dispossession for the weakest sectors of rural society as opportunities also arose for the peasant population (Millán, 2000).

It is important to note that the crisis of the Old Regime had a fundamental consequence for the future of Spanish agriculture: a new institutional framework in which to develop. This is undoubtedly its principal effect. Therefore, the transformations, changes or crises thereafter would occur within a different institutional context that would modulate and condition the future growth possibilities and the distribution of this growth among the different participating agents.

3. The persistence of food crises

Food shortages during the first half of the nineteenth century were not an exceptional feature of Spain within the European context. Even in 1840, the availability of enough food for the population was a weak point in the economic prosperity of Western Europe (Vanhaute et al., 2007). Nonetheless, and with respect to the previous century, there was an overall improvement. In fact, from the end of the 1820s, there were no serious food crises in Europe until the end of the 1840s, thanks to the improvement in agricultural productivity and in transport and communications. Despite this, there are doubts regarding the scope of these improvements in productivity, and it is estimated that 10% of the low income population was still structurally malnourished. This more favourable situation emerged within a context of improved trade terms of agricultural products due to the fall in prices of industrial products and the reduction in subsistence production, which implied that a growing part of output was sold on the market. However, in the 1840s, and particularly in the years 1845–8, the situation changed dramatically, especially in certain places such as Ireland. The whole of Europe suffered the potato plague of 1845 simultaneously and then the poor harvests of the main cereal crops in 1846. Nevertheless, this serious food crisis had traditional characteristics and other more modern features such as the fact that it occurred in a context of considerable market integration and a significant trading of foods between countries (Vanhaute et al., 2007).

In Spain, and also in Europe, the food crises at the beginning of the century (1803–5 and 1811–12) were followed by a relatively calm period (Barquín, 2003). The crisis of 1847 coincided with the critical situation that most of Europe was undergoing at that time. It is perhaps more remarkable that serious situations that we would consider as food crises could have occurred as late as 1856–7 and 1868.

These crises took place in Spain in a context of expanding agricultural production, which can be seen as a prolongation of the extensive growth experienced in the eighteenth century, but facilitated by the institutional changes of the liberal agrarian reform. Support for the expansion of domestic production explains the prohibitionist policy with respect to wheat imports which was implemented in 1820.

However, the wheat trade policy generated problems in the years of shortage as it was slow to react when prices rose. This situation was more serious for inland regions which, due to their lower prices and higher transport costs, suffered greater shortages than peripheral regions during times of crisis. Neither exports prior to the food crises, which were considerable, or the imports which took place once prices reached a sufficiently high level, were decisive in the price formation processes of wheat, which were fundamentally determined by the harvest movements. A less restrictive import policy would have enabled a more regular supply during times of crisis (Barquín, 2003). It could be said that the prohibition, as well as having social costs, was not vital for maintaining the interests of the cereal producers, as even with a less rigid policy, Spanish prices would not have moved too far away from international prices after the British abolition of the Corn Laws (Gallego, 2005: 278). As in other European countries, the strong wheat protectionism was a response to the fall in prices after the Napoleonic wars and the owners' concern about the fall in their income (Federico, 2012b). However, it should be understood that the solution that was adopted tended to profit the ownership laws that had been recently acquired or consolidated in the liberal agrarian reform. The supply of food to the population became a secondary priority after these types of considerations.

4. The integration of world agricultural product markets: the end-of-the-century depression

From the end of the first third of the nineteenth century, an increasing international integration of the Spanish agricultural sector occurred. This took place mainly through a growth of exports to more advanced countries and of imports that were not competitive with domestic output.

This occurred in the context of the beginning of the first wave of globalisation (O'Rourke and Williamson, 1999). The international trade of agricultural products grew significantly due to the increase in demand caused by the rise in income in countries undergoing an industrialisation process, the increase in supply generated by the incorporation of technological change, and the effects of the globalisation process on trade, basically the falling transaction costs generated by the reduction in maritime and land transport costs and the liberalisation of trade with the subsequent reduction in customs barriers.

The end-of-the-century agricultural depression was precisely the result of the growing integration of the international agricultural products markets. The strong increase in arrivals of agricultural products to the continent from the Russian Empire or the American continent with lower prices than those of domestic output, called into question the feasibility of many farms. The responses of the different European countries were varied and ranged between the adoption of protectionist measures, the reorientation of production and attempts to increase productivity by incorporating more innovative technology (O'Rourke, 1997; Lains and Pinilla, 2009).

In Spain, the crisis had two very different sides. On the one hand, the increased competition in the domestic markets of fundamentally agricultural products such as cereals or livestock. Production contracted as a consequence of the abandonment of large areas of land and reduced dedication to farming in an attempt to bring down production costs. Given the large size of the agricultural sector in the Spanish economy, the intensity of the crisis had significant consequences. Therefore, the first measure taken in order to counter the difficulties in the short term was an increase in customs protection in 1891.The main objective was the protection of wheat production and processed agricultural products (Gallego, 2001). Second, it was necessary to modernise production. This was achieved through the implementation of the new technology which had been developed in the United States since the mid-nineteenth century and was appropriate for the ecological conditions of most of Spain. The introduction of machinery and chemical and inorganic fertilisers, the beginning of seed selection processes and the introduction of new varieties were the most salient factors of this process, together with the expansion of irrigation either through the construction of canals and reservoirs by the State or the extraction of underground water by the farmers themselves. Finally, the difficulties encountered by the wheat sector fostered a significant reorientation of land uses. Here, the expansion of vegetable crops or fruit trees which were highly export oriented can be highlighted. Thus, fruit and horticultural products represented 7.4% of total agricultural production in 1890, but by 1931 the figure was 14%. Their export volumes increased by 1,100% between 1850 and 1930 (Pinilla and Ayuda, 2010). Furthermore, in other areas, sugar beet or forage plants to feed livestock replaced wheat on the irrigated land.

But the crisis also affected the most dynamic and buoyant sectors of Spanish agriculture that were enjoying notable success in foreign markets, namely, wine and oil.

Wine exports had experienced spectacular growth as a consequence of the phylloxera plague affecting French vines from the end of the 1870s. From 1891, exports to France faced discriminatory customs tariffs as a result of the political preference of this country for Algerian wines with similar characteristics to the Spanish wines and which where fundamental in the colonisation process in the north of Africa (Pinilla and Ayuda, 2002). The contraction in exports was brutal. The customs policies of other importing countries, such as Argentina or Uruguay, to support domestic production aggravated the situation even further (Pinilla and Serrano, 2008; Ayuda et al., 2020).

In the case of oil, export growth had been based largely on the industrial use of olive oil. At the end of the nineteenth century, however, the replacement of this product with industrial oils and fats delivered a hard blow to Spanish exports. The growing competition in the food applications of olive oil with other vegetable oils accentuated the problems (Zambrana, 1985).

The crisis and the policies adopted in response to it gave rise to a polarisation between two types of agriculture in Spain. One was oriented towards and dependent on external markets. It was therefore interested in gaining easy access to them which required both a trade policy that facilitated the entry of their exports and a higher level of productivity. The other agriculture was related more to the domestic market. Although the improvement in productivity was an indisputable requirement to ensure its continuity, the demand for a sufficient level of protection to be able to compete with more efficient producers was also a key factor.

5. Agrarian crisis in the 1930s?

The international economic crisis, which began in 1929 and lasted for the whole of the following decade, severely affected agriculture. Although production did not plummet, it basically stagnated during this decade and agricultural prices fell considerably (Federico, 2004 and 2005). Another feature of the crisis was the contraction of international trade. Although the volume of the quantities traded did not fall significantly throughout the decade, their prices fell considerably (Aparicio et al., 2009; Ocampo and Parra-Lancourt, 2010).

The international economic crisis also affected Spain. Although its effects were visible, with very little delay, its impact was more moderate and it was shorter in length. This was due to the lower degree of development of the Spanish economy. Its greater dependence on agriculture and the weak connection between the Spanish and international financial sectors explain why this crisis was weaker and shorter. In 1935, Spain's GDP had recovered its level of 1929 (Comín, 2012). However, in Spain, as in other European countries, the situation became more complex due to the political and social instability that affected the country for the whole for the 1930s. In the case of

Spain, this instability gave rise to a bloody Civil War in 1936, which lasted three years when a military coup against the democratic government of the Spanish Republic failed.

When referring to agriculture, we must analyse the two aspects of this situation. On the one hand, the impact of the international crisis. On the other hand, the high degree of social conflict existing in the Spanish countryside as a result of the opposition of the *latifundistas* (large land owners) and conservative sectors to the reforms developed by the centre-left governments and the impatience of certain sectors, particularly those linked to anarchist and socialist trade unionism, with the implementation of these reforms which could contribute to improving the situation of the most disadvantaged sectors.

Agricultural production fluctuated widely. This was normal due to its considerable dependence on rainfall, although record harvests were obtained of cereal crops in the years 1932 and 1934. In 1929–35, production stagnated while prices fell slightly (and decreased with respect to the prices of manufactured goods) (Comín, 2011). Agricultural production oriented towards the domestic market could have benefitted from the increase in real wages that took place from the beginning of the 1930s, especially in the case of the products with higher elasticity of demand with respect to income (Carreras and Tafunell, 2003). However, the situation in the countryside was affected by the problems experienced in other sectors, especially industry, and by the economic downturn in general. In particular, we should highlight that the crisis paralysed intense rural-urban migratory flows which, since 1910, had increased in intensity and led to a significant decrease in the percentage share of the active agricultural population of total population (Silvestre, 2005). Breaking this trend, with the crisis unemployed industrial or construction workers returned to their villages to work on the family farms or look for seasonal work as day labourers. Simpson and Carmona (2020) estimate that the farm population increased by 20% between 1930 and 1936 and it was this situation of tension in the agricultural labour market that caused most rural hardship. The impact of this situation was greater in southern regions, such as Andalusia, where there were more landless workers.

From the point of view of external trade, the Spanish policy sought to avoid the entry of agricultural product imports, particularly cereals. From 1922, not only were the tariffs on wheat and flour increased but their import was also banned except when prices surpassed certain limits established in the regulatory markets. This policy sought to protect the production that had reached sufficient capacity to supply the domestic market in a context of growing tension in international grain markets (Aparicio and Pinilla, 2019). The volume of agricultural imports contracted by around 20% between 1929 and 1935. However, the volume of exports was also seriously affected by the problems in the destination countries, falling by a slightly smaller amount (Gallego and Pinilla, 1996). As the prices of the exported agricultural products behaved better than the imported products, the coverage ratio of agricultural exports with respect to imports improved during the crisis years

(Pinilla, 1995). The impact on Spanish exports of agricultural products varied. At the beginning of the crisis, in 1929–30, the Spanish exporters of Mediterranean fruit and vegetables obtained their historical maximum sales volumes, both in current and constant values. However, after 1931, their sales fell significantly, as did their prices after 1932 at a rapid pace, although slightly less than overall agricultural prices (Pinilla and Ayuda, 2009 and 2010). In the case of wine exports, the tightening of the French trade policy generated a severe contraction of exports (Pinilla and Ayuda, 2002).

During the 1930s, a crisis on a social level emerged in the countryside. The reformist policies of the centre-left republican governments, the profound inequality suffered in many rural areas, particularly visible in the distribution of land ownership and the will of many social agents to improve their situation, generated a high level of tension in some parts of rural Spain which reached its highest point with the fight for agrarian reform. However, this opposition was made up of many other facets particularly related to the resistance to apply the new agricultural legislation approved by the first republican governments, which affected mainly the hiring of labour and conditioned the management of farms and increased wage costs (Comín, 2002: 302–306; Domenech, 2013; Robledo and González, 2017; Simpson and Carmona, 2020; Cobo and Garrido, 2021). In the case of the agrarian reform, despite its slow and scarce application, at least until February 1936, the large rural landowners felt that their rights were being threatened and developed an intense opposition on many different fronts. On the contrary, the impatience of the landless peasants with the slowness of the reform led them, on occasions, to occupy the lands of the large latifundios in southern Spain.

The high degree of rural conflict during the 1930s was due, therefore, both to the impact of the Great Depression, particularly resulting from the high level of unemployment in rural areas that used more wage-earning workers, and, most of all to the open emergence of a significant distributive conflict between the large landowners and the day labourers and small farmers. This occurred in an unprecedented democratic context in Spain, which enabled the centre-left governments, pressured by the rural unions, to implement a broad legislative programme to favour the latter. The failed military coup of 1936, which rapidly escalated into a Civil War, from the outset was supported by the landed elites and generated an explosion of violence in the Spanish countryside, which affected particularly those who had defended the interests of the peasants (Preston, 2012; Casanova, 2013).

6. Autarchy, black market and the technological backwardness of the early years of the Franco regime

The Spanish Civil War had a severe impact on Spain's economy. This is usually the case in these types of situations (Collier et al., 2003). The Spanish case is exceptional because it took an extraordinarily long period of time for things to return to normal. The policy followed by the Franco regime has been identified as the main cause for this, particularly the repression and exile of the highest qualified segment of the workforce, the high military costs and difficulty in importing capital goods (Rosés, 2008).

In the case of agriculture, the considerable drop in the volume of production that occurred in 1936 was followed by generally lower values in the subsequent years, although the destruction by the war to crops, means of production, livestock and installations was limited (Barciela, 1986; Martínez, 2006). The pre-war levels of production were not regained until 1951. The contraction in labour productivity was brutal. Throughout the 1940s, this was, on the whole, lower than pre-war levels by more than 30% and the pre-conflict levels were not obtained again until 1962 (Prados de la Escosura, 2017). The other available indicators provide data that is equally bleak: a fall in production per hectare, the abandonment of land, a fall in the use of machinery with no replacement of obsolete or broken machines, a fall in the level of fertilisation per hectare, a severe reduction in real agricultural wages, delays in agricultural research and innovation, a strong contraction of exports of the products in which Spain had leadership positions in the world market. All of this suggests that what was taking place was more than a crisis in the traditional agriculture and was more related to a crisis in the agricultural modernisation process that had been in progress since the depression at the end of the nineteenth century. The innovation progress stopped completely, giving rise to a spectacular technological backwardness (Fernández Prieto, 2007). At the same time, hunger returned to the Spanish rural areas, while a formidable black market emerged as an alternative to the failed policy to force the sale of output, particularly basic foods, at prices too low to be able to expand supply profitably (Barciela, 1986; Christiansen, 2012).

Such a profound and long-lasting collapse of agriculture can be explained by the combination of the extraordinary consequences caused by the world war, a critical situation generated by the international isolation resulting from Franco's policy of aligning with the Axis powers and an economic policy which was grossly interventionist and deliberately isolationist.

In terms of agriculture, the war mainly affected livestock, which reduced considerably and, in a context, plagued by difficulties to replace machinery or to import new machines, this seriously affected the crops and meat production. With a substantial reduction in the availability of organic and inorganic fertilisers and the complete halt of rural-urban migration, productivity experienced a huge setback. Meanwhile, wages dropped as a result of the abundance of labour and the dictatorial framework in which labour relations were developed. All of this affected the production of basic foods which did not meet demand. The creation of the National Wheat Service to control the purchase of basic products, assigning obligatory quotas of production, acquired at low prices, pushed production levels down even further. This output was sold on the market through the official channels, determined by rationing and also through a flourishing black market which was tolerated by the authorities (Barciela, 1986).

The crisis completely paralysed the process of technical transformations that had begun after the end-of-the-century agricultural depression. The Spanish agricultural sector returned to productivity levels characteristic of the beginning of the twentieth century and although this process did not come to a complete standstill it was substantially delayed.

7. Conclusion. The final crisis of traditional agriculture

From the beginning of the 1950s, there was a gradual return to the transformation process that had been interrupted by the war and previous crisis. This was facilitated by the change in agricultural policy from 1951, the end of Spain's international isolation, the arrival to Europe of the technology previously developed in the United States and the strong economic growth of the European continent.

From the mid-1950s and during the successive decades, Spanish agricultural production experienced rapid growth. This growth occurred in a context of a slight increase or fall in the use of land and labour and a significant increase in the use of capital. Consequently, the overall productivity of the factors or labour productivity experienced impressive growth, not only comparable to that of the other Western European countries but somewhat higher (Martín-Retortillo and Pinilla, 2015). If the increases in production and productivity were among the highest in Europe, can we talk about a crisis? There was no crisis in the agricultural sector, in fact, it was experiencing explosive growth. However, there was a final crisis of the traditional agricultural model upon the completion of a series of changes that had been implemented earlier which had come to a complete standstill due to the war and the problems of the 1940s. The new agricultural model was to be based on an intense capitalisation process, an enormous reduction in the use of the labour force and a complete transformation of the function of production.

The traditional production methods that still prevailed or that had re-emerged as a result of the problems in the 1940s disappeared from the Spanish countryside. The end of this traditional way of life and, most of all, the ensuing rural exodus took the form of a radical crisis in those areas where the intensity of the emigrations was so great that they gave rise to intense processes of rural depopulation (Collantes and Pinilla, 2011).

The other side of this situation was an intense mechanisation of the agricultural activity, an intensive use of means of production such as inorganic and chemical fertilisers, pesticides, new varieties of hybrid seeds and a formidable extension and improvement of irrigation.

The results of all of this was an agricultural sector that was much more closely linked to the industrial sector for the purchase of inputs and the sale of its output to be transformed in the agro-industry, a higher agricultural income due to the strong growth in productivity, a strong rise in the percentage represented by livestock production of total agriculture and a clear dependence on the financial sector for obtaining the necessary capital (Clar and Pinilla, 2009). From the institutional point of view, although the crude interventionism of the 1940s was softened, the surge in intervention and regulation policies in agriculture also affected Spanish agriculture in a similar way as in other developed countries (Fernández, 2008).

The acceleration and culmination of the industrialisation process in Spain played a key role in the final modernisation of Spanish agriculture. Industry and the cities were demanding labour which caused a mass exodus from the rural areas. At the same time, the strong increase in per capita income generated a profound change in the diet of Spaniards, with an increase in products with higher income elasticity. The production of livestock products such as meat or dairy goods increased considerably as did that of animal fodder, and they became the drivers for the growth of the agricultural output. Similarly, fresh fruit and vegetables also experienced significant increases in production. The interactions between agriculture and industry were also reversed. The agricultural sector became an important purchaser of industrial goods.

From the mid-1950s, Spanish agriculture returned to being a sector with enormous export potential, although the misalignments between demand and supply, partly explained by the errors in the agricultural pricing policy, determined that during a good part of the 1960s, the agricultural trade balance was negative. After the 1970s, particularly after Spain's entry into the then European Community, Spanish agriculture reinforced its traditional exporting vocation, occupying a leading position in international markets in many products (Clar et al., 2015).

In short, the technological supply for agriculture which was available from the beginning of the 1950s, the culmination of the industrialisation process in Spain and the growing connection with the international economy rendered the social and technological model of the country's traditional agriculture unfeasible.

Note

1 This study has received financial support from Spain's Ministry of Science and Innovation, project PGC2018-095529-B-I00 and from the Government of Aragon, through the Research Group S55_20R. I thank the editors for their comments and suggestions.

Bibliography

Acemoglu, D., Cantoni, D., Johnson, S. and Robinson, J.A., 2011, 'The Consequences of Radical Reform: The French Revolution', *American Economic Review*, 101(7), pp. 3286–3307.

Aparicio, G. and Pinilla, V., 2019, 'International Trade in Wheat and Other Cereals and the Collapse of the First Wave of Globalisation, 1900–1938', *Journal of Global History*, 14(1), pp. 44–67.

Aparicio, G., Pinilla, V. and Serrano, R., 2009, 'Europe and the International Agricultural and Food Trade, 1870–2000', in P. Lains and V. Pinilla (eds.), *Agriculture and Economic Development in Europe since 1870*, London: Routledge, pp. 52–75.

Ayuda, M.I., Ferrer-Pérez, H. and Pinilla, V., 2020, 'Explaining World Wine Exports in the First Wave of Globalization, 1848–1938', *Journal of Wine Economics*, 15(3), pp. 263–283.

Barciela, C., 1986, 'Introducción', in R. Garrabou, C. Barciela and I. Jiménez Blanco (eds.), *Historia Agraria de la España contemporánea. 3. El fin de la agricultura tradicional (1900–1960)*, Barcelona: Crítica, pp. 383–454.

Barquín, R., 2003, 'El comercio exterior de trigo y harina y las crisis de subsistencias en España', *Transportes, servicios y comunicaciones*, 5, pp. 127–148.

Brassley, P., Segers, Y. and Van Molle, L. (eds.), 2012, *War, Agriculture, and Food: Rural Europe from the 1930s to the 1950s*, London: Routledge.

Carreras, A. and Tafunell, X., 2003, *Historia económica de la España contemporánea*, Barcelona: Crítica.

Casanova, J., 2013, *A Short History of the Spanish Civil War*, London: I.B. Tauris.

Chatriot, A., 2016, *La politique du blé: crises et régulation d'un marché dans la France de l'entre-deux-guerres*, Paris: Institut de la gestion publique et du développement économique.

Chevet, J.M., Fernandez, E., Giraud-Héraud, E. and Pinilla, V., 2018, 'France' in K. Anderson and V. Pinilla (eds.), *Wine Globalization: A New Comparative History*, New York: Cambridge University Press, pp. 55–91.

Christiansen, T., 2012, *The Reason Why. The Post Civil-War Agrarian Crisis in Spain*, Zaragoza: Prensas Universitarias de Zaragoza/SEHA.

Clar, E. and Pinilla, V., 2009, 'The Contribution of Agriculture to Spanish Economic Development, 1870–19173', in P. Lains and V. Pinilla (eds.), *Agriculture and Economic Development in Europe since 1870*, London: Routledge, pp. 311–332.

Clar, E., Martín-Retortillo, M. and Pinilla, V., 2018, 'The Spanish path of Agrarian Change, 1950–2005: From Authoritarian to Export Oriented Productivism', *Journal of Agrarian* Change, 18(2), pp. 324–347.

Clar, E., Pinilla, V. and Serrano, R., 2015, 'El comercio agroalimentario español en la segunda globalización', *Historia Agraria*, 63, pp. 183–213.

Cobo, F. and Garrido, P., 2021, *La República en los pueblos. Conflicto, radicalización y exclusión en la vida política local durante la Segunda República española (19314–1936)*, Albolote (Granada), Comares.

Collantes, F. and Pinilla, V., 2011, *Peaceful Surrender: The Depopulation of Rural Spain in the Twentieth Century*, Newcastle upon Tyne: Cambridge Scholars Publishing.

Collier, P., Elliott, V.L., Hegre, H., Hoeffler, A., Reynal-Querol, M. and Sambanis, N., 2003, *Breaking the Conflict Trap: Civil War and Development Policy. A World Bank Policy Research Report*, Washington, DC: World Bank and Oxford University Press.

Comín, F., 2002, 'El periodo de entreguerras, (1914–1936)', in F. Comín et al. (eds.), *Historia Económica de España. Siglos X–XX*, Barcelona: Crítica, pp. 285–330.

Comín, F., 2011, 'Política y economía: los factores determinantes de la crisis económica durante la Segunda República (1931–1936)', *Historia y política: ideas, procesos y movimientos sociales*, 26, pp. 47–79.

Comín, F., 2012, 'La Gran Depresión internacional y la Segunda República', in E. Llopis and J. Maluquer de Motes (eds.), *España en crisis. Las grandes depresiones económicas, 1348–2012*, Barcelona: Pasado y Presente, pp. 133–164.

Domenech, J., 2013, 'Rural Labour Markets and Rural Conflict in Spain before the Civil War (1931–6)', *Economic History Review*, 66(1), pp. 86–108.

Federico, G., 2004, 'The Growth of World Agricultural Production 1800–1938', *Research in Economic History*, 22, pp. 125–182.

Federico, G., 2005, *Feeding the World: An Economic History of Agriculture, 1800–2000.* Princeton: Princeton University Press.

Federico, G., 2012a, 'Natura non fecit saltus: The 1930s as the Discontinuity in the History of European Agriculture', in P. Brassley, Y. Segers, and L. Van Molle (eds.), *War, Agriculture, and Food: Rural Europe from the 1930s to the 1950s*, London: Routledge, pp. 15–32.

Federico, G., 2012b, 'The Corn Laws in Continental Perspective', *European Review of Economic History*, 16(2), pp. 166–187.

Fernández Prieto, L., 2007, *El apagón tecnológico del franquismo. Estado e innovación en la agricultura española del siglo XX*, Valencia: Editorial Tirant Lo Blanch.

Fernández, E., 2008, 'Las políticas redistributivas de la España no democrática: Del objetivo industrializador al sostenimiento de los ingresos de los agricultores (1950–1975)', *Investigaciones de Historia Económica*, 12, pp. 11–42.

Findlay, R. and O'Rourke, K.H., 2007, *Power and Plenty: Trade, War, and the World Economy in the Second Millennium*, Princeton: Princeton University Press.

Gallego, D., 2001, 'Historia de un desarrollo pausado: integración mercantil y transformaciones productivas de la agricultura española (1800–1936), in J. Pujol et al. (eds.), *El pozo de todos los males. Sobre el atraso en la agricultura española contemporánea*, Barcelona: Crítica, pp. 147–214.

Gallego, D., 2005, 'La formación de los precios del trigo en España (1820–1869)', *Historia Agraria*, 36, pp. 263–285.

Gallego, D., Iriarte, I. and Lana, J.M., 2010, 'Las Españas rurales y el Estado (1800–1931)', in R. Robledo (ed.), *Sombras del progreso. Las huellas de la historia agraria*, Barcelona: Crítica, pp. 85–116.

Gallego, D. and Pinilla, V., 1996, 'Del librecambio matizado al proteccionismo selectivo: el comercio exterior de productos agrarios en España entre 1850 y 1935', *Revista de Historia Económica*, XIV(2 and 3), pp. 371–420 and pp. 619–639.

Gerhard, G., 2014, 'The Modernization Dilemma: Agrarian Policies in Nazi Germany', in L. Fernández-Prieto, J. Pan-Montojo and M. Cabo (eds.), *Agriculture in the Age of Fascism*, Brepols: Turnhout, Rural History in Europe, 13, pp. 139–58.

González de Molina, M., Soto Fernández, D., Guzmán Casado, G., Infante-Amate, J., Aguilera Fernández, E., Vila Traver, J., García Ruiz, R., 2020, *The Social Metabolism of Spanish Agriculture, 1900–2008*, Cham: Springer.

Grando, S. and Volpi, G., 2014, 'Backwardness, Modernization, Propaganda: Agrarian Policies and Rural Representations in the Italian Fascist Regime', in L. Fernández-Prieto, J. Pan-Montojo, and M. Cabo (eds.), *Agriculture in the Age of Fascism*, Brepols: Turnhout, Rural History in Europe, 13, pp. 43–84.

Grigg, D., 1992, *The Transformation of Agriculture in the West*, Oxford: Blackwell.

Hynes, W., Jacks, D.S and O'Rourke, K.H., 2012, 'Commodity Market Disintegration in the Interwar Period', *European Review of Economic History*, 16(2), pp. 119–143.

Jacks, D., Meissner, C. and Novy, D., 2011, 'Trade Booms, Trade Busts, and Trade Costs', *Journal of International Economics*, 83(2), pp. 185–201.

Koning, N., 1994, *The Failure of Agrarian Capitalism. Agrarian politics in the United Kingdom, Germany, the Netherlands and the USA, 1846–1919*, London: Routledge.

Lains, P. and Pinilla, V. (eds.), 2009, *Agriculture and Economic Development in Europe since 1870*, London: Routledge.

Llopis, E., 2002, 'Expansión, reformismo y obstáculos al crecimiento (1715–1789)', in F. Comín, M. Hernández and E. Llopis (eds.), *Historia Económica de España. Siglos X–XX*, Barcelona: Crítica, pp. 121–202.

Martiin, C., Pan-Montojo, J. and Brassley, P. (eds.), 2016, *Agriculture in Capitalist Europe, 1945–1960. From Food Shortages to Food Surpluses*, London: Routledge.

Martín-Retortillo, M. and Pinilla, V., 2015, 'Patterns and Causes of Growth of European Agricultural Production, 1950–2005', *Agricultural History Review*, 63(I), pp. 132–159.

Martínez, E., 2006, 'El campo en guerra: organización y producción agraria', in P. Martín Aceña and E. Martínez (eds.), *La economía de la guerra civil*, Madrid: Marcial Pons, pp. 107–159.

Millán, J., 2000, 'Los poderes locales en la sociedad agraria: una propuesta de balance', *Historia Agraria*, 22, pp. 97–110.

Moser, P. and Varley, T. (eds.), 2013, *Integration through Subordination. The Politics of Agricultural Modernisation in Industrial Europe*, Brepols: Turnhout, Rural History in Europe, 8.

Ocampo, J.A. and Parra-Lancourt, M., 2010, 'The Terms of Trade for Commodities since the Mid-19th Century', *Revista de Historia Económica-Journal of Iberian and Latin American Economic History*, 28(1), pp. 11–43.

O'Rourke, K.O., 1997, 'The European Grain Invasion, 1870–1913', *Journal of Economic History* 57(4), pp. 775–801.

O'Rourke, K.O. and Williamson, J.G., 1999, *Globalization and History: The Evolution of a Nineteenth-Century Atlantic Economy*, Cambridge: The MIT Press.

Pinilla, V., 1995, 'Cambio agrario y comercio exterior en la España contemporánea', *Agricultura y Sociedad*, 75, pp. 153–179.

Pinilla, V., 2009, 'The Impact of Markets in the Management of Rural Land', in V. Pinilla, (ed.), *Markets and Agricultural Change in Europe from the 13th to the 20th Century*, Turnhout: Brepols, Rural History in Europe, 2, pp. 11–36.

Pinilla, V. and Ayuda, M.I., 2002, 'The Political Economy of the Wine Trade: Spanish Exports and the International Market, 1890–1935', *European Review of Economic History*, 6(1), pp. 51–86.

Pinilla, V. and Ayuda. M.I., 2009, 'Foreign Markets, Globalisation and Agricultural Change in Spain', in V. Pinilla (ed.), *Markets and Agricultural Change in Europe from the 13th to the 20th Century*, Turnhout: Brepols, Rural History in Europe, 2, pp. 173–208.

Pinilla, V. and Ayuda, M.I., 2010, 'Taking Advantage of Globalization? Spain and the Building of the International Market in Mediterranean Horticultural Products, 1850–1935', *European Review of Economic History*, 14(2), pp. 239–274.

Pinilla, V. and Serrano, R., 2008, 'The Agricultural and Food Trade in the First Globalization: Spanish Table Wine Exports 1871 to 1935: A Case Study', *Journal of Wine Economics*, 3(1), pp. 132–148.

Prados de la Escosura, L., 2017, *Spanish Economic Growth, 1850–2015*, London: Palgrave Macmillan.

Preston, P., 2012, *The Spanish Holocaust*, Harper Collins: London.

Robledo, R. and González, A. L., 2017, 'Tierra, trabajo y reforma agraria en la Segunda República española (1931–1936): algunas consideraciones críticas', *Historia Agraria*, 72, pp. 7–36.

Rosés, J., 2008, 'Las consecuencias macroeconómicas de la guerra civil', in E. Fuentes Quintana and F. Comín (eds.), *Economía y economistas españoles en la Guerra Civil*, Madrid: Real Academia de Ciencias Morales y Políticas/Galazi Gutenberg, pp. 339–364.

Silvestre, J., 2005, 'Internal migrations in Spain, 1877–1930', *European Review of Economic History*, 9(2), pp. 233–265.

Simpson, J. and Carmona, J., 2020, *Why Democracy Failed. The Agrarian Origins of the Spanish Civil War,* Cambridge: Cambridge University Press.

Vanhaute, E., Paping, R. and Ó Gráda, C., 2007, 'The European Subsistence Crisis of 1845–50: A Comparative Perspective', in C.Ó Gráda, R. Paping and E. Vanhaute (eds.), *When the Potato Failed. Causes and Effects of the Last European Subsistence Crisis, 1845–1850,* Turnhout: Brepols, CORN series, 9, pp. 15–40.

Vivier, N., (ed.), 2008, *The State and Rural Societies. Policy and Education in Europe, 1750–2000,* Brepols: Turnhout, Rural History in Europe, 4.

Zambrana, F., 1985, *Crisis y modernización del olivar,* Madrid: Ministerio de Agricultura, Pesca y Alimentación.

Part II

The mechanisms of the crisis

4 The 1929 crisis from the perspective of a food-importing country – The United Kingdom, 1928–35

Paul Brassley

1. Introduction

This chapter examines the topic of this book from the viewpoint of the major food importer of the time. The idea that the problems of agriculture were responsible for the wider crisis of the Crash of 1929 or the Great Depression has been advanced recently by Joseph Stiglitz and his co-workers (Delli Gatti et al., 2012), but they are not entirely alone. Twenty years ago a study of the European economy between the wars concluded that the declining incomes of the food-exporting countries reduced their demand for manufactured exports, and more recently a study of the aftermath of the First World War pointed out that agrarian interest groups had 'little to lose in abandoning internationalism' in the early 1930s, and so embraced the protectionism that rose rapidly between 1929 and 1934 (Feinstein et al., 1997: 101; Tooze, 2015: 503; Tracy, 1982: 145–6).

However, it seems easier to find historians writing of the agricultural industry and those in it as victims of wider economic forces: '... those who earned their living from the land .... suffered grievously from the economic blizzard' especially in less-industrialised eastern Europe (Kershaw, 2016: 200; Steiner, 2005: 668). Another economic history of Europe argues that farm prices fell in the 1920s because expanding production was not met by a comparable growth in food consumption, whereas in the 1930s the problems were caused by protectionism (Munting and Holderness, 1991: 18). Studies produced at the time in the 1930s identified three contributory factors: over-production in relation to diminished purchasing power, tariff and non-tariff trade barriers, and monetary fluctuations (League of Nations, Economic Committee, 1931: 18–35; RIIA, 1932: 245). Living in a food-importing country, the people and governments of the United Kingdom (UK) were interested in two issues: where would their food come from and at what cost, and second what impact would international market changes have on the country's own farmers?

2. The UK as the major world agricultural importer

Writing in 1930, C.S. Orwin, one of the most prominent agricultural economists in the UK, observed that '... of the sum total of our [food] requirements

DOI: 10.4324/9781003105466-6

it may be said that we live from Saturday to Monday on our own supplies, and for the rest of the week we draw on all the world' (Orwin, 1930: 2). In 1929 cereals and livestock products accounted for about half of world agricultural trade, the UK was the dominant importer, and it was in the process of taking an increasing share of the market, as Table 4.1 demonstrates. A study by the Oxford- based Agricultural Economics Research Institute, of which Orwin was the Director, found that in 1930 the UK 'with less than 3% of the world's population, took about 99% of the world's exports of bacon and hams, 96% of the mutton and lamb, 63% of the butter, 62% of the eggs, 59% of the beef, 46% of the cheese, 32% of the wool, and 28% of the wheat and wheat flour (Murray and Cohen, 1934: 5).

The next biggest importer of wheat and rye by the late 1930s was Germany, but its combined imports of these two grains amounted to only a little over a million tonnes, compared with UK imports of well over 5 million tonnes. The only item for which the UK was not the major importer was fresh pork, which the Germans imported from Denmark and the Netherlands (Brassley, 2012: 34). The UK was also a major importer of tropical crops such as cane sugar, coffee, tea and cocoa, and fats and oilseeds, but the discussion in this chapter will be largely limited to temperate agricultural products.

The UK's position in the world market for these temperate crops, together with meat and dairy products, had been growing since the 1870s. By 1932 food, drink, and tobacco imports were over 52% of the UK's total visible trade (Mitchell, 1988: 458). The UK's position in interwar international agricultural markets was therefore nothing new, but a continuation of a pattern that had been established in the last three decades of the nineteenth century. It was only slightly disturbed by submarine warfare between 1917 and 1918, as Offer (1989) has argued, so that the whole period from 1870 to at least the early 1930s, if not the outbreak of the Second World War can be seen as one of a consistent free-trading agricultural policy (Perren, 1995). It was, furthermore, a policy differed fundamentally from the more protectionist policies followed by the major continental European countries (Tracy, 1982: 22–5).

The essentials of the story of international trade in agricultural products between the wars are now well known, having been explored by authors

Table 4.1 UK imports as a percentage of total world exports *(by weight)*

	1924–8	*1929–33*	*1934–8*
Wheat and rye	23.1	26.2	30.5
Beef, mutton and pigmeat	66.7	77.5	80.6
Butter	63.0	67.6	79.1

Source: World export data from Tracy, 1982: 143; UK import data from Ministry of Agriculture and Fisheries, *Agricultural Statistics, England and Wales* (annual). Slightly different figures for 1934–8 are reported in Brassley, 2012: 34.

from Tracy (1982) to Aparicio et al. (2009). World agricultural output increased between the wars, albeit to different extents in different countries, as Federico's calculations demonstrate. His figures suggest that world output, having fallen during the First World War, had regained its pre-war level by 1924, and then rose steadily until 1929. For the first half of the 1930s it fluctuated, but only by 3 or 4%, before beginning to increase again in 1937 (Federico, 2005: 234). Similarly, the volume of agricultural and food trade regained its pre-war level by 1925, rose to 1929, and then fell away a little, but never by more than 12% or so (Aparicio et al., 2009: 70). Specifying world price trends during the interwar period is a more difficult exercise, as they varied between one region and another, as Federico (2005: 22–3) points out, but it is clear that they fell from their relatively high wartime levels in the early 1920s, then began to rise again, until they hit the depression in 1929 and fell dramatically. They then remained below their 1929 levels until the outbreak of the Second World War (Tracy, 1982: 129).

As the UK was the world's major importer of agricultural products it would have been astonishing if these price changes had not affected its food import bill, and it did indeed benefit from these lower world prices in the 1930s. As Table 4.2 indicates, the effects differed from one commodity to another, but the overall pattern was much the same. High post-war prices were still affecting the import bill in 1921, but prices then decreased in the following two periods, covering the remainder of the 1920s. Wheat was most affected, and maize the least so. Then from 1930 onwards the prices of all these principal imports fell rapidly, reaching a minimum in 1934 in the cases of wheat, butter, and cheese, and in 1935 as far as maize and meat were concerned. Since imports formed a large proportion of total supplies, the internal market price received by UK farmers, as measured by the officially calculated Agricultural Price Index, reflected these international price changes, as the right-hand column in Table 4.2 demonstrates. The slow recovery that would generally

Table 4.2 World and UK product price indices *(1921 = 100)*

	Wheat	*Maize*	*Meat*	*Butter*	*Cheese*	*UK API*
1921 prices (£)	17.5	10.0	97.8	240.2	124.0	100
1922–5	69	87	76	75	80	74
1926–9	66	81	73	70	76	67
1930	47	58	71	57	65	61
1933	31	40	50	32	40	49
1934	30	43	55	29	38	52
1936	42	44	55	38	47	56

Source: Calculated from Ministry of Agriculture and Fisheries, *Agricultural Statistics, England and Wales* (annual). UK API (column 2) is the UK all products domestic agricultural price index, calculated from MAFF, 1968: 85 rebased to 1921. Individual product price indices are all import prices.

Table 4.3 UK import costs (*£million*)

	Wheat	*Maize*	*Meat*	*Butter*	*Cheese*
1921	89.7	18.4	131.7	42.3	17.4
1922–5	71.2	14.8	108.2	46.1	14.2
1926–9	69.1	14.3	106.4	50.8	14.1
1930	49.7	9.9	107.6	46.9	12.6
1933	34.6	10.3	74.9	34.3	7.6
1934	30.8	13.3	79.1	33.3	7.0
1936	41.8	16.3	76.6	44.4	7.8

Source: Calculated from Ministry of Agriculture and Fisheries, *Agricultural Statistics, England and Wales* (annual).

continue up to the outbreak of war in 1939 could be detected by 1936 in the prices of all these commodities. As Table 4.3 shows, the total cost of importing each of them tracked the price changes remarkably closely.

Clearly these were not the only agricultural commodities imported into the UK in the interwar period. The annual statistical publication of the Ministry of Agriculture, upon which Table 4.2 is based, listed 47 different agricultural commodities in 1925. The smallest individual item was the £82,000 spent on importing haricot beans, and the largest the £76.157 million on wheat and wheat flour. The figures for meat in Table 4.2 include several types that were individually listed, such as beef and veal, mutton and lamb, pork, bacon, hams, and 'meat, unenumerated'. One of the largest items not listed in Table 4.2, which otherwise covers the most important imported products, was, perhaps surprisingly, 'eggs in shell', upon which UK importers spent more in 1925 than they spent on maize or cheese. Another major absentee from this list is sugar, which did not appear in the agricultural statistics because UK production at that point was negligible. The implication, if import costs fell as prices fell, is that the quantities imported varied little, or at least less than the costs of importing them. The extent to which this is true is tested in Table 4.4, which lists the quantities of these principal agricultural imports. What becomes clear from these figures is that there was no significant change in the level of imports of wheat, meat, and cheese, whereas maize and butter imports were both higher after 1930 than before.

The other major changes were in the sources of these imports, as Table 4.5 demonstrates. In this table the British Empire countries most often mentioned are Canada, Australia, New Zealand, and India. Argentina, as far as trade regulations were concerned was, as we shall see below, often treated almost as an Empire country.

One thing that emerges clearly from Table 4.5 is that the sources of butter and cheese imports changed very little in these years. The major butter suppliers were New Zealand and Denmark, although Australia was also a regular supplier, as was the country initially listed as the 'Irish Free State' and later as

Table 4.4 Physical quantities of UK imports

	Wheat (million tons)	*Maize (million tons)*	*Meat (million tons)*	*Butter (thousand tons)*	*Cheese (thousand tons)*
1921	5.1	1.8	1.3	176	141
1922–5	5.9	1.7	1.5	256	144
1926–9	6.0	1.8	1.5	302	150
1930–2	6.2	2.3	1.6	387	150
1933–6	5.8	3.1	1.5	474	143

Source: calculated from Ministry of Agriculture and Fisheries, *Agricultural Statistics, England and Wales* (annual).

Table 4.5 Sources of imports
(percentage of each commodity)

	Wheat and flour	*Maize*	*Meat*	*Butter*	*Cheese*
1922					
British Empire countries	44.6	22.8	26.1	47.6	84.4
Argentina	16.3	34.5	37.2	–	–
USA	37.9	39.6	15.7	–	–
Other countries	1.1	3.1	20.9	44.0	15.6
1929					
British Empire countries	37.6	16.5	17.3	41.2	84.3
Argentina	37.1	69.3	40.0	4.7	–
USA	20.6	10.4	6.0	–	–
Other countries	4.7	3.8	36.7	54.0	15.7
1933					
British Empire countries	67.5	5.7	29.2	52.7	92.0
Argentina	20.0	79.6	32.6	2.3	–
USA	0.1	0.7	2.4	–	–
Other countries	12.4	14.0	35.8	45.0	8.0
1936					
British Empire countries	83.2	2.9	38.7	52.7	89.9
Argentina	1.2	91.8	34.4	1.5	–
USA	0.1	0.2	1.3	–	–
Other countries	15.5	5.0	25.6	45.9	10.1

Source: Calculated from Ministry of Agriculture and Fisheries, *Agricultural Statistics, England and Wales* (annual).

Eire. The Netherlands and Sweden were also regular butter suppliers, and by the mid-1920s even the USSR (still appearing in the official publications as 'Russia') was sending more than 10,000 tons of butter to the British market each year. Canada and New Zealand were the principal sources of cheese, with the Netherlands as the principal regular supplier listed among the other countries. The aggregated meat import figures hide considerable variations from one type of meat to another. Denmark was by far the most important source of bacon and ham, with the Netherlands and Poland also making a significant contribution among those listed as 'other countries', and only Canada as a significant Empire supplier. On the other hand, Empire suppliers such as New Zealand and Australia had virtually the whole of the mutton and lamb trade, with some additional supplies from Argentina, whereas Argentina, and to a much lesser extent Uruguay and Brazil, were the main sources of chilled beef, with frozen beef coming from Australia and New Zealand.

The major changes in the pattern of imports were found in the cereal trades. Suppliers of maize, the principal feed grain, were evenly split between Empire countries (mainly South Africa), Argentina, and the USA in the early 1920s, but by 1936 Argentina dominated the trade. Conversely, from being a significant source of wheat up to the mid-1930s, Argentina appeared to drop out of the market in 1936, by which time Australia and Canada almost had the trade to themselves, although Russia and Rumania were listed among the suppliers from other countries. Perhaps the most interesting feature of these figures in Table 4.4 is the disappearance of the USA from the British market, not only for wheat and flour, but also for feed grains and meat. Given the importance of comments on the decline of agriculture and its impact on the depression in the USA (Delli Gatti et al., 2012: 62, 67), it is worth examining some statistical evidence for that country, as in Table 4.6. This shows how exports of two important agricultural commodities fell away to a greater extent than exports in general.

It is important to remember that there was a general fall in world prices after 1929, so the decline in total (i.e. not just agricultural) exports to the UK can be explained to some degree at least by this. However, a study measuring trade in constant 1992 US dollars found that total agricultural exports halved between the mid-1920s and the early 1930s (Gardner, 2002: 150). Moreover, as far as agriculture is concerned, the Table 4.6 data are in physical units, and they show that wheat output per hectare decreased slightly, wheat exports plummeted after 1933, and meat exports declined steadily. A study commissioned by the National Bureau of Economic Research in New York not long after these events confirmed these trends, although its figures differed in detail from those in Table 4.6. For example, it found that 40.5% of the net

Table 4.6 USA – production and exports

	1921	*1922–5*	*1926–9*	*1930–3*	*1934–6*
Total exports to the UK ($million, current prices)	942	941	877	434	419
Wheat area (million ha.)	26	23	24	23	19
Wheat output (million tonnes)	22	21	23	21	16
Wheat exports (million tonnes)	8	4	3	2	0.2
Meat exports (thousand tonnes)	361	354	180	128	94

Source: Mitchell, 2003: 145, 171, 279, 289–90, 479.

output of wheat was exported in 1921, a figure that was halved by 1930 and reduced to 3.5% in 1935 (Barger and Landsberg, 1942:53). It blamed the decline on increasing self-sufficiency in Europe, expanding production on the part of Canada, Argentina, and Australia, and 'so far as the United Kingdom is concerned, to the preferential treatment it has accorded Canada and Australia for political, and Argentina for commercial, reasons'.

While the UK remained 'inspired by the chimera of Imperial self-sufficiency', little change was to be expected (Barger and Landsberg, 1942: 55). In fact, as Table 4.6 demonstrates, both wheat and meat exports from the USA had halved during the 1920s, before the notion of imperial preference had had any legislative effect, so the extent to which it can be blamed for the decline in US trade might be questioned. On the other hand, as Murray and Cohen (1934: 13–16) point out, by 1933 foreign (i.e. non-Empire) supplies had decreased so much that Empire countries accounted for half of UK food imports, compared with only 38% five years earlier.

3. Explaining the changes in trade

The preceding section argues that the UK maintained, or even increased, its contribution to the demand for agricultural products from the world market throughout the pre- and post-1929 periods, although Empire and quasi-Empire suppliers were increasingly favoured. Given that other European countries were increasingly protectionist, why was this?

Apart from a brief period between 1917 and 1921, when cereal prices were guaranteed, albeit at a lower level than the market prices then prevailing, the UK market had operated at world prices since 1846 (Brassley, 2015: 112). During the 1920s successive UK governments operated agricultural policies that maintained free trade in farm products and emphasised the need for farmers 'to organise themselves on an economic basis' (Howkins, 2003: 50; Sheail, 2010: 237). It was a decade in which UK agriculture suffered from a lack of domestic demand, as unemployment in the heavy industries that had expanded during the war – coal mining, iron and steel, heavy engineering – together with textiles meant that unemployment was normally over 1 million, so that, in Edith Whetham's words, 'there remained over a million families who could not afford to buy the food which farmers in England and Wales had difficulty in selling' (Mowat, 1968: 165, 274–5; Whetham, 1978: 153).

Farm incomes fell: one estimate calculates that the average for 1924–9 was only 77% of the average for 1904–10 (Brassley, 2014: 189), although the effects were seen more in arable farming areas than in livestock districts. In June 1929, when UK agricultural economists met at the annual conference of the learned society they had formed in 1926, they heard a series of papers which put the blame for 'the present agricultural depression' on falling world food prices and monetary factors following the UK's return to the Gold Standard (Enfield, 1929: 121–2; Thompson, 1929: 42–8).

Like both of the two main political parties, Labour and Conservative, the agricultural economists were anti-protectionist (Cooper, 1989; Griffiths, 2007). One of their leading members, C.S. Orwin, argued that the UK felt no need to protect agriculture, which only occupied 7% of its population, in the same way as France or Germany, with their much higher agricultural populations. The real competitor of the UK farmer, he felt, was the exporting manufacturer. Protecting agriculture would reduce the demand for manufactured exports, which provided work for far more people (Orwin, 1930: 36). A later report agreed, pointing out that restricting major import commodities such as wheat and beef would 'inevitably arouse the deepest resentment in the agricultural exporting countries. These are largely the countries which constitute what we have come to call the sterling area and it is mainly in them that the British Government has been attempting to secure a larger market for our exports by means of trade agreements and reciprocal concessions' (Astor and Rowntree, 1935: 28–9).

Britain was an industrial country. Manufactures accounted for 77% of the value of its merchandise exports in 1929, and 34% of its national product came from manufacturing and construction, which employed 31.7% of the workforce in 1930. In agriculture, in contrast, 7.6% of the labour force produced 4% of the national product (Daunton, 2007: 14; Feinstein et al., 1997: 59; Mitchell, 1978: 433). As Rooth (1985) has argued, there was little possibility of international trade negotiations prioritising the agricultural industry over the need to maintain manufacturing exports, especially as invisible exports such as shipping, financial services and overseas investment earnings were declining at the same time (Kennedy, 2001: 269). The argument that a prosperous agriculture could have replaced export customers as a market for UK manufactured products was refuted at the time by Astor and Rowntree (1939: xiv), who pointed out that the most valuable exports, such as steel rails, locomotives and machine tools, were of little interest to farmers.

What Astor and Rowntree did not mention, probably because it was so obvious to them that it did not need to be said, was that the main exporters of the temperate agricultural products – wheat, beef, butter, cheese, etc. – that competed with UK domestic production were former British colonial possessions. For the UK consumer, discriminating against farmers in these countries would have meant taking action against people who shared history, culture, and in some cases family connections. In this the UK was different from France, Germany, the Netherlands, and Belgium, whose colonial connections in the interwar years produced Mediterranean or tropical agricultural products. Where there were similar interests between home and colonial countries, as in the case of French and Algerian wine production, it is worth noting that access to the domestic market was maintained (Tracy, 1982: 144, 178). These differences between the UK, with its temperate colonies, and other European countries, appear to have been under-explored, and deserve further investigation.

4. Changing UK agricultural policies

By 1931, therefore, countervailing forces were at work on UK agricultural policy makers. On one side there was pressure to do something for agriculture; on the other, it was important to safeguard the interests of the industrial majority. During the 1920s protectionist policies in other European countries that had previously been food importers increasingly closed their markets and thus made the UK market more attractive. The volume of imports gradually increased, as Table 4.3 indicates. Then came what the League of Nations Economic Committee (1931) called 'the Agricultural Crisis', and a UK Ministry of Agriculture economist at the time termed 'the world crisis' (Street, A.W., 1933: 4). He argued that monetary disturbances and cutbacks in manufacturing led to unemployment and reduced consumer purchasing power and consequently 'a more or less complete breakdown of the exchange mechanism over the greater part of the world'.

World non-agricultural production, according to League of Nations data, fell by 36% between 1929 and 1932, but agricultural supply was less elastic, and fell by only 2% (Murray and Cohen, 1934: 90). As small producers operating in more competitive markets, farmers either could not or would not reduce production, so farm prices fell further. Faced with declining world prices, some exporting country governments tried to reduce world market volumes by supply restrictions or stock building, while others tried to help their own producers with export subsidies. Continental European importers increased tariffs. Since the UK market was still open in 1931 there was an 'unparalleled inrush' of food. Disaggregating the data in Table 4.4 suggests that the tonnage of the five imports listed there increased by 23% between 1928 and 1931. Although it was initially hoped (at least by farmers) that the UK's departure from the Gold Standard in September 1931 would increase import prices and so cut volumes, many of the main exporters to the UK devalued their currencies at the same time, so that there was little net effect (Murray and Cohen, 1934: 7; Street, A.W., 1933: 4–5).

The actions of the National government that came into office in the autumn of 1931 indicated that it was less wedded to free trade than its predecessors for the last ten years (or indeed for the previous 80 years) had been. In November 1931 import duties were imposed on some types of fruit, flowers and vegetables, and in March 1932 the Import Duties Act imposed a ten% duty on some agricultural products, although not wheat, meat or wool (Murray and Cohen, 1934: 7). British wheat producers, who were responsible for less than 20% of the national supply, were supported by the 1932 Wheat Act, which set a 'standard price' of 10 shillings per hundredweight (112 lb or 0.05 ton) for a 'standard quantity' of national output of 27 million hundredweights. Since the average market price of wheat in 1932 was 5s-11d per hundredweight this was a significant subsidy, and wheat producers responded accordingly, so that the standard quantity was exceeded in 1933 and the standard price correspondingly reduced (MAFF, 1968: 82, 109; Whetham, 1978: 243–4).

The introduction of protectionist policies, especially for agricultural products, was complicated by the fact that many of these products came from British Empire countries. Leaving aside any sentimental attachment to their peoples, they were a major market for UK manufactured exports (Youngson, 1960: 116). The problem was discussed at the Imperial Economic Conference held in Ottawa in the summer of 1932. The conference recognised the principle of quantitative regulation of imports into the UK, coupled with Imperial Preference, meaning that Empire products would pay lower, or zero, duties on importation to the UK. In effect, the needs of the UK producer came first, those of Empire producers second, and others last. These measures were enshrined in the Ottawa Agreements Act, passed in November 1932 and due to be operative from 1st January 1933, although rapid decreases in livestock prices in the autumn of 1932 led to a number of informal agreements to restrict meat imports before the Act came into force.

The farmer and writer A.G. Street, looking back on 1932, argued that, although it had been a most productive year, and the government had 'used practically every political method of helping the farming industry' the position of the farming industry was 'materially worse' than it had been at the beginning of the year. Prices had continued to fall (see Table 4.2) and Street laid the blame 'at the door of our present inadequate money system' (MAF, 1934: 141; Street, A.G., 1933: 279–81; note that there are more detailed discussions of these events in Tracy, 1982: 159–61 and Whetham, 1978: 243–6).

The other important component of government intervention in agriculture in this period was the passing in July 1933 of the Agricultural Marketing Act. There had been a previous Act of the same name in 1931, but it had little effect because although it encouraged farmers to come together to arrange the marketing of their produce, it did nothing to control imports. The 1933 Act, coming after the Ottawa conference, allowed the regulation of both imports and home production, and resulted in time in Marketing Boards for milk (the most successful), potatoes, hops, and pigs. The effects of these boards have been much discussed (e.g. Tracy, 1982: 161–5), but in the context of this paper, concerned with the position of the UK as the dominant food importer of this period, what mattered more was that agricultural products became an important feature of the trade agreements negotiated with various non-Empire countries in the following two years.

The annual report on agricultural statistics for 1933 noted agreements with Argentina, Denmark, Sweden, Norway, Iceland, Finland, Latvia and Estonia and indicated continuing negotiations with other countries (MAF, 1934: 143). A table of import regulations agreed for agricultural products between 1932 and June 1934 occupied 8 pages of small print. It covered wheat and wheat flour, meat and bacon, dairy products, potatoes, fruit, and vegetables. There were different regulations depending on slight differences in products: three sets of arrangements for condensed milk, for example, depending upon whether it was whole milk sweetened, whole milk unsweetened, or separated. From November 1932 to March 1934 eggs in shell were subject to three different rates of duty depending upon their size, and eggs not in shell four different rates depending upon whether they were liquid, dried whole, dried yolk or dried albumen. Empire products were generally free of duty, foreign products were dutiable, and Irish Free State products mostly but not always dutiable (Murray and Cohen, 1934: 98–106).

In short, what all these negotiations had attempted to do was to afford some degree of assistance to UK farmers without compromising the interests of the country's manufacturing exporters. Since Empire countries were the principal recipients of their exports, the food that they sent to the UK remained duty-free, while trade agreements were negotiated with other countries, notably Argentina and the Scandinavian countries, which were important both as agricultural suppliers and recipients of UK manufactures. If agriculture was to receive support, it had to be done in a way that did not interfere with foreign trade, which is why the 1932 Wheat Act was largely financed by the taxpayer (Rooth, 1985: 174, 190), and why the Milk Marketing Board established under the 1933 Agricultural Marketing Act was more successful, because there was no foreign competition for liquid milk, than the pigs or bacon boards.

5. The impact on UK agriculture

The result of all these negotiations and agreements was that UK farm prices rose, slowly at first (see Table 4.2), and the sources of imports changed significantly (see Table 4.5). But in 1934 Murray and Cohen were still concluding that only demand increases would have much effect on UK farm prices, and the president of the Agricultural Economics Society remained sceptical that all the government assistance given to agriculture since the end of the war had had much effect on the UK's arable acreage (Murray and Cohen, 1934: 93; Venn, 1934: 20–1). To judge from the official statistics (see Table 4.7) he was correct, since they show that the areas of the main arable crops were lower in 1928 than they had been in 1922, and lower still by 1936, except for wheat, which, as we have seen, was subject to government assistance.

Table 4.7 Crop areas and outputs in Great Britain

	Wheat		*Barley*		*Oats*		*Potatoes*	
	Area (million acres)	*Output (million tons)*	*Area (million acres)*	*Output (million tons)*	*Area (million acres)*	*Output (million tons)*	*Area (million acres)*	*Output (million tons)*
1922	2.0	1.7	1.5	1.1	3.2	1.9	0.7	5.2
1928	1.5	1.3	1.3	1.1	2.6	2.1	0.6	4.5
1929	1.4	0.3	1.2	1.1	2.7	3.3	0.7	4.7
1932	1.3	1.2	1.0	0.8	2.4	2.0	0.7	4.5
1936	1.8	1.5	0.9	0.7	2.2	1.7	0.6	3.8

Source: MAFF, 1968: 98–116.

Table 4.8 The grass area and livestock population in Great Britain

	Grass area (million acres)	*Cattle numbers (million)*	*Sheep numbers (million)*	*Pig numbers (million)*	*Fowl numbers (million)*
1922	20.0	6.9	20.1	2.5	29.0*
1928	20.9	7.2	24.0	3.2	45.3
1929	20.9	7.2	23.7	2.5	48.4
1932	21.4	7.6	26.4	3.4	65.2
1936	21.0	7.9	24.2	4.0	65.7

*the fowl number is for 1921.
Source: MAFF, 1968: 96–7, 122–8.

Table 4.8, in contrast, shows that the grass acreage was fairly stable after 1929, as were sheep numbers, but cattle, pig, and especially poultry numbers were rising.

As A.G. Street argued, whether they were arable or livestock products, farmers had to produce something in order to pay their debts (Street, A.G., 1933: 279). At a time when prices were falling, they could only continue in business by reducing their costs, and the cost that was most obviously reduced was that of labour. Between 1929 and 1936 the full-time employed (i.e. excluding farmers) labour force in Britain decreased by 100,000, and a further 35,000 part-time and casual workers also left the industry. Nearly 200,000 farm horses went too (MAFF, 1968: 62, 129). They could, and did, also reduce their machinery purchases. Ransomes, the largest maker of ploughs and other farm implements in the country, found that their sales fell by over 20% between 1928 and 29 and 1930 and 31, although they may have seen that as a relatively minor problem compared to the early 1920s, when sales were only half of what they had been in 1920. For the industry as a whole, domestic sales were only a part of their market. The big problem was that export earnings had fallen dramatically compared with their level in 1913. On the other hand, sales of cream separators, sterilising equipment and milking machines rose as the dairy herd expanded, and tractor production increased rapidly after the establishment of the Dagenham factory to produce Fordsons from 1933 onwards (Dewey, 2008: 187, 200–8).

For UK agriculture as a whole, the net effect was that costs were reduced in line with reductions in output, so that net farm income, in constant price terms, was no worse in the early 1930s than it had been in the late 1920s, and after 1935 farm incomes increased as output rose (Brassley, 2006: 198; 2014: 189). The impact of direct subsidies by 1937–8 was estimated to be worth £33million to UK agriculture. Half of this sum resulted from the relief from local taxation from which farmers benefitted. Against this, it was estimated that the effect of the Agricultural Wages Board in increasing farm workers' wages, and thus farmers' costs, was about £16 million. However, by the year

1937–8 it was also estimated that the effect of higher prices received by farmers as a result of 'the influence of the Marketing Acts and their supplementary legislation' was considerably greater, of the order of £40 million, at a time when the value of UK agricultural output was about £215 million (Astor and Rowntree, 1935: 18; Venn, 1939: 39–44). But those who farmed and worked on farms in the late 1920s and early 1930s could not know that they would be made better off by wars and rumours of wars.

The writers of the time, and those who subsequently produced their memoirs, remembered their difficulties. Those writers that based their books on their experiences in East Anglia, in particular, such as Adrian Bell (1940: 24) or Hugh Barrett (1994) emphasised the hardship of the time, although A.G. Street, who farmed on lighter land in southern England argued that part of their difficulties arose from their determination to adhere to traditional methods (Street, 1937: 74–5). Those who farmed in other parts of the country told a more complex story, in which hard times and the effects of change were intermixed. Ronald Firbank (1946) took over a large Welsh hill farm at the age of 21 and not only survived but expanded. Hubert Snowdon (1998) and Arthur Court (1987) in different parts of western England benefitted from the impact of the Milk Marketing Board on dairy farming, and there were several large farmers on the downland of southern England, such as the Hosier brothers (1951), A.G. Street (1932), John Cherrington (1979), and Rex Paterson (Martin, 2013) who survived and thrived by converting their arable to pasture for outdoor dairy herds. And Barrett admits that even in East Anglia 'the tide turned' by 1937 or 1938, and the farmers who had survived did well thereafter (Barrett, 1994: 102).

6. Conclusions

In discussing the role of agriculture in the economic crises of the interwar period, there are two principal questions concerning the UK agricultural industry: did it have an impact on the UK economy, and how did it affect the world economy? There is also a subsidiary question about the way in which interwar changes affected UK agriculture.

As we have seen, UK agriculture, responsible for only about 4% of the national gross national product (GNP), was too small to have much effect on the UK economy as a whole. It employed a greater proportion of the labour force – a little less than 8% – and contributed to the unemployment problem by releasing some of them over the course of these two decades, but it had little impact on the domestic demand for industrial products. Even in the agricultural machinery sector, more problems were caused by the decrease in export demand than by decreased purchases by UK farmers. It therefore seems difficult to argue that UK agriculture was responsible for the country's interwar economic problems. If anything, it was the reverse. The maintenance of free trading policies in the 1920s, and the design of food import policies after 1929, provided little protection for UK farmers but maintained food imports from many if not most of the main importers. Examining these events from a wider – i.e. non-agricultural – perspective, a recent economic history of the country as a whole concluded that the result was to keep food prices relatively low, 'so that more spending power could be released for consumer goods', whereas increasing food prices, while assisting the small minority that formed the agricultural population, would have had a serious impact on the general standard of living (Daunton, 2007: 185, 236).

Since the UK was the major agricultural importing country, changes in its traditional free-trade policies clearly had the capacity to create problems for the countries exporting agricultural products. In the event, as Table 4.5 and the discussion associated with it demonstrates, the principal effect of changing UK agricultural trade policy in the early 1930s was trade diversion, in this case to member states of the British Empire from other trading partners. This was what the Ottawa negotiations of 1932 were designed to achieve, and in large measure they did so. There were, of course, good reasons, deriving from the need to maintain industrial exports, to ensure that some of the UK's major non-Empire trading partners were not disadvantaged, and that is what the bilateral trading agreements with countries such as Argentina and Denmark which followed shortly afterwards were designed to do. There was no such agreement with the USA, which lost its important position in the UK market, but, as Table 4.6 demonstrates, this was a trend that was already in progress ten years before any trade-diverting agreements were concluded. In contrast with some other European importers, the UK's contribution to world demand for farm products was maintained throughout the interwar period.

The significance of continental protectionism was a feature that UK and British Empire economists were at pains to emphasise in the 1930s. In 1935 Sir Frederick Leith Ross, a civil servant in the UK Treasury, was commissioned by the Economic Committee of the League of Nations to make a study of the effects of increased agricultural protectionism. C.S. Orwin used two pages of the *Journal of the Royal Agricultural Society of England* to summarise his report for the benefit of its members. Leith Ross had concentrated particularly on the imposition of tariffs and milling quotas, mainly in Germany, France and Italy, but also in other Western and Central European countries. The biggest increases had been imposed after 1930, and he concluded that although there were many reasons for the present 'world crisis', one of the measures that would promote recovery 'would be the gradual relaxation of the present intensive agrarian protectionism of the industrial countries of Europe' (Orwin, 1936: 238–40).

In the opinion of R.R. (later Sir Ralph) Enfield, a senior economist in the UK Ministry of Agriculture and Fisheries, such a relaxation of protection was unlikely. In his Presidential Address to the Agricultural Economics Society in 1935 Enfield attempted to assess the possibilities of agricultural recovery in a detailed analysis of the current position of the industry. He argued that slowing population growth coupled with industrial depression across Europe had reduced demand, while agricultural output had been maintained. Inevitably prices had fallen, although putting the unemployed back to work would soon remove any excess food production. However, that was not happening; what was happening was agricultural protectionism, which had reduced continental European imports, by a half in the case of wheat and a third in the case of beef and butter, while German, French, and Italian domestic agricultural prices were more than twice UK prices by 1933, and farm output was increasing.

In addition, the food exporting countries had been affected by decreased capital transfers from the USA and Europe in the wake of the Crash, and in consequence protected their own industries, thus worsening the position of the manufacturing exporters. The effects of protectionism, he concluded, were unlikely to be undone, so non-European exporters were unlikely to recover their markets, while at the same time there was still a great potential demand for food among the poorer people of Europe (Enfield, 1935, 15–31). These, according to Frank McDougall, an Australian working for the League of Nations, were the 'disastrous results' of protectionism, which was producing a 'ridiculous' world agricultural situation (McDougall, 1936: 209).

Thus contemporary agricultural economists, and more recent economic historians, appear to agree with the conclusions that emerge from the evidence set out in this paper: UK agriculture, agricultural policies, and import policies were not responsible for the crisis in 1929. From the reverse perspective, if the events of 1929 and after had a limited impact on farming, it might be argued that they had a greater effect on agricultural policy. Professor Ashby argued at the time that neither the state nor the farmers had defined their policy aims. The farmers, he suggested, kept thinking that agricultural policy should enable them to maximise output; fortunately 'the State has been wise enough to repudiate the idea of using the last acre and the last man for the last ounce of production' (Ashby, 1939: 85–6). But among the policy measures that were introduced in the 1930s were some, such as drainage, lime and fertiliser subsidies, marketing boards, and using deficiency payments to support wheat production that would be maintained or extended during or after the Second World War.

Finally, there is the question of whether 1929 and the few years after represented a crisis for UK agriculture or just a temporary acceleration of existing trends. If it was a crisis, it was not the first to stress UK farmers with lower prices, but the third, after the late nineteenth century and 1920. Perhaps therefore it is better to see the whole 1870–1939 period, following the title of Richard Perren's book, as one of depression (Perren, 1995). This is not to say that it was an unrelieved price depression, because prices were beginning to rise a little before the First World War, and rose significantly during that war, but the agricultural price index was lower in real terms in 1913 than it had been in 1873, and lower again at its minimum point in 1934 than it had been in 1913. With the exception of the years between about 1913 and 1921 two or three generations of farmers had therefore coped with relatively low prices, and especially lower cereal prices. In the south-western county of Devon, for example, the arable area fell by 20% between 1875 and 1900, and the wheat acreage more than halved, but dairy cattle numbers increased by 30% (Anon, 1876; Board of Agriculture, 1901). Farmers adjusted their farming to reflect different circumstances. The years between 1929 and 1932 were therefore just more than usually difficult ones in a long series of difficult years. Can the same be said of agriculture in other European countries?

Bibliography

Anon, 1876, *Agricultural Returns of Great Britain, 1876*, London: HMSO, C.1635.

Aparicio, G., Pinilla, V., and Serrano, R., 2009, 'Europe and the International Trade in Agricultural and Food Products, 1870–2000', in P. Lains and V. Pinilla (eds), *Agriculture and Economic Development in Europe since 1870*, London: Routledge, pp. 52–75.

Ashby, A.W., 1939, 'Agricultural Conditions and Policies 1910–1938', in Anon (ed.), *Agriculture in the Twentieth Century: Essays on Research, Practice and Organization to be Presented to Sir Daniel Hall*, Oxford: Oxford University Press, pp. 57–86.

Astor, Viscount, and Rowntree, B. Seebohm, 1935, *The Agricultural Dilemma*, London: P.S.King and Son.

Astor, Viscount, and Rowntree, B. Seebohm, 1939, *British Agriculture: The Principles of Future Policy*, Harmondsworth: Penguin.

Barger, H., and Landsberg, H.H., 1942, *American Agriculture, 1899–1939: A Study of Output, Employment and Productivity*, New York: National Bureau of Economic Research, Inc.

Barrett, H., 1994, *Early to Rise: a Suffolk Morning*, Ipswich: Farming Press (originally published by Faber and Faber, 1967).

Bell, A., 1940, *The Cherry Tree*, Harmondsworth: Penguin (originally published in 1932).

Board of Agriculture, 1901, *Agricultural Returns for Great Britain, 1900*, London: HMSO, Cd.576.

Brassley, P., 2006, 'British Farming Between the Wars', in P. Brassley, J. Burchardt and L. Thompson (eds), *The English Countryside Between the Wars*, Woodbridge: Boydell, pp. 187–99.

Brassley, P., 2012, 'International trade in agricultural products, 1935–55', in P. Brassley, Y. Segers and L. Van Molle (eds), *War, Agriculture and Food: Rural Europe from the 1930s to the 1950s*, London: Routledge.

Brassley, P., 2014, 'Agricultural output, costs and incomes in the United Kingdom, 1919–1940', in J.-M. Chevet and G. Béaur (eds), *Measuring Agricultural Growth: Land and Labour Productivity in Western Europe from the Middle Ages to the Twentieth Century (England, France and Spain)*, Turnhout: Brepols, CORN series, 15.

Brassley, P., 2015, 'Britain, 1750–2000', in E. Thoen and T. Soens (eds), *Struggling with the Environment: Land Use and Productivity. Rural Economy and Society in North-Western Europe, 500–2000*, Turnhout: Brepols.

Cherrington, J., 1979, *On the Smell of an Oily Rag: My 50 Years in Farming*, London: Northwood Books.

Cooper, A.F., 1989, *British Agricultural Policy 1912–36: A Study in Conservative Politics*, Manchester: Manchester University Press.

Court, A., 1987, *Seedtime to Harvest: A Farmer's Life*, Bradford on Avon: Ex Libris Press.

Daunton, M., 2007, *Wealth and Welfare: An Economic and Social History of Britain 1851–1951*, Oxford: Oxford University Press.

Delli Gatti, D., Gallegatti, M., Greenwald, B.C., Russo, A., and Stiglitz, J.E., 2012, 'Sectoral Imbalances and Long-Run Crises', in F. Allen, M. Aoki, J.-P. Fitoussi, N. Kiyotaki, R. Gordon and J. Stiglitz (eds), *The Global Macro-Economy and Finance*, Basingstoke: Palgrave Macmillan, pp. 67–91.

Dewey, P., 2008, *'Iron Harvests of the Field': The Making of Farm Machinery in Britain since 1800*, Lancaster: Carnegie Publishing.

Enfield, R.R., 1929, 'Some Economic Causes of the Depression', *Journal of Agricultural Economics*, vol. 1(2), pp.117–129.

Enfield, R.R., 1935, 'The Expectation of Agricultural Recovery', *Journal of Agricultural Economics*, vol. 4(1), pp.14–43.

Federico, G., 2005, *Feeding the World: An Economic History of Agriculture, 1800–2000*, Princeton, NJ: Princeton U.P.

Feinstein, C., Temin, P., and Toniolo, G., 1997, *The European Economy Between the Wars*, Oxford: Oxford University Press.

Firbank, R., 1946, *I Bought a Mountain*, London: Harrap.

Gardner, B.L., 2002, *American Agriculture in the Twentieth Century: How It Flourished and What It Cost*, Cambridge, MA: Harvard U.P.

Griffiths, C.V.J., 2007, *Labour and the Countryside: The Politics of Rural Britain 1918–1939*, Oxford: Oxford University Press.

Hosier, A.J. and Hosier, F.H., 1951, *Hosier's Farming System*, London: Crosby Lockwood.

Howkins, A., 2003, *The Death of Rural England: A Social History of the Countryside since 1900*, London: Routledge.

Kennedy, P., 2001, *The Rise and Fall of British Naval Mastery*, London: Penguin.

Kershaw, I., 2016, *To Hell and Back: Europe 1914–1949*, London: Penguin.

League of Nations, Economic Committee, 1931, *The Agricultural Crisis*, vol. 1, Geneva: League of Nations.

MAFF [Ministry of Agriculture, Fisheries and Food], 1968, *A Century of Agricultural Statistics: Great Britain 1866–1966*, London: HMSO.

Martin, J., 2013, 'Rex Paterson (1903–1978): Pioneer of Grassland Dairy Farming and Agricultural Innovator', in R.W. Hoyle (ed.), *The Farmer in England, 1650–1980*, Farnham: Ashgate, pp. 295–324.

McDougall, F.L., 1936, 'World Agriculture and the Problems of Nutrition', *Journal of Agricultural Economics*, vol. 4(3), pp. 203–222.

Ministry of Agriculture and Fisheries [UK], *Agricultural Statistics, England and Wales* (annual).

Mitchell, B.R., 1978, *European Historical Statistics, 1750–1970*, London: Macmillan, abridged edition.

Mitchell, B.R., 1988, *British Historical Statistics*, Cambridge: Cambridge University Press.

Mitchell, B.R., 2003, *International Historical Statistics: The Americas 1750–2000*, Basingstoke: Palgrave Macmillan.

Mowat, C.L., 1968, *Britain between the Wars, 1918–1940*, London: Methuen.

Munting, R., and Holderness, B.A., 1991, *Crisis, Recovery and War: An Economic History of Continental Europe 1918–1945*, London: Philip Allan.

Murray, K.A.H. and Cohen, R.L., 1934, *The Planning of Britain's Food Imports: A Quantitative Study of the Effects of Recent Legislation*, Oxford: Agricultural Economics Research Institute.

Offer, A., 1989, *The First World War: An Agrarian Interpretation*, Oxford: Oxford University Press.

Orwin, C.S., 1930, *The Future of Farming*, Oxford: Oxford University Press.

Orwin, C.S., 1936, 'Farm Economics', *Journal of the Royal Agricultural Society of England*, vol. 97, pp. 237–257.

Perren, R., 1995, *Agriculture in Depression, 1870–1940*, Cambridge: Cambridge University Press.

RIIA [Royal Institute of International Affairs], 1932, *World Agriculture: An International Survey*, London: Oxford University Press.

Rooth, T., 1985, 'Trade Agreements and the Evolution of British Agricultural Policy in the 1930s', *Agricultural History Review*, vol. 33, part 2, pp.173–90.

Sheail, J., 2010, 'The White Paper, *Agricultural Policy*, of 1926: its Context and Significance', *Agricultural History Review*, 58(2), pp. 236–54.

Snowdon, H.N., 1998, *Born to Farm in Devon: By Horse and Handtool at Thurlestone 1918 to 1939*, Newton Abbot: Orchard Publications.

Steiner, Z., 2005, *The Lights that Failed: European International History 1919–1933*, Oxford: Oxford University Press.

Street, A.G., 1932, *Farmer's Glory*, London: Faber and Faber.

Street, A.G., 1933, *Hedge Trimmings*, London: Faber and Faber.

Street, A.G., 1937, *Farming England*, London: Batsford.

Street, A.W., 1933, 'The Agricultural Marketing Act 1933', *Journal of the Royal Agricultural Society of England*, vol. 94, pp.1–21.

Thompson, R.J., 1929, 'Some Indications of the Nature and Extent of the Present Agricultural Depression', *Journal of Agricultural Economics*, vol. 1(2), pp.38–51.

Tooze, A., 2015, *The Deluge: The Great War and the Remaking of Global Order*, London: Penguin.

Tracy, M., 1982, *Agriculture in Western Europe: Challenge and Response 1880–1980*, 2nd edn., St.Albans: Granada.

Venn, J.A., 1934, 'Presidential Address: The State and Agriculture', *Journal of Agricultural Economics*, vol. 3(1), pp.13–24.

Venn, J.A., 1939, 'Agriculture and the State: The Financial and Economic Results of Control', in Anon. (ed.), *Agriculture in the Twentieth Century: Essays on Research, Practice and Organization to be Presented to Sir Daniel Hall*, Oxford: Oxford University Press, pp. 21–49.

Whetham, E.H., 1978, *The Agrarian History of England and Wales, Vol. VIII, 1914–1939*, Cambridge: Cambridge University Press.

Youngson, A.J., 1960, *The British Economy 1920–1957*, London: Unwin University Books.

5 International markets, policy, and mobility. 'Rural Italies' in the 1930s recession

Francesco Chiapparino and Gabriele Morettini

1. Introduction

The example of Italian agriculture in the recession of the 1930s is more significant than the limited influence of the country on the international market for at least two reasons. First, the large variety of rural contexts makes the peninsula a useful framework of reference for observing the performance of a wide range of agricultural environments during the crisis. 'The differences – as stated by Ghino Valenti (1911: 1), one of the founders of national rural statistics – that emerge in agricultural Italy between one compartment and another, and sometimes between parts of the same compartment, are such and so great that it can be affirmed without exaggeration that our country contains in its restricted territory, of just over 286,000 square kilometers, all that is more typical, from the agricultural point of view, of the most distant countries in Europe'.

The marked heterogeneity of these 'rural Italies' (Jacini, 1881) allows us to appreciate, within the same institutional framework, the dynamics triggered by the crisis in a manifold set of agricultural contexts, ranging from the Apennine or Alpine subsistence economies to the sharecropping polyculture of Central Italy and the tree cultivations specialized for export in Sicily and Apulia, from the 'high farming' of Low Lombardy, to the industrial crops of the reclaimed Po Delta and the large cereal estates of the Mezzogiorno. A second feature that makes Italy remarkable, or in some respects even exemplary, concerns State intervention. Dictatorship guaranteed relatively wide freedom of action for Fascist policies such as ruralization or the *Battaglia del Grano*. Given that internationally the 1930s represented a turning point for the role played by State support in the primary sector (Federico, 2012), the rapid activism of Fascism in this field acquires considerable relevance. This chapter aims to both highlight the diversified effect of the recession on the various rural economies of the peninsula and outline the selective impact of regime policies. In addition, it tries to appraise the role played by both the population and labor mobility in these dynamics.

DOI: 10.4324/9781003105466-7

2. Clustering the 'rural Italies' on the eve of the crisis

With half or more of its workforce employed in the primary sector, Italy could be defined for the whole first half of the twentieth century as an only partially industrialized country, where agriculture maintained considerable importance although, in particular since the 1880s, it no longer represented the leading economic branch (Ciocca, 2007). Between the two wars the contribution of this sector to the national GDP decreases very gradually from 32% to around 25%, while the trendline in its added value, after sharing the slight grow of the first half of the twenties, actually stagnated from 1926 to the late 1930s (Figure 5.1). As regards employment, the structural shift from the primary to other sectors, which characterizes Italy during most of the first part of the twentieth century with a final crescendo at the time of the post-war 'economic miracle', seems to slow down in correspondence with the drop in prices in the 1930s (Figures 5.2 and 5.3).

According to official statistics, agriculture employs a slowly decreasing share of the active population in Italy from the late nineteenth century onwards. This contraction stops in the first half of the 1930s: from 10,449 million persons in 1931 the number of employees grows progressively to 10,503 million in 1936, then drops again the following year (10,401), falling to below 10 million only during the war, in 1941 (Broadberry et al., 2011: 53–4). National trends in agricultural output, therefore, are not in contrast with the idea of the agricultural stagnation which can be inferred from the collapse in rural prices or with the block in the labor force outflow hypothesized by recent literature (Delli Gatti et al., 2012). Data on the added value, however,

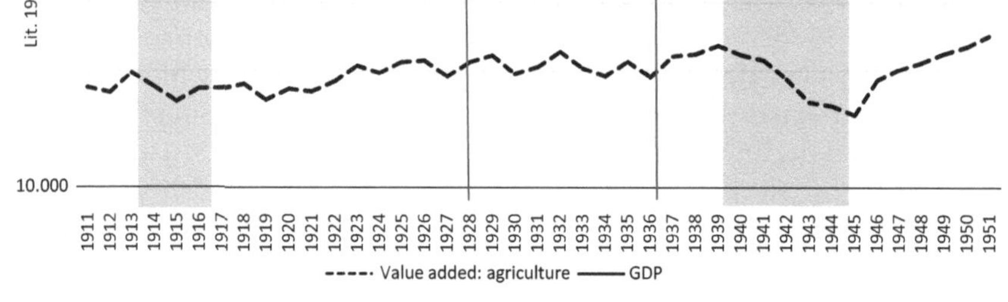

Figure 5.1 GDP and added value in agriculture, Italy 1911–51.

Source: Banca d'Italia, https://www.bancaditalia.it/statistiche/tematiche/stat-storiche/stat-storiche-economia/

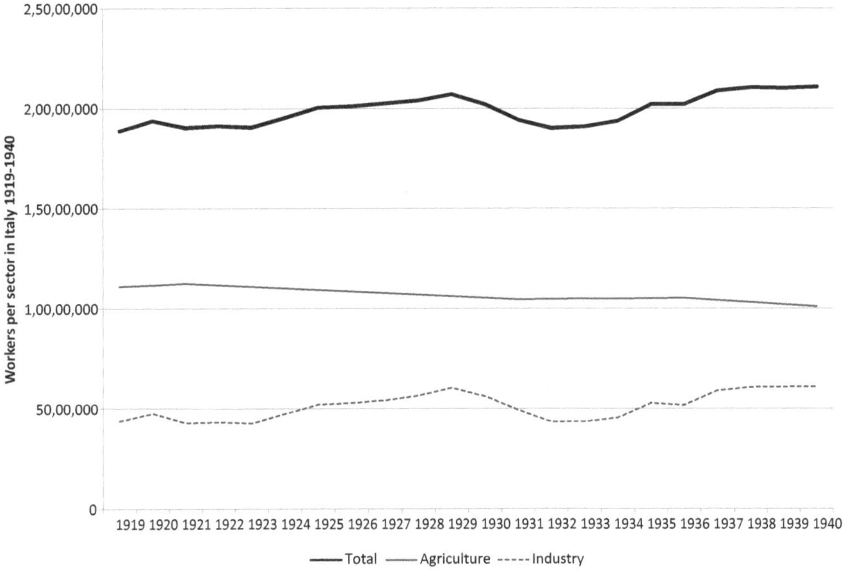

Figure 5.2 Workers per sector in Italy 1919–40.
Source: Broadberry et al., 2011: 53–4.

Figure 5.3 Wholesale price index 1928–38.
Source: Istat, 1935. 14; 1937, 149ff.; 1939, 197ff.

provide clear evidence of neither a fall in production (and incomes) nor a significant crisis in the primary sector.

Nonetheless, these data are not surprising if one considers the diversity of Italian agriculture. Italy was (and to a certain extent still is) a mosaic of countryside which is highly differentiated as to geographic, morphologic, and even climatic conditions, as well as to contracts and farm management systems (small and large ownership, tenancy, sharecropping, etc.), cultural and social configurations (with reference, for instance, to the density of the urban networks), level of capital investments (in terms of infrastructures, zootechnical heritage, endowment of rural buildings, etc.), or commercial targets (export-led, domestic market oriented, subsistence productions, etc.). Frequently the trends in all these components, which are often divergent, tend to offset one another, and thus to disappear or emerge only very weakly at a national scale.

The first step in analyzing the dynamics of the crisis is therefore the disaggregation of Italian agriculture into areas which are as homogeneous as possible, in order to discriminate the performance of the different rural settings within the country. To that end, the regional partitioning, commonly used for local analyses (Zamagni, 1978, Daniele and Malanima, 2011) is not adopted here, but on the contrary the investigation is carried out at provincial level, which allows a significantly fine scale to be reached as well as a reduction in the heterogeneity of the units of analysis. At the same time, a great deal of information has been collected at the detailed level of the agricultural zones[1]. The latter aggregate, however, is used only partially, unlike in other surveys (Martinelli, 2014), because it does not allow to cross the data with most of the historical statistics (and especially those on agricultural crops), which are available only at provincial level.

The sources of information are the 1931 Population Census, the 1930 Livestock Census and the 1929 *Catasto agrario* (Land register). The latter is probably the most reliable statistical inquiry on agriculture in the interwar period, the result of 20 years of efforts to improve the national agricultural data (Albertario, 1938, D'Onofrio, 2016). Over 50 variables, relative to conduction systems and cultivated lands (areas and production data for single crops), have been utilized to carry out a Principal Component Analysis, which allowed ten typologies of agriculture to be identified empirically, i.e. recurrent associations of crops, yields and conduction forms, in the 279 agrarian regions of the Kingdom (considering the national borders of the time). Through a further Cluster Analysis, the Italian provinces have then been grouped according to the relative incidence of these types of agriculture, obtaining 18 rural areas with a far higher degree of homogeneity than is found for the administrative regions (Chiapparino and Morettini, 2018). The resulting geography of Italian agriculture on the eve of the crisis is illustrated in Figure 5.1.

A wide range of agricultural systems emerges. The Northern plains are characterized by the agricultural capitalism of the Low Po Valley (Cluster Nr. 5), based on large tenancy, wheat-corn rotation, artificial meadows, and high livestock loads, together with the variant of Western Piedmont (3), featuring rice cultivation, and the plain provinces of Veneto (6), where peasant conduction is more common, and crops are more varied. Hilly Piedmont (Asti, 1) also constitutes a different context, where small ownership prevails in association with mixed crops, a good livestock endowment, and a marked specialization in wine production. The recently reclaimed area of the Po Delta (7), and above all the Province of Ferrara (8), are on the contrary characterized by an industrial agriculture, focused, among other productions, on sugar, hemp, and fruit connected with large agro-business companies and widespread trading networks. Although often integrated with small and medium farms, this agriculture relies on good capital availability, and modern cultivation systems, albeit with a more modest livestock endowment than in Lombardy.

Central Italy, on the other hand, is mainly characterized by its peculiar sharecropping and polyculture organization, *Mezzadria* (Cluster Nr. 9), combined with small peasant property at the higher altitudes. The Mezzogiorno, in turn, presents three areas of specialized (mainly export-led) cultivations: Sicily (17), where large cereal estates co-existed with tree crops, principally citrus fruits and, in the central part of the island, almonds; Central (13) and Southern Apulia (Lecce province, Nr. 14), specialized in wine, olives, and respectively almonds and tobacco; and the province of Naples (12), the traditionally richest and most diversified agriculture in Southern Italy (and in the whole peninsula), that produces vegetables, citrus fruits, wine, fruits, etc., as well as livestock, hemp and rye (!).

Other clusters concern inner and mountain areas. In the North, the longitudinally elongated provinces of the Alpine Arc (1) in fact comprise three different zones: the flat strip, which can be assimilated to the Po plain and often to the (not specialized) Veneto cluster; the pre-alpine hillsides, with their own agriculture (where, for example, silk was traditionally important), and the mountains, with valleys and subsistence economy. Further rugged environments are Liguria and High Tuscany (4) and, in the South, the provinces of the Strait of Messina (15), both featuring a poor subsistence agriculture associated with specialized productions, such as olives or citrus fruits, and goats in the South.

The rest of the Central and Southern part of the peninsula is composed of two clusters: the Arable plains (Agro Romano, Capitanata, etc., 11) characterized by large cereal estates in association with sheep breeding, and the residual internal areas (Southern Apennine, 10), mostly mountainous and hilly, where these same features are combined with small mixed subsistence farming. Similar characteristics are also shared by Sardinia (18), that represents the poorest Italian countryside (Zattini, 1924).

For the sake of simplicity, it can be stated that there are at least six different types of agriculture in interwar Italy: agricultural capitalism in the Po Valley (with different variants), industrial farming in the Po Delta, Southern specialized and export-oriented agriculture, *Mezzadria* in the Center, a large

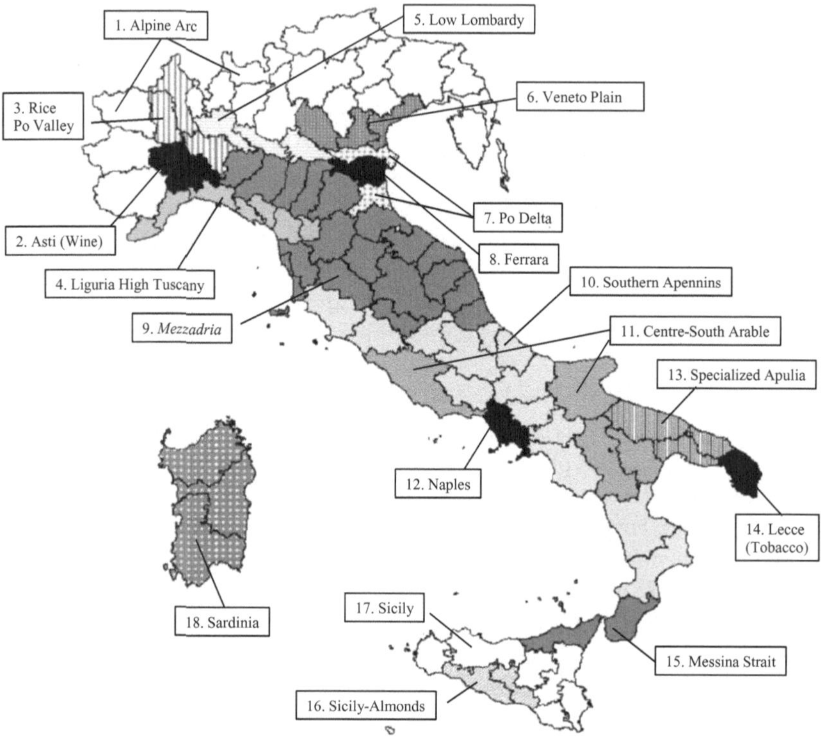

Figure 5.4 Provincial clusters in Italian agriculture, 1929.
Source: Chiapparino and Morettini, 2018.

estate economy based on cereals and sheep breeding, and subsistence farming in the inner areas (mainly, but not only in the South), which are the so-called 'bone', as opposed to the 'pulp' of the more fertile coastal areas (Rossi Doria, 1958: XIX) (Figure 5.4).

3. Winners and losers in the recession

As previously mentioned, a reconstruction of agricultural production at provincial level can take advantage of official statistics, which at least from 1929 report the physical quantities of a large set of crops with a good degree of reliability. Nonetheless, a monetary picture of agricultural output also requires a thorough knowledge of prices, which may differ greatly on single local markets and therefore represents one of the major drawbacks in the historical statistics (Federico, 2003: 376). Both contemporary and recent (Maroi, 1946; Baffigi, 2011) attempts have been made to assess the gross agricultural output between the two wars, but these reconstructions are restricted to single years and not aimed at diachronic comparisons. One exception is represented by an unpublished analysis, carried out at the end of the 1930s and explicitly based on homogeneous criteria over time (Chiapparino and Morettini, 2018). The author of this study is a fairly well-known agricultural statistician and geographer of the time, Luchino Franciosa, who estimated gross agricultural production both in 1929, using the Cadastral data as a basis, and in 1936–7 as soon as new reliable statistics were available. Although already used in 1942 by Guglielmo Tagliacarne, who was a forerunner in the field of modern market analysis, Franciosa's work was first published in a synthetic form only after the war (Franciosa, 1947). It is however an important reconstruction by an authoritative expert of the time, who had a prominent position in the Statistical Office of the Ministry of Agriculture as well as in Istat, the national statistics institute which was established in 1926. Access to privileged sources and a vast network of local informants and scholars enabled him to limit some inevitable errors and approximations. The results of this estimate are included within the cluster pattern in Figure 5.5.

Table 5.1 shows how diversely Italian agriculture is affected by the crisis. In 1936–7 as a whole it is still losing 10% of its output in comparison with 1929. However, many rural economies are in considerably worse conditions, while others record a better performance, and some have even exceeded their pre-crisis results. The Northern plain clusters, in particular, successfully withstand the recession. Positive dynamics are to be observed in the case of Low Lombardy, which features an agricultural capitalism that experienced the 1930 recession as little more than a conjunctural episode along a consolidated path of growth and accumulation dating back to at least the eighteenth century

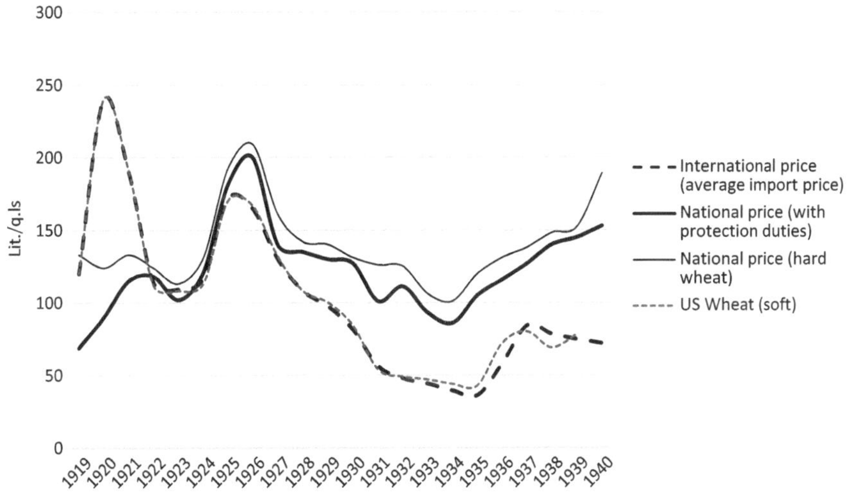

Figure 5.5 National and international (import) wheat prices 1921–39.
Source: Istat 1958: 173; Federico et al., 2011: 234–6.

Table 5.1 Gross salable agricultural product (Gsp) per hectare of Agrarian and forestry area (Afa) in the clusters of Italian agriculture, 1929 and 1936–37

	Afa	*Gsp per hectare (in Liras)*		*Italy = 1.00*		*Variation*
Cluster	*% of Italy*	*1929*	*1936–37*	*1929*	*1936–37*	*1929 = 100*
1. Alpine Arc	22.4	1,402	1,195	0.9	0.8	85
2. Asti (Wine)	0.5	2,151	2,508	1.4	1.8	117
3. Rice Po Valley	2.8	2,206	2,246	1.4	1.6	102
4. Liguria High Tuscany	3.0	1,750	1,345	1.1	0.9	77
5. Low Lombardy	2.2	3,828	3,954	2.4	2.8	103
6. Veneto Plain	2.3	3,113	3,050	2.0	2.1	98
7. Po Delta	1.1	3,251	3,513	2.0	2.5	108
8. Ferrara	0.7	3,229	3,394	2.0	2.4	105
9. *Mezzadria*	17.2	1,905	1,784	1.2	1.3	94
10. Southern Appennine	16.6	1,185	1,023	0.7	0.7	86
11. Central South Arable	8.2	1,089	946	0.7	0.7	87
12. Naples	1.0	4,676	3,132	2.9	2.2	67
13. Apulia Specialized	3.2	1,818	1,576	1.1	1.1	87
14. Lecce (Tobacco)	0.9	1,32	1,289	0.8	0.9	98
15. Messina Strait	2.1	1,763	1,092	1.1	0.8	62
16. Sicily-Almond	1.7	1,915	1,796	1.2	1.3	94
17. Sicilia	5.7	1,550	1,400	1.0	1.0	90
18. Sardinia	8.1	507	421	0.3	0.3	83
Italy	100	1,590	1,425	1.0	1.0	90

Source: Elaborations on estimations of Franciosa, 1947 and Cadastral data.

(Cafagna, 1989). A variant of this rural system, such as that of the large Piedmontese rice-growing property, achieves similar results, while a relatively worse trend is recorded in the Veneto plain, with its greater incidence of small and medium-sized farms. A leading position among the rural areas of the peninsula is also represented by the industrial agriculture of the Ferrara province and the surrounding provinces of Rovigo and Ravenna (the Po Delta cluster). Well-endowed with capital and land assets, these recently reclaimed areas prove to be the most capable in facing the recession. Nor should it be forgotten that the large tenants and landowners of these regions were one of the main interest groups supporting the Fascist regime (Fano, 1975; Cohen, 1979).

The example of the Asti province was fairly different because this specialized peasant agriculture remained, as will be seen later, almost deaf to the appeal of the *Battaglia del grano*. Nonetheless, in this case there were relevant investment efforts both in terms of capital (above all livestock) and labor, combined with particular attention to the manufacturing innovation and commercial enhancement of limited and sometimes high-quality wine productions (Cirio and Rapetti, 1984).

As regards Central Italy and most of Sicily, these areas experience a milder deterioration than elsewhere albeit for different reasons. The former (*Mezzadria*) can rely on the resilience of family farming and its prevailing integration in local market, less exposed to the fall of the prices. Whereas the whole of Sicily, excluding the North-Eastern part which belongs to the Messina Strait cluster, receives State support for the extensive cultivation of wheat (here typically associated with broad beans), which compensates for the reduction in specialized tree crops. For a further set of regions, on the contrary, the first half of the 1930s, and probably the whole decade after the revaluation of the lira in 1927, represents a period of great recession. This is the case, firstly, in the mountain areas characterized by a diffuse subsistence economy both in the Southern Apennines and in the Northern clusters, where, nonetheless, the Alpine regions are associated with richer hilly and flat areas.

Liguria and Upper Tuscany, lacking this combination, experience a heavier impoverishment, which also involves olives and other, formerly very profitable, specialized productions. Similarly, and to an even larger extent, the Southern export-oriented agriculture collapses in the 1930s, in the Naples province as well as in the central and Southern part of Apulia, Calabria, and North-Eastern Sicily. The fall is greatest in the latter cluster, the Messina Strait, where the ruggedness of the territory hinders the offset of specialized productions by extensive crops, and therefore this area represents the sum of three cumulative elements of weakness: as a mountain area, as an export-oriented agriculture (especially citrus), and as part of the *Mezzogiorno*. Finally, a further rural context that was severely affected by the recession is the poorest and most archaic part of Italian agriculture: the large arable estate areas of the continental South (including Rome in the Center) and Sardinia, which are affected by consistent contractions in their already very limited monetary output per hectare.

There are many causes for such a heterogeneous performance, all of which are mainly related to the different crop specializations and environmental potential of the various clusters. With the crisis market trends and related price movements impact above all on these specializations, producing the diverging results described above. Government policies, often with selective characteristics aimed at supporting single productions or social groups, also play a crucial role in determining these diverse outcomes. Moreover, together with prices and policies, many further elements may influence the different dynamics of the 'rural Italies', from the endowment of natural and reproducible capital, which eases the adaptation to the new conditions created by the recession, to the integration of the primary sector with manufacturing processes, that again focus the analysis on markets and the outlets for agricultural output. Among these factors, labor mobility, stressed in the hypothesis advanced by Delli Gatti et al. (2012), is of particular importance and will be discussed here to consider its connection with the intensity of the recession in the various clusters.

4. Markets and policies

The drop in agricultural prices, dating back to 1926 onwards, and hence prior to the 1929 crisis, has a decisive role in the international crisis of rural economies. In Italy, moreover, the decline is aggravated by the strong deflationary policy implemented by the regime in 1927. Above all, the crisis has a very selective impact on the different rural branches. In some of these, such as citrus fruits, the collapse in prices on international markets, which represent the major outlet for these productions, is reflected in a dramatic decline. In 1933 the average price of oranges falls to 36% of the 1929 price (28% of 1925), for lemons it drops as low as 31%, less than one-third compared with four years before (Istat, 2011, tab. 21.1). In the latter case, the situation is worsened by the loss of the profitable market of citric acid since, during this period, Pfizer and other international producers begin to extract this substance from sugar instead of low-quality lemons, as a reaction to the monopolistic rise in prices carried out by Messina firms at the end of the twenties (Lupo, 1990, pp. 264–6). The crisis, however, affects all branches of citrus production, from bergamot (Bevilacqua, 1980: 51–2) to high-quality lemons such as *Verdelli*, up to the point that in 1932–3 many fruits were not harvested from orchards (Lupo, 1990: 266). The slump in this crop has a decisive weight in the reduction in output in the Messina Strait cluster, where in 1936–7 lemon yield is 47% lower than in 1929, and it also significantly affects the other Sicilian areas.

Almonds, which were sold mainly to the North and Central European confectionery industry, also suffered a significant price contraction, losing in 1933 about half their 1929 value. Prices decline more moderately for other commodities like olive oil, which in 1933 loses around 1/3 of its 1929 value. What is interesting in this case is that olive production presents quite a diverse trend in North and Central Italy in comparison with the South, although the entity of this production in the former areas is much smaller. Ligurian oil in 1929–33 suffers a price drop of about 32% while Apulian oil prices decrease by 38%, starting from a cost already 5–10% lower than in Liguria (Istat, 1931: 15 and Istat, 1934: 15). The dynamics of the sector allow us to hypothesize that the limited production in the Center-North is more enhanced by the processing industry, mainly oriented to the internal urban market, compared to the South and the Islands, which are therefore severely affected by the collapse in exports (Franciosa, 1940: 72–83).

The case of grapes seems to be similar, although its analysis is further complicated by the extreme variety of wine types, qualities and therefore prices. In this branch too, Northern production reacts better to the crisis. The excellent performance of the Asti cluster is the fruit of articulated strategies which, on the one hand, imitate French producers and introduce the first Italian quality brands, and on the other aim to win over popular consumption on the large Milanese urban market. Generally speaking, cultivations oriented to domestic demand, from legumes to vegetables (if for local consumption), wood or industrial crops supplying national manufacturers, are less prone to the price depression than export commodities, such as fruits (Table 5.2).

Table 5.2 Estimation of the Italian gross agricultural production per groups of crops and macro-areas[a]

	Italy			*North*			*Center*			*South*			*Islands*		
	1929	*1936–7*	*Idx*	*1929*	*1936–7*	*Idx*	*1929*	*1936–7*	*Idx*	*1929*	*1936–7*	*Idx*	*1929*	*1936–7*	*Idx*
Cereals	10.7	11.3	*106*	5.3	5.8	*110*	1.8	1.8	*104*	2.3	2.2	*94*	1.3	1.5	*117*
Indust. crops	1.1	1.1	*98*	0.8	0.7	*89*	0.1	0.1	*74*	0.2	0.3	*116*	0.1	0.1	*191*
Legumes: chickpeas, lentils, beans, etc.	1.0	0.9	*93*	0.2	0.2	*95*	0.2	0.2	*85*	0.4	0.4	*92*	0.2	0.2	*99*
Vegetable	3.3	2.8	*85*	1.4	1.2	*83*	0.6	0.5	*90*	1.1	0.8	*77*	0.2	0.3	*120*
Grapes	4.5	2.7	*59*	1.6	1.1	*70*	1.2	0.7	*58*	1.2	0.6	*53*	0.6	0.3	*46*
Olives	1.5	1.4	*91*	0.1	0.1	*166*	0.2	0.3	*113*	0.9	0.8	*87*	0.3	0.2	*63*
Fruits	3.7	2.5	*69*	0.9	0.6	*68*	0.2	0.1	*69*	1.4	0.9	*66*	1.1	0.8	*73*
Livestock	15.7	14.9	*95*	9.7	9.3	*96*	2.8	2.7	*97*	2.0	2.0	*101*	1.3	1.0	*78*
Other crops	1.6	1.1	*68*	0.9	0.6	*67*	0.3	0.2	*83*	0.3	0.2	*61*	0.1	0.1	*60*
Forest products	2.3	2.0	*85*	1.3	1.1	*82*	0.5	0.4	*81*	0.5	0.4	*95*	0.1	0.1	*106*
Gross agric. prod. (Gsp)	45.4	40.7	*90*	22.1	20.6	*93*	7.7	6.9	*90*	10.3	8.6	*84*	5.2	4.5	*86*

Source: Chiapparino and Morettini, 2018.
Note: a in millions of Liras, index 1929 = 100

The best result in recovering 1929 levels is achieved by cereals. This is not surprising since, starting from 1925, wheat was the focus of an intense policy by the Fascist regime. The *Battaglia del Grano* was officially aimed at achieving a sort of strategic self-sufficiency, which is all the more invoked ten years later when faced with the sanctions introduced by the League of Nations following the invasion of Ethiopia. This target however was never fully reached. In fact, this policy was more simply a way to alleviate the difficulties of the balance of payments, which were burdened by the need to import raw materials and technologies and, after World War I by the contraction of emigrants' remittances. Nonetheless, wheat is the focus of an articulated set of measures, ranging from the increase in customs duties to the introduction of new selected varieties, and intense propaganda efforts to promote its cultivation – or, rather, in the original purpose, its yield improvement.

Alongside these guidelines, Fascist rural policies mainly concern the confirmation (and increase) of protectionism for some other products, such as rice (Brianta, 1983) and sugar (Sabbatucci Severini, 2004), the relaunch of the reclamation campaign, including a wide range of interventions (such as the construction of roads) which were not always directly related to agricultural production, and the so-called 'ruralism', as will be discussed later. At the center of these measures, the 'Wheat battle' consists mainly in a progressive reprise of the traditional protection duties, reintroduced with 7.5 Liras per quintal in 1925 and progressively raised to 75 in 1931. At the end of 1936 protection is progressively reduced to 18 Liras, but by that date, the internal wheat trade was administered by the State through a system of mandatory storages (Banca d'Italia, 1938: 329–44).

Several studies concerning the impact of wheat protectionism on Italian agriculture (Profumieri, 1971; Tattara, 1978, and others) have highlighted the selective character of this policy. As indicated in Figure 5.6, it has very diverse results in the various rural areas of the country in terms of both yield improvements and growth of arable surface dedicated to grain. Some Northern clusters, generally characterized by a high level of productivity, significantly increase their wheat areas, such as the rice plain in Piedmont, Low Lombardy, Ferrara, and the Po Delta. Others, like the Veneto plain and mountain regions, improve yields without any enlargement of wheat cultivation. Asti on the contrary even seems to ignore the *Battaglia del Grano*. In the Center and the South, some rural contexts, for example Mezzadria and Central Apulia, improve their efficiency. In other clusters, such as Southern Apulia, a large part of Sicily, the Southern arable area and even Naples, the growth in production is prevalently based only on the wider extension of grain areas. Finally, in the mountain regions like the Southern Apennines or the Messina Strait, such a policy has very limited results.

In very general terms, the richest rural economies benefit from the regime's policy by focusing on a protected market and improving their profitability. Mainly located in the North but also including, for example, Central Apulia (Cluster 13), these areas are flexible, better capital endowed and can

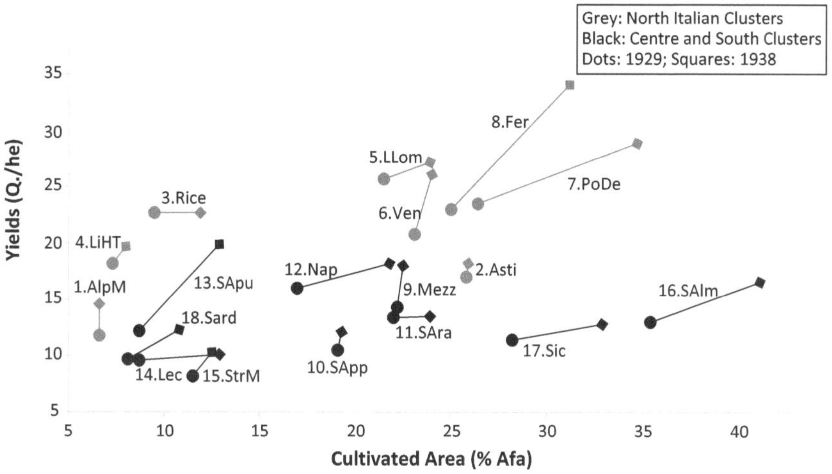

Figure 5.6 Wheat yields and cultivated areas 1929 and 1938.
Source: Chiapparino and Morettini, 2018.

achieve significant yield improvements. For other territories, prevalently in the South, grain protectionism only extends wheat cultivation, while sacrificing richer and more consolidated productions.

5. The relevance of mobility

According to some scholars, the 'trapping' of the workforce in a stagnant sector has the effect to decrease its incomes and thus contributes significantly to depressing aggregate demand and prolonging the recession (Delli Gatti et al., 2012). Emigration was the traditional solution to this problem for the large portions of Italian agriculture that were unable to react to the Great Depression of the late nineteenth century (Sori, 1979: 69–118; Fauri, 2015: 13–27). The interruption to these outflows, initially with World War I and then, above all, due to the closing of the US borders in the mid-1920s, deprives the rural world of important compensation mechanisms. It worsens the relative overpopulation of many rural areas and curbs the flow of remittances that sustain their income. The consequence is a depression of local purchasing power, which, also considering the weight of the primary sector, affects whole regional economies. Italy, however, lacks the reverse migration processes, from market to subsistence agriculture, observed, for instance, in the USA (Boone and Wilse-Samson, 2021).

In the peninsula, like in many other countries especially in Europe, there is no clear-cut separation between market and subsistence agriculture. Even in richer settings, market crops are always coupled with food crops for peasant subsistence. In the countryside, in other words, the recession can aggravate underemployment but generates unemployment only in those rare areas where the presence of landless laborers depending entirely on their wages for subsistence is massive. One of these cases is the industrial agriculture of Ferrara and the Po Delta region, where the unemployment of landless laborers becomes an explosive question, and the Fascist regime is active in relocating at least some of these workers in the newly reclaimed areas all over the country. Elsewhere, and in most of Italy, agriculture is a sort of sponge-sector, capable of absorbing unemployment by compressing incomes and the standard of living, even to the very limits of subsistence if necessary.

Despite the fact that emigration comes to a halt, Italy continues to experience other forms of mobility after the mid-1920s. It has been observed that, from 1923 onwards, internal mobility increases throughout the period up to World War II (Treves, 1976: 17–20 and 127–31; Gallo, 2012: 75ff.). Alongside traditional seasonal mobility, typical of the preindustrial economy and declining in perspective, the interwar period is above all characterized by a significant urbanization process. The Regime's 'ruralistic' policy promotes bans on mobility towards cities, with the intent to preserve traditional rural values and avoid the social tensions of the urban context – the countryside as a sponge sector, as mentioned above. Such restrictions on internal migrations, however, are largely disregarded. They hardly achieve anything apart from hiding the official data on these movements of the population and hence complicating their retrospective reconstruction today (Ipsen, 2002). In any case, besides the urbanization process, internal mobility also involves a broader set of often smaller scale migrations, occurring within the same province or between neighboring areas, and not necessarily directed towards large cities.

Together with changes in population, Table 5.3 shows some basic indices of mobility for the 18 clusters indicated above, obtained from the 1931 and 1936 demographic censuses. The mobility index is the sum of changes of residence (registrations and cancellations) recorded by the municipal offices in this period as a percentage of the average population in 1931–6. It includes shifts out of the cluster, as well as simple inter-municipal mobility. The migratory effectiveness index, on the other hand, is the ratio of net migration to total in- and out- migration of the period. It measures the direction of net movements, if inbound (positive values) or outbound (negative values).

The mobility index tends to be high in the North of the country, with peaks in Eastern Piedmont (both Asti and the rice cluster) and the province of Ferrara. It is considerably lower in the South and the Islands. The Low Lombardy and Central South Arable clusters are particular because they include the two major cities of Milan and Rome, which represent strong poles of attraction, despite the restrictions on urbanization imposed by the regime. It is significant in this regard that they are the only two clusters with a positive migratory efficacy index. More specifically, if Milan belongs to a highly mobile area, Rome is an outlier within the Central South Arable cluster, otherwise characterized by scarce population mobility, which was almost exclusively outbound.

Table 5.3 Population growth, mobility, and its 'efficiency' per cluster in Italy 1931–6

Cluster	*1931*	*1936*	*Mobility 1931–36*	*'Efficiency'*
	millions of inhabitants		*% average pop.*	*1931–36*
1. Alpine Arc	8.45	8.56	7.2	−6.0
2. Asti (Wine)	0.25	0.24	10.5	−10.2
3. Rice Po Valley	1.23	1.23	9.7	−1.2
4. Liguria High Tuscany	2.17	2.20	6.5	−1.7
5. Low Lombardy	2.76	2.91	9.1	4.6
6. Veneto Plain	1.79	1.86	8.0	−7.2
7. Po Delta	0.59	0.60	8.5	−8.8
8. Ferrara	0.37	0.37	9.7	−9.1
9. *Mezzadria*	6.70	6.86	7.4	−4.6
10. Southern Appennine	4.79	4.95	4.1	−18.6
11. Central South Arable	2.59	2.86	6.2	11.6
12. Naples	2.08	2.18	4.6	−8.1
13. Apulia Specialized	1.49	1.58	4.7	−7.1
14. Lecce (Tobacco)	0.49	0.51	4.1	−12.6
15. Messina Strait	1.15	1.17	4.3	−22.4
16. Sicily-Almond	0.64	0.66	4.2	−24.5
17. Sicilia	2.65	2.66	5.0	−21.2
18. Sardinia	0.97	1.02	5.1	−5.6
Italy	41.18	42.44	6.5	−5.7

Source: Elaborations from Population Censuses and Municipal records.

Finally, Figure 5.7 combines the variations in agricultural output per hectare of Agricultural and forest area (Afa, in monetary value) and mobility for the 18 clusters. Both the indexes are standardized on the national data. The Italian average is therefore placed at the intersection of the chart axes.

The significant, positive relationship between mobility and agricultural production is clearly evident. At the top of the scale, Asti is the cluster with the highest population mobility (mostly outgoing in the North) and the best agricultural performance. In this case, as seen above, there is no reallocation of land for wheat: the cereal policy supported by the regime seems to be almost ignored, whereas it is the workforce to be reallocated efficiently. The other Northern plain clusters, from Veneto (Nr. 6) to Ferrara (8) or Low Lombardy (5), also lie in the first quadrant of the graph. Unlike Asti, these clusters take great advantage of the Fascist regime policy, although they resemble that area for their heavy reliance on mobility. The destinations of these displacements are the large productive centers of the North, such as Milan, Turin, Genoa, which in the 1930s benefit from the industrial policies of recovery and rearmament. Besides these, a whole series of minor industrial poles is equally supported by the regime, from Aosta to Marghera (Venice) to the cities snatched from Austria with the war and destined to be Italianized, such as Bolzano or Trieste. Furthermore, a role in these changes in population is also played by the dense network of small and medium-sized towns in

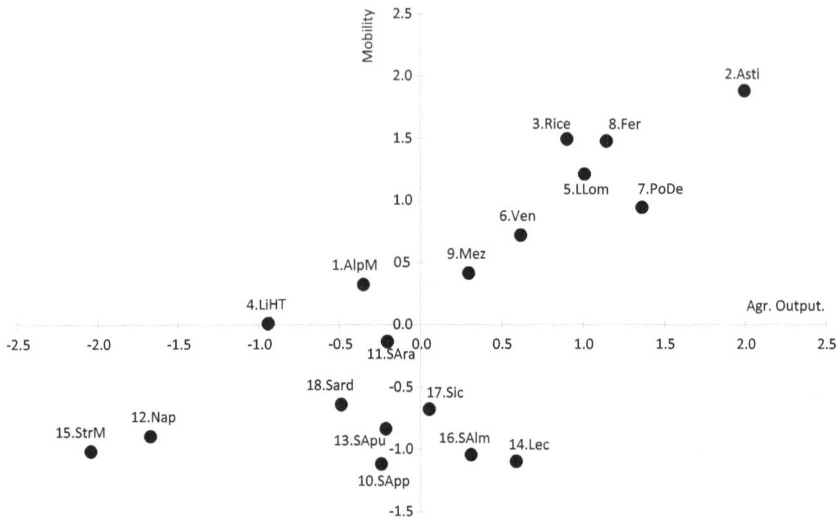

Figure 5.7 Variation in agricultural output of Afa (1929–36/7) and mobility (1931–6).
Source: Elaborations on data in Tables 5.1 and 5.3.

the Po Valley, with their intense social and economic relationships, as well as perhaps by rural mobility itself, even beyond traditional seasonal migrations. The Mezzadria area (9), in Central Italy, has an intermediate position, in line with a resilient system *par excellence*, based on polyculture, endowed with strong flexibility, and largely dependent on crops which were less affected by crises, such as those aimed at peasant subsistence or local markets.

The Alpine Arc, among the Northern mountain clusters, has only a slightly worse collocation in the second quadrant. As mentioned above, the composite nature of these provinces should also be considered. Most of them include very heterogeneous areas, from flat plains, similar to the rest of the fertile Po Valley, to the dynamic pre-Alpine belt, up to the mountain area. The latter region is seriously affected by the crisis and, unlike the Apennines, suffered a strong depopulation process already in the 1930s. Considered on its own, the strictly alpine area would have a worse performance, probably similar to Liguria-High Tuscany.

Sicily (Cluster 17), Sicily-Almonds (16), and Southern Apulia (14), in the fourth quadrant, are of special interest. These territories combine a significantly lower mobility than the national average with a relatively good agricultural performance. This result is strictly connected to the Fascist regime policies. These areas largely convert their production into a protected and incentivized crop like wheat. Alongside the cereal policy, tobacco also plays a role in Southern Apulia, where this traditional specialization is relaunched by large investments promoted by the State to exploit the domestic market (Mastrolia, 2008).

The third quadrant includes clusters which are severely hit by the recession and lack policy support. The Southern specialized agriculture of Naples and the Strait of Messina suffers heavily from both the international trade crisis and the population 'entrapment' once the possibility to emigrate comes to a halt. At the same time, its rugged territory is unsuitable or, in the case of Naples, too limited to benefit from the grain policy. Other parts of the *Mezzogiorno* have a scarce mobility but a better agricultural outcome, although lower than the national average. The impact of the recession is mitigated here by the governmental support provided for cereals, which represent their major production. The case of the South and Central Arable cluster (Cluster 11) is similar, apart from the higher mobility, related however exclusively to Rome, that represents by far the greatest and the almost unique domestic pole able to activate mobility flows in the South and a large part of the Center of the peninsula in these years.

6. Some general considerations

In conclusion, disaggregating is a sort of methodological imperative in order to investigate the diverse rural economies, all the more so in the case of the Italian primary sector and its large variety of environmental and productive contexts. The partitioning of the country into a set of agricultural clusters on a provincial basis, which are much more homogeneous than the administrative regions themselves, first of all shows how the gaps broaden because of the crisis. In a large part of the Northern lowland and hill farming area, the recession is only a contingent obstacle. Falling prices cause losses, but these economies are ready to recover and are often even able to successfully exploit the opportunities provided by the regime, primarily its cereal policy.

For other rural contexts the crisis has, on the contrary, a much more dramatic impact. Alpine mountain areas experience severe difficulties that trigger significant, and in some respects definitive, depopulation processes. The Apennine areas, in the Center and the South, show even greater resilience in this phase, thanks to the adaptability of the sharecropping system of the Mezzadria or the benefits of the Battaglia del Grano, both elements destined in any case to disappear with the modernization that started after World War II. However, above all it is the specialized Southern export-oriented rural systems, centered on the prized trees (such as citrus or almond) and horticultural (especially in Naples) crops, to be hit by the depression. Similar to the North, they were the result of accumulation processes dating from the nineteenth century, and sometimes even before, that had required conspicuous investments, risk propensity, and entrepreneurial skills (Lupo, 1990; Bevilacqua, 2000: 163ff.). For the South as a whole, their crisis implied the failure of a long-term economic and social hypothesis of endogenous growth and modernization. The example of Naples has an even wider significance. This province, which until 1929 was the richest rural area in the peninsula, suffered a collapse that made it lose this traditional primacy forever. Its decline signals how the interwar recession widened the gap between North and South, turning it into a furrow that has never been bridged again.

In general terms, moreover, the different trajectories of the 'rural Italies' show the selective impact of policies, beyond that of market dynamics and falling prices. Protectionism and cereal policy play a role in supporting the output of both clusters suited for wheat or other crops for the domestic market, as occurs mainly in the South and the Center, and those, often in the North, with resources that allow them to shift to these productions. Despite sacrificing more valuable productions, the *Battaglia del Grano* shows the effectiveness of policies to support agriculture, as testified by the relatively good performance of the clusters that enlarge their wheat cultivations and, above all, yields. In some respects, therefore, it anticipates the great role that protections and incentives are destined to have for the Italian (and European) primary sector in the second half of the twentieth century (Federico, 2012).

Finally, what is of primary interest here is the fact that the manifold dynamics of the peninsula's rural economies provide good evidence of the important role of mobility in the evolution of the crisis. Once the outlets for international emigration are closed, territories with better domestic migrations tend to have better performance, with all other conditions being equal and regardless of the effect of support policies. Thus, for instance, among specialized mountain areas, Liguria-High Tuscany, which are characterized by better mobility than the Messina Strait, also maintains higher levels of output. Similarly, a specialized province such as Asti achieves much better results than the analog Naples cluster both in terms of economic performance and population mobility. More in general, Northern territories, featuring higher mobility, present better productive trends than those in the South, with the significant exception of the areas benefiting from the grain policy.

Simplifying, it could be stated that a set of territories is trapped in productive specializations affected by the crisis (Naples, Strait of Messina, Central Puglia), or in poor and inefficient productive structures (Sardinia, Apennines, large arable properties in the South and Center). A second group (Southern Puglia, the rest of Sicily) are also trapped, but in resilient specializations, which resist the crisis thanks to State support despite sacrificing their best productions. In both cases, the lack of emigration opportunities in the mid-1920s has profoundly negative consequences. It lays the foundations for a great delay in development in the *Mezzogiorno* and contributes significantly to transforming its diversity into a permanent gap (Gallo, 2018). Further areas, such as Liguria or the Alpine mountains, on the contrary, experience little or no entrapment of their workforce – which in the Italian context actually means that they have a limited degree of underemployment. Consequently, they suffer the recession comparatively less than other regions, similar to the *Mezzadria* in Central Italy, although in the latter case thanks to this area's resilience and intrinsic ability to adapt. Finally, the remaining Northern regions of plains and hills survive the depression relatively easily through flexible and well-capitalized agriculture as well as high internal mobility and a corresponding capacity to limit underemployment.

Note

1 The agricultural zones (groups of municipalities with common rural characteristics), or preferably the agricultural regions (their grouping per altitude – plain, hill, mountain – within the same province) were used in the Principal Component Analysis in order to identify the different agricultural systems of the peninsula on the basis of the 1929 Land register.

Bibliography

Albertario, P., 1938, 'Catasto agrario e rilevazione annuale delle superfici e delle produzioni agrarie', *Bollettino mensile di statistica agraria e forestale*, 9/4, pp. 430–468.

Baffigi, A., 2011, 'Italian National Accounts, 1861–2011', *Quaderni di Storia Economica*, Economic History Working Papers, 18, Bank of Italy, Economic Research and International Relations Area.

Banca d'Italia, 1938, *L'economia italiana nel sessennio 1931–1936*, Rome: ISP.

Bevilacqua, P., 1980, *Le campagne del Mezzogiorno tra fascismo e dopoguerra*, Turin: Einaudi.

Bevilacqua, P., 2000, *Tra natura e storia. Ambiente, economia, risorse in Italia*, Rome: Donzelli

Boone, C. and Wilse-Samson, L., 2021, 'Structural Change and Internal Labor Migration: Evidence from the Great Depression', https://drive.google.com/file/d/1Wc0GlKHPJabLGpFTEk1hWaKZaaAPpnlb/view (Working paper available the 11.16.2021)

Brianta, D., 1983, 'Risicoltura e fascismo negli anni della crisi. Alle origini dell'Ente nazionale risi 1927–1933', *Agricoltura e forze sociali in Lombardia nella crisi degli anni trenta*, Milan: FrancoAngeli, pp. 255–290.

Broadberry, S., Giordano, C. and Zollino, F., 2011, 'A Sectoral Analysis of Italy's Development, 1861–2011', *Quaderni di Storia economica*, Economic History Working Papers, 20, Bank of Italy, Economic Research and International Relations Area.

Cafagna, L., 1989, *Dualismo e sviluppo nella storia d'Italia*, Venice: Marsilio.

Chiapparino, F. and Morettini, G., 2016, 'Un contributo dimenticato: Luchino Franciosa e la produzione lorda vendibile dell'agricoltura italiana negli anni trenta', *Proposte e ricerche*, 77, pp. 113–38.

Chiapparino, F. and Morettini, G., 2018, 'Rural 'Italies' and the Great Crisis. Provincial Clusters in Italian Agriculture Between the Two World Wars', *Journal of Modern Italian Studies*, 23/5, pp. 640–77.

Ciocca, P., 2007, *Ricchi per sempre? Una storia economica d'Italia (1796–2005)* Milan: Bollati Boringhieri.

Cirio, P. and Rapetti, V., 1984, 'Alle origini dello spumante italiano. L'industria enologica di Canelli (fine '800–1939)', *Quaderno ISR Alessandria*, 14, pp. 103–22.

Cohen, J., 1979, 'Fascism and Agriculture in Italy: Policies and Consequences', *Economic History Review*, 32/1, pp. 70–87.

Daniele, V. and Malanima, P., 2011, *Il divario Nord-Sud in Italia 1861–2011*, Soveria Mannelli: Rubbettino.

Delli Gatti, D., Gallegati, M., Greenwald, B.C., Russo, A. and Stiglitz, J.E., 2012, 'Mobility Constraints, Productivity Trends, and Extended Crises', *Journal and Economic Behavior & Organization*, 83/212, pp. 375–393.

D'Onofrio, F., 2016, *Observing Agriculture in Early Twentieth Century Italy*, London: Routledge.

Fano, E., 1975, 'Problemi e vicende dell'agricoltura italiana tra le due guerre', *Quaderni storici*, 29–30, pp. 468–96.

Fauri, F. 2015, *Storia economica delle migrazioni italiane*, Bologna: Il Mulino.

Federico, G., 2003, 'Le nuove stime della produzione agricola italiana 1860–1910: primi risultati e implicazioni', *Rivista di storia economica*, 19/3, pp. 357–81.

Federico, G., 2012, 'Natura non fecit saltus: The 1930s as the Discontinuity in the History of European Agriculture', in P. Brassley, Y. Segers and L. Van Molle (eds.), *War, Agriculture and Food: Rural Europe from the 1930s to the 1950s*, New York: Routledge, pp. 15–32.

Federico, G., Natoli, S., Tattara, G. and Vasta, M., 2011, *Il commercio estero italiano 1862–1950*, Roma-Bari: Laterza.

Franciosa, L., 1940, *L'olivo nell'economia italiana*, Rome: Failli.

Franciosa, L., 1947, 'Il valore della produzione agraria dal 1929 al 1938', *Rivista di politica economica*, 3/1, pp. 128–42.

Gallo, S. 2012, *Senza attraversare le frontiere*, Rome-Bari: Laterza.

Gallo, S. 2018, 'Migrazioni interne al Meridione e politica della mobilità tra le due guerre', *Meridana*, 92, pp. 143–68.

Ipsen, C., 2002, *Dictating Demography. The Problem of Population in Fascist Italy*, Cambridge: Cambridge University Press.

Istat (various years), *Annuario statistico italiano*, Rome.

Istat, 1931 and 1934, *Riassunto dei prezzi all'ingrosso e dei prezzi del pane*, Rome.

Istat, 1958, *Sommario di statistiche storiche italiane 1861–1955*, Rome.

Istat, 2011, *L'Italia in 150 anni. Sommario di statistiche storiche 1861–2011*, Rome.

Jacini, S., 1881, *Atti della Giunta per la inchiesta agraria e sulle condizioni della classe agricola*, Rome: Forzani.

Lupo, S., 1990, *Il giardino degli aranci*, Venice: Marsilio.

Maroi, L., 1946, *Lezioni di economia agraria*, Naples: IES.

Martinelli, P., 2014, 'Von Thünen South of the Alps: Access to Market and Inter-war Italian Agriculture', *European Review of Economic History*, 18/2, pp. 107–43.

Mastrolia, F. A., 2008, 'La coltivazione e la lavorazione del tabacco in Terra d'Otranto tra Otto e Novecento', *Proposte e ricerche*, 61, pp. 125–52.

Nützenadel, A., 2001, 'Economic Crisis and Agriculture in Fascist Italy, 1927–1935. Some New Considerations', *Rivista di storia economica*, 17/3, pp. 289–312.

Profumieri, P.L., 1971, 'La 'Battaglia del grano': costi e ricavi', *Rivista di storia dell'agricoltura*, 11/2, pp. 153–72.

Rossi Doria, M. 1958, *Dieci anni di politica agraria nel Mezzogiorno*, Bari: Laterza.

Sabbatucci Severini, P., 2004, *Il capitalismo organizzato*, Venice: Marsilio.

Sori, E. 1979, *L'emigrazione italiana dall'Unità alla Seconda guerra mondiale*, Bologna: Il Mulino.

Tattara, G. 1978, 'La battaglia del grano', in G. Toniolo (ed.), *L'economia italiana 1861–1940*, Rome-Bari: Laterza, pp. 337–80.

Treves, A. 1976, *Le migrazioni interne nell'Italia fascista*, Turin: Einaudi.

Valenti, G., 1911, *L'Italia agricola dal 1861 al 1911*, Rome: Lincei.

Zamagni, V., 1978, *Industrializzazione e squilibri regionali in Italia*, Bologna: Il Mulino.

Zattini, G. 1924, 'Valutazione della produzione lorda dell'agricoltura italiana', *Notizie periodiche di statistica agraria*, 15/4, pp. 47–223.

6 From boom to burst – Argentine's primary sector and the 1930s Crisis

Julio Djenderedjian and Juan Luis Martirén

1. Introduction

Between 1895 and 1914 Argentina experienced a remarkable economic growth, ranking among the wealthiest countries in the world (Díaz Alejandro, 1982; Korol, 1991; Taylor, 1992; Cortés Conde, 1997; Gerchunoff and Llach, 2004; Villarroya-Sanz, 2005; Míguez, 2008). A great boom on the primary sector –particularly of wheat and corn production since the mid-1980s– boosted a fast industrial development and a construction fever.

Nevertheless, these 'best days' started to fall behind at the end of the 1920s, and promptly the so-called 'Belle Époque' turned into a grim reality. The new conjuncture began with a commodity price crisis that preceded the outbreak of World War I (WWI), negatively affecting the Argentine economy for a longtime.

This period attracted much attention in academic literature. There are, however, different interpretations about the reasons of the economic stagnation. Most of the research is based on a comparative perspective of Argentina with 'settler' (e.g., Canada and Australia) and OECD economies. For some scholars, the 'diverging' turning point started in 1913 (Di Tella and Zymelman, 1967; Taylor, 1992; Cortés Conde, 1997). This position argues that growth rates began to decline from 1913 onwards, and that policies implemented in the 1920s were not strong enough to modify this structural trend. In addition, the depletion of the agricultural soil and the end of the Pampean inland frontier affected the cereal production, generating a slower pace of growth. Other studies place this phenomenon at the turn of the century (Villarroya-Sanz, 2004). On the other hand, the 'optimistic' stance extends the 'Belle Époque' cycle till 1929. According to this position, supported by Carlos Díaz Alejandro (1975, 1982), the export-led growth could overtake the black clouds of the 1914–18 years, reaching laudable results during the 1920s (which were even better than those of Australia, for example).

As Míguez pointed out (2008: 262–4), both positions have well-grounded reasons, but there is not an overt consensus. The main question could be summarized as follows: the negative effects generated by the WWI were only temporary, being overcome in the 1920s? Or they definitely ended up

DOI: 10.4324/9781003105466-8

showing a drift that was already clear since 1913? About that, we still have no answers. Despite these positions, what is undeniable is that the 1930 crisis was a watershed in Argentine economic history, and there are still many gaps to explain its effects. Argentine serial evidence before 1906 is problematic (or unreliable), so any retrospective statistical analysis could be calculated on weak bases (in particular, the commonly used GDP per capita). Besides, there have been no sector-specific approaches to analyze this period.

In the last decade, academic research shed new light to the Great Depression and its consequences around the world. The role of the primary sector has been underlined as an interesting variable to evaluate large-scale crisis (Delli Gatti et al., 2012). In the same track, this chapter will focus on agricultural sector to propose new interpretations about the effects of the Great Depression on the Argentine economy. In order to do so, three strategies will be followed: (1) we will present and analyze some macro-magnitudes related with the primary sector role in the whole economy. (2) Agricultural sector Total Factor Productivity (hereafter TFP) will be measured between 1895 and 1937, to consider its evolution as a key explanation not properly attended until now. (3) We will study labor factor reallocation, particularly between agriculture, construction, and manufacturing, and the impact of international migrations, in order to assess why and how they affected (or even determined) the effects of the Great Depression in Argentina.

We seek to discuss the position that argues that Argentine agriculture reached a key productivity frontier (by land occupation under dry farming) in 1914. On the contrary, we hold that that frontier was only reached in 1930. In addition, we will show that, beyond the impact of the 1930 crisis, its local long-term effects were reduced due to the particular characteristics of the Argentine labor market. In that context, construction sector was the key adjustment factor, in order to deal with the worst effects on labor demand in major crises. But, curiously, it was not hitherto addressed with the importance it deserved. During the period under analysis, it underwent greater expansion than other sectors in times of prosperity, and deeper falls during crisis. This explains the reallocation of labor supply: while the agrarian sector does justify the seasonal fluctuations, the construction sector explains the cyclical ones.

2. The Argentine economic expansion: Some magnitudes

Considerable debate took place on the economic effects derived from independence of Spain at the beginning of the nineteenth century. While some scholars hold a pessimistic position (Coatsworth, 1993), others have addressed that the revolutionary decade (1810s) was the symbolic baseline of a long-run expansive economic cycle (Schmit and Rosal, 2000). In essence, both positions have solid background: it is undeniable that the effects of the Revolution (long war, capital destruction) strongly affected several regions of present-day

Argentina, as well as the Atlantic orientation acquired by its economy after 1810 generated broad benefits, particularly for the Pampean region. Taking advantage of the wide availability of land, this area achieved a notable expansion of internal borders on the basis of livestock and agricultural production (Barsky and Gelman, 2003; Djenderedjian et al., 2010). So, when literature refers to Argentine nineteenth-century economic and demographic growth, it is basically pointing out to a few districts: Buenos Aires, Santa Fe, Entre Ríos, Córdoba (all located in the Pampean region), and to a lesser extent the inland provinces of Mendoza and Tucumán.

This growth cycle achieved great expansion from 1880 onwards, and the export-oriented growth promoted by the so-called First Globalization transformed the Argentine economy[1]. The attraction of European labor force, particularly from Italy and Spain, was also crucial in that process (Figure 6.1)[2].

Economic growth during the period under analysis had five main stages. The first one took place during the two last decades of the nineteenth century, and the expansion of the primary sector had a huge centrality. The second stage went from 1902 to WWI. The distinctiveness of this period lied not only in a remarkable growth of the agricultural production (and much more of the crop area), but also in the takeoff of the industrial and commercial sector (Rocchi, 2006). Many scholars have stressed that these two stages were unique in the Argentine economic development: the annual

Figure 6.1 Total GDP and GDP per capita in Argentina (1890–1935).
Source: Cortés Conde and Harriague, 1994: Appendix.

growth rates achieved in several sectors had been unrepeatable (Di Tella and Zymelman, 1967; Cortés Conde, 1997). The third stage, between 1914 and 1918, was shaped by the international context, being the first caveat for the productive conditions. The fourth one started after the recessive effect produced by the end of WWI and was abruptly interrupted by the Great Depression. Beyond the different positions about the turning point of Argentinean economic 'divergence' (at least compared with other settler economies like Canada, Australia or New Zealand), the available evidence accounts for an outstanding economic growth, mainly in the primary sector (driven by the high prices of commodities). The last stage run from the Great Depression till the end of the analyzed period, and was characterized by strong recessive impact, succeeded by a subsequent rebound since 1933.

The main discussion in the extant literature does not focus on the economic growth *per se*, but on GDP per capita (at considerably lower rates over time). On this aspect, it should be noted that while, at the end of the period, the GDP still hold an upward trend, the per capita figures returned to the 1914 levels. This evolution has led many researchers to tag this year as the real turning point of the divergence (Di Tella and Zymelman, 1967; Taylor, 1994; Cortés Conde, 1997), some focusing on falling GDP growth rates per capita, and others on financial indicators.

In essence, both GDP growth evidence and other macro-magnitudes do not seem to suggest a considerable stagnation in growth, at least until the Great Depression.

Table 6.1 Investment and export growth (1900–39)

	1900–04	*1905–09*	*1910–14*	*1915–19*	*1920–24*	*1925–29*	*1930–34*	*1935–39*
Saving/ GDP (%)	7	10	4	10	4	11	6	11
Investment/ GDP (%)	9	16	15	7	10	13	9	11
Terms of trade (1913=100)	88	103	104	88	64	83	73	95
Total exports (1913=100)	38	64	83	140	135	177	85	107
Exports per capita (1913=100)	58	81	86	127	110	123	52	61
Exports/ GDP (%)	27	27	24	30	24	24	16	17

Source: Della Paolera and Taylor, 2001:147. Total and per capita exports estimations taken from Ferreres, 2010 and Maddison, 2001.

Moreover, if we consider other macroeconomic indicators, the end of the economic prosperity can be clearly seen in the first half of the 1930s. Foreign trade was the most affected sector: both exports per capita and the share of exports over total GDP fell sharply when the 1929–30 crisis started.

This would indicate that the primary sector surpluses, which previously subsidized less productive economic sectors, were running out.

Therefore, what was the outlook when the 1929–30 crisis erupted? Apparently, and beyond its ups and downs, the primary sector continued to have a strong primacy in economic development. It had been the main basis of this economic take off since towards the end of the nineteenth century. The dynamic livestock production and a burgeoning agriculture activity drove a radical transformation of the economic structure and heightened other sectors of the economy, particularly manufacturing, services, and construction, which grew at a similar pace in relative terms.

But this dependence at some point was going to generate problems. Some alerts were activated during the WWI, but finally became clearly visible in 1929 onwards. In general, income was reduced through agricultural exports, and the arrival of foreign investment was also closed. In an economy with low levels of savings and high debt, this situation forced an economic turnaround. The times of huge prosperity were running out, and other sectors that had grown thanks to the agricultural boom – e.g., industry and commerce-faced sustainability issues. This was perhaps the main effect of the Great Depression over the Argentine economy.

However, it is necessary to delve a little more in the intersectoral behavior analysis in order to shed light on some aspects still discussed. In other words, it would be interesting to know if this phenomenon, so clear in 1929, had been developing before. Let's start by the agricultural sector.

3. An alternative analysis: Total factor productivity in Argentine agriculture

The aggregate statistics on the activity of the primary sector (especially agriculture) present a remarkable growth during the period under analysis. Regarding to the cultivated area, it had a strident increase between 1895 and 1914, a relative stagnation from WWI to 1923, and a new expansion until 1937. The crops evolution had similar trends, but logically it accused the effects of climatic contingencies in some years (vg. 1897, 1911, 1917, 1922) (Figure 6.2).

At the same time, it is important to stress the high volatility of agricultural prices, which had real effects on the activity, unlike the terms of trade, whose evolution did not converge with production trends (as could be seen in Table 6.1). Particularly, the three biggest falls of the period resulted in huge shocks. The 1911 fall prompted the largest agrarian protest of the entire twentieth century. A new drop in 1917 implied a considerable strike for both the agrarian economy and the international trade of Argentina. Finally, the great impact generated by the Great Depression must be highlighted above all. Although the magnitude of the drop in cereal prices was not reflected in the crops volume, it affected to a large extent the wheat culture, which suffered a notable decline in cultivated area, being replaced by corn.

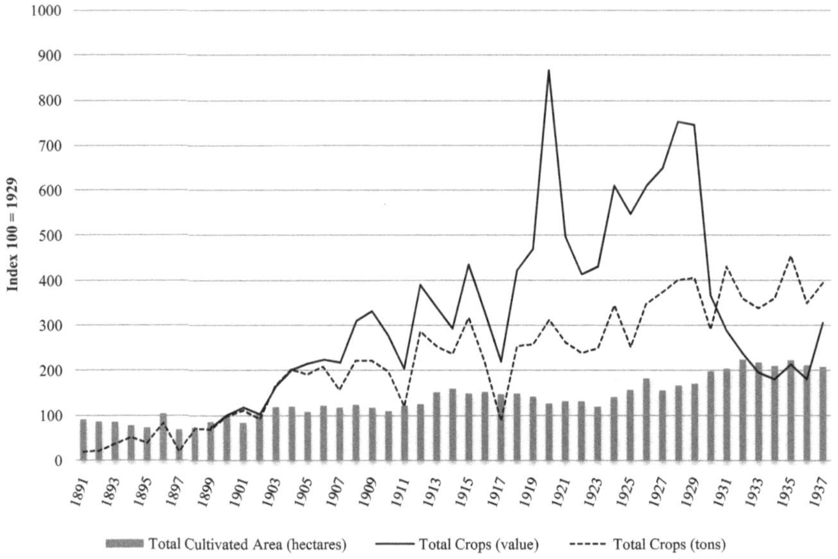

Figure 6.2 Cultivated area and cereal production (main crops: wheat, corn, flax).
Source: Own elaboration from Frank, 2005.

Despite this evidence, there are still many questions about the agrarian sector achievement during the 'Belle Époque' and, particularly, how it was affected by the crisis. If we rely on aggregate information, we could think that despite the sharp drop in crops value during the Great Depression, neither the production volumes nor the cultivated areas were affected in equal measure. But what were the bases of this growth? Where did the key to that expansion reside?

On this matter, a useful measure of the overall economic efficiency of a particular country or sector is Total Factor Productivity (hereafter TFP). It is not easy to assess the evolution of Argentine agrarian productivity in the nineteenth and early twentieth centuries. Some key data has not been collected or is not available for the entire country. For this chapter, we have calculated the TFP for the agricultural sector (excluding livestock not used for agricultural production) from a variety of sources, particularly three censuses: 1895, 1914, and 1937. They provide rich and abundant evidence, which has been processed together with statistical information from additional sources, in order to show the respective evolution of the production factors. Not including the livestock should be debatable, as it was a key part of the primary sector and accounted for nearly 50% of the exports. But available data make a really difficult task to measure the output and the capital cost of this sector.

We have estimated the annual TFP growth rate from 1895 to 1937, by periods, using the respective growth rates of the factors involved in agricultural production, and aggregated agricultural output. We use the dual approach[3], according to which the real value of the output is equivalent to the real income of the factors of production:

$$Y_s = r_t K_t + r_t T_t + w_t L_t$$

where Y represents the total output value and K, T, and L the respective factors (Capital, Land, and Labor). At the same time, r and w represents the factor remunerations (real wages and cost of land and capital). Taking logarithms and considering annual rates, we get the following expression:

$$\hat{Y} = s_k\left(\hat{r} + \hat{K}\right) + s_t\left(\hat{r} + \hat{T}\right) + s_l\left(\hat{r} + \hat{L}\right)$$

where '$s_k = rK / Y$'; '$s_t = rT / Y$' and '$s_l = rL / Y$' are the shares of the factors of production in the total income and the symbols on the letters (ˆ) indicate growth rates. So, the dual PTF or 'Solow residual'[4] is obtained as a weighted sum of the growth of real factor prices and would result from the next formula:

$$\widehat{PTF} = s_k\hat{K} - s_l\hat{L} - s_t\widehat{T}$$

This period included, according to the usual academic knowledge, the best performance of Argentine agrarian sector, and also experienced two of its worst crises (1914–16; 1929–33) (Table 6.2).

As can be seen in the upper table, the results are controversial, at least considering the growth and weight of the agricultural sector. Contrary to what it might be supposed, TFP had negative growth from 1895 to 1914, and a moderately positive one from 1914 to 1937. The striking point here is that TFP was negative just during the greatest boom in the primary sector

Table 6.2 Annual growth rates (%) in the value of production factors, output, and TFP, Argentina, 1895–1937

	1895/1937	*1895/1914*	*1914/1937*
Years	37	19	23
Land (*T*)	−0.17	−1.80	1.14
Capital (*K*)	0.22	−1.32	1.45
Labour (*L*)	−0.10	−1.92	1.36
Factors (tot.)	4.20	6.90	2.03
Output	4.07	5.12	3.22
TFP	−0.13	−1.78	1.19

Source: Argentina, Censuses, 1895; 1914; 1937. Frank, 2005; Miatello, 1904 for man-hour cost; República Argentina. Ministerio de Agricultura, 1916. Data covers the whole country, but considering only main crops (wheat, corn, linseed, oats, barley). Anyway, it must be taken into account that these cultures embrace roughly 80% of the total area under cultivation, depending on year. Prices in gold Pesos, at constant values (year 1914).

(1895–1914). The main explanation seems to lie in the fact that, until the first decade of the twentieth century, there was still a large stock of barren land (in southern and western Pampean region) that was being put progressively in production[5]. By 1910, the productivity of these stocks was not necessarily high, but frontier lands had been a key for Argentine agrarian expansion in the nineteenth century. They promoted an increase in the average extension of the farms, many of which were among the largest in the world in its field[6]. This was extremely important on factor endowments, because capital and labor were very expensive, so feasibility of farms was based in low relative prices of land. Therefore, while cultivated area was growing at an accelerated rate (and thus the factor remuneration), the main output increased, but not at the same pace[7].In addition, by 1910, frontier arable land was about to end, as most of the Pampas has been or was near to be reached by railways[8]. This pushed up land prices – until then the key of agricultural growth – and all this resulted in negative or low TFP values. In other words, these results would be suggesting than economic growth rested basically on factor accumulation, and not in productivity, which had a negative performance, at least till 1914.

The evolution of the terms of trade would also explain this behavior. That is, just when they were beneficial, the sector was consistently capitalized with European machinery, and this allowed the putting into production of important frontier land settlements, despite these had modest yields. From 1914 onward, the role of those previous technological changes showed all their potential; and capital investment became more and more crucial. This is what 1914–37 data is showing: even including two major crises (1914–16; 1929–33), factor productivity went to a positive field. Thus, the explanation for this phenomenon seems to be based on two variables: on the one hand, a more efficient capital amortization, particularly in machinery, during the 1920s (as we said, it is worth noting that a large part of that machine stock had already been acquired during the preceding period). On the other hand, evidently output rates per hectare/work unit grew considerably. We cannot identify the concrete reasons for this output growth, but perhaps key aspects such as better soil management or a more moderate profitability than in previous period (which required prioritizing crop quality to quantity) had a role.

Anyway, TFP indicators are consistent with the aggregate evidence. This fact is probably suggesting that the primary sector growth during the 1920s was based more on an increasing productivity than on total factor accumulation. However, this glimpse is not so clear if we add an extra variable: the labor productivity, which seemed to be decreasing during that decade.

4. Labor productivity in the agriculture and industrial sectors

When the frontier lands run out, theoretically the choice of agriculture over other sectors of the economy should became irrelevant for labor and capital investment. That is, yields and productivity of all sectors should converge, as it was no more one key factor at relatively low prices. This is probably what happened in the Argentine economy, as far as we could know by some signs: by 1900–10 local interest rate converged with that of international capital markets, roughly to 5–6% annually, breaking almost a century with very high rates (and volatility)[9]. This generated a strong increase in investment rates during that period, as noted in Table 6.1.

Unfortunately, the available evidence does not give us licence to go deeper into the evolution of sectoral grade investment over time. In aggregated terms, we know that after the logical stroke derived from WWI, rates started to grow anew during the 1920s, and then fell again after the Great Depression. This information allows us to infer that investment was a key-factor in the growth cycles of 1902–14 and 1919–29. But it impedes to make broader assertions about the different sectors of the economy. Hence, we will focus on labor productivity, whose evolution can be calculated for both the agricultural and manufacturing sectors. Following graph shows this interesting evidence, which again offers hitherto surprising results (Figure 6.3).

According to this graph, labor productivity in the industrial sector generated a growing gap with respect to agriculture. Although in a jagged path, it is evident that labor productivity in agriculture, even from 1900 onwards, accumulated a progressive delay, at least compared to manufacturing, being from 1918 onwards quickly overtaken by the rising industrial sector productivity. In some sense, this is also reflected in the GDP evolution: for the 1900–4 five-year period, primary sector accounted for an average 12.9% of total GDP; by 1909–13, that figure dropped to 9.45%. Despite it had increased

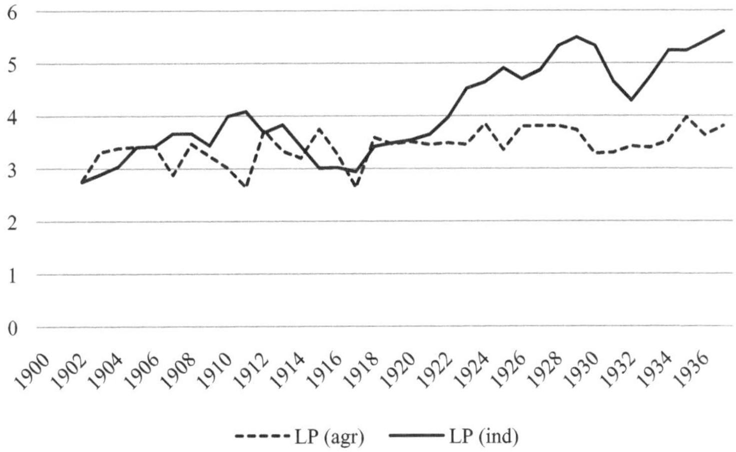

Figure 6.3 Labor productivity (LP) in agricultural and industrial sectors. Argentina, 1900–37.

Source: Aggregate value (VA) and Economically Active Population (EAP) for each sector, in constant 1970 prices, taken from MOXLAD database (http://www.lac.ox.ac.uk/moxlad-database, accessed May to July 2018). LP = VA/EAP[10].

its share to 11.7% during the stagnation derived from WWI, by the end of the 1920s dropped again, ending at 9.75% in 1929–33. It should be noted that during the 1920s, international demand of agrarian commodities had a very significant growth: wartime's high prices for the main products exported by Argentina remained in top levels throughout the decade (wheat, corn, wool, and linseed combined price index, at 100 for 1900–4, was 181.55 in 1914–18, and 186.15 in 1924–8)[11].

What does this suggest? That since at least 1918 agriculture was probably no longer the most dynamic sector of the Argentine economy. Of course, this does not mean that it was not the most profitable. But although it had been essential as a builder of the country's international purchasing power, in terms of productivity it had begun to lose ground to other sectors[12]. This starts a new interpretative point. The first consequence is the growing reallocation of labor from agriculture to manufacturing, a phenomenon already noted by sources and scholars (Bunge 1928–30). Being labor productivity higher and growing in manufacturing, capital investment probably also shifted from primary to secondary sector. As horizontal frontier expansion had ended, increases in agricultural productivity should be propelled, above all, by capital investment[13]. But if capital flowed to manufacturing instead of agriculture, in the medium term this would end in a slower growth rate of the last.

So, we could suggest that despite its growth (and its positive TFP), the primary sector was already losing dynamism in the 1920s. This problem was at the same time disguised by the substantial increase in commodity prices during that decade. But it became evident when the 1930 crisis arose. The result was an increasing fragility for the primary sector, as it was highly dependent on international demand, which by 1930 accounted for about 80% of corn national production, or 50% of wheat (Barsky and Gelman, 2003). This fragility can be observed in the following graph (Figure 6.4).

Therefore, it is not surprising to see that the primary sector lagged when compared to the evolution of the rest of the economy, prior to and after the Great Depression[14]. But not only on that occasion: as we can see in the graph, the 1926–35 period was preceded by a similar movement of both lines in the 1913–19 conjuncture, which, by the way, was far more critical for the Argentine economy than the Great Depression. In both cases, it seems clear that the performance of the agriculture sector was worse than that of the others and used to precede both critical turning points. Considering the weight of the primary sector in aggregate demand, it would be interesting to study the impact of this situation in labor demand (Delli Gatti and others 2012).

5. The key for reallocation. Construction sector

First of all, it is important to address that the rising manufacturing sector obviously allowed labor reallocation from the primary one. But probably, if it had to balance labor factor remuneration until achieving high enough levels to compensate the losses in the agricultural sector, it will finally be ended

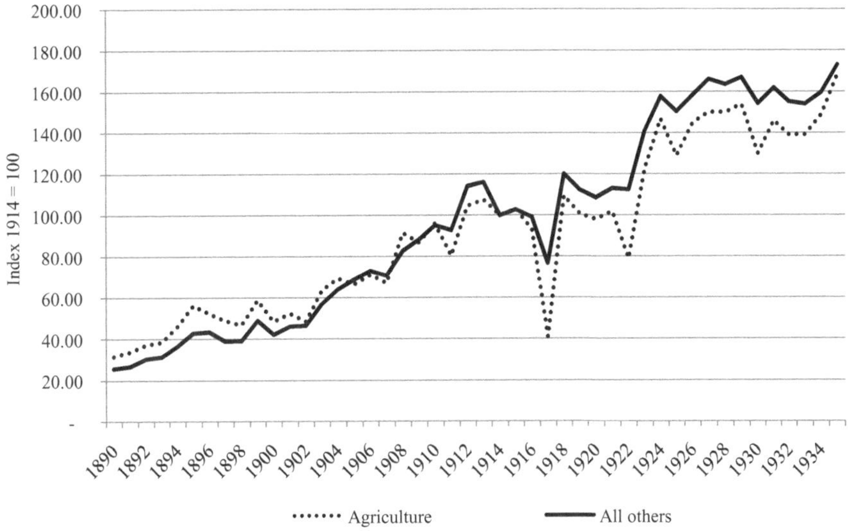

Figure 6.4 Agricultural GDP, compared to all other sectors. Argentina, 1890–1935.
Source: Cortés Conde, 1997. Agriculture includes both livestock and farming.

in lower productivity, as worker's income in Argentina was higher than in Europe (a traditional source for manufactured goods).

It is particularly difficult to quantify labor resource reallocation by sector for early-twentieth-century Argentina. Available data is dispersed, and includes lots of adults with unspecified profession, or as members of too broad categories ('day laborers', 'peons', 'foremen'). Besides, there is only one complete census for the first four decades of the twentieth century (1914). Anyway, it seems that those broad categories reflected at least in part the structure of the labor market: a more specialized group, large enough, and a consistent unskilled one, composed by foreign young males of recent immigration (e.g., Sabato and Romero 1992). Following table shows the professions declared by all adults (over 14 years) in the 1914 census, distributed by sectors and specifying number and percentage of foreigners (Table 6.3).

Those that did not declare profession were mostly 'non-working' people: housewives, children, retirees, etc. In this aggregate, women accounted for 1.535.990 out of the total of 1.793.661. So, by 1914, for a whole economically active population of 3.233.253, labor force included 530.770 professionals and specialized workers in the primary sector, 212.199 in construction, 509.407 in manufacturing, 1.166.963 in services, and 813.912 non-specialized workers in all sectors. In other words, the former ones reached the 25% of the total workforce[15]. Of them, 48% were foreigners; and the presence of foreigners was even more obvious in the construction sector (62%). It is important to note that Italian masons and architects built most of the private and public

Table 6.3 Professions declared by adults aged 14 years and over, Argentina, 1914

Sector		*Total*		*Foreigners*	*% foreign*
Agriculture		530,772		212,164	40%
Construction		212,199		132,197	62%
Manufacturing		509,407		210,293	41%
Services		1,166,963		516,422	44%
Undetermined					
Day laborers	702,528		330,909		
Peons	111,384	813,912	59,115	390,024	48%
No profession declared		1,793,661	690,432	690,432	38%
		5,026,914		**1,080,456**	

Source: 1914 Census, in Argentina, 1916–17, IV: 383–97.

buildings in major Argentinean cities of that time. But foreigners were also present in many activities: as can be seen in the table, its share was never less than 40%. Aside from construction, agriculture was the main sector where foreigners massively took low quality jobs.

This outlook is clearly evidenced when analyzing immigration flows. As can be noted from the following graph, the structure of the Argentine labor market was highly determined by the economic situation. In other words, by depending heavily on the entry of foreign labor, the impact of the crises was transitory (Figure 6.5).

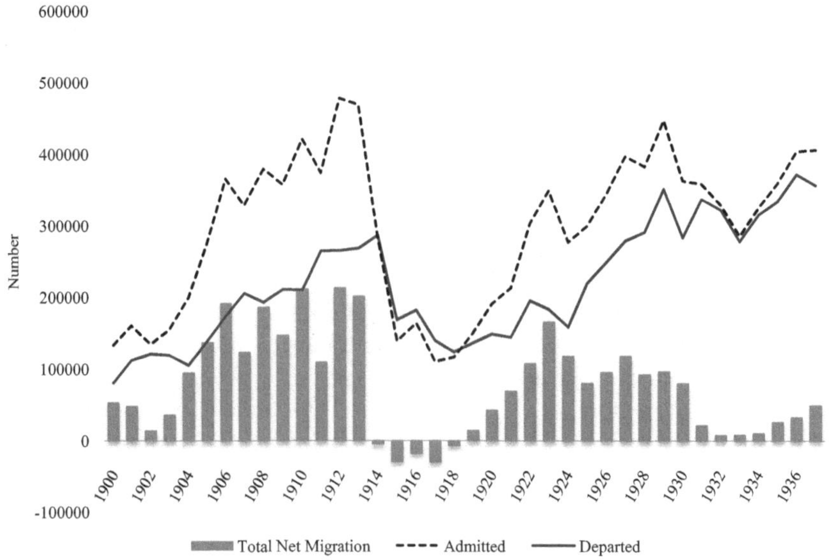

Figure 6.5 European immigration to Argentina (1900–30).
Source: Ferreres, 2010.

Literature and qualitative sources emphasized the role of temporal immigration (or 'swallow migration'), going mostly from southern Europe to Argentina, with crowds leveraging the transatlantic traffic facilities and the inverse seasons, seeking massively to be hired by the harvesters at both sides of the Atlantic in subsequent periods of the year. This seasonal migration clearly influenced Argentina's rural and urban labor markets; any reduction in arrival flows, immediately altered the production costs (Frid 2001: 80–6). But if crops failed, or if by any reason agriculture did not offer good jobs, construction was undoubtedly the most appreciated field to earn some money. Easy sectorial reallocation, at least for non-specialized workers, was granted by this mechanism. After their arrival, the immigrants simply found out available jobs, no matter if urban or rural activity, through official or private information networks[16]. It is to be noted that skilled foreigners were also a significant proportion of labor supply; intersectoral reallocation was difficult for these workers, but if a crisis arose, part of them could return to Europe, easing the pressure on the respective labor market.

If sectorial reallocation, particularly for labor, was easy, so the problems in Argentine agriculture did not excessively burden the whole economy. But the matter was the pro-cyclical role of the key reallocation sector: construction (Figure 6.6).

In this sense, construction sector operated as a pro-cyclical activity, strongly overcoming GDP level in good times, and inversely falling sharply in critical moments. So, it probably absorbed a growing percentage of unskilled workers from the primary sector, when this one was experiencing a slow

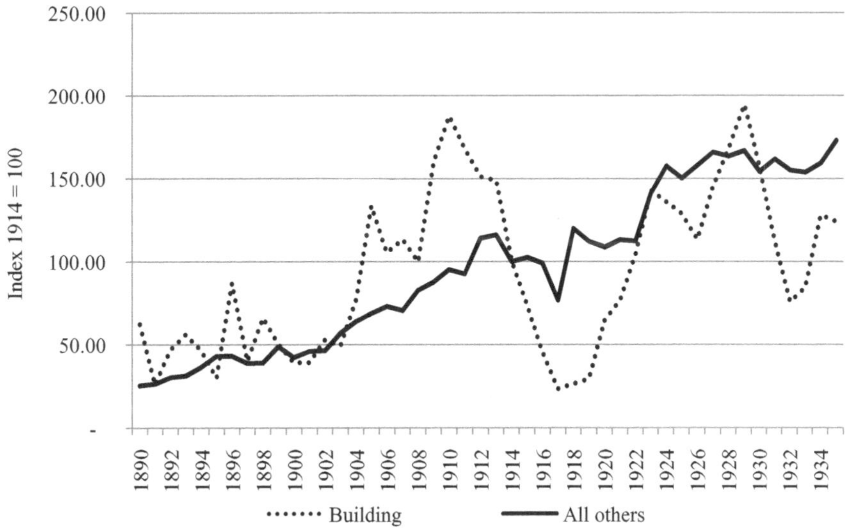

Figure 6.6 Construction GDP compared to all other sectors. Argentina, 1890–1935.
Source: See Figure 6.4

decay, even competing with more dynamic sectors (e.g., manufacturing). And, when crises arose, construction sector rapidly contracted, expulsing not required workers. If this did not result in massive unemployment, it was due to the immediate stopping of arriving immigrants, warned about these constraints by the information networks circulating at both sides of the Atlantic. If the crisis was serious enough, many immigrants simply returned, as it was the case, e.g., in 1891 (Alsina 1910).

Therefore, international workforce movements allowed the Argentine economy to export a consistent share of the detrimental effects of decayed agricultural productivity. That occurred during the worst moments of the WWI, when immigration flows suddenly dropped. But when a new crisis, and unemployment, arose by 1929–30, returning people added deflationary pressures on salaries. This situation probably explains the relatively fast recovery of Argentine economy, but obviously contributed in aggravating the situation in Europe during the Great Depression.

6. Conclusions

Undoubtedly, the primary sector was a crucial point in Argentina's economic development. However, there is no consensus among economic historians about when it began to lose dynamism. Although the limits of internal frontier had already been reached by 1914, it was still possible to expand the cultivated area and increase crop volume in the 1920s. In that context, the growth of the agricultural product continued to fuel the economy and improving prosperity in the 1920s. However, the Great Depression put in evidence the fact that primary's sector strength was no longer such.

In this chapter we sought to show some aspects of primary sector evolution, in comparison to the rest of the economy. We also analyzed the TFP and labor productivity, aiming to provide alternative approaches that could shed new light to a complex phenomenon.

What did we find? By the side of macroeconomic indicators, the primary sector did not seem to show signs of stagnation until the Great Depression. Despite the critical junctures in terms of prices or climate contingencies, there was a continuous growth cycle that motorized other sectors. Nevertheless, the stagnation in the cultivated area from 1930 onwards showed that previously agriculture had been losing ground to other sectors. On this point, some scholars argued that the preeminence of the primary sector was unnecessarily prolonged. The industrial sector had been taking off since the 1920s and the comparative advantages of the country were positioning it as a viable alternative. However, economic policy remained focused on an export-oriented growth, and exports were absolutely led by agricultural products.

In any case, we hold that already in the 1920s, and despite its growth, the primary sector would have begun to lose ground to the industry. This is evident in the strong loss of labor productivity, even in a context of solid crop growth. So, in that decade, labor, and capital probably started a reallocation process, which was still developing when the Great Depression erupted. Manufacturing was the faster developing sector, and labor demand surely allowed it to assimilate part of the workers not yet taken by agriculture. But key sector was construction, as it allowed the economy to capture higher amounts of labor in boom times, expelling them inversely in bust ones. If this phenomenon did not end in unbearable unemployment rates, or higher economic impact when in crisis, this was due to the fact that seasonal migration was quite considerable as a part of labor supply. Therefore, at critical moments, that flow was greatly reduced, and workers returned or remained in Europe, adding pressure to its own labor market.

Notes

1 About First Globalization in Latin America, see among others Bértola & Williamson, 2003.
2 Argentine population went from 4 million in 1895 to 8 million in 1914. Estimates for 1937 set the total population at 13.5 million. See Vázquez Presedo, 1978 and 1977.
3 Current methodology was taken from Sanchis Llopis, 2007.
4 It is commonly called 'residual' because it is the part of growth that cannot be explained by the increase of input factors.
5 As it can be noted in Figure 6.2, the cultivated area grew constantly until 1914, driven by the annexation of frontier lands. For the rest, the increase in cultivated area carried out in the 1930s was due to livestock movements.
6 Even compared with its US counterparts, the average area of Argentinean farms was larger. By 1890/95, in the states of Illinois, Iowa, Kansas and Missouri, the ratio between agricultural land and owners/overseers ranged at 41-61 hectares (101 to 150 acres); in the Argentine provinces of Buenos Aires, Santa Fe, and Entre Ríos, same figure was between 90 and 147 (222 to 363 acres). Djenderedjian, Bearzotti & Martirén, 2010, II: 870.
7 Míguez, 2008: 303-04, had already noted that land productivity (measured in yields per hectare) before the WWI depended to a large extent on the cultivation of new lands, due to progressive soil depletion in older farms. Maybe the production of marginal frontier lands and the depletion of soils have been central reasons for the lower growth of agricultural output in relation to other factors.
8 This included only irrigation-free arable lands. See on that, e.g., Cortés Conde, 1979.
9 Obviously, this need further research; it was also due to currency stabilization, which began in 1899. Data on interest rate in Tornquist, 1919.
10 Astorga, 2011, used the same aggregated data to measure labor productivity in Latin America during the twentieth century.
11 Frank, 2005 database; prices in the Buenos Aires Stock Exchange.
12 It is impossible to fully develop this point here, but Miguez, 2008: 302 and ff., offers a nice explanation on that.
13 About the end of frontier lands by 1910, see Cortés Conde, 1979.
14 Besides, since 1916 there were specific years of high drop in Agricultural GDP, mainly due to crop failures.
15 Argentina, Census, 1916–17, IV: 383-397.
16 There were government offices devoted to the managing of the immigrants' flow. They kept a record of available jobs that was presented to the immigrants, who were also provided with free accommodation, food, train tickets, and useful

information. Ochoa de Eguileor & Valdés, 2000. Guides, handbooks, travel diaries, etc., usually recommended how to earn money in most sectors of the bulging turn-of-the-century Argentinean economy. See, e.g., Spiotti, 1905 and 1906.

Bibliography

Adelman, J., 1994, *Frontier Development. Land, Labour and Capital in the Wheatlands of Argentina and Canada, 1890–1914*, Oxford: Clarendon Press.

Alsina, J. A., 1910, *La inmigración en el primer siglo de la independencia*, Buenos Aires: Felipe S. Alsina.

Argentina,1916–17,*Tercer Censo Nacional Levantado el 1° de Junio de 1914,* Buenos Aires: L. J. Rosso y Cia.

Astorga, P., Bergés, A. and FitzGerald, V., 2003, 'The Oxford Latin American Economico History Database,OxLAD', The Latin American Centre, Oxford University, http://oxlad.qeh.ox.ac.uk/, Oxford.

Astorga, P., Bergés, A. and FitzGerald, V., 2011, 'Productivity Growth in Latin America Over the Long Run', *Review of Income and Wealth*, 57/2, pp. 203–223, DOI: https://doi.org/10.1111/j.1475-4991.2011.00447.

Barsky, O. and Gelman, J., 2003, *Historia del agro argentino. Desde la conquista hasta comienzos del siglo XXI*, Buenos Aires: Sudamericana.

Bértola, L. and Williamson, J., 2003, 'Globalization in Latin America before 1940',*NBER Working Papers,* 9687, Cambridge, MA.

Bulmer-Thomas, V., 1994, *The Economic History of Latin America since Independence*, Cambridge: Cambridge University Press.

Bunge, A. E., 1928/1930, *La economía argentina*, Buenos Aires: Agencia General de librerías y Publicaciones/Compañía Impresora Argentina S.A. 4 vols.

Coatsworth, J., 1993, 'La independencia latinoamericana. Hipótesis sobre los costos y beneficios', in L. Prados de la Escosura and S. Amaral (eds.), *La independencia americana. Consecuencias económicas*, Madrid: Alianza, pp. 17–30.

Cortés Conde, R., 1979, *El progreso argentino 1880–1914*, Buenos Aires: Sudamericana.

Cortés Conde, R., 1997, *La economía argentina en el largo plazo, siglos XIX y XX,* Buenos Aires: Sudamericana/Universidad de San Andrés.

Cortés Conde, R. and Harriague, M., 1994, 'Estimaciones sobre el PBI en Argentina 1874–1935'. *Documento de Trabajo,*Nr. 3, Universidad de San Andrés, Buenos Aires.

Della Paolera, G. and Taylor, A., 2001, *Straining at the Anchor: The Argentine Currency Board and the Search for Macroeconomic Stability, 1880–1935*, Chicago: The University of Chicago Press.

Delli Gatti, D., Gallegati, M., Greenwald, B. C., Russo, A. and Stiglitz, J. E., 2012, 'Mobility Constraints, Productivity Trends, and Extended Crises', *Journal of Economic Behavior & Organization*, 83/3, pp. 375–393, DOI: https://doi.org/10.1016/j.jebo.2012.03.011.

Di Tella, G. and Zymelman, M., 1967, *Las etapas del crecimiento económico argentino*, Buenos Aires: Eudeba.

Di Tella, G. and Zymelman, M., 1973, *Los ciclos económicos argentinos,* Buenos Aires: Paidós.

Diaz Alejandro, C. F., 1975, *Ensayos sobre la historia económica argentina*, Buenos Aires: Amorrortu.

Diaz Alejandro, C. F., 1982, 'No Less Than One Hundred Years of Argentine Economic History, Plus Some Comparisons', *Center Discussion Paper, 392*, Yale University, Economic Growth Center, New Haven, CT.

Diéguez, H.,1972, 'Crecimiento e inestabilidad del valor y el volumen físico de las exportaciones en el período 1864–1963', *Desarrollo Económico*, 12, pp. 333–349, DOI: https://doi.org/10.2307/3466227

Djenderedjian, J., Bearzotti, S. and Martirén, J. L, 2010, *Expansión agrícola y colonización en la segunda mitad del siglo XIX*, Buenos Aires: Teseo/Universidad de Belgrano.

Duncan, T. and Fogarty, J., 1984, *Australia and Argentina: on parallel paths*, Carlton: Melbourne University Press.

Ferreres, O. (dir.), 2010, *Dos siglos de economía argentina*. Buenos Aires: Fundación Norte y Sur.

Frank, R., 2005, [On Line Database, Historical Price Series for Agricultural products,by month, Argentina, 1826–2005], http://www.anav.org.ar/sites_personales/5/, accessed March to July 2018.

Frid, C., 2001, 'Migrants, Farmers, and Workers: Italians in the Land of Ceres', in D. R. Gabaccia and F. M. Ottanelli (eds.), *Italian Workers of the World: Labour Migration and the Formation of Multiethnic States*, Urbana/Chicago: University of Illinois Press, pp. 79–101.

Gerchunoff, P. and Llach, L., 2004, *El ciclo de la ilusión y el desencanto: un siglo de políticas económicas argentinas*, Buenos Aires: Ariel.

Korol, J., 1991, 'Argentine Development in a Comparative Perspective', *Latin American Research Review*, 26, pp. 201–212.

Maddison, A., 2001, *The World Economy: A Millennial Perspective*, Paris: Organization for Economic Co-operation and Development.

Miatello, Hugo, 1904, *Investigación agrícola en la Provincia de Santa Fe*, Buenos Aires: Cía. Sub [sic]-Americana de Billetes de Banco.

Míguez, E., 2008, *Historia económica de la Argentina. De la conquista a la crisis de 1930*, Buenos Aires: Sudamericana.

Ochoa de Eguileor, J. and Valdés, E., 2000, *Dónde durmieron nuestros abuelos? Los hoteles de inmigrantes en la ciudad de Buenos Aires*, Buenos Aires: Centro Internacional para la Conservación del Patrimonio.

República Argentina, Ministerio de Agricultura, 1916, *Estadística Agrícola del año 1914–1915*, Buenos Aires: Talleres Gráficos del Ministerio de Agricultura.

Rocchi, F. 2006, *Chimneys in the Desert. Industrialization in Argentina during the Export Boom Years, 1870–1930*, Stanford, CA: Stanford University Press.

Sabato, H. and Romero, L. A., 1992, *Los trabajadores de Buenos Aires. La experiencia del mercado: 1850–1880*, Buenos Aires: Sudamericana.

Sanchis Llopis, T., 2007, '"Enfoque dual" versus "enfoque primal" en la cuantificación del crecimiento de la productividad sectorial de la economía española, 1958–1975', *Revista de Historia Industrial*, 33/XVI, pp. 147–163, DOI: https://doi.org/10.1344/rhi.v16i33.19797

Sanz Villarroya, I., 2005, 'The Convergence Process of Argentina with Australia and Canada: 1875–2000', *Explorations in Economic History*, 42, pp. 439–458, DOI: https://doi.org/10.1016/j.eeh.2004.10.003

Sanz Villarroya, I. and Prados de la Escosura, L., 2004, *Institutional Instability and Growth in Argentina: A Long-Run View*, IFCS - Working Papers in Economic History, WH from Universidad Carlos III de Madrid/Instituto Figuerola.

Schmit, R. and Rosal, M., 2000, 'Del reformismo colonial borbónico al libre comercio. Las exportaciones pecuarias del Río de la Plata,1768–1854', *Boletín del Instituto de Historia Argentina y Americana 'Dr. E. Ravignani'*, 3rd Serie, 20, pp. 69–109.

Spiotti, E., 1905–1906, *La Repubblica Argentina. Annuario dell'Emigrante Italiano.* Anno I -1905/II – 1906, Genova/Buenos Aires: Alfredo Cantinello.

Taylor, A., 1992, 'External Dependence, Demographic Burdens, and Argentine Economic Decline After the Belle Epoque', *Journal of Economic History*, 52/4, pp. 907–936. DOI: https://doi.org/10.1017/S0022050700011955

Taylor, A., 1994, 'Tres fases del crecimiento económico argentino', *Revista de Historia Económica*, 12/3, pp. 649–683, DOI: https://doi.org/10.1017/S021261090000478X

Tornquist, C. A (ed.), 1919, *The Economic Development of the Argentine Republic in the last Fifty Years*, Buenos Aires: Ernesto Tornquist & Co., Limited.

Vazquez-Presedo, V., 1978, *crisis y retraso. Argentina y la economía internacional entre las dos guerras*. Buenos Aires: EUDEBA.

Vazquez-Presedo, V., 1979, *El caso argentino. Migración de factores, comercio exterior y desarrollo, 1875–1914*, Buenos Aires: EUDEBA.

7 The effects of the Great Depression on the agricultural economy of the tobacco-exporting countries in South-eastern Europe

Socrates D. Petmezas

1. Introduction. The long-term financial and demo-economic constraints

The purpose of this chapter is to comparatively examine the effects of the Great Depression on the agricultural economy of three neighbouring South-eastern European countries, Greece, Turkey and Bulgaria, which specialised in tobacco exports. The three neighbouring countries were primarily agrarian exporting economies, which almost monopolised the production and export of oriental tobacco, producing, in the early 1920s, 84% of the 121 thousand tons that was the average world volume of this highly valued type of tobacco (Dagkas, 2003: Table 62). In the beginning of the Interwar period, the largest part of their populations (60–75%) was rural and the primary sector (extractive industries excluded) was responsible for 45–55% of their Gross Domestic Product (GDP). The productivity of labour and the wage rate were relatively low, as their industries were technologically backward and labour intensive, with a low ratio of invested fixed capital per labourer. The domestic industrial production was concentrated in only some sectors of the light consumer industry, producing almost exclusively for the low-income section of their domestic consumption.

Another common characteristic of the three countries was the fact that they had mutually engaged in a long series of bloody wars (1911–22) that culminated in a series of compulsory (Greco-Turkish) or voluntary population exchanges (between Bulgaria and its two neighbours). This was by no means a unique result of the long European War frenzy that covered four decades (1911–49), nonetheless, it was one of the most intense experiences of demographic engineering. It involved the exodus of 12% of the total population of Greece in 1920, before the massive population exchange, and the subsequent entry of maybe 1.5 million people. After the population exchange, according to the 1928 population census, one out of five citizens was an incoming refugee while, in the recently annexed northern Greek provinces, refugees formed 40% of the population and were the majority in most urban centres, other than Salonica (Petmezas, 2012: 158). The percentage of the refugee population in the other two countries was not so large, but it was

DOI: 10.4324/9781003105466-9

still substantial. For a population of 5.48 million, in 1926, the refugees in Bulgaria constituted 4.7%, but they were mostly located in Pirin Macedonia (Dragostinova, 2006: 553).

The Turkish government chose to play down the extent of the population exchange and did not encourage the expression of refugee identity, in a country where more than 3 million Christians either left or were killed, while half a million Muslim refugees moved in (Kirişci, 1996: 408; Pamuk, 2018: 50–1 and 166–7). The total population of 16.5 million in 1913, in the area that became the future Turkish Republic, shrunk by maybe 3.5 million (−20%), the incoming refugees constituting around 3% of the total population. One cannot conclude the presentation of adverse demographic developments in the Southern Balkans and Anatolia without insisting upon the direct effects of the long war decade on the population: deaths and widespread material destruction.

Furthermore, in all three countries the economic consequences of the wars and of the peace treaties were having a destabilising effect on the post-war economic and agrarian structures and the larger part of the elsewhere roaring twenties was lost in an effort to return to full and efficient employment of their economic resources. The reconstruction of the GDP series for the three countries clearly demonstrates that – contrary to most other European economies – the per capita GDP, which had fallen precipitously during the war decade, did not regain its 1911/14 levels before the mid-1930s! (Petmezas 2012: 242–60) Effectively, substantial growth was observed only after 1933, in all three countries (with Turkey demonstrating a lag of 2–3 years) (Figure 7.1).

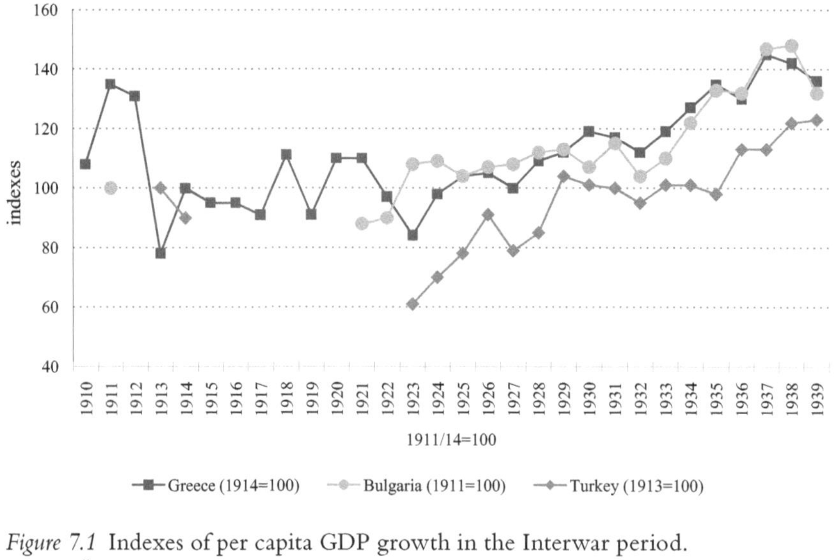

Figure 7.1 Indexes of per capita GDP growth in the Interwar period.
Source: Özel, 2000: 142; Kostelenos et al., 2007: Table 9-I; Ivanov, 2012: 518-23, Table 50.

Death, destruction and forced population exchange were not the only results of wars. Peace treaties imposed devastating territorial losses and financial reparations on the defeated nations, while the 'victors', like Greece, had to make good for the growing sovereign debt incurred during the war. In effect, a long series of post-war financial conferences and plans, under the aegis of the League of Nations, had finally reached a consensual agreement whereby the defeated states (Germany, Bulgaria etc.) were obliged to pay annual war reparations, on top of their pre-war debt service. Victors were no less indebted themselves. Greece ended in 1927 with a positive financial position *on paper*: it owed to his creditors less that it was owed from war reparations (Mazower, 1991: 102–12). In fact, it was a financially overburdened country (much like Turkey and Bulgaria), dependent on the inter-mediation of the financial committee of the League of Nations to find new loans at a reasonable cost in the international capital markets. In all three countries, capital was urgently needed for long-term public investment projects of land amendments and other such endeavours, which were indirectly related to their agricultural-export economy and to the necessary modernisation of their urban and administrative network.

To secure unimpeded access to foreign capital markets, Greece and Bulgaria had to abide by the rules of the powers that were represented by the Financial Committee of the League of Nations. A broad range of financial reforms, which would ensure that each country stabilise its currency by adhering to the Gold Exchange Standard, were imposed upon them, like the foundation of an independent central bank, along the lines of the League of Nations Financial Committee (Christodoulaki, 2002; Tooze and Ivanov, 2011: 39). Turkey was a special case: the 1920s was a period of direct foreign disinvestment in Turkey. No new foreign loans were contracted and most foreign-owned companies (those which were not nationalised) sold out their assets and left the country. The Turkish Central Bank was not founded under the aegis of the League of Nations Financial Committee, but as a public response to the 1929 currency crisis (Görmez and Yiğit, 2014: 380–3).

A currency convertible to gold or to the principal foreign currencies (Sterling Pounds and US Dollars) and the prompt service of their foreign debt and war reparations was thus to be maintained at all costs. This could only be assured with a tightly controlled monetary and fiscal policy and 'sustainable' trade balance and budgetary deficits, a policy which was sanctified by the mainstream economic thought. This constraint was not without its contradictions. The tremendous financial needs for the settlement of refugees or the land amendment projects would of course demand an increase in public spending and of foreign debt. The service of foreign debt was an absolute priority, and a steady inflow of foreign exchange was necessary for that, if the reserves of the Central Banks in gold and foreign exchange (and thus their adherence to the Gold Standard) were to be preserved.

At the same time, ever since the end of the war in 1918, agricultural-export countries faced an extremely negative international conjuncture: prices of manufactured goods (some of them inputs for farms producing for the export markets) rose much faster that the prices of their agricultural products. The terms of trade have decisively turned against agricultural prices and the producers of the agricultural-export economies (*The Agricultural Crisis,* 1931, i: 9–11). This meant that for these countries, agricultural exports had to rise *faster* that manufactured imports in order to be able to maintain a sustainable trade balance and the necessary volume of foreign exchange earnings. The structure of their foreign trade demonstrated their fragile and vulnerable position. Only a few agricultural products had a dominant position in the composition of their exports and were of paramount importance for their financial stability.

Furthermore, the tax revenues of these governments were usually disproportionately dependent upon the production and export of these few products. The fact that agricultural prices were, by definition, volatile and that their terms of trade were steadily declining vis-à-vis industrial imports was not a good sign. More concretely, in our case, tobacco was the prime export product in each country (Figure 7.2). Only one or two other agricultural products were an important part of exports in the relatively smaller countries like Greece (currants) or Bulgaria (grains, animal products), while in a larger country like Turkey, the number of the exported agricultural goods was a bit larger (Stefanoff, 1938: 43; Tezel, 1982: 119), giving it *in theory* a somewhat greater latitude in case of abrupt international price fluctuations.

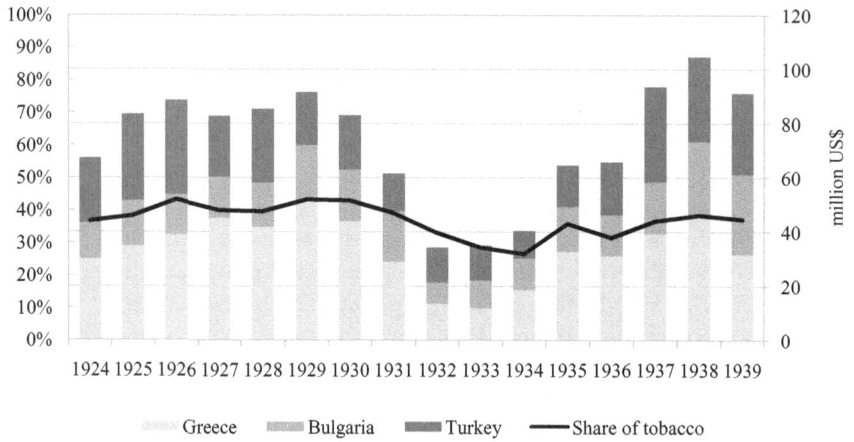

Figure 7.2 Aggregate export of oriental tobacco (in million US$) by country of origin and its aggregate share in the total exports of the three countries.

Source: Lambros and Tzanidis, 1939: 118; South-Eastern European Monetary and Economic Statistics from the Nineteenth Century to World War II, 2014, online data-series : BG6C_A, BG6D_A, GR6E_A, GR6F_A, TR6C_A, TR6D_A).

2. The slackening oriental tobacco economies before the crisis

What made matters worse was the fact that tobacco was also a product which had a key role in the maintenance of the income equilibrium of a substantial part of small rural households producing the plant and having few or no alternative crops to grow, if tobacco prices decreased. The decline in the price of tobacco would have a direct effect on the income of a large percentage of agricultural households in many densely populated provinces of Northern Greece, Southern Bulgaria and the Turkish Aegean and Pontic littoral. The income of these households was barely in equilibrium, and price volatility had *asymmetric* effects on it. Soaring prices were a temporary blessing but this ephemeral 'surplus income' had little long-term impact, while low prices led to a cycle of indebtedness at high interest rates.

Furthermore, many urban wage earners (in large part destitute refugees) were making ends meet thanks to their temporary work in the commercial processing of tobacco leaves in the large warehouses of tobacco merchants. In Northern Greece and in Pirin Macedonia, in Bulgaria, the urban wage earners of the tobacco export sector constituted the largest part of the working poor, and thus had a quasi-oligopsonistic position for the retail traders and small craftsmen in these towns. In 1929, it was estimated that almost 15% of the active labour force of the Greek economy was directly or indirectly associated with the production, commerce and export of unprocessed tobacco or cigarette manufacture for the domestic market (Petmezas, 2012: 198). Any decline in tobacco prices and exports had a direct impact on the aggregate demand of a substantial part of the rural and urban population and a strong negative effect on tax revenues and public spending.

In that sense, price volatility and, even worse, a long-term decline in tobacco prices and/or exports would have a debilitating effect both on the financial stability of the country and on the modest budget of small rural households, especially the smaller-sized farms, which had no alternative to a labour-intensive culture like tobacco. A demand crisis would simply force them to sell at lower prices, restrain their unnecessary monetary outlays and consumption, intensify the use of their land and eventually accumulate arrears in debt service. To make matters worse, many of them were refugees or land reform 'allottees' who were supposed to reimburse the public treasury for lands they were allotted. A large part of the Greek, Turkish and Bulgarian peasantry was also heavily indebted to private bankers and usurers (Tantcheff, 1931: 127; Keyder, 1981: 121–4; Koç, 1990, 37–9; Akçetin, 2000, 84–5; Petmezas, 2012, 238–42).

In the mid-1920s oriental tobacco exports had reached a record level and fetched relatively high prices in world markets. This was due to the recovery of German, Austrian and Central European demand and the effects of the expansion of smoking to new consumers (women and former soldiers). A few years after the catastrophic wars and their aftermath, smokers in the former

German and Austro-Hungarian space could return to their pre-war habits. Two countries absorbed the largest part of oriental tobacco exports, Germany and the US, while countries of the former Hapsburg Empire (Austria, Hungary, Czechoslovakia and Poland) also held together a substantial share. If we aggregate Greek, Bulgarian and Turkish exports, we have a robust proxy of the total oriental tobacco demand worldwide. During the war decade, international demand boomed from a record 54.5 thousand tons in 1912 to a peak of 78.1 thousand tons in 1920. In 1926, the aggregate exported volume of the three countries reached a record magnitude of 123.5 thousand tons for a total production of 136 thousand tons. It is only in 1938 that such a high volume of exports (124.5 thousand tons) will be again registered (Figure 7.3).

For all practical reasons, the world demand for oriental tobacco had reached its epochal peak well before 1929. The volume of production showed considerable volatility since 1926 but exports in volume were less volatile. The price of tobacco in the 1920s had also reached a peak level. The price of imported tobacco (of all varieties and qualities) in the US showed a rapid rise after the war, with a zenith of 98 cents per pound in 1924, followed by a notable contraction and stabilisation in 1928–9 (Figure 7.4).

By the same token, the total valuation of aggregate exports of the three countries followed a different pattern: the total value of exports grew rapidly until 1925, and then stagnated at a level slightly above US$200 million, the share of oriental tobacco in the aggregate exports of the three countries fluctuating around 40% until 1930 (Figure 7.2). The Great Depression abruptly reversed this situation.

To sum up, since 1925, the previously growing impetus of oriental tobacco exports (and, in general, of the aggregate agricultural exports) lost

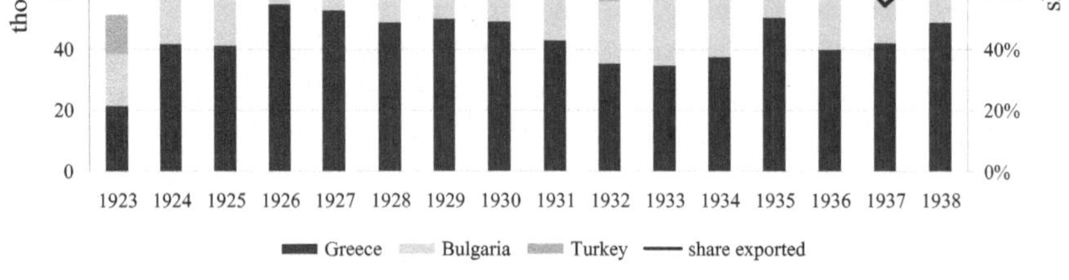

Figure 7.3 Aggregated oriental tobacco exports (in thousand tons) and the share of exports in the aggregated volume of tobacco production of the preceding year.

Source: Lambros and Tzanidis, 1939: 118.

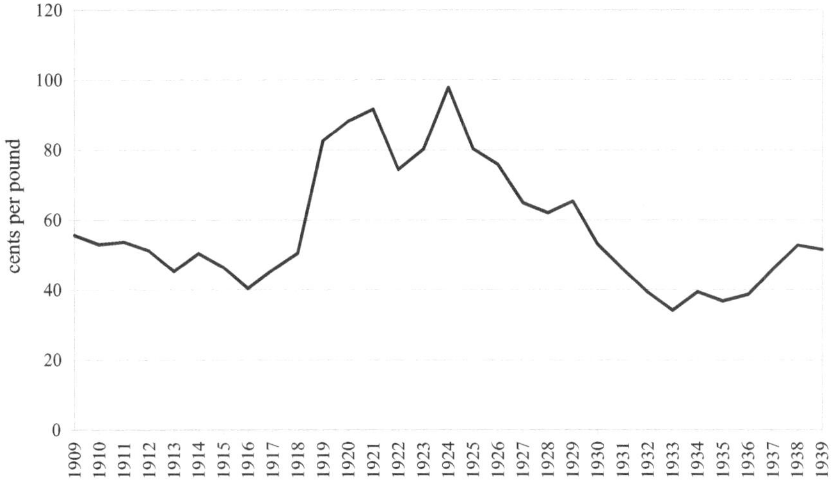

Figure 7.4 The price of imported unprocessed tobacco leaves in the US.
Source: *Statistical Abstract of the USA, 1940*: 334.

momentum and prices seemed to reach an upper threshold. Economists, businessmen and civil servants in these countries were already alarmed by world demand obviously running out of steam. *Ex post facto*, we can assert that tobacco exports in the 1920s had been instrumental in providing the ailing economies with rural and urban employment, precious foreign exchange and fiscal revenues and a significant push to the domestic aggregate demand, at a difficult time of anaemic productive recovery from the war destruction and the debilitating burden of population movements and destitute refugees. Nonetheless, even without the world depression, oriental tobacco economies had lost their dynamism by the end of the 1920s.

3. Shock transmission mechanisms and policy reactions to the Great Depression

In 1929, the aggregate value of tobacco exports registered a peak with US$91 million (almost 16.5 million Sterling Pounds), a substantial sum of foreign exchange for the three economies. Then, in October 1929, the stock market crashed on Wall Street and later, in the summer of 1931, a series of banking defaults in Austria and Germany signalled that the financial system in the European continent was, in its turn, profoundly shaken. In September 1931, the unimaginable happened: the British government devalued the Pound Sterling, suspended its convertibility and published a law imposing unprecedented import tariffs. The International Gold Exchange Standard was practically abandoned: the countries that did not devalue their currency protected their exchange rate by measures controlling exchange outflows.

The world demand for oriental tobacco was already stagnating in the late 1920s, but in 1932 it fell into a trough: from 103 thousand tons in 1929–30 and 84–89 thousand tons in 1931–3 to just 76 thousand tons in 1934, while, in aggregate value, it contracted to a greater degree from US$91.5 million in 1929, to US$61.5 million in 1931 and just US$34.3 million in 1932 (just one third of the corresponding figure in 1929) and US$40.5 million in 1934 (when prices had picked up a little). Other agricultural exports of the region had also suffered price and volume regression: grains, currants and other grapes and fruit (Evelpidis 1931; Stefanoff, 1938: 35–46). The aggregate exports of the three countries were almost halved (from little more than US$210 million in 1929 to just over US$100 million in 1932)! In fact, in South-eastern Europe, the 1929 depression was transmitted through the falling prices of agricultural exports, and mainly impacted the rural income and the public finances. Industrial employment and wages were affected less, protected by their small scale. The wage rate is estimated to have fallen only by 4% between its peak (1929) and trough (1932), while employment had fallen by 20% (Lazaretou, 2014: 167).

This was a contraction of epic proportions for these heavily indebted countries, at a moment when all international capital markets were practically dried out. It was impossible to obtain new international loans and the situation could only be dealt with by using extreme measures, as the foreign exchange reserves were dwindling. Initially, Turkey, Bulgaria and Greece responded with a rise of import tariffs and later with the imposition of import quotas (Bobtcheff, 1938: 6–8; Tezel, 1982: 167–70; Mazower, 1991: 203–12). Since they continued to cherish the hardly fought for and won anti-inflationary war for currency stabilisation, their governments were reluctant to formally abandon the Gold Standard, especially when their huge foreign debt was denominated on gold or foreign exchange (Tooze and Ivanov, 2011: 41–2). They chose to continue servicing their foreign debt and war reparation obligations. Only Greece defaulted and devalued its currency in April of 1932. It did so with the implicit consent of the British government and the League of Nations Financial Committee (Mazower, 1991: 189–98; Tooze and Ivanov, 2011: 40). This was the first of a series of devaluations until 1936 when the drachma was finally pegged again to the Sterling at a rate of 550 drachmas to the pound (losing 46% from a rate of 375 drachmas in 1928–31).

The other two countries did not follow the Greek example of devaluation but chose to continue servicing their foreign debt and preserve their adherence to the Gold Standard. Thus, their foreign debt and war reparations expressed in gold were not re-evaluated. Nonetheless, this *formal* adherence was combined with strict regulations that restricted the free outflow of exchange and imposed high import tariffs and quotas (Bobtcheff, 1938: 15–18; Tezel, 1982: 170–3). Turkey and Bulgaria have thus defended their gold and foreign exchange reserves by directly manipulating the volume of import trade and the flow of foreign exchange. Imports declined faster than exports (Table 7.1)

Table 7.1 The compound annual rate of change of the value of imports and exports of Greece, Bulgaria and Turkey, and their average trade surplus or deficit

Imports				
	Greece	*Bulgaria*	*Turkey*	*aggregate*
1923 to 1929	10.6%	6.3%	6.0%	8.1%
1929 to 1933	−23.4%	−24.6%	−22.3%	−23.2%
1933 to 1939	8.8%	21.2%	12.7%	12.6%
Exports				
	Greece	*Bulgaria*	*Turkey*	*aggregate*
1923 to 1929	14.6%	4.7%	6.7%	9.0%
1929 to 1933	−18.6%	−14.1%	−6.1%	−12.7%
1933 to 1939	10.8%	19.1%	9.4%	12.2%
Average trade surplus or deficit as percentage of exports				
5-year averages	*Greece*	*Bulgaria*	*Turkey*	
1923/1929	−108%	−11%	−36%	
1929/1933	−78%	+17%	+9%	
1933/1939	−50%	+11%	+10%	

Source: My own estimates using data from *South-Eastern European Monetary and Economic Statistics from the Nineteenth Century to World War II*, 2014, online data-series : BG6C_A, BG-6D_A, GR6E_A, GR6F_A, TR6C_A, TR6D_A).

and the trade deficit was reduced (as in Greece) or reversed (as in Bulgaria and Turkey) (Figure 7.5).

All three countries had also tried to follow a policy of fiscal consolidation (*i.e.* contraction of public spending) in order to reduce their budgetary deficit to sustainable levels, while they needed to also continue their policy of productive public investments in agriculture and other key sectors. Greece was leading a policy of budgetary surplus, since 1924 (when its access to world financial markets was practically blocked), and after the stabilisation of its currency in 1928, it continued the policy of fiscal restraint in order to improve its standing as a safe sovereign debtor and profit from low-interest foreign loans that were directed to a large programme of productive public works[1]. Initially, the Venizelos government, after responding to the urgent financial needs in 1930–1, resumed its policy of fiscal restraint which ameliorated its budgetary balance and drastically reduced the share of government expenditure to GDP. The substantial devaluation of the Greek drachma and import controls (tariffs and quotas) reduced the large trade deficit (although the Greek trade deficit remained the largest of the three) and, with a budgetary surplus, the administration was able to continue financing its public works programme. Meanwhile, devaluation had a benign effect on nominal

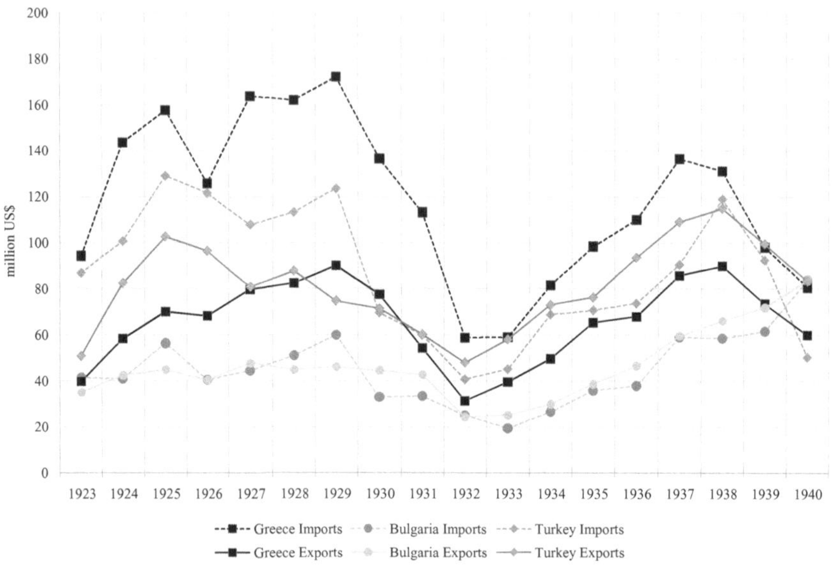

Figure 7.5 The Foreign Trade of Greece, Bulgaria and Turkey.
Source: South-Eastern European Monetary and Economic Statistics from the Nineteenth Century to World War II, 2014, online data-series : BG6C_A, BG6D_A, GR6E_A, GR6F_A, TR6C_A, TR6D_A).

domestic prices: the Greek Price Index grew in a period of world price deflation (Figure 7.6).

Bulgaria and Turkey, on the contrary, followed a different policy mix. Their governments had opted to insist on adhering to the Gold Standard and service their gold-denominated foreign debt. Consequently, they were obliged to assume a policy of exceptional import reduction and strict exchange controls (Nenovsky, Pavanelly and Dimitrova, 2008, 92–102). They achieved a trade surplus but servicing their foreign debt meant that they had to accept a substantial budgetary deficit, and we observe that during the 1930s, the share of government revenues to GDP was, contrary to the Greek case, growing, largely financed from domestic capital holders in both Bulgaria (Ivanov and Dimitrova, 2014: 223) and Turkey (Görmez and Yiğit, 2014: 390).

This was by no means an unprecedented choice of economic policy. Many central European countries (among them Germany and Hungary) with a substantial gold-denominated foreign debt had made the same choice (Eichengreen and Irwin, 2010). Turkey, which officially adhered to the Gold Standard in February 1930 and founded a central bank as late as October 1931, also adopted a policy of import and exchange controls leading to a trade surplus and a growing budgetary deficit (Görmez and Yiğit, 2014: 389–90) in order to finance an ambitious programme of public investment. Both countries' formal adherence to a fixed exchange rate relative to the gold standard

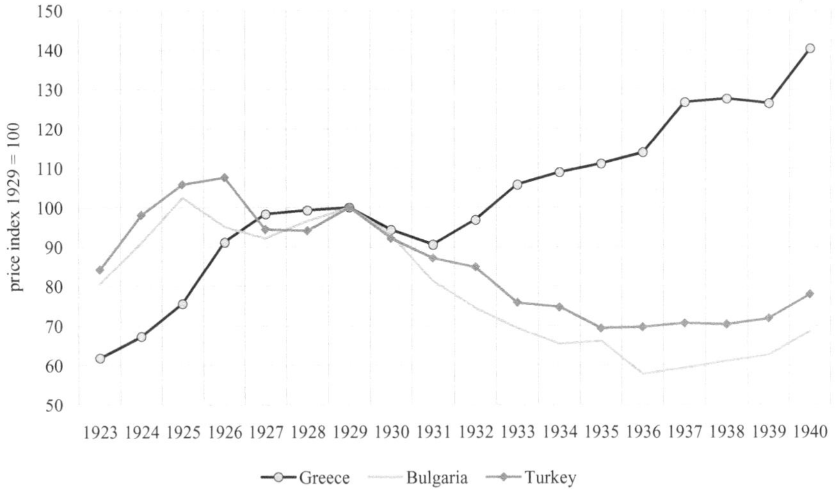

Figure 7.6 The price index in Greece, Bulgaria and Turkey.
Source: South-Eastern European Monetary and Economic Statistics from the Nineteenth Century to World War II, 2014, online data-series: BG5A_A, GR5A_A, TR5A_A).

was an obstacle to any effort to fully reflate their economy: prices remained below the 1929 level (Figure 7.6) and the broad money supply grew at substantially lower rates than Greece (Lazaretou, 2014: 153; Ivanov and Dimitrova, 2014: 213; Görmez and Yiğit, 2014: 386).

4. The initial negative effects of the world crisis

All three countries had faced an extremely adverse situation in the first four years of the crisis (1930–4), which showed its teeth in the summer of 1931 and subsequently grew in intensity until 1934. In fact, observing the evolution of the GDP (Figure 7.1) we can assert that the index of per capita GDP had returned to its 1929–30 level and registered a slight relative amelioration only in 1934, for Greece and Bulgaria, and in 1936 for Turkey. Since the mid-1930s, in all three countries the per capita index registered a modest but real increase above the 1929–30 level. This growth should be attributed, on the one hand, to the expansion of domestic manufacturing, behind the protective walls of tariffs and import quotas, and on the other hand, to the surprisingly rapid growth of their agricultural production (Kopsidis and Ivanov, 2017: 95; Pamuk, 2018: 187–91). But this growth dynamic became observable only after around 1934. It should be underlined that this increase was not only a result of policy choices and developments taking place in the 1930s, but that it was intrinsically related to the growing public intervention in agriculture, which had already begun in the mid-1920s but actually crystallised as a new policy regime in the second half of the 1930s. It was thus, in part, a delayed effect of earlier institutional transformation and public investment which finally began to bear fruit in the mid-1930s.

The earlier years of the depression (1930–3) were the most difficult. Deflation was 'imported' and the per capita GDP in constant prices stagnated. The crisis hit the agricultural sector through the abrupt decline of prices and of the demand for the few exported agricultural products (tobacco, fruit and vegetables, Bulgarian wheat). In Bulgaria, the agricultural income had fallen by 50% in 1930–3, and the farmers were unable to service their debts, a recurrent pattern in all three countries. In fact, the high prices of the late 1920s had pushed the farmers into borrowing[2] and the reversal of the situation had the typical asymmetrical effects. Indebted farmers were unable to make ends meet, and, in late 1930, the government had to reluctantly step in with a National Debt Relief Act which covered 1.2 million rural households for a debt of 6.6 million, out of 10 million leva of non-performing agricultural credits (a quarter of the GDP) that the National Debt Relief Act addressed (Tooze and Ivanov, 2011: 45–6).

Bulgarian peasants faced with falling returns for their principal export products (tobacco and wheat), expanded their subsistence cultures and retreated to the familiar 'peasant self-subsistence' model, which was the standard culprit – or justification – of economists for the inelastic response of the Bulgarian economy to monetary stimulus. On the positive side, Bulgarian peasants had also adopted better-rewarded labour-intensive export cultures (like fruit, vegetables, and industrial plants other than tobacco), which helped them remedy their households' budgetary deficit (Kopsidis and Ivanov, 2015: 18). Nonetheless, initially, in 1930–3, returns to land and labour were shrinking rapidly, while the ratio of land to labour was also rapidly deteriorating showing that there was a deceleration of labour release from the countryside (see Table 7.2).

The Turkish farmers had also felt the double impact of falling international prices and shrinking household income on the one hand and growing indebtedness on the other. The majority of the small-owner farmers were producing for export and for the domestic urban markets: tobacco in the regions of Izmir and the Black Sea coast; cotton in Izmir and Adana regions; figs and grapes in the provinces of Izmir, Denizli, Aydin and Manisa; wheat in Thrace, central

Table 7.2 Bulgaria: annual rates of change of main agricultural indexes *(between 5-year averages)*

	Return to land (Q/L)	*Return to labour (Q/T)*	*Ratio of land to labour (T/L)*
1905–1911	0.65	0.05	0.59
1912–1920	−4.14	−3.11	−1.03
1921–1929	2.22	2.74	−0.52
1930–1933	−2.16	−1.16	−1.00
1934–1939	5.73	4.79	0.94

Source: Kopsidis and Ivanov, 2015: 13.

and western Anatolia. They were perennially indebted to local merchants and usurers and usually paid off and 'renewed' their debt every year (Keyder, 1981: 121–3). The crisis dried out the credit market, bankrupted the merchant houses and left a part of the poorer peasants desperately unable to renew their debt, purchase seeds and other necessities (Keyder, 1987: 95–6).

The situation was worsened by the earlier introduction in 1925 of a new 'modernized' agricultural taxation system that eliminated the tithe (a tax in kind proportional to the gross physical output of their farm) in favour of a fixed cash tax relative to the size of farm or livestock, and consequently disproportionally heavy when prices crashed. There were incidences reported in December 1930 of starving peasants in the highly commercialised Izmir hinterland, who were forced to feed themselves with weeds (Akçetin 2000: 92). The state-owned Agricultural Bank, influenced in its credit choices by the influential local municipal elite, as well as the credit cooperatives, failed to offer the necessary funds to the small-owner farmers (Akçetin, 2000: 91–3).

The poorer peasants responded to the challenge by adopting a 'predatory' strategy (squatting on public and private lands, engaging in contraband trade and other illegal activities) and diversifying their income sources through temporary emigration to the towns. They changed their culture mix, expanding the area of subsistence crops and adopting – whenever they had the opportunity – new export cultures. Peasants abandoned tobacco for wheat, except for tobacco small owners of the Black Sea coast, who had no alternative to tobacco due to the very small size of their farms (Akçetin 2000: 96). In fact, Turkish farmers were diversifying from export-oriented tobacco to wheat, which was channelled to the domestic market (Akçetin, 2000: 95–6). In these difficult years (1930–3) the total crop acreage initially regressed and then took an upward trend, although wheat and tobacco regressed more, while yields began a slow rise (always excepting tobacco). There is no indication that commercial inputs (like fertilisers) were adopted and probably in Turkey the rise of yields is the result of more diligent labour invested in weeding, seeding etc. (Table 7.3).

In Greece, the same pattern is observed: the decrease in export prices had forced peasants to change their crop mix in favour of subsistence crops (Kostis, 1987: 137–9; 1990: 111–7), or wherever it was possible, of other more profitable export or commercial crops (fruit, vegetables, cotton). A large part of Greek farmers were also indebted to merchants and local usurers, and found themselves in a very precarious position. Moreover, allottees of the land reform and agriculturally settled refugees were also heavily indebted to the treasury, but were also the first to enjoy a moratorium of debt servicing. In 1931, the government decided to suspend all taxation on agricultural production, except of taxes and tariffs imposed on tobacco and currants (mainly exported items whose taxation was carried by the merchants and foreign consumers). In 1934, it has been estimated that an average small rural household had a budgetary deficit of 18% of: its agricultural income (Petmezas 2012: 238). The deficit of the rural households was covered with earnings from non-agricultural activities and wage labour.

Table 7.3 Turkey: the compound annual rates of change of basic indexes of agricultural production and acreage

(between 5-year averages)

	Wheat			*Tobacco*		
	acreage	*volume*	*yield*	*acreage*	*volume*	*yield*
1909 to 1914–25	1.2%	−4.6%	−5.7%	2.0%	2.4%	0.4%
1925/29 to 1930/34	−0.7%	6.8%	7.6%	−4.5%	−6.2%	−1.8%
1930/34 to 1935/39	4.9%	7.6%	2.6%	7.6%	10.3%	2.5%
	aggregate indexes of the agricultural economy					
	total acreage	*total value*	*rural labour*	*return to labour (Q/L)*	*return to land (Q/T)*	*ratio of land to labour (T/L)*
1909 to 1914–25	1.1%	−2.2%	−0.8%	−1.4%	−3.2%	1.8%
1925/29 to 1930/34	1.4%	9.8%	2.1%	7.5%	8.3%	−0.7%
1930/34 to 1935/39	4.6%	1.1%	1.8%	−0.7%	−3.4%	2.7%

Source: see Table 7.6 in the Annex.

The Interwar crisis had hit particularly hard this rural population that was dependent on wage labour or the culture of export products (tobacco, currants) and especially those poorer households who were not able to even secure their own food consumption (Evelpidis 1939: 144–70). The parliamentary Greek governments had been too timorous to radically address the problem of agricultural indebtedness: in 1936, the total agricultural debt had reached 9–10 billion drachmas (half of the average value of the annual agricultural output) and was owed to public and private creditors in an almost equal share. It took eight years of vacillation (and a royal dictatorial government in search of popular legitimisation) to finally confront the problem by writing off a large part of the privately owned debt in May of 1937 (Petmezas, 2012: 238–42).

The initial reaction of Greek farmers to the export crisis was to expand the tilled acreage in favour of subsistence products (grains). On the contrary, the area (and the volume of production) of the main export products, like tobacco and currants, had significantly decreased until 1932–4 (Table 7.4). The Greek agricultural economy and state finances had to initially deal with the problem of the collapse of the tobacco export sector (which not only provided income to rural producers but to a substantial number of urban wage labourers). In October 1930, the government intervened to absorb the unsold tobacco and stabilise its export prices, principally in order to provide some relief to the tobacco merchant exporters. But it was clear that the national policy of protecting the income of the tobacco producers and regulating the exported volume (and prices) of tobacco was inadequate.

In October 1931, after many months of negotiation, the three tobacco-exporting countries had managed to convince the League of Nations

Table 7.4 Greece: the compound annual rates of change of basic indexes of agricultural acreage and production
(between 5-year averages)

the annual rate of change (between the 5 year averages)	*1920/24 to 1925/29*	*1925/29 to 1930/34*	*1930/44 to 1935/38 (*)*
Surface of cultivated arable land and vineyards without fallow (thousand ha)	3.4%	4.7%	3.2%
Wheat (thousand ha)	3.3%	5.2%	4.9%
Tobacco (thousand ha)	12.9%	−2.6%	3.0%
Currant vineyards (thousand ha)	−2.1%	−0.3%	1.2%
Wheat (thousand tons)	5.3%	8.6%	8.1%
Tobacco (thousand tons)	10.6%	−5.7%	4.9%
Currants (thousand tons)	0.8%	−1.9%	2.0%
Net value of Agricultural production (millions Swiss Frs)	1.8%	−2.7%	6.3%
Return to land (Q/T)	−0.7%	−0.7%	0.8%
Return to labour (Q/L)	0.4%	2.6%	3.3%
Ratio of land to labour (T/L)	1.1%	3.6%	2.3%

(*) the 1935/38 is a four-year average.
Source: See Petmezas, 2021: Table 1.

Economic and Financial Section to expand the definition of agrarian-exporter country to include not only countries exporting grains but oriental tobacco as well. It was at that moment hoped that, through international conferences, the agrarian exporting countries and their industrial importers would be able to reach mutually advantageous agreements, which would stabilise prices (protecting the rural income and exchange receipts of the exporting countries) and guarantee that agricultural countries would receive enough exchange to be able to pay for the import of manufactures and the unimpeded service of their foreign debt and war reparations (Prontzas, 1996: 287–307). In other words, this initiative was an attempt to safeguard the international monetary system based on the Gold Exchange Standard.

Nonetheless, all these international efforts for the collaboration of industrial and agricultural export countries to address the problem of volatile and falling agricultural prices failed, while the last-ditch effort to save the Gold Standard itself was doomed as soon as the newly elected US President, Franklin D. Roosevelt, made clear he did not intend to sacrifice the American interests on its 'golden altar'. After the failure of the Geneva Conference to deal with the question of agrarian-exporting countries in March 1933, it was clear that international trade in general and the tobacco export trade in particular would be conducted through special bilateral or multilateral agreements inside larger currency zones. Already since late 1931, many countries had begun to sign bilateral clearing agreements.

5. Export reorientation and introverted growth in the late 1930s

The months that followed the failure of the Geneva Conference in March 1933, and especially the London World Economic Conference in June 1933, were paramount in the formation of separate trade blocs, around 'strong' industrial and financial poles: Great Britain, the US, France and the gold-bloc countries and Germany. Greece had already signed bilateral clearing agreements first with France, in July, and then and more importantly with Germany, in August 1932. Bulgaria also signed clearing agreements with Germany in June 1932, and Turkey, in its turn, in 1934. These agreements locked the three countries into the larger German economic/trade area (Asenova, 2013: 94–106; Mazower, 1991: 218–24; Tezel, 1982: 177–9). Many Central and Eastern European countries (Romania, Hungary, and Yugoslavia) had signed comparable clearing agreements with Germany. Germany, and its Reichsmark (RM), thus became the main trade partner of each country, while from the German point of view, each of these countries held a minor share of German interests.

This asymmetric relationship was even more lopsided because each small 'agrarian' country founded its export trade with Germany on a handful (at best) of substitutable primary export products, which could not easily find an alternative 'free-trade' market at equally high prices, while German trade interests were distributed to a large number of high-technology industrial products (Raupach, 1969: 83–86). Furthermore, it was soon made evident that most of Germany's trade partners held a long-term positive position in the bilateral clearing trade balance, with their blocked (*Sperrmark*) Reichsmark bank-accounts bloated. In a free market situation, this trade surplus would have been a blessing, but in this particular case their positive bank accounts were blocked until their importers could find an equivalent solvable domestic demand for German goods. In fact, each country was practically making an implicit RM-denominated loan to Germany, running the risk of a possible devaluation of the RM.

Contrary to the widely held view, Nazi Germany did not try to immediately capitalise on this unique opportunity of monopsonistic profit (for instance by forcing low prices on its partners' main export goods), or to impose any bilateral agreement that would jeopardise the formal political or economic sovereignty of its trade partners. Furthermore, the positive surplus of the clearing agreements of each trade partner could serve as legally accepted collateral for its central bank to legitimately expand its monetary base, providing domestic loans in proportion to the bilateral surplus of their blocked RM accounts, partly 'monetising' this surplus (Neal, 1979, 398–404). Not all German trade partners adopted such an expanding monetary policy, but Greece did so in 1935, followed later by Bulgaria and Turkey (Psalidopoulos, 2014: 125–30; Ivanov and Dimitrova, 2014: 211), expanding their money supply and further reflating their economy (Figure 7.6).

The most obvious effect of the clearing agreements was the almost immediate redress of the agrarian export trade (tobacco sold at relatively high prices) which coincided with other positive counter effects of the (forced) protection of the domestic market for import-substituting manufactures. Germany absorbed on average in 1933–9 a record 52.4% of Bulgarian, 47.9% of Greek, and 38.3% of Turkish tobacco exports. Greece and Turkey were able to channel a part of their product to the US, the other major buyer of oriental tobacco, a market that was freely importing and paying in gold-denominated exchange (Table 7.5). Nonetheless, Germany was a larger and more rapidly expanding market for tobacco in the late 1930s. Thus, the German demand redressed and stabilised agricultural prices and rural incomes in all three countries. The German economy, with an 11% growth rate in 1934–8 (Neal, 1979: 393) was becoming the locomotive for the growth of its peripheral South-eastern European economies. A growing percentage of the foreign trade of these countries was directed towards Germany (which absorbed Austria in 1938). This implied that other trade partners, usually the important industrial exporters and the large consumer markets of North-western Europe, saw their own share equally diminish (Neal 1979: 397, Table 2).

The domestic demand offered equally beneficial results to the expanding agricultural production. Cotton production, encouraged by positive policy

Table 7.5 Unprocessed tobacco imports in the US and German markets

In tons (five year averages) and share of US and German markets in the tobacco exports of each exporting country.

Country of origin	*USA*			*Germany*		
	1925–29	1930–34	1935–39	1925–29	1930–34	1935–39
Greece	20,377	16,065	18,962	16,085	15,884	21,558
Turkey	12,710	12,595	19,261	9,025	9,116	14,030
Bulgaria	–	–	–	9,266	9,657	11,573
Total	69,705	53,881	56,507	98,022	82,828	94,982
Share of oriental tobacco in the total value of tobacco imports	47.5%	53.2%	67.6%	35.4%	41.8%	49.7%

Share of US and German markets in the tobacco exports of each exporting country

Country of origin	*USA*			*Germany*		
	1925–29	1930–34	1935–39	1925–29	1930–34	1935–39
Greece	41.2%	40.2%	42.8%	32.5%	39.8%	48.7%
Turkey	36.5%	49.3%	60.7%	25.9%	35.7%	44.2%
Bulgaria	–	–	–	35.5%	43.5%	43.0%

Source: *Agricultural Yearbook* [since 1938 *Agricultural Statistics*] (annual issues of the years 1925–40); *Statistisches Jahrbuch für das Deutsche Reich* (annual issues of the years 1925–40).

initiatives, expanded in Greece and Turkey to meet the demand of the growing domestic cotton industry for raw materials (Petmezas, 2012: 246–8; Tekeli and Ilkin, 1988: 58–61; Karakoç, 2014: 169). The ambitious Turkish industrialisation programme was not particularly successful, nonetheless, large scale public investment had expanded the railroad network in the 1930s and reinforced the dynamic commercialisation of agricultural production which, in its turn, provided growing demand for the domestic industry (Pamuk, 2018: 189–90). To a large degree, the upward swing of the agricultural and industrial output in all three countries was the result of this positive interaction between agriculture and domestic industry.

In Greece, the mid-1930s coincided with the partial completion of the large-scale land amendment projects in Northern Greece that added 300 thousand hectares (ha) of high-quality arable land to the existing 3 million ha in 1934: a rise of 10%. Almost at the same time, there was a positive reversal of the previous 20-year long decline of grain yields; in the next few years, yield grew on average from less than 60 to more than 90 metric quintals per ha (Petmezas, 2012: 187). The expansion of the acreage is equally noticed in Bulgaria (Tooze and Ivanov, 2007: 701), Greece (Petmezas, 2012: 241–50) and Turkey (Karakoç, 2014: 82, Table 2.4) even-though there is practically no evidence of rise in labour productivity. Nonetheless, according to Kopsidis and Ivanov (2015: 14–22), Bulgarian agriculture underwent the beginning of a 'Green Revolution' in the 1930s (Table 7.2) with high rates of productivity growth and an amelioration of the ratio of land to labour! Nonetheless, in spite of its growth, labour productivity was low by international standards and its increase had always been fragile and intermittent, due to the anaemic demand for labour in the urban sector.

In fact, in the Interwar period and especially in the 1930s, all migratory destinations that would have eased rural unemployment, in the absence of domestic urban pull, were sealed. Without emigration, an underdeveloped agrarian economy with low rural incomes and a non-dynamic domestic industry was unable to provide enough demand for the expansion of the domestic urban labour demand. Consequently, the rural population surplus could not find profitable employment and thus settle permanently in the towns. The large rural economy, dominated by under-capitalised small family farms, absorbed the growing labour surplus exacerbating their under-capitalisation and orienting them towards labour-intensive products and activities. A constant check was exerted on rural labour productivity and on the wage rate of unqualified labour in the larger economy. On the other hand, such an agrarian structure reduced the immediate negative effects of the Great Depression on national employment and even on industrial wage rates, *i.e.* concealed the increase in unemployment on a national level and alleviated its most obvious pauperising effects. But it had a long-term negative impact on labour supply and especially on labour productivity, primarily in the countryside, but also in the urban/industrial sector.

6. Conclusion. A fundamental policy regime shift

From the mid-1930s and onwards, a more fundamental transformation was produced due to the urgent necessity to reflate the economy and boost output growth. The political, academic and economic elite opted for a profound change of the policy regime. Industrial protectionism and import substitution industrialisation were favourable *but unintended* by-products of the urgent priority to restrain imports, but the swift implementation of a self-conscious interventionist policy in the agricultural economy was of epochal importance, because this policy regime continued, expanded and became dominant after the Second World War.

The expansion of extension services took off in the early 1930s in all three countries. Institutes were founded for the protection and support of specific products for domestic industrial demand (like cotton, sugar beet, olive oil). Networks of experimental and educational public farms and seed producing centres for the diffusion of the best cultural practices, modern agricultural equipment, high-quality seed and animal breeds, fertilisers and pesticides were organised. Finally, the acceleration of an earlier effort for the improvement and expansion of the educational and research structure (agronomic, forestry and veterinary schools, scientific centres of research for plant and epizootic diseases, etc.) was observed (Petmezas, 2012: 246–55; Tekeli and Ilkin, 1988).

In the second half of the 1930s, tobacco (and other) exports and prices had recovered, the industrial and agricultural output and land yields increased and, to a great extent, the average rural household's income was redressed. A new policy regime of state intervention, applied and regulated by specialised public institutions, was imposed upon the agricultural economy. The rise of authoritarian royal dictatorships and one party regimes facilitated the adoption of a new spirit of corporatism, and seemed to be the only road to a dynamic recovery.

Nonetheless, this was only a temporary respite. In the Greek case, in spite of amelioration of land and labour productivity, rural regional specialisation regressed. It was the 'less developed' regions of the North that profited from the new interventionist policy regime while the economically more competitive provinces had shown little dynamism. The regional rates of growth of the indices of aggregate land and labour productivity grew in the 1930s faster in the less advanced regions (Petmezas, 2021, Annex 1). Regional convergence was achieved thanks to the slower growth of the rates of productivity change in the most commercialised provinces. In general, the small under-capitalised family farms survived in the 1930s (and even increased their returns to land and labour) thanks to public price and income support, relatively cheap credit from the Greek Agricultural Bank, partial debt relief and almost complete fiscal immunity. Both the cost of production in agriculture and the rate of latent rural unemployment remained high, and many of these farms became unsustainable in the post-war environment of trade liberalisation.

Annex

Table 7.6 Turkey: basic indexes of agricultural acreage and production

	Wheat			*Tobacco*		
Five-year averages	*Acreage (ha)*	*Volume (tons)*	*Yield (quintals per ha)*	*Acreage (ha)*	*Volume (tons)*	*Yield (quintals per ha)*
1909–14	2,477,883	3,736,790	15.1	51,070	36,249	7.1
1925–29	2,945,676	1,850,592	6.3	68,766	52,074	7.6
1930–34	2,842,064	2,577,345	9.1	54,639	37,871	6.9
1935–39	3,613,249	3,717,345	10.3	78,681	61,731	7.8
	Aggregate indexes of the agricultural economy					
Five-year averages	*Total acreage (ha)*	*Value (million constant TL in 1927 prices)*	*Rural labour (thousands)*	*Return to labour (Q/L)*	*Return to land (Q/T)*	*Ratio of land to labour (T/L)*
1909–14	4,730,888	1,058	6,027	175.5	223.6	0.78
1925–29	5,542,254	759	5,376	141.1	136.9	1.03
1930–34	5,935,918	1,211	5,979	202.5	204.0	0.99
1935–39	7,446,754	1,279	6,551	195.3	171.8	1.14

Source: My estimates using Karakoç, 2014: 82–6; Güran, 1997: Tables 1.1–1.3).

Notes

1 Macroeconomic data, collected under the aegis of the Austrian and Balkan Central Banks, for Greece, Bulgaria and Turkey are available online in the *South-Eastern European Monetary and Economic Statistics from the Nineteenth Century to World War II* (2014). The following data-series have been used: on M3 money supply: BG1Q_1, GR1H_A, TR1L_A; on Foreign Trade: BG6C_A, BG6D_A, GR6E_A, GR6F_A, TR6C_A, TR6D_A; on Consumer price index: BG5A_A, GR5A_A, TR5A_A; on public revenue and expenditure: BG4A_A, BG4B_A, GR4A_A, GR4E_A, TR4A_A, TR4B_A; on Industrial growth TR5B_A, GR5H_A; on industrial employment and wages: GR5H_A, GR5I_A.

2 The expansion of rural indebtedness was a result of the relatively abundant supply of money available after the two large international loans of 1926 ('refugee loan') and 1928 ('stabilisation loan') as well as the inflow of short-term US loans to the private sector (Kolev, 2009: 10).

Bibliography

The Agricultural Crisis, 1931, 2 vols, Geneva: League of Nations, Economic and Financial Section. Available at https://digital.nls.uk/league-of-nations/archive/191866195.

Agricultural Yearbook [since 1938 *Agricultural Statistics*], annual issues 1900—1941, Washington, D.C.: US Department of Agriculture. Available at https://catalog.hathitrust.org/Record/002137878.

Akçetin, E., 2000, 'Anatolian Peasants in the Great Depression 1929–1933', *New Perspectives on Turkey*, 23, pp. 79–102. doi: 10.1017/S0896634600003393.

Asenova, V., 2013, *Small State Autonomy in Hierarchical Regimes. The Case of Bulgaria in the German and Soviet Spheres of Influence 1933–1956* (Unpublished doctoral dissertation), Central European University, Budapest, Hungary.

Bobtcheff, C., 1938, 'La Politique du Commerce extérieur de la Bulgarie après la guerre', *Трудове На Стопанският Институте За Социални Поручвания При Софийския Дарявен Университет* [*Proceedings of the Economic Institute for Social Studies at Sofia State University*], 4, pp. 1–49.

Christodoulaki, O., 2002, 'Η Μεταρρύθμιση Του Τραπεζικού Συστήματος Και η Ίδρυση Της Τράπεζας Της Ελλάδος [The Reform of the banking system and the Foundation of the Bank of Greece]', in Ch. Hadjiiossif (ed.) *Ιστορία της Ελλάδας του 20ού αιώνα* [*History of Greece in the 20th Century*], Athens, II(2), pp. 250–67.

Dagkas, A., 2003, *Recherches sur l'histoire sociale de la Grèce du Nord: Le mouvement des ouvriers du tabac, 1918–1928*, Paris. http://users.auth.gr/adagkas/texts/final,6-2003.pdf.

Dragostinova, T., 2006, 'Competing Priorities, Ambiguous Loyalties: Challenges of Socioeconomic Adaptation and National Inclusion of the Interwar Bulgarian Refugees', *Nationalities Papers, 34*(5), pp. 549–74. doi: 10.1080/00905990600952970.

Eichengreen, B., and Irwin, D.A., 2010, 'The Slide to Protectionism in the Great Depression and the Protectionist Temptation: Who Succumbed and Why?', *Journal of Economic History*, 70(4), pp. 871–97. doi: 10.1017/S0022050710000756.

Evelpidis, Ch., 1931, *Η Γεωργική Κρίσις ιδία εν Ελλάδι* [*The Agricultural Crisis, Especially in Greece*, Athens.

Evelpidis, Ch., 1939, *Θεωρία και πράξις αγροτικής πολιτικής και οικονομίας* [*Theory and Practice of Agrarian Economy and Policy*], Athens.

Görmez, Y. and Yiğit, S., 2014, 'Turkey: From 1923 to 1947', in *South-Eastern European Monetary and Economic Statistics from the Nineteenth Century to World War II*, Athens, Sofia, Bucharest, Vienna: Bank of Greece, Bulgarian National Bank, National Bank of Romania, Oesterreichische Nationalbank, pp. 379–400. Available at: www.bankofgreece.gr/Pages/en/Publications/Studies/seemhn.aspx.

Güran, T., 1997, *Agricultural Statistics of Turkey during the Ottoman Period*, Ankara: DIE.

Ivanov, M., 2012, *The Gross Domestic Product of Bulgaria 1870–1945*, Sofia: Bulgarian Statistical Service. Available online at: https://www.nsi.bg/biblioteka/2018/04/23/-the-gross-domestic-product-of-bulgaria-1870-1945/, (Accessed: 21 August 2020).

Ivanov, M. and Dimitrova. K., 2014, 'Bulgaria: From 1879 to 1947', in *South-Eastern European Monetary and Economic Statistics from the Nineteenth Century to World War II*. Athens, Sofia, Bucharest, Vienna: Bank of Greece, Bulgarian National Bank, National Bank of Romania, Oesterreichische Nationalbank, pp. 199–241. Available at: www.bankofgreece.gr/Pages/en/Publications/Studies/seemhn.aspx.

Karakoç, U., 2014, *Sources of Economic Growth in Interwar Egypt and Turkey: Industrial Growth, Tariff Protection and the Role of Agriculture* (Unpublished doctoral dissertation), London: London School of Economics and Political Science (University of London). Available at: https://ethos.bl.uk/OrderDetails.do?did=1&uin=uk.bl.ethos.634512.

Keyder, Ç., 1981, *The Definition of a Peripheral Economy: Turkey, 1923–1929*, Cambridge, New York: Cambridge University Press.

Keyder, Ç., 1987, *State and Class in Turkey: A Study in Capitalist Development*, London, New York: Verso.

Kirişci, K., 1996, 'Refugees of Turkish Origin: 'Coerced Immigrants' to Turkey since 1945', *International Migration*, 34(3), pp. 385–412. doi: 10.1111/j.1468-2435.1996.tb00534.x.

Koç, M., 1990, 'The Transformation of Oriental Tobacco Production in the Aegean Turkey', *New Perspectives on Turkey,* 4, pp. 31–55. doi: 10.15184/S0896634600000200.

Kolev, S., 2009, 'The Great Depression in the Eyes of Bulgaria's Inter-War Economists', *Bulgarian National Bank Discussion Paper 79.* Available at: https://papers.ssrn.com/sol3/papers.cfm?abstract_id=2888701.

Kopsidis, M. and Ivanov, M., 2015, 'Was Gerschenkron Right? Bulgarian Agricultural Growth During the Interwar Period in Light of Modern Development Economics.' Working Paper 82. European Historical Economics Society Working Papers, in Economic History. Available at: http://www.ehes.org/EHES_82.pdf.

Kopsidis, M. and Ivanov, M., 2017, 'Industrialization and De-Industrialization in Southeast Europe', in K.H. O'Rourke and J.G. Williamson (eds.) *The Spread of Modern Industry to the Periphery since 1871,* London, New York: Oxford University Press.

Kostelenos, G., Petmezas, S., Kounaris, E., Sfakianakis, M. and Vasiliou, D., 2007, *Ακαθάριστο Εγχώριο Προϊόν 1830–1939.* [*The Gross Domestic Product 1830–1939*]. Sources of Economic History of Modern Greece], Athens: ΚΕΠΕ and HA/NBG.

Kostis, C.P., 1987, *Αγροτική Οικονομία και Γεωργική Τράπεζα. Όψεις της Ελληνικής Οικονομίας στο Μεσοπόλεμο (1919–1928)* [*The Agricultural Economy and the Bank of Agriculture. Aspects of the Greek Economy in the Interwar period*]. Athens: Cultural Foundation /National Bank of Greece.

Kostis, C.P., 1990, *Αγροτική Οικονομία και Γεωργική Τράπεζα. Όψεις της Ελληνικής Οικονομίας στο Μεσοπόλεμο (1919–1928): Τα Τεκμήρια* [*The Agricultural Economy and the Bank of Agriculture. Aspects of the Greek Economy in the Interwar period: Documentation*], Athens: CF/NBG.

Lambros, G. and Tzanidis, M., 1939, *Τα Ανατολικά Καπνά. Συγκριτική μελέτη της οικονομικής θέσεως και κινήσεως των καπνών Ελλάδος, Τουρκίας και Βουλγαρίας* [*The Oriental Tobacco. Comparative Study of the economic position and movements of the tobacco output of Greece, Turkey and Bulgaria*], Athens.

Lazaretou, S., 2014, 'Greece: From 1833 to 1949.' in *South-Eastern European Monetary and Economic Statistics from the Nineteenth Century to World War II,* Athens, Sofia, Bucharest, Vienna: Bank of Greece, Bulgarian National Bank, National Bank of Romania, Oesterreichische Nationalbank, pp. 101–70. Available at: www.bankofgreece.gr/Pages/en/Publications/Studies/seemhn.aspx.

Mazower, M., 1991, *Greece and the Inter-War Economic Crisis,* Oxford, New York: Clarendon Press.

Neal, L., 1979, 'The Economics and Finance of Bilateral Clearing Agreements: Germany 1934–1938', *Economic History Review,* 32(3), pp. 391–404. doi: 10.2307/2595705.

Nenovsky, N., Pavanelly G., and Dimitrova, K., 2008, 'Exchange Rate Control in Italy and Bulgaria in the Interwar Period: History and Perspectives.' in *The Experience of Exchange Rate Regimes in Southeastern Europe in a Historical and Comparative Perspective,* Vienna: Citeseer (Proceedings of Oesterreichische Nationalbank Workshops 13), pp. 80–117. http://citeseerx.ist.psu.edu/viewdoc/download?doi=10.1.1.394.8847&rep=rep1&type=pdf.

Özel, I., 2000, 'An Evaluation of the Economic Performance of Turkey in the 1930s Based on Late-Ottoman Economy', *New Perspectives on Turkey,* 23, pp. 125–46. doi: 10.1017/S0896634600003411.

Pamuk, Ş., 2018, *Uneven Centuries: Economic Development of Turkey since 1820.* Princeton, NJ, Oxford: Princeton University Press.

Petmezas, S., 2012, *Προλεγόμενα Στην Ιστορία Της Ελληνικής Αγροτικής Οικονομίας Του Μεσοπολέμου* [*Prolegomena to the History of the Greek Agricultural Economy during the Interwar Period*], Athens: Alexandria Publ.

Petmezas, S., 2021, 'Οι επιπτώσεις της Κρίσης του 1929 στην Ελληνική αγροτική παραγωγή [The Impact of the 1929 Crisis upon the Greek Agricultural Production]', in A. Kakridis and S. Rizas (eds.) *Η κρίση του '29 και η Ελλάδα: οικονομικές, πολιτικές και θεσμικές όψεις* [*The 1929 Crisis and Greece: Economic, Political and Institutional Aspects*], Athens: KEINE/Academy of Athens and Bank of Greece, pp. 19–45.

Prontzas, E.D., 1996, *Οικονομικός Προστατευτισμός Και Βαλκανική Συνεργασία: Τα Ανατολικά Καπνά Στο Μεσοπόλεμο [Economic Protectionism and Balkan Cooperation: Oriental Tobacco during the Interwar Period*], Thessaloniki: University Studio Press.

Psalidopoulos, M., 2014, *Ιστορία της Τράπεζας της Ελλάδος 1928–2008: Από τράπεζα του κράτους εγγυήτρια της χρηματοπιστωτικής σταθερότητας* [History of the Bank of Greece 1928–2008: From Bank of the State to Guarantor of Financial Stability], Athens: Bank of Greece.

Raupach, H., 1969, 'The Impact of the Great Depression on Eastern Europe', *The Journal of Contemporary History,* 4(4), pp. 75–86. doi: www.jstor.org/stable/259837.

South-Eastern European Monetary and Economic Statistics from the Nineteenth Century to World War II, 2014). Athens, Sofia, Bucharest, Vienna: Bank of Greece, Bulgarian National Bank, National Bank of Romania, Oesterreichische Nationalbank. The online Database is available at https://www.bankofgreece.gr/en/publications-and-research/research/research-networks/seemhn/the-seemhn-data-volume, Accessed: 27 May 2017).

Statistical Abstract of the USA, 1940, Washington, DC. Available at https://www.census.gov/library/publications/1941/compendia/statab/62ed.html (Accessed: 27 November 2020).

Statistisches Jahrbuch für das Deutsche Reich. [1880–1941/42], Berlin: Statistisches Reichsamt. Available at http://www.digizeitschriften.de/dms/toc/?PID=PPN514401303, (Accessed: 20 May 2020).

Stefanoff, I., 1938, 'Foreign Trade of Bulgaria after the World War', in *Трудове На Стопанският Институте За Социални Поручвания При Софийския Дарявен Университет [Proceedings of the Economic Institute for Social Studies at the Sofia State University]*, (2–3), pp. 1–117.

Tantcheff, M., 1931, 'Bulgaria', in *The Agricultural Crisis*, 1, Geneva: League of Nations, Economic and Financial Section, pp. 117–33. Available at https://digital.nls.uk/league-of-nations/archive/191866195.

Tekeli, I. and Ilkin, S., 1988, 'Devletçilik Dönemi Tarim Politikalari (Modernleşme Çabalari) [Agricultural Policy in the era of Statism (Modernisation Efforts)]', in Ş. Pamuk and T. Zafer (eds.) *Türkiye'de Tarımsal Yapılar* [*Agrarian Structures of Turkey*], Ankara: Yurt Yayınevi, pp. 37–90.

Tezel, Y., 1982, *Cumhuriyet Döneminin İktisadi Tarihi 1923–1950* [*Economic History of the Republican Period, 1923–1950*], Istanbul: Yurt Yayınevi.

Tooze, A. and Ivanov, M., 2007, 'Convergence or Decline on Europe's Southeastern Periphery? Agriculture, Population, and GNP in Bulgaria 1892–1945', *Journal of Economic History,* 67(3), pp. 673–703. doi: 10.1017/S0022050707000277.

Tooze, A. and Ivanov, M., 2011, 'Disciplining the 'Black Sheep of the Balkans': Financial Supervision and Sovereignty in Bulgaria, 1902–38', *The Economic History Review,* 64(1), pp. 30–51. doi: 10.1111/j.1468-0289.2010.00544.x.

8 The 1929 crisis in Hungary's dual agriculture

Zsuzsanna Varga

1. Introduction

Between the two world wars agriculture constituted Hungary's largest economic sector. The agricultural export was of high importance in terms of the import-export balance and, therefore, the balance of state budget. In 1920 agricultural commodities made up 80% of total exports and 20 years later still 65%[1]. Moreover, approximately half of the population of the country still lived on agriculture (Figures 8.1a–8.1c).

Another characteristic feature was the duality of farm structure as a consequence of the extremely unequal land distribution inherited from the nineteenth century. In the interwar period still nearly half of the country's total land was owned by a few dozen of aristocratic families, yet the proportion of non-aristocratic large estates was high. As a contrast, only about 20% of the total land belonged to the peasant holdings, smaller than 5.7 ha (10 kh), that made up some four-fifths of all agricultural holdings[2] (Figure 8.2).

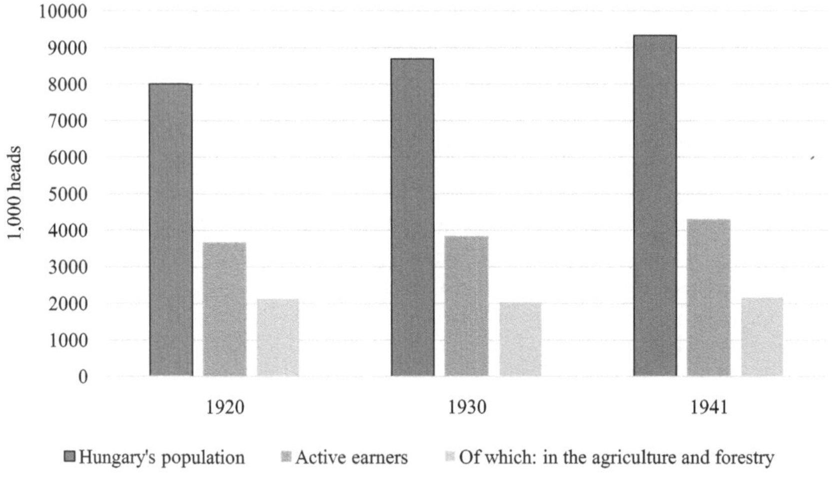

Figure 8.1a Population and the number of employees in agriculture.
Source: Hungarian Agriculture 1851–2000. (CD–ROM) Hungarian Central Statistical Office, Budapest, 2000. Statistics at the beginning of the year.

DOI: 10.4324/9781003105466-10

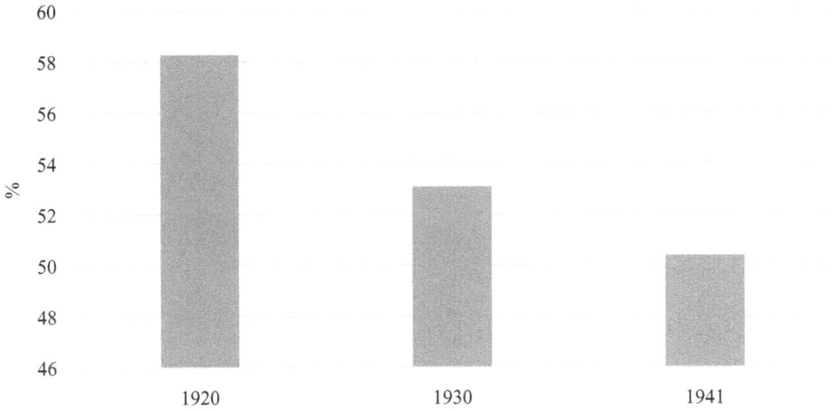

Figure 8.1b Share of agricultural employees.
Source: Hungarian Agriculture 1851–2000. (CD–ROM) Hungarian Central Statistical Office, Budapest, 2000. Statistics at the beginning of the year.

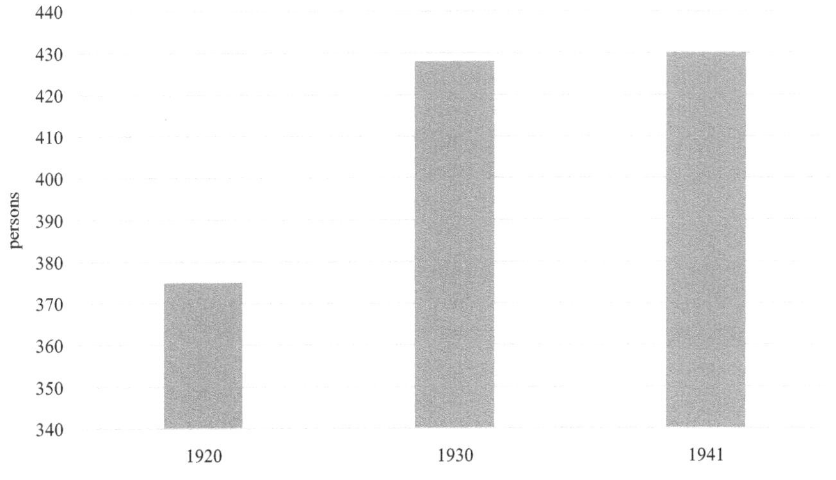

Figure 8.1c Population per 100 active agricultural employees.
Source: Hungarian Agriculture 1851–2000. (CD–ROM) Hungarian Central Statistical Office, Budapest, 2000. Statistics at the beginning of the year.

This chapter is aiming to analyse how the growing state intervention after 1929 affected different actors of the dual Hungarian agriculture. To understand the political, social and economic context of the crisis years a short historical introduction is necessary. It covers the nineteenth-century socio-economic heritage of the sector and the consequences of the First World War (WWI). In the second part, the effects the crisis had on the various actors in the dual Hungarian agriculture will be analysed. Special attention will be paid to the heterogeneity of the agrarian society in Hungary (as only a minority of the peasant

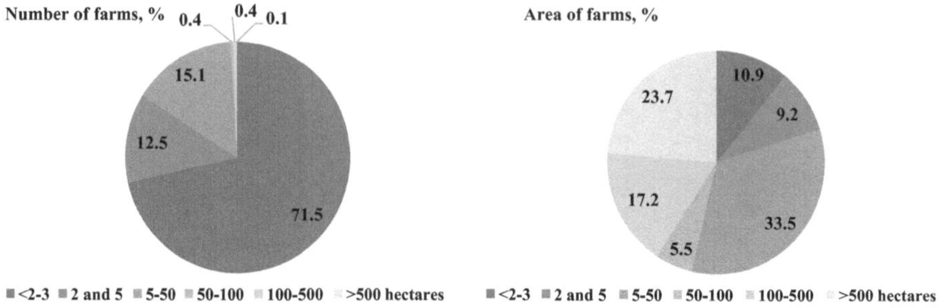

Figure 8.2 Land distribution in Hungary in 1935.
Source: Hungarian Agriculture 1851–2000. (CD–ROM) Hungarian Central Statistical Office, Budapest, 2000.

farms were family-run farms in the Western-European sense of the word.) In the third section a review will be given on the different crisis-management taken by the Hungarian governments in the period between 1929 and 1936.

2. The origin of the dual structure

To give a historical background, one has to go back as far as the abolition of serfdom. As a consequence of this approximately half of the land remained in the property of landowners' (Eddie, 1967: 293–310; Orosz, 1998: 59–75). By this way the system of latifundia was preserved. It was also helped by the survival and extension of entailed estates too. Between 1870 and 1900, 64 new entailed estates were created; their area increased five-fold (Püski, 2020: 295–308). Some large estates started modernization, it was indicated by their specialization and the appearance of processing industry connected to agriculture (alcohol distilleries, sugar factories, mills, lumberyards). A special type of agricultural modernization was the land lease system based upon large estates. However, in the majority of large estates the methods of land farming changed only little in the last third of the nineteenth century concerning their work organization and production structure (Kaposi, 2001: 239–45).

Those peasant farms that received enough land when serfdom was abolished, started on the way of capitalist development. Those with good market opportunities specialized, especially around the capital and other major cities. The biggest problem peasant estates had to cope with was the so-called real inheritance system, due to which the size of inherited plots decreased at each change of generations (Vári, 2010: 179–93). The small plot was not enough to sustain a family, therefore those peasants with small holdings were forced to work for wages. Many of them emigrated overseas at the turn of the century. Between 1899 and 1914 half of all emigrants came from the ranks of agricultural day-labourers and servants (Kövér, 2004: 80–3).

The Austro-Hungarian Customs Union and its rising agricultural tariffs became beneficial for Hungarian agriculture (Schulze, 2000: 311–40). The food industry (especially the milling industry) stood at the head of industrial development, providing extremely favourable conditions for agricultural development. The following data show clearly the importance of agriculture in generating and contributing to national income. Before the WWI agriculture provided more than half (54–60%) of the national income (Szuhay, 1998a: 99–101). During the entire period of the Austro-Hungarian Monarchy (1867–1918), agriculture played an important role in the country's exports, considering especially the export of agricultural-based industrial products. Between 1909 and 1913, 50% of the total export value was comprised of agricultural products while within the common customs area this figure was 55%. Among agriculture-based goods, grain and flour, as well as slaughter and draft animal products, played the largest role in export (Eddie, 1977: 329–58). It is important to emphasize that the exceptional growth of the Hungarian agriculture during the 1870s and 1880s was accomplished without purchased industrial inputs. As a result of river regulations, huge tracts of lands were gained for cultivation. Most mechanical and technical changes concentrated on the improvement of traditional hand tools or better draft animals. Only threshing was mechanized significantly (Szuhay, 1998a: 104–6).

Relying on new development economics, Michael Kopsidis summarized the structural weakness of Hungarian agriculture at the end of the dualist period in the following:

> ...agricultural growth and its capability to absorb labour was very likely hampered in the long run by the fact that serf emancipation transformed serf labour mainly into inefficient wage labour, and that heavily distorted land markets prevented the transfer of land to the more efficient peasant producers.
>
> (Kopsidis, 2009: 293–4)

As a consequence of WWI, the Austro-Hungarian Empire was defeated and it disintegrated. Hungary remained kingdom, run by a Regent, Admiral Miklós Horthy. The nature of the interwar political regime can be characterized as a limited parliamentary state with strong elements of authoritarianism and a hegemonistic party structure (Romsics, 1999: 130–4; Kontler, 2002: 345–51). The economic unity of the Monarchy and the work distribution between Austria and Hungary was finished. It posed a great challenge to the industrial and financial sectors. Some missing industries (like textile) had to be replaced, in other cases – for example, in milling industry – the remaining production capacity was disproportionately huge, which caused difficulties. A national bank was to be established in Hungary together with a national currency. The development of agriculture after Trianon was affected by the fact that the traditional trade connections were cut off and the favourable prices provided by the protected market also disappeared (Berend and Ránki, 1995: 149–63; Tomka, 2018: 47–79).

Moreover, out of the problems of agrarian society heaped up in the nineteenth century, the issue of land became an acute problem. With WWI lingering on, more and more promises were made to introduce land reforms. The wartime governments were well aware that this is the buzzword that could motivate the army whose majority was made up of peasants. Therefore at the end of WWI, one of the most urgent problems was the distribution of land in Hungary. The social pressure was so strong that already at the time of the disintegration of the Monarchy, some measures were taken to solve this problem. The bourgeois revolution of 1918 incorporated land reform in its programme, but the law – declaring expropriation of estates over 500 kh (285 ha) – was never enacted. Instead of land reform, the Hungarian Bolshevik Government saw the road to agricultural development in the socialization of some large and medium-sized estates (over 75 kh/42.7 ha), creating Soviet-style cooperatives on these estates (Gunst, 1998: 200–3; Kontler, 2002: 328–38).

The so-called counter-revolutionary governments, which took over after the revolutions were crushed, had to face the land reform issue. Although at the 1920 elections the United Agrarian Labourers' and Smallholders' Party received the most mandates, they could not realize their concept concerning land reforms. The landed aristocracy was more successful in enforcing its interests. The land reform of 1920 concerned a mere 8.5% of the agricultural land of the country. The 412 000 applicants received 699,000 kh (398,430 ha), in other words, an average 1.7 kh (0.96 ha) per applicant (Szuhay, 1998b: 178–9). If we compare the Hungarian land reform of 1920 to the land reforms in Central- and East European countries, it could be stated that it was the most modest one, and it barely changed the unhealthy estate structure (Brassley, 2010: 151).

Parallel to the 1920 land reform (Law XXXVI: 1920) the system of the representatives of agrarian interests (Law XVIII: 1920) was also established. In the literature important connections between the two laws have been pointed out. During the connected preparations of the act on land reform and the act on the establishment of the chamber, the political activities of the participating political agents was aimed to prevent any possible independent initiatives started by peasantry and to ensure that only non-peasant land owners and the authorities might start initiatives (Bódy, 2010: 105–19). All this goes to show that in Hungary the different groups of agrarian society had quite different abilities to enforce their interests. It must be noted that after 1922, the United Agrarian Labourers' and Smallholders' Party ceased to exist, in consequence of their government in coalition with the Christian National Unity Party, they merged into a new government party which, up until 1932, was universally referred to as the *Egységes Párt* (Unity Party) (Romsics, 1999: 112–13).

3. Survival and adaptation strategies during the crisis years

Following the chaos of the disintegration of the Monarchy, Hungarian agriculture started to recover from the mid-1920s. The second half of that decade saw a slow and moderate upturn. Sales and the availability of loans improved following the 1924 currency stabilization. The increase in mortgage loans also made technical development possible to a certain extent. Accordingly, the mechanization and use of fertilizers also increased. Compared to the 1,183 tractors in 1925, by 1929 there were 6,800. The number of steam threshing machines increased by 66% between 1925 and 1929. Fertilizer consumption per land unit increased by 60% in the same period -14.65 kilograms per 1 kh (0.57 ha) – but this only surpassed the pre-war level by 22% (Szuhay, 1998b: 180).

The effects of technical development are also reflected in the transformation of production: results and averages increasing slightly (Figures 8.3 and 8.4). However, the rise in production results meant that only wheat and corn exceeded the pre-war level somewhat, while the other products did not reach this level. The situation was similar in the development of production averages.

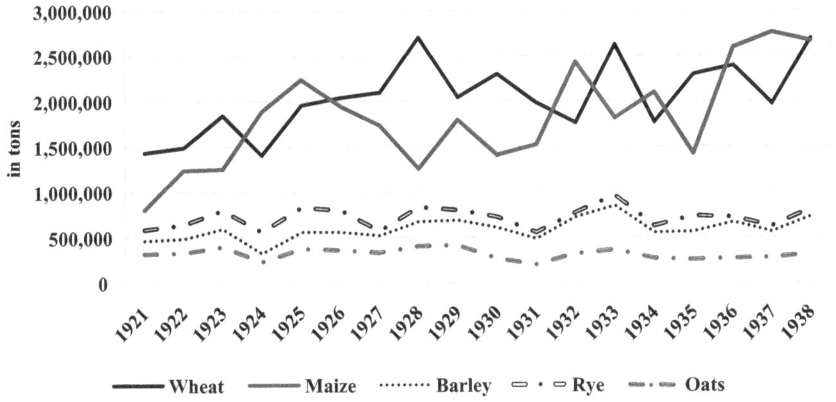

Figure 8.3 Production of main cereals.
Source: Hungarian Agriculture 1851–2000. (CD–ROM) Hungarian Central Statistical Office, Budapest, 2000.

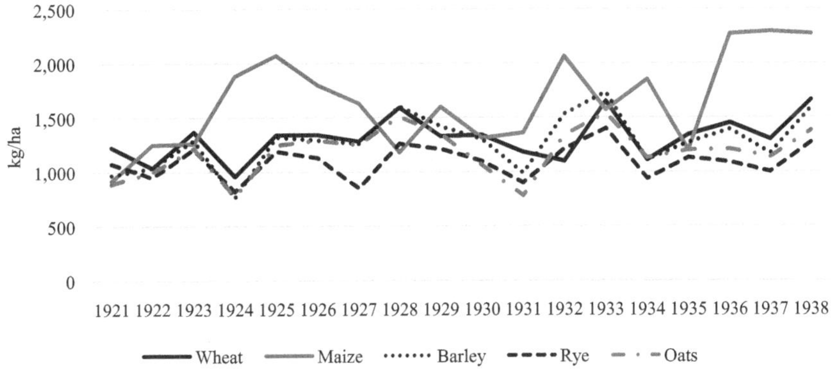

Figure 8.4 Average yield of main cereals.
Source: Hungarian Agriculture 1851–2000. (CD–ROM) Hungarian Central Statistical Office, Budapest, 2000.

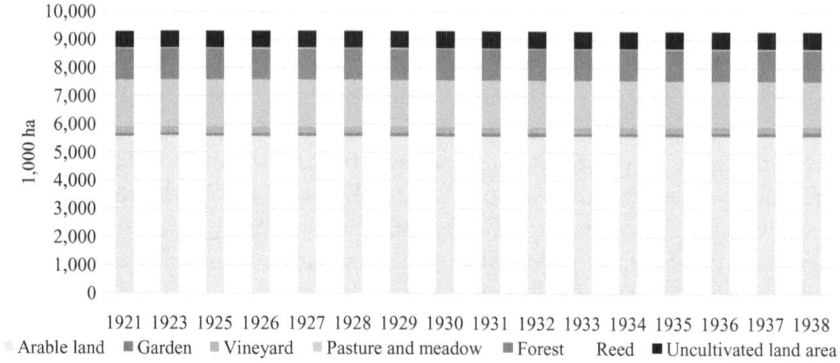

Figure 8.5 The agricultural land area of Hungary by land use categories.
Source: Hungarian Agriculture 1851–2000. (CD–ROM) Hungarian Central Statistical Office, Budapest, 2000.

There were also no significant changes in the structure of sowing territory (Figure 8.5). Keeping the structure unchanged and the slow technical development was related to the abundant cheap labour force in the countryside.

During the 1920s with regard to sales – with the exception of 1926 – there weren't any major difficulties until the second half of 1928. The Hungarian agricultural products were purchased on the former export markets despite these countries' efforts towards self-sufficiency. The majority of Hungarian exports were directed at Austria and Czechoslovakia. Between 1925 and 1928 close to 80% of corn crops, 78% of wheat comprising close to half of the grain exports, 85% of flour, 77% of homed cattle and 99% of hog exports were directed to these countries (Horváth, 1940: 525–6).

In the meantime, signs of overproduction were to be seen in Europe (Berend, 1998: 255–9). As a result of this, Hungary's balance of trade went into deficit in 1928. With an increase in imported goods, the export levelled (or according to other data, it decreased). The reason for this was the fact that Europe was full of the cheap overseas agricultural products and the market for the Hungarian agricultural products shrank. Even if they could be sold, they were sold at a much lower price. It must be emphasized that in Hungary the issue of agriculture was a problem of external trade and therefore it affected the state budget and consequently the whole economy. So, the agricultural backwardness of Hungary was made very obvious by the Great Depression. Hungary's excessive grain production only made matters worse. Compared to other exporting countries, Hungary was in a much more disadvantageous situation because production costs were higher.

The crisis caused massive price drops, thus, for example, wheat's average wholesale price taking the wholesale price of 1924–8 as 100%, dropped to 36.6%. The price of plant-based products dropped by 54% between 1929 and 1933, while the price drop in livestock and animal-based products was 48%. It is essential to emphasize that this crisis affected all agricultural products. Another aggravating factor was the large scale widening of the 'agricultural scissor' ('agricultural scissor' refers to the relative high price of industrial products vis-a-vis the low price of agrarian products), but this was not only characteristic in Hungary.

Contrary to the large scale drop in income, debt burdens increased. The proportion between agriculture's debts and income caused difficulties already in the 1920s, but the price crashes following 1928 created a catastrophic situation. The annual 1.17 billion Pengő debt burden in 1928/29 increased to 2.18 billion by 1932/33. In 1932/33 only the interest- and repayment burden – despite the various debtor protection measures – amounted to 25% of income compared to 9% in 1929. Due to debt accumulation, non-payment and the collapse in prices, agricultural debt in 1932/33 loan repayment liabilities increased almost three-fold.

Having observed the general phenomena of the crisis, it must be analysed how it influenced certain groups of agrarian society. In 1935, 29% of the total land consisted of large estates with more than 1,000 kh (570 ha) and landowners with estates larger than 100 kh (57 ha) owned 48% of the land. On the other hand, landowners with farms smaller than 5 kh (2.8 ha) only held 10% of the land and those with less than 20 kh (11.4 ha), 32% (Figure 8.2). The flagrant disproportion of land distribution is also indicated by the fact that 42% of the agrarian population did not have land or held less than a hectare in territory.

The latifundia owning half of the land did not carry out any considerable modifications on their production structure after 1918, they went on growing mainly crops (mostly wheat), which was sold abroad. They were affected by the price fall and the sales crisis at the same time, therefore when considerable foreign market share was lost, the aristocracy was the first to demand state support. Their other response to the crisis was to reduce the production cost on their own latifundia, mainly labourers' wages (Figure 8.6). Moreover,

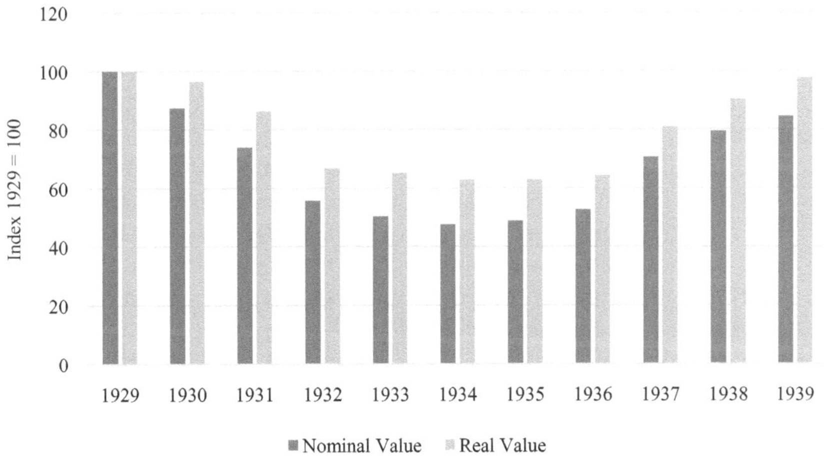

Figure 8.6 The evolution of day labour wages in agriculture in Pengős
Source: Matolcsy, 1944: 35.

even wages could be cut, due to the huge abundance of workforce in this sector. Those latifundia had a greater chance to survive the depression which had also built the system of processing industry earlier, that is, they had mills, distilleries, sugar factories, etc. However, only some of them had such a modern structure.

Concerning the other elements of dual agricultural structure, we must draw attention to an important difference in terminology. In Hungary, but also in the rest of Eastern Europe, in addition to certain strata of landowning peasants, the dwarfholders and the landless agricultural workers also had to be considered part of the peasant society. It is quite different from most of the Western agricultural development where only those people were considered peasants who had enough land to support themselves. The main reason lying behind these phenomena is the above-mentioned difference in the inheritance system. The traditional Germanic stock inheritance system created the clear separation between the peasant (the first born or the youngest son) inheriting the plot from the parents and the rest of the siblings, who either stayed on the farm as farm hands (or served elsewhere in the near vicinity) or moved to other regions where they found land for themselves. This system ensured that family farms would not be divided up into small pieces but would continuously remain sufficiently large, and at the same time it directed the majority of the peasant population to new, uncultivated land.

As a result, the majority of peasant society was made up of semi-peasant strata who had no option but to remain peasants. They were difficult to distinguish from the relatively small number of land-owning peasants and those cultivating their own family farms. Eastern European development also differed from Western Europe in that there was not such a substantial difference between the way of life of self-supporting peasants and that of agricultural workers. There, the lifestyles of land-owning peasants and agricultural workers were already very different by the sixteenth and seventeenth centuries. In Eastern Europe, as a consequence of inheritance and land division, a deterioration in their financial situation quickly ensued and the section of the peasantry owning partial plots lived lives similar to those of ex-smallholder peasants, that is, the wage labourer stratum. This explains the magnetic attraction for them of even the smallest amount of land. They aspired to create their own small peasant farm, and a plot with a vegetable garden represented the illusion of an independent family farm (Gyáni, 2004: 399–403).

Among the peasant farms it is important to make a distinction between those that specialized and produced for market sale regularly and those that were self-sufficient and took only the superfluous part of the annual produce to the market. In the beginning, the price fall had little effect on the peasant farms that produced for the internal market as they were not selling wheat but animal products, vegetables or fruit. Their time came when the depression affected the industrial sector and the consumption in the cities decreased due to the spreading unemployment. Those peasant farms were in a really difficult situation whose owners took loans in the second half of the

1920s to develop the farms by purchasing threshing machines or modernizing the farms in other ways (Held, 1980: 216–23). Those that specialized in one kind of produce were more likely to be affected. In the case of products of such special quality, export could have made up for the reduced internal market, but the network of sales cooperatives was by far not so developed as in Netherlands or Denmark for example. There they helped farmers appear in foreign markets.

Peasant farmers were brought into a difficult situation by the decrease in their cash income. It did not only affect those who had to serve their loans but a much wider group as fewer and fewer of them could pay the ever increasing taxes. At first it was the rising taxes that burdened the dwarfholders and the landless contracted workers who constituted two thirds of the peasants, too. Those who were the beneficiaries of the 1920 land reform constituted a separate group. For them, it was a huge problem to pay the redemption fee in cash as they did not have any extra produce that could have been taken to the market. If they sold any part of their produce, it could have had a detrimental effect on their families' standard of consumption (Gyáni, 2004: 399–416).

The aforementioned facts may explain why tens of thousands of peasant farms were sold in the first half of the 1930s (Központi Statisztikai Hivatal, 1941: 63–4). As the annual reports of the Országos Mezőgazdasági Kamara [National Agricultural Chamber] prove that even in 1935 more than 10,000 peasant farms were sold[3].

Concerning that in the agricultural sector of the time, payment was characterized by some feudal features, it seemed that it would be easier for seasonal agricultural workers to survive the depression owing to their wages paid in kind. Those who had a one-year-long contract to work on the latifundium, the farmhands were better protected as their wages meant that they were provided with accommodation, fuel, grain to make bread and the right to use a small vegetable patch (Gunst, 1998: 205–6). By this way their wages kept their value, but in return they were completely dependent.

Most seasonal workers were also bound to the latifundia as they were employed there from spring until autumn. As has already been mentioned, big and middle-sized land owners employed them for fewer working days, trying to cut their expenses by this way (Heller, 1941; Schrikker, 1943). However, there were plenty of workers to choose among. The huge oversupply of labour resulted in the reduction of wages, especially in the overpopulated towns and villages in the Great Plain (Perneczky, 1941).

4. Changing governments – Changing crisis management

Analysing the governmental measures taken to handle the crisis, it is conspicuous that so many approaches could be observed in the disputes often with references to various foreign examples (Ormos, 2004: 289–332). However, real governmental decisions were much more restricted.

In the beginning, they tried to counteract the losses resulting from the price fall. The so-called Boletta System was introduced in 1930. According to this system, wheat and rye could only be sold with crops tickets (bolettas). It was worth 3 Pengő (Hungarian currency at that time) per 100 kg, and the sum had to be paid for the producer. A separate fund was created to carry out the payments which were financed by the state. It was only valid for consumption grain and as the government provided an extra price after the sold wheat and rye, it was clear that mainly the great grain growers, the owners of the great estates benefitted from it. It is not surprising since this group of agricultural producers was the strongest to make their influence felt in politics. It is symbolic that the Ministry of Agriculture was led by aristocrats in that period (Estók, 2004: 285–9). Another measure was the 'bonus' system, which played an extremely important role in agricultural product sales. It was closely related to the foreign currency control system. Payments in Pengő of foreign currency received from export sales were always made at a rate higher than the official exchange rate; that is, a mark-up or bonus price was applied. In other words, the system was actually a disguised form of devaluing the Pengő in foreign trade. Considerable sums from the fund created from mark-up surplus were used to subsidize the sale of agricultural products.

These measures triggered a deep political crisis in the governing party (Romsics, 1999: 181–4). Those groups who felt that the government preferred the interests of the large estates to those of the smallholders broke away. This led to the formation of the Independent Smallholders' Party, which became the strongest opposition party in the 1931 elections. However, the opposition had little influence on taking measures for the benefit of peasants. In 1931, István Bethlen, the head of the party that had been governing for ten years, resigned due to the crisis. In the literature it is stated that Bethlen intended to leave the government only temporarily until an interim government had taken the most serious constringency measures and then he wanted to regain the power. An interim government led by Gyula Károlyi was really formed but afterwards it was not the conservative political elite, which was represented by Bethlen that formed a government. In connection with the right shift in international politics and the Hungarian attempts at the revision of the Trianon peace treaty, the Governor, Miklós Horthy appointed Gyula Gömbös, paramilitary-turned-politician, admirer of Mussolini, and the most prominent advocate of radical right policies (Kontler, 2002: 364–71; Vonyó, 2001: 9–29).

This turn of the events brought several new elements not just into the discourse on the depression but also into the actual policy measures. By that time, there was so much social tension in agriculture that it begged for immediate intervention. The 'policy of the strong hand' represented by Gömbös and his group became more appreciated by the governing conservatives after the usual 'techniques' in handling the world economic crisis had failed. It was not only because of the crisis that agriculture became an essential area for the new government. Gömbös and the groups of gentry, military officers and civil servants had proclaimed from the 1920s on that the borders laid down in the Trianon Treaty could only be modified by force of arms (Zeidler, 2007: 325–68). What was required was an army and this army could only have been based on a peasantry reinforced morally and financially to make them independent and thus, fit for the great task. It is therefore not surprising that an essential element of the governmental programme entitled National Workplan issued in October 1932 was the preference of agricultural interests (Gergely-Glatz-Pölöskei, 2003: 288–302). Not only did the programme discuss agricultural matters first but boosting other sectors of economy would be subordinated to agricultural development.

Putting agriculture first was more than a mere slogan and the measures taken in the first year clearly proved this. The 'Christian idea of agriculture' had been an integral part of Gömbös' political views ever since the 1920s. His plan was first to protect smallholders, and then to establish new and viable small and medium-sized farms within the framework of a 'healthy settlement policy'.

The laws regulating the debts of farmers in 1933 and 1935 had been an important tool in the crisis-management policy of the state (Szuhay, 1998b: 183). Estates with a debt above a critical level were, at the request of the debtor declared protected by the government which was later designated in the real estate register. Such landed property was – in case the proprietor had been paying the interests of the credit – protected from being sold by auction. The state spent a significant amount of money on settling the so-called 'smallholders debts'. In the budgetary years 1933–4 and 1934–5, a total amount 32.5 million, whereas in 1935–6 and 1936–7 some 75.6 million Pengő were allotted for this purpose. According to the reports of the Ministry of Agriculture the majority of the subsidies connected to the protection had been given to large landowners, since some 61% of all 1,100,000 hectares declared protected fell into the category larger than 60 hectares[4].

The second step would have been a large-scale reform of landed property. The Gömbös government came up with the idea that some parts of the large estates should be divided among the part-time smallholders and agrarian workers who lived in abject poverty. In the 1920s, Gömbös urged a radical land reform under any circumstances, even if it had proven economically disadvantageous in the short run. When he rose to power, however, this was exactly where he was bound to make a serious compromise. Due to the serious counter-interests and immense political power of the class of large landowners, he had only been able to put across a law on modest settlement policy shortly prior to his death in 1936. The act on settlements estimated some 240,000 hectares of land for subdivision within a period of 25 years[5].

These experiences along with the persisting resistance from the large landowners made the government look for other ways out. In order to modernize the farming of small-owners, they intended to accelerate the process of the consolidation of holdings. This means a redistribution of landed property where the different parts of land of one certain owner (his parcels) being in different parts of the village are united in one piece of land with the consensus of all owners under the guidance of a legal authority. The decree 34.700/1935 issued by the Ministry of Justice regulated consolidations and other forms of redistribution of landed property. The primary aim of the new order was to make consolidations easier, quicker while at the same time professional and most of all, cheaper. On the one hand, consolidation processes started in earlier years has become easier to complete, on the other hand, the increased role of the state enabled new further villages to start the consolidation process. 1936 saw 24, 1937 18, 1938 15 and 1939 some 20 villages – altogether in 77 villages – start consolidation. According to data from the Consolidation Department of the Ministry of Agriculture, the period between 1935 and 1941 saw completed consolidations in some 98 villages on a total of nearly 180,000 hectares[6].

Even though the pace was far from what had been needed, it is vital to underline that in the villages concerned, the positive effects showed quite quickly. The consolidated estates were suitable for sowing and threshing with machines. There was an increased readiness to build farmsteads, too. The majority of the consolidated villages saw an average increase of 20% in their total produce, the purchase price of landed property increased and the quality of farming improved also[7].

The other part of state intervention in agriculture had been the subsidization of product marketing. This was largely due to Hungary being a major exporter of agrarian products. Beside the necessary immediate measures Gömbös had the intention to base long-term development on the involvement of new foreign markets. His first official visit abroad was to Mussolini in Rome. Six months later he was the first prime minister in Europe to visit recently inaugurated chancellor Hitler. One month later representatives of Hungary and Germany signed a trade agreement supplementing the one in 1931 that opened the German market to the Hungarian export of wheat, rye, barley and corn (Gerhard, 2014: 139–58; Vonyó, 2001: 28–30).

Via supplementary treaties to a 1931 German-Hungarian trade agreement, Germany opened its markets to Hungarian produce. In addition to the high exports to Germany – which in late 1930s made up 50–60% and in 1944 close to 74% of exports – Italy's buyer's market was also significant (12–20%). In view of the general squeeze on currency liquidity, the bulk of these transactions were organized within bilateral settlement mechanisms in which deliveries of goods in each direction were mutually balanced (Szuhay, 1998b:186–90).

In the crisis management policy of Gömbös' government, a new period started in 1934. The tripartite agreement concluded in Rome in 1934 between Italy, Austria and Hungary was an important landmark in the advancement of monopolization. Introduced was the minimal wheat price system based on the high wheat purchase price ensured in the agreement (Berend-Ránki, 1974: 319–41). The Futura Corporation (a Hungarian firm engaged in agrarian product commerce) was commissioned to purchase the wheat and export it to the Italian and Austrian markets.

The effectuation of the German economic policies was an important factor in the rise of monopoly organizations. The German government preferred having Hungarian monopoly organizations deal with similar German organizations in foreign trade sales. In 1934, Hungary signed an agreement with Germany to increase agricultural exports. The monopolization of sales also coincided with the large estate owners' interests (Berend, 1998: 273–8). It led to the purchase price increase of certain crops and products, and since the large estate owners were granted the majority of export quotas, they received most of the high export prices. The large estate owners' organizations processed the increasingly larger part of foreign trade sales.

5. Closing remarks

In the second half of the nineteenth century the appearance of market economy in Hungary involved a considerable state contribution. State intervention, which increased in the years of the WWI, did not fall after 1918 either, when it could have been explained by the building of the new national economy after the disintegration of the Austro-Hungarian Monarchy. When the Great Depression reached Hungary, the necessity of state intervention was not a question. It had had a long tradition and acceptance. However, it was subject to debates which branch should be helped by state intervention and the amount allocated to this purpose from the state budget was also disputed.

This chapter has observed the various stages of state intervention in agriculture between 1929 and 1936. It was also distinguished whether a measure was to remedy a problem that arose from a concrete situation or whether it offered a solution to a structural problem of the sector that had not been solved for a long time. Paying attention to the power relations, the chapter has also revealed how the different ability of the participants of dual agriculture to enforce their interests influenced the measures taken by the three governments studied here.

The case studies in this volume are intended to analyse the experiences of various European countries in crisis treatment, so they can enrich the theses defining of the role of the State (for instance Stiglitz, 1989) with interesting historical lessons. The case of Hungary highlights the following: when the success of state intervention is assessed, it is important to take into account the 'path-dependency content' of the targeted problem. It has been demonstrated in this study that in Hungary only the symptoms of the crisis were treated by a wide range set of governmental measures (public procurement, price interventions, export promotion, etc.) which caused a considerable delay in the treatment of the long lasting structural deficiencies of dual agriculture. The price of delay could hardly be measured by economic terms due to the discontinuity after 1945, but the social price became obvious in the process of the radical land reform in the spring of 1945 (Swain-Varga, 2013).

Notes

1 In most cases the source of the statistical data of this chapter: Hungarian Agriculture 1851–2000. (CD–ROM) Hungarian Central Statistical Office, Budapest, 2000. The exceptions are indicated.
2 In Hungary before 1972 the official unit of land measurement was *kataszträlis hold* (abbreviated: kh). 1 katasztrális hold (kh) = 0.57 hectare (ha). In this chapter, I calculate land measurement in hectares, to facilitate comparison with other countries.
3 Magyar Nemzeti Levéltár Országos Levéltár (National Archives of Hungary, hereafter cited as MNL OL) P-1064 Országos Mezőgazdasági Kamara éves jelentései [The annual reports of the National Agricultural Chamber] 1929–1935.
4 MNL OL FM K–184–a 1938. 4532.
5 Law XI:1936. In: Corpus Iuris, 1936. 125–56.
6 MNL OL FM K–184. 1941. 5699.
7 MNL OL FM K–184. 1941. 7823.

Bibliography

Berend, I. T., 1998, *Decades of Crisis: Central and Eastern Europe before World War II*, Berkeley: University of California Press.

Berend, I. T. and Ránki, G., 1974, *Economic Development in East-Central Europe in the 19th and 20th Centuries*, New York and London: Columbia University Press.

Berend, I. T. and Ránki, G., 1995, 'The Economic Problems of the Danube Region after the Breakup of the Austro-Hungarian Monarchy', in B. K., Király and L. Veszprémy (eds), *Trianon and East Central Europe: Antecedents and Repercussions*, New York: Columbia University Press, pp. 149–63.

Bódy, Z., 2010, 'Ungarn als Sonderfall des mitteleuropaeischen Agrarismus in der Zwischenkriegszeit', in H. Schultz and A. Harre (eds), *Bauerngesellschaften auf dem Weg in die Moderne Bauerngesellschaften au dem Weg in die Moderne. Agrarismus in Ostmitteleuropa 1880 bis 1960,* Wiesbaden: Harrassowitz, pp. 105–19.

Brassley, P., 2010, 'Land Reform and Reallocation in Interwar Europe', in R. Congost and R. Santos (eds), *Contexts of Property in Europe. The Social Embeddedness of Property Rights in Land in Historical Perspective,* Brepols: Turnhout, Rural History in Europe, 4, pp. 145–64.

Eddie, S. M., 1967, 'The Changing Pattern of Landownership in Hungary 1867–1914', *Economic History Review*, 20(2), pp. 293–310.

Eddie, S. M., 1977, 'The Terms and Patterns of Hungarian Foreign Trade, 1882–1913', *Journal of Economic History*, 37(2), pp. 329–58.

Estók, J., 2004, *History of Hungarian Agriculture and Rural Life, 1848–2004*, Budapest: Magyar Mezőgazdasági Múzeum.

Gergely, J., Glatz, F. and Pölöskei, F., 2003, *Magyarországi pártprogramok, 1919–1944*, [The Programmes of the Political Parties in Hungary, 1919–1944], Budapest: Eötvös Kiadó.

Gerhard, G., 2014, 'The Modernization Dilemma: Agrarian Policies in Nazi Germany', in F. Prieto, J. Pan-Montojo and M. Cabo (eds), *Agriculture in the Age of Fascis: Authoritarian Technocracy and Rural Modernization, 1922–1945,* Turnhout: Brepols Rural History in Europe, 13, pp. 139–58.

Gunst, P., 1998, 'Hungarian Agrarian Society during the Inter-war Period (1919–1945)', in P. Gunst (ed.), *Hungarian Agrarian Society from the Emancipation of Serfs*

(1848) to the Re-privatization of Land (1998), New York: Columbia University Press, pp. 199–253.

Gyáni, G., 2004, 'Social History of Hungary in the Horthy Era', in G. Gábor, G. Kövér, and G. T. Valuch (eds), *Social History of Hungary from the Reform Era to the End of the Twentieth Century*, New York: Columbia University Press, pp. 271–507.

Held, J., 1980, 'The Interwar Years and Agrarian Change', in J. Held (ed.), *The Modernization of Agriculture: Rural Transformation in Hungary, 1848–1975*, New York: Columbia University Press, pp. 197–317.

Heller, A., 1941, 'Munkáscsoportok és vándormozgalom a mezőgazdasági munkásszerződések alapján', [Work Teams and the Migration Movement on the Basis of Agricultural Work Contracts], *Magyar Statisztikai Szemle*, [Hungarian Statistical Review], 19(8), pp. 572–85.

Horváth, J., (ed.), 1940, *Trianoni Magyarország mezőgazdasága I–II*, Budapest: Uj barázda.

Hungarian Agriculture 1851–2000. (CD–ROM) Hungarian Central Statistical Office, Budapest, 2000.

Kaposi, Z., 2001, 'A magyarországi uradalmi rendszer változásai a XVIII–XX. Században', [Changes in the Large Sacale Farming in Hungary between the XVIII–XX Centuries], *Agrártörténelmi Szemle* [Agrarian History Review], 43(1–2), pp. 239–60.

Kontler, L., 2002, *A History of Hungary*, New York: Palgrave Macmillan.

Kopsidis, M., 2009, 'Hungary', in P. Lains and V. Pinilla (eds), *Agriculture and Economic Development in Europe since 1870,* London and New York: Routledge, pp. 286–310.

Kövér, G., 2004, 'Inactive Transformation: Social History of Hungary from the Refom Era to World War I', in G. Gábor, G. Kövér and G. T. Valuch (eds), *Social History of Hungary from the Reform Era to the End of the Twentieth Century*, New York: Columbia University Press, pp. 3–267.

Központi Statisztikai Hivatal, 1941, *Magyarország mezőgazdaságának főbb üzemi adatai az 1935. évben a gazdaságok (üzemek) nagysága szerint.* [Major Farm Data of Hungarian Agriculture in 1935] Budapest: Központi Statisztikai Hivatal.

Matolcsy, M, 1944, *Az életszínvonal alakulása Magyarországon 1924–1944.* [The Development of the Standard of Living in Hungary 1924–1944]. Budapest: Magyar Ipari Munkatudományi Intézet

Ormos, M., 2004, *A gazdasági világválság magyar visszhangja*, [The Hungarian Reception of the Great Depression], Budapest: PolgArt.

Orosz, I., 1998, 'Peasant Emancipation and After-effects', in P. Gunst (ed.), *Hungarian Agrarian Society from the Emancipation of Serfs (1848) to the Re-privatization of Land (1998)*, New York: Columbia University Press, pp. 53–97.

Perneczky, B., 1941, 'A mezőgazdasági munkanélküliség', [Agricultural Unemployment], *Magyar Gazdák Szemléje*, [Hungarian Farmers Review], 46(7), pp. 164–75.

Püski, L., 2020, 'Vélemények és adatok: hitbizományok a két világháború közti Magyarországon', [Opinions and Data: Entailed Estate in the Interwar Hungary], in K. Papp, A. Bárány, R. Kerepeszki and L. Pallai (eds), *Kultúra, művelődés, agrárium. Tanulmányok ifj. Barta János 80. Születésnapjára,* [Culture and Agriculture. Papers Dedicated to the 80th Birthday of Professor János Barta], Debrecen: Debreceni Egyetem Történelmi Intézete, pp. 295–308.

Romsics, I., 1999, *Hungary in the Twentieth Century*, Budapest: Corvina-Osiris.

Schrikker, S., 1943, 'A sommások alkalmazásának és kereseti viszonyainak üzemi vonatkozásai', [The Farm Relations of Employing Seasonal Labourers and the

Wage Conditions], *Magyar Gazdák Szemléje*, [Hungarian Farmers Review], 48(3), pp. 134–56.

Schulze, M.-S., 2000, 'Patterns of Growth and Stagnation in the Late Nineteenth Century Habsburg Economy', *European Review of Economic History*, 4(3), pp. 311–40.

Stiglitz, J. E., 1989, 'On the Economic Role of the State', in A. Heertje (ed.), *The Economic Role of the State*, London: Basil Blackwell, pp. 9–85.

Swain, N. and Varga, Z., 2013, 'Postwar Land Reforms in Comparative Perspective', *Öt Kontinens. Az Új- és Jelenkori Egyetemes Történeti Tanszék Tudományos Közleményei*, 11(1), pp. 141–58.

Szuhay, M., 1998a, 'The Capitalization of Agriculture', in P. Gunst (ed.), *Hungarian Agrarian Society from the Emancipation of Serfs (1848) to the Re-privatization of Land (1998)*, New York: Columbia University Press, pp. 99–124.

Szuhay, M., 1998b, 'Evolution of Hungarian Agriculture during the Inter-War Years (1918–1945)', in P. Gunst (ed.), *Hungarian Agrarian Society from the Emancipation of Serfs (1848) to the Re-privatization of Land (1998)*, New York: Columbia University Press, pp. 177–98.

Tomka, B., 2018, 'Az első világháború és a trianoni béke gazdasági hatásai Magyarországon', [The Economic Effects of the WWI and the Trianon Peace Treaty in Hungary], in Z. Bódy (ed.), *Háborúból békébe. A magyar társadalom 1918 után: Konfliktusok, változások a háború és az összeomlás nyomán*, [From the War to the Peace: The Hungarian Society after 1918], Budapest: MTA BTK, pp. 47–79.

Vári, A., 2010, 'Agrarians, Peasant Party and Rural Co-operatives in Hungary 1886–1922', in H. Schutz and A. Harre (eds), *Bauerngesellschaften au dem Weg in die Moderne. Agrarismus in Ostmitteleuropa 1880 bis 1960*, Wiesbaden: Harrassowitz, pp. 179–93.

Vonyó, J., 2001, *Gömbös Gyula és a jobboldali radikalizmus*, [Gyula Gömbös and the Radical Right], Pécs: Pannónia Könyvek.

Zeidler, M., 2007, *Ideas on Territorial Revision in Hungary, 1920–1945*, New York: Columbia University Press.

9 The impact of the crisis on the Polish agriculture (1929–35)

Tadeusz Janicki

1. Introduction

The circumstances of the functioning of Polish agriculture throughout practically the whole interwar period were unfavourable. Destructions which took place during the First World War and the wars on borders (1918–21), the post-war economic recession and the 1923 hyperinflation were so many hurdles connected with the integration of the land of former annexations and the construction of the national internal market. In the following years, they turned out to be particularly unfavourable for agriculture economic policy (favouring industry and consumption in the cities) and they led to the economic crisis of 1929–35, with tragic consequences for the Polish countryside.

2. Agriculture in interwar Poland

In interwar Poland, agriculture was a fundamental part of the national economy. In 1931, at the foot of 32.3 m people in Poland, the countryside was inhabited by over 23.2 million people, which accounted for over 71% of the total population. From agriculture, horticulture, fisheries and forestry, about 19.6 m residents supported themselves. According to the estimates from the interwar period, the value of agricultural production in 1929 was estimated at the sum of 13 billion zlotys, while the value of industrial production was calculated at 5 billion zlotys (*Little Statistical Yearbook*, 1939: 11).

Polish agriculture – like all sectors of the economy, owing to the long affiliation to the three partitioning annexations (Prussia, Russia and Austria) – was characterized by different level and character of economic development. Polish agriculture was strongly diversified in terms of agrarian structure, agricultural culture and social relations. Depending on the former partitions, agriculture differed in terms of the size of farms, the amount of plans per hectare and the total volume of production, the level of agrotechnical technology and knowledge, relations with the market and relations between rural inhabitants, especially between peasants and large landowners.

Relatively high concentrations of land and agricultural modernization were achieved in Greater Poland (Wielkopolska) and Pomerania (former Prussian partition), where agriculture was intensive. In turn, the agriculture

DOI: 10.4324/9781003105466-11

Figure 9.1 The borders of modern and interwar Poland and the areas of the former Prussian, Russian and Austrian partitions.

of the former Russian and Austrian annexations was heavily fragmented and largely extensible (Kozłowski, 1989: 97–106) (Figure 9.1).

According to data from 1931, small farms – up to 5 hectares – and medium farms – from 5 to 10 hectares – prevailed in Polish agriculture; 82.6% of the agricultural population inhabited farms up to 10 hectares. Larger farms – from 10 to 50 ha – accounted for 10.5% of total farms. Great land ownership was relatively small (0.5% of households), but economically strong as it owned as much as 25.81% of the total land (18.0% of farmland and 50.0% of forest) (Mieszczankowski, 1960: 333–4; Landau and Tomaszewski, 1962: 241–7). This is evidenced by the data provided in Table 9.1.

With the rise of the independent Polish state in 1918, numerous economic ties with the former invaders were broken. This adversely affected agriculture as a whole, especially in the agriculture of Greater Poland and Pomerania. Breaking the market ties with Germany led to the collapse of agricultural

Table 9.1 Agrarian structure in Poland in 1931

Area of farms	*Number of farms (in thousands)*	*%*	*Population of farms (in thousands)*	*%*
In all	3,196.0	100	15,694.9	100
Under 2 ha	747.1	25.5	2,998.2	19.1
2–5 ha	1,136.1	38.7	5,531.0	38.4
5–10 ha	728.7	24.8	3,943.5	25.1
10–15 ha	190.9	6.5	1,105.0	7.0
15–50 ha	118.2	4.0	6,940.3	4.5
More than 50 ha	14.7	0.5	57.3	0.4
Unknown size	260.3	x	1,365.9	5.5

Source: *Little Statistical Yearbook*, Warszawa (1939: 68).

exports from these voivodeships and the fall in prices of agricultural products that did not reach the pre-First World War level during the entire interwar period. Negative effects of the cut off from the markets of the former Habsburg monarchy were also felt by the farming of Galicia. Only the voivodeships of the former Kingdom of Poland (so-called central) and partly Eastern voivodeships benefitted to some extent from the liquidation of competition in the supply of grain and animals from Russia (Mieszczankowski, 1983: 27–8).

In the years of relative stabilization and economic revival in Europe (1924–8), Poland also experienced an improvement in its economic conditions, and there was an increase in agricultural prices and an increase in purchasing power of the rural population. Prices of agricultural commodities reached the highest level in 1927, while price scissors between prices of agricultural products and industrial goods closed. Relatively high prices of agricultural products resulted from the lack of grain self-sufficiency of Poland, war damage and the bad economic situation of Polish agriculture in the post-war period. The lack of agricultural investment and the associated degradation of the agricultural economy (especially the reduction of production in western voivodeships leading intensive farming up to 1914) forced the import of grain and flour, which did not decline even in the boom of 1925–8. The fast birthrate and cereal prices on the world markets, which in this period were seasonally lower than in Poland, contributed to the import (Ciepielewski, 1965: 13).

Under conditions of relative prosperity and high prices of agricultural products in comparison to industrial goods, farmers commenced investments aiming to increase productivity and increase their households. For this purpose, they borrowed from state and private banks or from moneylenders (Mieszczankowski, 1963: 126; Kostrowicka, Landau and Tomaszewski, 1984: 315)[1]. Unfortunately, debts calculated and contracted in the pre-crisis years became a heavy burden for farmers after it started, when the prices of agricultural products fell sharply. The necessity of timely repayments of subsequent loan instalments (and other financial burdens) often led to the insolvency and auctioning of farms for debts.

3. Causes of the agricultural crisis in Poland

The fundamental causes of the agricultural crisis in Poland were: periodic crop overcapacity, shallow internal market resulting from the slow development of industry and its collapse of low level of urbanization in 1929, the link between the Polish agricultural market and the world market, and the so-called 'cheap bread policy'. Additionally, after a good harvest in 1928, from the autumn onwards, a constant and steady decline in grain prices began. At the same time, a temporary reduction in cash flow made it difficult to obtain credit and discourage the food industry from shopping. A good global cereal harvest and its falling prices on commodity exchanges and grain imports to Poland became an additional factor in decreasing agricultural prices on the domestic market (Ciepielewski, 1965: 65).

Moreover, in the mid-twenties, the Polish government launched a pro-consumer 'cheap bread' policy, therefore intervening into the agricultural market to reduce and stabilize food prices. Therefore, government guidelines for the marketing year 1927/28 recommended gathering grain reserves, introduction of export duties on cereals in the fall and duty-free import of wheat. In this way, the government supported the development of industry (interested in lowering production costs) and sought to reduce the cost of supporting urban populations as a way to improve the social atmosphere. All this was at the expense of the income of rural residents and agriculture.

With such policies did the Polish authorities enter the period of escalating crisis. In addition, despite the sharp decline in prices in agriculture since the autumn of 1928, the government circles' optimistic evaluation of the economic situation dominated. Among others, therefore, was why the reaction of the government to the economic downturn was late and as consequence ineffective. For example, the export duty on rye and rye flour was abolished on 4 March 1929, and from 1 September 1929 so too was the one on wheat. Customs duties on grain imports were introduced on 18 September 1929 and the export premium on 16 November 1929 (Ciepielewski, 1965: 15; *Przegląd Gospodarczy*, 1930, no. 6: 258)[2]. Meanwhile, imports had unambiguously influenced the national pricing system, especially in the first period of the emerging crisis, when American grain cheaper than Polish, pressed the prices on the internal market.

4. Decline in income and financial problems of the countryside

The decline in prices of agricultural commodities was the main manifestation of the agricultural crisis in Poland, as was the case around the world. As already mentioned, it began in the fall of 1928 when the prices of mainly plant products, especially cereals, fell, and continued incessantly until the marketing year of 1934/1935. In 1935, prices for agricultural products fell by about 65% compared to 1928, including wheat – by 65%, rye – by 68% and potatoes – by 66%. Similarly large reductions concerned animal products – the prices of live cattle decreased by 57%, pig prices by 66% and milk prices by 62%. In order to receive the same amount of money as in 1928, in 1935 a farmer had to sell three times as many products (Musiał, 2009: 157).

However, despite the first signs of a worsening economic climate at the turn of 1929, the first year of the agricultural crisis was, in fact, the 1929/30 economic year. Initially, the peasants did not experience the effects of it severely because the price collapse covered only plant production, while the smaller peasant farms concentrated on farming. It was only in the economic year of 1930/31 that there was a deep collapse in the prices of animals and animal products. Consequently, the income of peasant farms began to fall sharply. Compared to 1928/29, in the 1930/31 economic year they fell by over 30%, and in the worst of 1934/35 they fell by almost 65% (Mieszczankowski, 1983: 35). Generally speaking, the decrease in income occurred in farms larger than 50 ha (see Table 9.2), but per capita it was the opposite. The biggest drop in income per capita was in farms up to 5 hectares.

In general, the main causes of falling agricultural commodity prices during the crisis was the shrinkage of the domestic and foreign markets, first for products of plant origin, and then also for products of animal origin (Kozłowski, 1989: 129; Little Statistical Yearbook, 1936: 183; Ciepielewski, 1965: 314).

Given the discounted prices of agricultural products of plant origin and relatively high prices of animal products, breeding was far more profitable than growing cereals and other crops. By adapting to this new market situation, farmers devoted cheap grain to feed and, until the beginning of 1931, quickly increased the stock of livestock. Unfortunately, both on the domestic market and abroad, the demand for breeding products decreased, and from the spring of 1930 there was a collapse in the price of farm products, which particularly affected the owners of small farms where traditionally breeding industry dominated (Ciepielewski, 1965: 17–18).

Despite such a drastic drop in prices, farmers could not refrain from selling their products because they had to pay taxes, pay off debts, and buy some of the most essential industrial products, etc. Therefore, in order to obtain the necessary cash at low prices, they were forced to sell more and more of their products, which further increased the supply advantage over demand and lowered prices even further. The need for cash also led to the so-called

Table 9.2 Income of agricultural farms in Poland 1929–36
(in million zloty)

Year	*Farms > 50 ha*	*1929=100*	*Farms < 50 ha*	*1929=100*
1929	1,677	100	2,459	100
1930	1,184	70.6	2,090	85.0
1931	1,023	61.0	1,667	67.8
1932	826	49.2	1,314	53.4
1933	757	45.1	1,036	42.1
1934	666	39.7	946	38.5
1935	685	40.8	906	36.8
1936	789	47.1	1429	58.1

Source: Kozłowski (1989: 131).

hunger supply, a situation in which farmers as food producers did not consume its certain types (especially meat and dairy), and even starved because they sold everything that was in demand.

As a result of the decline in incomes, the capacity of agricultural payments deteriorated considerably, leading to difficulties with servicing current financial obligations and the gradual reduction of purchases of industrial products. These aforementioned difficulties were primarily related to the repayment of loans taken in the boom years of 1925–8.

According to estimates based on official data and the survey of the Institute of Social Economy of 1934, the general agricultural debt at the end of 1932 amounted to 5,204.8 million zlotys, including a debt of 2,676 million in banks and credit institutions and 2437.2 min for private persons. At the same time, the value of total agricultural production in Poland was estimated at PLN 4,197 million (Mieszczankowski, 1963: 132).

The additional burdens for poorer villages were various state and local taxes. The most serious of these was the land tax, which in 1928 burdened the village with the sum of PLN 70 million, and in 1935, despite a deep decline in rural incomes, amounted to PLN 68 million. Apart from the land tax, local government taxes, such as self-government land taxes, amounted to PLN 37.8 million in the fiscal year 1933/34; in addition, road charges and rural compensatory tax in the same year amounted to PLN 35.4 million and PLN 31.6 million respectively (Mieszczankowski, 1961: 114–58).

5. Decline in purchases of industrial products and the autarkization of the rural economy

Agriculture, burdened with all sorts of necessary credit and tax payments, began to save on the purchase of industrial goods. The first was consumer goods considered luxury (including household appliances, clothing, sugar, newspapers and books) and then machinery and other means of production, especially artificial fertilizers. In the latter case, the decline occurred despite the state crediting fertilizers and price reductions and introduction of instalment sales by the state-owned chemical concern (United Nitrogen Factories) (Zaremba, 1998: 74–5).

With the prolonging and deepening of the crisis, restrictions on purchases also included such basic rural products as kerosene, matches and even salt. As a result, there was a sharp decline in sales and, consequently, the production of agricultural machines. In three years the production of horse ploughs fell by 80%, horse harnesses by 97%, threshing machines by 93% and winders (grain cleaners) by 93%.

Similar to the purchase of agricultural machinery, the consumption of fertilizers decreased. Moreover, expenditure on construction investments, dead livestock, etc., also fell (Ciepielewski, 1966: 102–5; Kubiczek, Wyczański, Jezierski, 2006: 386–8). As a result, the countryside almost completely ceased acquiring factory supplies; instead it met its needs for tools, equipment, and clothing through repairs and own production, or bought the goods needed by local craftsmen, often on a basis of interchangeable transaction.

The overall level of purchase by the village of agricultural machinery and equipment in 1932 compared to 1928 was only 8.8%. Thus, the decline in production in this section of industrial production was over 90%. For comparison, the overall decline in industrial output in Poland in 1932 was 41% (Ciepielewski, 1965: 316).

The above limitation of the purchase of industrial goods by farmers, in addition to the decrease in income, also resulted from the sharp rise in the price scissors between agricultural and industrial products and, consequently, the purchasing power of agriculture. In the years 1928–35, prices of agricultural products and animal products fell by more than 60% and prices of industrial products were less than 30%. This phenomenon occurred both in wholesale prices of agricultural and industrial goods and in retail prices. The opening of the price scissors during the crisis years (1930–6) was consistently above 30 points. In the following years, it ranged from 20–30 points (Mieszczankowski, 1983: 39; Konopka, 2009: 16; Orczyk, 1971: 108, 184) (Figure 9.2).

Particularly high prices remained on the monopolized articles. During the crisis, industrial companies in Poland, defending themselves from falling incomes, created a number of cartels that controlled about 60–70% of the newly manufactured industrial production in 1935. Cartel prices concerned, among others, metal products, artificial fertilizers, cement, kerosene, matches, sugar, salt, textiles, and vodka and tobacco, so products massively acquired by the village before the crisis (Mieszczankowski, 1983: 39; Kostrowicka, Landau, Tomaszewski, 1984: 322).

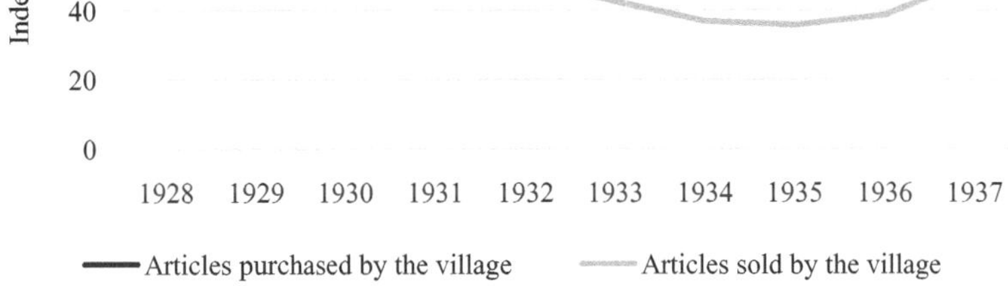

Figure 9.2 Price indices of goods purchased and sold by the village ('price scissors'), 1928–37.

Source: Kozłowski (1989: 128).

The food industry was also experiencing severe difficulties. Regress came in all its departments except for the production of bacon, which was massively exported to the Great Britain (Krupin, 2019: 987)

Reaction to falling incomes and high prices of industrial products was the autarkization of the rural economy, namely the pursuit of basic needs for industrial goods by way of self-supply. Farmers, either by themselves or by local craftsmen, produced yarns and fabrics, utility and construction ceramics, wicker baskets, shoes and other leather goods, tools and metal objects, and many other things necessary to survive (Kostrowicka, Landau, Tomaszewski, 1984: 316)[3]. Thus, in Poland there was a significant separation of the capitalist economy in the industry and smallholder economy in the countryside, and the market linkages between agriculture and industry were limited, which further exacerbated and prolonged the crisis. At the same time, in relation to a significant part of the Polish countryside, there was a return to the natural economy, which resulted in a large part of agricultural production being outside the market. Another manifestation of autarkization of a significant part of the Polish countryside was the return to the natural economy, which resulted in a large part of agricultural production being outside the market (Kostrowicka, Landau and Tomaszewski, 1984: 316).

It is worth mentioning here the positive role of cooperatives, especially dairy, in mitigating the effects of the crisis in its first period, when the membership of the cooperative provided the receipt of milk produced and the declining but regular income. However, due to the deep decline in prices for farm products and dairy products, many cooperatives went bankrupt, which often led to peasants' additional indebtedness; accordingly, in line with the principle of material responsibility, they had to pay the cooperative obligations. Nevertheless, villages with cooperative traditions tried to revive fallen cooperatives, which allowed them to benefit from the government assistance for agriculture and relatively quicker access to the path of economic (Ciepielewski, 1965: 130–1).

6. Changes in the structure and agricultural production

The crisis also affected the agrarian structure and agricultural production. Under the influence of falling rural incomes, the pace of agricultural reform slowed down. Starting from 1929 until 1934, the amount of arable land decreased (from 164.5 thousand hectares to 56.5 thousand hectares) decreased. Nevertheless, as a result of this and as a result of family divisions and land acquisition, the number of farms increased. Unfortunately, most of the new farms were less than 5 hectares, which aggravated the agrarian fragmentation in Poland (Landau and Tomaszewski, 1982: 177; Mieszczankowski, 1983: 94–5).

In the sphere of agricultural production from the beginning of the crisis, the overall area of the crop was systematically growing (from about 16.5 million hectares in 1929 to 17.1 million hectares in 1935) and the structure of the crop was changing at the same time. On the one hand, the area of four crops of cereals and potatoes increased, and on the other, the area of sugar beet and other industrial crops decreased (Landau and Tomaszewski, 1982: 180, 190). Negative changes occurred in the cultivation technique. The level of mechanization and the use of artificial fertilizers decreased. In general, those cultivation techniques that required cash were resigned from. However, despite this, the average yield from ha (except sugar beet) declined slightly. Only in western voivodeships, where mass fertilizers had been applied before the crisis, was the fall in yields larger (Landau, Tomaszewski, 1982: 197). In the sphere of breeding, the number of horses decreased by more than 300 thousand and the number of bovine and ovine animals was about the same. The pig population was fluctuating significantly depending on the market situation (Mieszczankowski, 1983: 191–2) (Tables 9.3 and 9.4).

Table 9.3 The yield of the major field crops in Poland by regions (1926–30 and 1931–35)

	Wheat	*Rye*	*Barley*	*Oats*	*Potatoes*	*Sugar beets*
	Yields from hectares					
Central region						
1926–1930	13.2	11.3	13.1	13.0	116	190
1931–1935	12.2	11.8	12.8	13.1	122	198
Eastern region						
1926–1930	11.0	8.7	9.8	9.0	90	152
1931–1935	9.9	8.8	10.3	9.2	95	165
Western region						
1926–1930	18.8	13.8	18.3	16.3	124	235
1931–1935	16.8	13.6	16.6	14.9	126	213
Southern region						
1926–1930	10.0	9.6	9.7	9.4	101	189
1931–1935	9.2	9.7	9.9	9.7	100	182

Source: *Little Statistical Yearbook* (1931: 20, 1936: 42).

Table 9.4 Farm animals in Poland between 1929 and 1935 *(thousands)*

Year	*Horses*	*Cattle*	*Pigs*	*Sheep*
1929	4,047	9,057	4,829	*
1930	4,103	9,399	6,047	2,492
1931	4,124	9,786	7,321	2,599
1932	3,940	9,461	5,844	2,488
1933	3,773	8,985	5,753	2,557
1934	3,764	9,258	7,091	2,554
1935	3,760	9,759	6,723	2,802

Source: *Little Statistical Yearbook* (1938: 86).

To sum up, it can be stated that in Polish agriculture, in the period of crisis, there was an extensification of agricultural production, in which the decrease in capital expenditures was compensated by increased workload.

The crisis also led to changes in agricultural policy. Under the influence of economic growth in the second half of the twenties, the Polish government did not expect a downturn and was surprised by the crisis. In the period from the autumn of 1928 and throughout 1929, state authorities, institutions and people involved in shaping agricultural policy, agricultural prices, and other signs of depression were considered to be transitional. Only a sharp collapse in prices, rapidly deteriorating general economic situation, and rising rural discontent forced the authorities to make decisions and take action against the crisis.

At the beginning of 1930, an emergency relief plan for agriculture was developed, which indicated the need for specific measures in the fields of grain, credit, tax, insurance, customs, tariff, etc. The main objectives of government intervention in the field of agriculture were to counteract the sharp fall in prices of agricultural commodities and a diminution in the price scissors between agricultural and industrial goods, while the reduction in tax burden and debt relief were secondary (Ciepielewski, 1966: 294–5; Mieszczankowski, 1961: 154; Landau and Tomaszewski, 1982: 88–90).

In order to raise agricultural prices, a state purchase of cereals was introduced and anti-cartels were launched to reduce the prices of industrial products. It was believed that lowering prices for industrial and monopolistic products would benefit not only the whole economy, but also the industry itself, which would increase production, reduce fixed costs, etc. Industrial spheres had a different opinion but despite that, in March 1933 the government decided to publish a policy on the issue of the anti-cartel law and reduce some of the prices of docked industrial goods. Unfortunately, this did not produce significant results and price scissors continued. The government's anti-crisis measures were limited by running a deflationary fiscal policy that is an aversion to moderate inflation as a prompt for market conditions, and by a strong and convertible currency. The monetary circulation in Poland decreased from 1,600 million zlotys in 1929 to 1,411 million in 1935 (Kozłowski, 1989: 270–4).

7. Conclusion. Social problems in the countryside in times of crisis

The major social problem of the Polish countryside in the interwar period was its agrarian overpopulation and the so-called 'Superfluous people' whose number in 1935 was estimated at 4–5 million. As a result, the common phenomenon in the country was unemployment, poverty, and hunger. The situation was further aggravated by the natural increase, which, despite falling during the crisis, was still around 300,000 people each year, and by blocking the possibility of economic migration from the village to the city and abroad.

As a result of industry redundancy, people who had lost their livelihood in the city even a returned to their home villages (Landau, Pański and Strzelecki, 1939; Stańczyk, 1955; Ciepielewski, 1968: 66–7).

Under conditions of declining income and extreme overcrowding in the country, poverty and hunger deepened, which in many cases forced the state authorities to feed the hungry rural population (Ciepielewski, 1968: 70). The decline in market consumption of the inhabitants of the village was extremely profound, almost twice deeper than the inhabitants of the cities (see Table 9.5 and Figure 9.3).

Under the influence of poverty and lack of prospects in the rural environment, moral and social norms eroded, so social conflicts and minor crimes, especially thefts, intensified. In addition, the number of marriages fell and the number of extramarital pregnancies and infanticides increased. As a result of the crisis, rural residents had limited access to secondary and tertiary education, which was paid in Poland at the time. In general, the civilization regression was triggered by poverty in the countryside.

Table 9.5 Market consumption index for villages and cities in Poland (1929–36). *Index 1929 = 100*

Year	*1929*	*1930*	*1931*	*1932*	*1933*	*1934*	*1935*	*1936*
Total	100	97	91	84	81	82	83	85
Cities	100	100	95	89	87	89	90	92
Villages	100	86	73	54	47	43	49	49

Source: Ciepielewski (1968: 284).

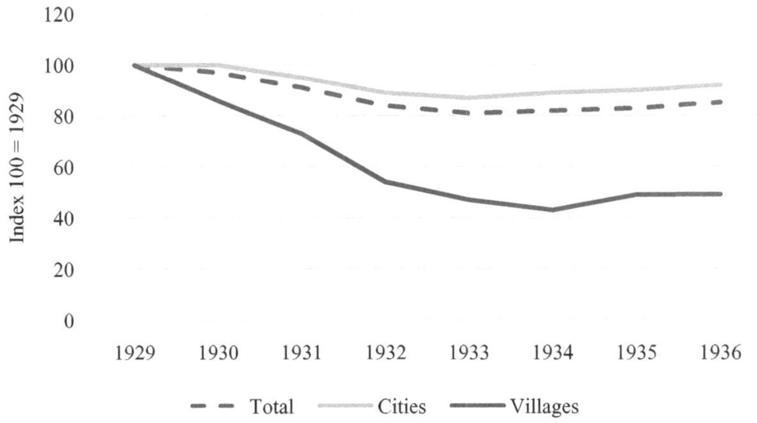

Figure 9.3 Market consumption index in Poland for villages and cities (1929–36).
Source: Ciepielewski (1968: 284).

Notes

1 M. Mieszczankowski estimates that the debt of agriculture, which amounted to about PLN 0.5 billion in 1924, amounted to approximately PLN 5 billion in 1931/32.

2 The neighbouring countries, and above all Germany, responded to the economic upswing faster and more decisively by introducing, for example, high export bonuses as early as 1928.

3 The number of peasant workshops in the farm was estimated at around one million, which meant that about 25–30% of the farms were able to produce their own fabrics.

Bibliography

Ciepielewski, J., 1965, *Polish village during the Great Depression of 1929–1935*, Materials and documents, Warszawa: Wydawnictwo 'Książka i Wiedza'.

Ciepielewski, J., 1966, *Agrarian Policy of the Polish Government in 1929–1935*, I–II, Warszawa: Wydawnictwo Szkoły Głównej i Statystyki.

Ciepielewski, J., 1968, *Agrarian Policy of the Polish Government in 1929–1935*, Warszawa: Wydawnictwo 'Książka i Wiedza'.

Drozdowski, M., 1963, *Economic Policy of the Polish Government in 1936–1939*, Warszawa: Państwowe Wydawnictwo Naukowe.

Konopka, K., 2009, 'Necessity of Agricultural Reforms in the Second Polish Republic (1918–1939)', *Ekonomia i zarządzanie. Kwartalnik Wydziału Zarządzania (Economy and Management. Quarterly Journal of the Faculty of Management)*, 1(1), pp. 7–19.

Kostrowicka, I., Landau, Z., Tomaszewski, J., 1984, *Economic History of Poland of the 19th and 20th Centuries*, Warszawa: Wydawnictwo 'Książka i Wiedza'.

Kozłowski, K. (ed.), 1989, *Economic Problems of the Second Republic Poland*, Warszawa: Państwowe Wydawnictwo Ekonmiczne.

Krupin, V., 2019, *Foreign Trade in Agri-Food Products*, in M. Halamska et al. (eds), *Continuity and Change. One Hundred Years of Development of the Polish Countryside 1918–2018*, Warszawa: Wydawnictwo Naukowe Scholar.

Kubiczek, F., Wyczański, A., Jezierski, A. (eds), 2006, *History of Poland in Numbers, II, Economy*, Warszawa. Zakład Wydawnictw Statystycznych.

Landau, Z., Pański, J., E. Strzelecki, E., 1939, *Unemployment among Peasants*, Warszawa: Instytut Gospodarstwa Społecznego.

Landau, Z., Tomaszewski, J., 1962, *Epitome of Poland's Economic History 1918–1939*, Warszawa: Wydawnictwo 'Książka i Wiedza'.

Landau, Z., Tomaszewski, J., 1982, *The Economy of Inter-war Poland*, III. Great Depression 1930–1935, Warszawa: Wydawnictwo 'Książka i Wiedza'.

Little Statistical Yearbook [Mały Rocznik Statystyczny], 1931, 1936, 1938, 1939, Warszawa: Główny Urząd Statystyczny (GUS).

Mieszczankowski, M., 1960, *Agrarian Structure of Inter-war Poland*, Warszawa: Państwowe Wydawnictwo Naukowe.

Mieszczankowski, M., 1961, 'Agricultural Taxes in Interwar Poland', *Roczniki Dziejów Ruchu Ludowego* (*Yearbooks of the Movement of the Peasant)*, 3, pp. 114–158.

Mieszczankowski, M., 1963, 'Debt of Agriculture of the Interwar Poland'. *Recent History of Poland: materials and studies from 1914–1939*, 6, pp. 123–148.

Mieszczankowski, M., 1983, *Agriculture of the Second Republic Poland*, Warszawa: Wydawnictwo 'Książka i Wiedza'.
Musiał, W., 2009, 'The Great Economic Crisis in Polish Agriculture - Reminder and Warning'. *Journal of Agribusiness and Rural Development*, 3(13), pp. 155–162.
Orczyk, J., 1971, *Agricultural Production of Poland in the Years of the Great Economic Crisis 1929–1935*, Poznań: Państwowe Wydawnictwo Naukowe.
Przegląd Gospodarczy (*The Economic Review*), 1930, 6, pp. 257–260.
Stańczyk, M., 1955, 'Agrarian Overpopulation in Capitalist Poland', *Ekonomista* (*The Economist*), 1, pp. 94–116.
Zaremba, J., 1998, *Eugeniusz Kwiatkowski. Romantic Pragmatist*, Warszawa: Instytut Naukowo-Wydawniczy Olympus.

Part III

The crisis and the policies

10 Swedish agriculture and the crisis of the 1930s

Mats Morell

1. Introduction

The world crisis of the 1930s appeared fully in Sweden by 1931. Export prices and incomes fell, deteriorating the spending power of households, which reinforced pressure on prices, investments and employment in a vicious circle. Unemployment peaked at 25% in 1932. Already by 1934, GDP figures superseded the previous all-time high of 1930. The quick recovery is explained by the 1931 depreciation as well as by the fact that much of the industry had been rationalised and stood strong after the 1920s. The role of the new Keynesian economic policy introduced after 1932 is played down (Schön, 2010).

This focus of this chapter is on clarifying how agriculture was thrown into this crisis, the interplay between efforts to solve the acute problems, and the long-term effects of these efforts.

World free trade was among all that was lost in 1914. From 1870 to 1914, the world's 'first food regime' ruled (Friedmann, 1987; Friedmann & McMichael, 1989; McMichael, 2009). It was symbolised by the gold standard and marked British economic hegemony. Brits had 'outsourced' their food provisioning to tropical colonies, delivering fruits, sugar, vegetable fats and tea to settler colonies/states providing grain. Imported foods reduced wage costs in the 'Workshop of the world'. Meanwhile, transatlantic and Russian grain arriving by cheapened steamship and railway freights put stress on commercial grain production in continental Europe (Aparicio et al., 2009). After the war, and the failed efforts to restore pre-war economic conditions, agriculture in most countries suffered from glutted markets. When they were confronted with the crisis that was escalating from 1929, most nations tried to regulate their agricultural sectors and protect their farmers' incomes. Following the next world war, the 'second food regime' developed under American dominance. Surpluses were produced in the USA and later in much of Europe. They were dumped on a segmented, distorted world market or transferred in the form of food aid to decolonising developing countries. Free trade in agriculture had to wait (Friedmann, 1987; McMichael, 2009).

DOI: 10.4324/9781003105466-13

2. Agriculture in the Swedish economy in the early twentieth century

By the outbreak of the First World War, Sweden was in a strong phase of industrialisation. Iron- and steel branches had been concentrated and modernised, many mechanical workshops worked for the domestic market, and a few large exporting companies in the telecommunication, electrification, and dairy branches had been established. Value added of manufacturing superseded agriculture's already around 1905 (Figure 10.1). In the interwar era, large Swedish firms adopted mass production technologies and Tayloristic managerial practices (Magnusson, 2000).

Although the value added of agriculture stagnated, food production per capita increased by 70% between 1870 and 1945 (Morell, 2001: 14). This is explained by the extended use of industrially produced inputs. Processing was increasingly performed in mechanised dairies mills. By the turn of the century, 25% of the sales of the mechanical industry went to agriculture (Kuuse, 1970). Thus, a reduction of farmers' incomes, risked reducing industrial profits.

Smallholdings and family farms dominated the farm structure. In 1937, over 75% of farms held 10 hectares of arable or less. Farms of a maximum of 20 hectares held 55% of the acreage and 69% of the dairy cows (SCB, 1937). Over three-quarters of the agricultural labour force was made up of farm family members (SCB, 1937); this proportion grew as paid farm labourers, particularly young women before the 1940s, left agriculture (SOU, 1944:65). About 60% of the total 428,000 farms combined farming with other income

Figure 10.1 Value added of agriculture and manufacturing in Sweden 1900–1940. *Constant (1910/12) prices.*
Source: *Schön and Krantz, 2015: 18.*

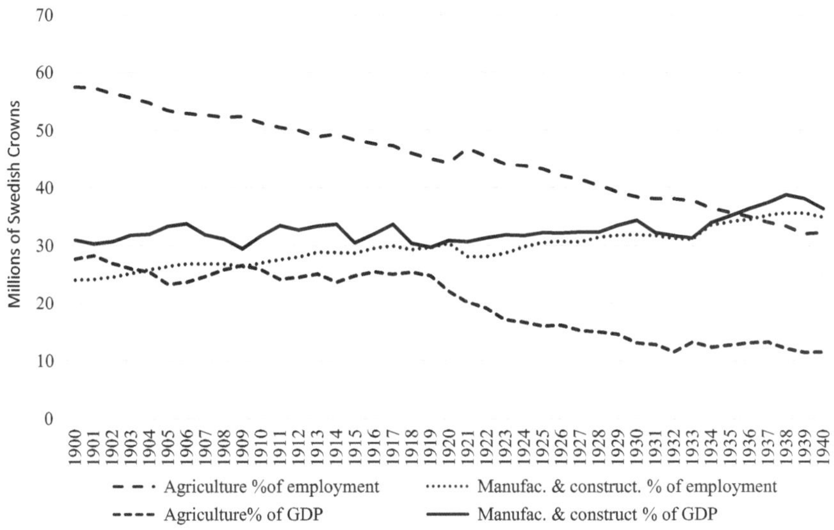

Figure 10.2 Sweden 1900–1940. Percentage share of employment and GDP of agriculture and manufacturing plus construction sectors.

Source: Employment: Edvinsson, 2005: 368–9. GDP: Schön & Krantz, 2015: 18.

sources to keep households afloat in *normal* years (Morell, 1998). Therefore, although most smallholders would keep on farming despite the crisis, falling farm incomes would create a pressing flow of labour power from the farm sector towards other sectors, aggravating unemployment. Furthermore, farming remained unproportionally important for employment (Figure 10.2).

3. Economic and agricultural development in the 1920s

Due to blockaded food imports and rising foreign demand for meat and livestock, agricultural prices soared during the war. Output prices rose more than wages and prices for inputs, including land. Credit was abundant and a mortgage-based agricultural investment boom in processing and electrification developed. Additionally, many new smallholdings were created from land sold by larger estates (Schön, 2010; Morell, 2011)[1].

By the summer of 1920, the feverish inflation halted. Consumption, investments, production, prices and asset values dwindled. Unemployment peaked around 25%. The crisis was aggravated by deflationary economic policy, aiming at restoring the crown at its 1913 value against gold. Many investors went bankrupt and banks with securities in stocks ran into problems. Ownership of banks and manufacturing companies were restructured and industrial plants were concentrated (Schön, 2010). Agricultural product prices fell more than other prices, as imbalances mounted on the agricultural world market (Figure 10.3).

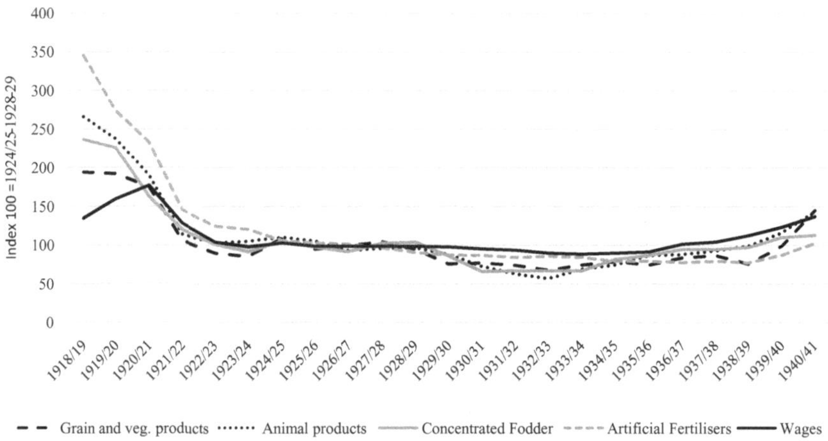

Figure 10.3 Index of agricultural prices 1918/19–1940/41.
Source: Nanneson, 1942: 256, 258.

By 1924, the acute crisis was over. The export branches, as well as new industries directed towards the home market, did well while restructuring of manufacturing continued. Nominal wages remained high despite persisting unemployment and employers substituting capital for labour. By the end of the 1920s, real incomes for those employed had doubled and this led to increasing demand for household durables (Schön, 2010). Population growth and household formation remained low. Therefore, there was little increase in the demand for inelastic agricultural goods, while per capita consumption of more price-elastic goods, such as butter, milk and cheese, grew (Morell, 1994). These trends were international. By the end of the 1920s, meat and dairy products made up 75% of sales from the farm sector. The export surplus of butter reached 74.9 million Swedish crowns in 1929, while the entire wheat harvest was worth only 90 million crowns. Still, agriculture did not prosper due to unfavourable relative price development (Schön, 2010; Figure 10.3). The nadir of Swedish agricultural prices occurred in 1922–3, but prices remained depressed throughout the 1920s. This meant that farmers' incomes fell in relative terms. During the war farmers earned on average 20–25% more than industrial workers. By the mid-20s, they earned 25–30% less (Schön, 2010).

The pattern of only slow growth for food demand was typical for industrialised countries. Simultaneously, former battleground countries restored their agricultural capacity while output from transoceanic countries, which had increased their agricultural export during the war, also grew. Russia, in the shape of the Soviet Union, re-entered the scene after some years. In the USA, agriculture and road transports were motorised, freeing large acreages previously devoted to fodder to now cultivate human food (Olmstead & Rhode, 1994). All this contributed to major gluts of the world markets for grain, sugar and vegetable fats. World stocks of wheat doubled between 1926 and 1929 but in 1929, after two bumper crops, the international grain market collapsed. In Sweden, wheat prices started to fall already in 1928 and more sharply in 1929[2].

Price pressure on vegetable fats favoured Swedish farmers, who imported such goods to raise milk yields. More problematically, exports of animal products to Europe increased from Australia, New Zealand and Argentina, but prices kept up due to rising household incomes (Åmark, 1942).

4. Agricultural crisis and recovery in the 1930s

The collapse of the international grain market in 1929 was the prelude to the depression. Unemployment rose everywhere, incomes fell and animal product prices on the Swedish export markets also fell (Nannesson, 1942). The situation was aggravated when many nations introduced import quotas or raised tariffs and Britain signed the 'Imperial preference' for commonwealth producers. Swedish agricultural prices reached a bottom in 1932–3 (Figure 10.4).

Falling prices did not reduce output. Animal fodder became cheaper and Swedish milk production increased until 1930, only to fall marginally following a bad fodder harvest in 1931. Increasing dairy and pork sales compensated for reduced incomes from grain. Exports of butter and pork reached all-time highs in 1929–30 and 1930–1, respectively (Åmark, 1942).

Farm profitability dropped but not to the level of the early 1920s (see Figure 10.5). Debt among farmers had significantly increased in the decade before the crisis. Investment taken on wartime loans turned out to be expensive when compared to the properties' sale value after the deflation of the early 1920s (Åmark, 1942: 233–4).

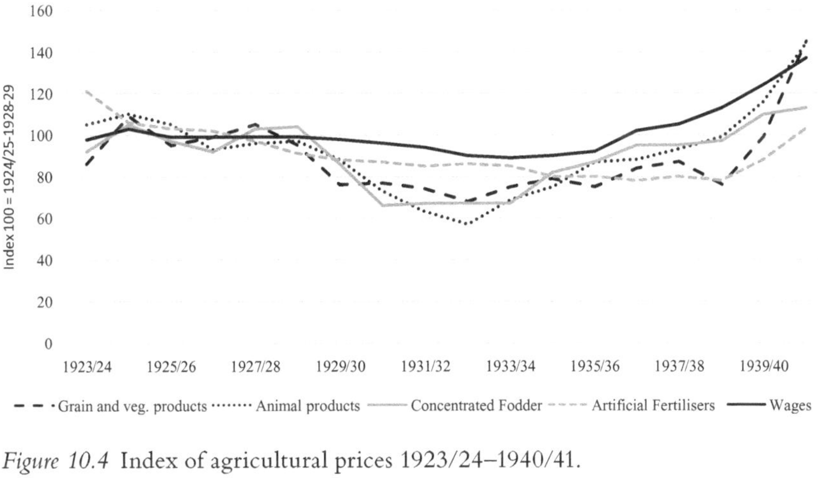

Figure 10.4 Index of agricultural prices 1923/24–1940/41.
Source: Nannesson, 1942: 256, 258. Detail of figure 3.

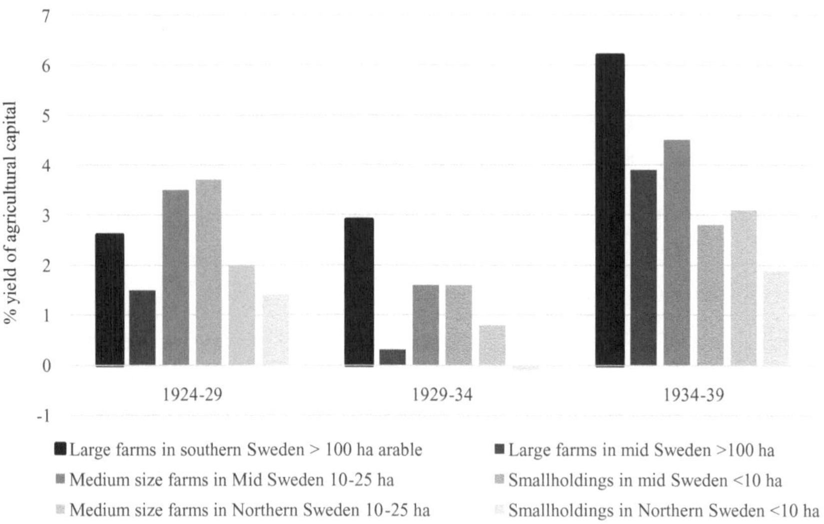

Figure 10.5 Profitability in the interwar years.

Five year averages. Different categories of farms.

Source: Nannesson, 1942: 283.

Note: Nannesson annually performed calculation according to the methods developed by Laur on a sample of farms (n = c. 900) with organised book-keeping. These farms were probably better run than farms in general.

In 1933, an investigation of farm debt, sampling 12,846 farms of different sizes, found that 9.5% of them had debts exceeding the asset values while 23.3% had debts exceeding 75% of asset values (see Table 10.1). The smallest and largest farms tended to be more indebted than middle-sized farms. Many of the smallest farms were newly established smallholdings, bought by workers with the help of premium governmental loans. Large estates invested more in buildings, machinery and groundwork than other farms.

These levels of debt led to problems with amortisations and interest payments when incomes fell. The frequency of liquidations and the number of forced farm sales increased (Table 10.2). In 1932, the combined debt of the liquidated farms reached 34.6 million crowns, while their combined asset value was 21.7 million crowns.

The development of prices, profitability, and farm incomes clearly indicated that the sector was in crisis. Having the total number of 428,000 holdings in mind, it might be argued, however, that comparatively few farmers actually went bankrupt or were forced into selling. In fact, the number of working farm units, foremost smallholdings, *increased* somewhat between 1927 and 1932 (SCB, 1959: 27, table 14). This reflected that for smallholders, it was hardly an alternative to leave their farms because of lowered farm incomes unless the failure to provide interest payments forced them to do so.

Table 10.1 Sweden 1933. Percentage of farms of different sizes with debts exceeding 75% and 100% of asset values

(sizes of the farms measured as rateable value in 1000 SEK)

Size group	*<5*	*5–10*	*10–25*	*25–50*	*50–100*	*>100*
75–100% debt	12.1	12.3	13.4	17.0	17.4	21.6
>100% debt	14.0	9,5	6.1	7.6	10.6	12.4
Total > 75% debt	26.1	21,8	19.5	24.6	28.0	34.0

Source: Bonow (1935: 290–291).

Table 10.2 Sweden 1929–33. Bankrupt farmers, farm properties sold on executive auctions and total value of executively sold farm properties

Year	*1929*	*1930*	*1931*	*1932*	*1933*
Bankrupt farmers (number)	435	402	656	846	574
Executively sold farms (number)	617	604	723	1018	1002
Total value of sold farms (millions SEK)	8.7	10.6	14.1	23.4	20.3

Source: Bonow (1935: 293).

For the smallholders, the farm was a direct source of livelihood rather than a capital investment (Chayanov, 1986), and they had no choice but to remain farming when possibilities for side incomes from wage work were reduced (see Figure 10.6). More farms closed down during industrial boom years than during recessions (Morell, 2001: 35–6, 79).

The agricultural crisis was thus tightly connected to the general crisis. The acute agricultural crisis resulted from decreased household spending power. Conversely, lowered farm incomes and investments reduced the farming sector's demand for industrial goods, thus reducing profits and investments among industrial firms. Moreover, with falling farm incomes, many smallholders/part-time workers searched for side incomes and contributed to the oversupply of labour.

As shown in Figure 10.5, farm profitability improved quickly after 1933. Wage costs and prices of inputs increased but, thanks to market regulations, so did output prices (Figure 10.4). Hectare yields improved and mechanisation was intensified (Nannesson, 1942, 269–77). It has been claimed that these improvements mostly concerned large and middle-sized farms, whereas smallholders failed to mechanise and were left behind, as they were not able to make full use of their labour power. For them, profitability (net profits in proportion to the capital invested) did not improve by a great deal (see Figure 10.5). Profitability in this strict sense was, however, less relevant for smallholders as capital yields made up a very small part of their incomes from agriculture. Compensation for work by family members was more important. In the accounting, farm-family wage incomes were imputed from notified working hours and current farm-hand wages. When farm-hand wages increased, the computed capital yields

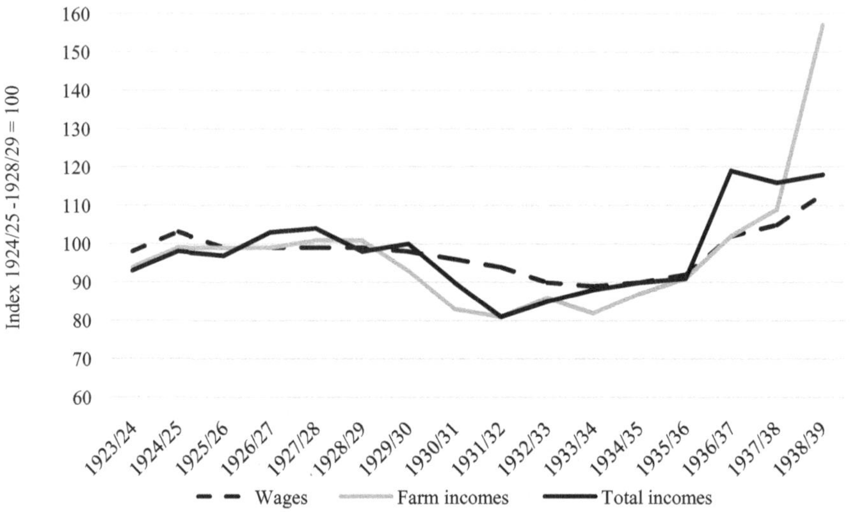

Figure 10.6 Income development among Northern smallholders in Sweden 1923/24–1938/39, compared to wage development in agriculture.

Source: Nannesson, 1923–39.

were pressed down among small farms where labour costs weighed heavily among running costs and were not so easily pressed down by mechanisation as on large farms (Nannesson, 1942). Therefore, the profitability measures present an unnecessarily dismal picture of the plight of the smallholders. Their *total incomes* grew more than profitability (Olsson, 1945).

5. Organisational efforts in the 1920s

The structural cause of agricultural distress was well formulated by the trade union economist, Clas-Erik Odhner:

> With rising living standards and stagnating population increase, demand for 'new commodities' produced by industry increases much faster than demand for food. With rising productivity within agriculture, this fact easily implies that the supply of agricultural products continuously tends to overrun demand. Surpluses press the prices, and the profitability of farming will remain on a level far below profitability in the expanding industry' (Odhner, 1953: 13).

Actors on the agricultural-political scene in the late 1920s, however, focussed on the fact that unorganised farmers sold more when prices fell and, therefore, further pressed prices down. Their envisaged solution was to achieve control of the supplies and stop farmers from competing with each other. Farmers, it was claimed, were less organised than industrialists and industrial workers. There was some truth in that. The 1920s was a high time for industrial cartels, not least in Sweden; trade unions had recovered after the disastrous conflicts a decade earlier (Magnusson, 2000).

In 1928, before the onset of the acute crisis, three initiatives for the organisation of agricultural producers were taken in order to regulate supply and market relations. First, a governmental agricultural committee, *Jordbruksutredningen*, was appointed with exactly that aim (Thullberg, 1979).

Secondly, plans were made up for unifying the producer co-operatives – which had developed since the late nineteenth century – under the leadership of the general agricultural society, SAL (*Sveriges Allmänna Lantbrukssällskap*).

In order to vitalise SAL, hitherto an elite organisation hosting no more than 3,000 members and consisting of mainly of large-scale farmers, a reform agenda was adopted. It aimed to establish cooperation between local co-operatives and convincing them to enrol collectively in SAL. The enrolled co-operatives should form national branch sections within SAL (the dairy section, the slaughterhouse section, etc.) and combine efforts in order to avoid 'unsound' competition. The goal was to engage all farmers in the co-operatives and to control supply via obligatory deliveries, implying delivering *only* to the cooperatives (Hellström, 1976).

The sale of milk was the most important source of monetary incomes for most farmers. Consumer milk (fresh milk) made up a third of milk sales; the rest, the so-called product milk, was processed into butter and cheese. Around one quarter of the sales of milk was exported as butter. Consumer milk attracted a higher price than product milk; that price was determined by the world-market price of butter. The development of motorised milk transports during the 1920s intensified competition in the market for consumer milk. Fresh milk produced further away from centres of consumption, which had previously been used for butter processing, was driven to the cities and marketed as consumption milk. This pressed down the price of consumption milk. Around large consumer centres, dairy cooperatives had merged to form regional associations that monopolised milk processing and retailing in their respective areas. MC, the largest regional dairy association, tried to compel its enrolled farmers near Stockholm to give up part of the premium on consumer milk so the organisation could subsidise payments to farmers that were further away, who delivered product milk, on the condition that these latter farmers refrained from entering the Stockholm market. The goal was to raise and stabilise milk payments to farmers by monopolising the supply of consumer milk. The SAL dairy section wanted to extend this model to the entire country. The regulation was to be handled without governmental influence (Hellström, 1976; Morell, 2009).

Thirdly, local activities in various parts of the country in 1928 finally led to the creation of the Farmers Union, *Riksförbundet landsbygdens folk* (RLF), in 1929[3]. The RLF came to organise, farmers of all descriptions. Initially, its relation to the cooperative movement was complicated as the new organisation argued that farmers should sell to anyone paying the best, whether or not they were in co-operatives. After some infighting, however, RLF emerged as the missing link, organising farmers on a mass basis. In time, the RLF and the cooperative movement enforced one another (Thullberg, 1977; Rydén, 1998; Just, 2009).

Neither any of the measures proposed by the agricultural committee, nor the recruitment to RLF or the cooperative reorganisation led by SAL, got far before the outbreak of the crisis. At the political level, a majority for non-intervention ruled throughout the 1920s (Åmark, 1942).

6. The creation of agricultural regulations

The political answer to the escalating crisis was the construction of a regulation apparatus for price support to farmers. Grain was not exported but partially imported. Thus, prices could be stabilised by reserving the domestic market for Swedish growers. Legislation for a quota of bread grain passed in the parliament in 1930. It was combined with an agreement that the large mills paid stipulated minimum prices to the cultivators. This was soon replaced by a guarantee that all bread grain good enough to grind would be purchased at fixed prices by the Swedish grain association, which, in turn, sold the grain to the mills. To cover losses, the association was allowed to charge fees when grain products were imported (Hellström, 1976).

Milk production generated considerable export surpluses and could not be handled like grain. SAL's work for price equalisation of the milk market was threatened when falling butter prices enlarged the price gap between consumer milk and product milk. Furthermore, too few producers were enrolled for the voluntary version of price equalisation to work. At SAL's request, therefore, the government granted the newly founded national association of Swedish dairies, SMR, the right to collect a 'price equalisation fee' on all milk sold or prepared for butter, cheese, or cream in Sweden, even from producers *not* engaged in SMR dairies. The fees financed a price subsidy paid to butter exporters. Thus, the price level of butter in Sweden could rise above world-market levels. Dairies became able to pay farmers more for the milk than the world-market prices implied. By 1938, 91% of Swedish dairy milk passed through SMR-enrolled dairies (Hellström, 1976)[4]. Thus, with the help of the governmental milk-market regulation, the cooperative movement achieved control over the milk supply.

A consumption tax on margarine was added to this in 1933, aiming to stop consumers from switching to margarine when butter prices rose. Proceeds from the tax were used for subsidising butter exports. Similar regulations with fees either on domestic sales or exports, depending on whether export prices or domestic prices were to be subsidised, were introduced in other branches such as beef, pork and eggs (Morell, 2009).

The regulations upset the balance between different branches and necessitated further regulations. The area for wheat increased at the expense of fodder grain: wheat prices were regulated while fodder grain prices were not. Guaranteed sales to fixed prices made fertilising and further cultivation of wheat worthwhile and wheat surpluses grew. A wheat fee for producers was introduced to hamper the expansion of wheat. Part of the crop was stored, but much was sold at discounted prices as fodder. Sellers received 'normal' wheat prices, as the state covered the difference (Åmark, 1942). The fees on domestically consumed milk were supposed to subsidise butter exports. The larger domestic consumption was in relation to exports, the better the regulation worked[5]. However, the guaranteed price for butter and the falling fodder prices induced farmers to increase production. Thus, the surplus needed to be exported, as subsidised butter grew. Therefore, taxes on concentrated fodder were introduced. Similarly, the import of maize was restricted in order to moderate pork production after the pork price had been stabilised (Åmark, 1942).

Productivity rose while employment in farming did not decrease particularly fast. Food consumption continued to grow only slowly. Neither the organisational efforts nor the regulations served to adapt agriculture to the trends of domestic demand. Instead, farmers were guaranteed sales at fixed prices, irrespective of the volume produced. Farming was disconnected not only from the signals of international markets but also from those of domestic consumers. The larger the surplus that the regulations led to, the larger the cost of subsidising the dumping of the surplus.

Some critics of the crisis policy wanted to abolish the domestic regulations and let demand govern prices. This would have led to a shrinking agricultural sector. Others promoted food subsidies to under-nourished social strata: 'the consumption reserve' (Bonow, 1935)[6]. But strong interest groups and an unexpected political alliance stood behind the established regulations.

7. The crisis policy and the crisis agreement of 1933

Most farmers voted for the Agrarian Party (*Bondeförbundet*), formed in 1913. It consistently promoted agricultural support measures. When grain support was discussed, the Conservative party proposed tariff increases, while the Agrarians preferred guaranteed minimum prices. The winning proposal of quotas was made by the liberal (*Frisinnade*) minority government. The problems for domestic grain-producing, large-scale farmers paved the way for the acceptance of this proposal by all non-socialist parties. The Social Democrats used free trade and income-distributional arguments and voted no to all these proposals[7].

The milk regulation requested by SAL was delivered by the *Frisinnade* government, which had substantial personal bonds both to SAL and the agricultural committee. Given the background of the crisis and the *perception* of crisis manifested by SAL, this proposal was also accepted by all non-socialist MP. The Social Democrats voted against it, but as the crisis escalated, they became convinced of the need for agricultural support. Thus, when the Social Democrats won the 1932 elections on their new labour market policy, based on loan-financed public works paid for at market wages, they sought alliances for solving the problems of both the agricultural sector and the labour market in one blow (Hellström, 1976; Morell, 2009).

The Social Democrats' need for support for their labour market policy (which all non-socialist parties objected to) and the readiness of certain leading Agrarians to accept anything as long as support for agriculture was secured, paved the way for the crisis agreement in May 1933. The Agrarians supported the new labour-market policy in exchange for Social Democratic acceptance of far-reaching regulation of the agricultural market, led by the cooperative movement. The Agrarians were criticised by Conservatives who claimed that they won nothing on the 'cow trade', which the non-socialists would not have been able to achieve without accepting the Social-Democratic labour-market programme. For the Agrarians, however, a solution including the Social Democrats was preferred, since it would not be threatened in forthcoming elections (Thullberg, 1977; Morell, 2009).

8. The crisis, the regulated market and the corporatist welfare state

In an earlier interpretation, the signs pointing towards agricultural overproduction already before the crisis is used to underpin an argument that in the modern industrial state, the agricultural sector would find itself in a 'permanent crisis', unless markets and prices were regulated (Thullberg, 1977; Pedersen et al., 1974: 162–3). From that followed the conclusion: the regulation of the agricultural market urged for by the farm-interest organisations concerned an adaptation of the agricultural sector to the modern industrial state. The crisis becomes unimportant for the choices that transformed agriculture into a regulated branch.

One can argue about how deep the agricultural crisis was. It is true that many of the critics of the turn that agricultural regulation took in Sweden (Myrdal, 1938 and Odhner, 1953) accepted a planned economy as a necessity. Structural change, however, is a normal outcome of long-term, sectorial-structural development. Normally, when production capacity in a branch overrides demand, producers leave that branch, either by plan or pressed by the price mechanism. This has happened to agriculture in all industrialised countries, not in the least in Sweden (Morell, Gadd & Myrdal, 2011).

I argue that subsequent long-term developments depended on the fact that major actors accepted that agriculture and the economy at large were in a crisis (Morell, 2001; Morell, 2009). Before the crisis, all parties except the agrarians opposed agricultural protection through government intervention. The SMR was not likely to have been granted the right to collect a *tax* (the milk fee from non-associated producers and consumers) without the influence of the crisis. Furthermore, the perception of a crisis convinced co-operative leaders that they could not manage the reorganisation of the milk market without governmental support[8].

Apart from motivating actions that brought about a regulated agricultural sector, the agricultural and general economic crisis of the early 1930s had four long-term consequences. Firstly, it triggered the agreement of 1933 that introduced the cooperation between Social Democrats and Agrarians; this became the political axis that agricultural policy would rest on until the late 1950s. Secondly, via the crisis agreement, the crisis contributed to the securing of the domination of Social Democracy in Swedish politics up to the 1970s, although the party rarely enjoyed a parliamentary majority of its own. Thirdly, the crisis manifested the establishment of interventionism in economic policy, which contrasted strongly with the relative laissez-faire policy of the 1920s[9]. Fourthly, it contributed to the construction of a corporatist welfare state, in which strong interest organisations became influential and even achieved public-administrative power.

Without a crisis, there would hardly have been any collaboration between the Agrarians and the Social Democrats. The compromise was hailed as signalling the unity of 'workers and peasants'. This is rhetoric. Had ideology mattered, the compromise would hardly have taken place. The Social Democratic party was – like its German counterpart – a reformist Marxist party for industrial wage workers. Its agricultural policy up to the 1910s mentioned land nationalisation; to Social Democrats, agricultural cooperatives had long meant collective farms. The ideological roots of the agrarians were distinctly anti-socialist. Early on, the party housed prominent members who, with various means, tried to restrict the breakthrough of political influence for labourers, which was the feared outcome of the common vote system. Also, the last stand of resistance against trade unions' right to organise workers was raised among farmers (Morell, 2001). The deep ideological cleavage between the two parties that formed the compromise in 1933 underlines the importance of the crisis for compromise to materialise.

The international trade crisis around 1930 offered arguments in favour of governmental intervention (cf. for USA, Rockoff, 1998). Prior to the crisis, there was little support for the far-reaching governmental intervention that became a hallmark of the economic policy up until the 1970s. The general economist view, and the view of all the non-socialist parties, at least up to 1933 was that 'market imperfections' – in the form of trade unions trying to keep up wages – caused unemployment (Schön, 2010).

In a seminal book, tracing the roots of Swedish corporatism, Bo Rothstein (1992) emphasises the interplay between farmers on the one hand and workers on the other. The interest organisations on both sides strove for control of supply of their principal commodity: food and labour, respectively. With help from the respective political parties closely connected to them, they both achieved their goal through the historical compromise of 1933. Rothstein, however, emphasises the importance of the non-socialist government's decision on milk market regulation in 1932, rather than the actual crisis agreement that followed one year later. He claims that the decisive steps towards corporatism and interventionism were taken by the non-socialists rather than by Social Democrats. The non-socialist government implemented the milk market regulation, which granted public administrative powers (in effect taxation right) to a private organisation[10]. Once this step towards providing the farmers' organisations a supply monopoly was taken, the door opened for granting similar concessions to the trade unions, particularly as the 1933 agreement safeguarded and extended the agricultural regulation.

Evidently, the non-socialists' acceptance of governmental market intervention in 1930 and 1932 was determined by the farming community – or their spokesmen – managing in making the argument that a severe crisis necessitated regulations to save farm enterprises. The crisis motivated rapid short-term action but the choice of action, and the political constellations that developed, transformed these measures into a long-term move towards interventionism and corporatism.

While it may be claimed that the labour market development, in a way, followed from the interventionism concerning agriculture in the early 1930s, there was one big difference. As for agriculture, the state remained heavily involved in price formation. From 1939, agricultural prices were determined using a general national calculus according to which the entire farm sector was viewed as one single company. Wage rates (shadow wages, for farm family members), input prices and goals of income levels were used in the equation in order to compute farm gate prices. Representatives of the state, the RLF and the cooperative movement (later a consumer delegation as well) were involved in the discussions. The prices that were arrived at were guaranteed by the state; the aim was to give medium-sized family farmers' income levels that were equal to incomes among industrial workers' families. For farmers, a governmental income policy was pursued. Arguably, farmers were transformed from market entrepreneurs into deliverers of homogeneous goods at fixed and governmentally guaranteed prices.

On the general labour market, on the other hand, the state was held at arm's length. The 1938 *Saltsjöbadsavtalet* agreement between the general trade union, LO, and the main employer's organisation implied that both labour market parties agreed on the definition of their respective roles. It also, however, manifested the unanimous consideration of the two parties: they should, without the influence of the government, negotiate and determine wage levels and labour relations (Magnusson, 2000).

Thus, the crisis agreement contributed to the acceptance of government interventions with the use of budget policy to fight crises. It contributed to the formation of a society resting heavily on interest organisations. According to an influential interpretation, the compromise between 'workers and farmers', manifested in the Swedish 1933 crisis agreement with similar agreements in Denmark and Norway, formed the basis for the Nordic Social Democratic welfare state and citizen-inclusive social reforms from the 1930s onwards. With the rapid shrinkage of the farm population in the post-war era and the growth of a new social composition with unionised urban white-collar workers, however, the foundation of this compromise and the welfare model derived from it was doomed to start dissolving (Esping Andersen, 1992).

9. Comparisons with Scandinavia and beyond

Despite cultural similarities, conditions differed among the Nordic countries. Farming employed the bulk of the population in Finland, Norway, and Sweden. However, its relevance for the national economy was smaller in Sweden, as it was heavily industrialising, while in Norway shipping and fishing had grown in importance. As much food was imported to these countries, it was, when fighting the crisis *symptoms* (falling farm incomes), possible to start by protecting domestic markets, easing the credit situation and, in the Swedish case, to subsidise agricultural exports in order to release the price pressure. The outcome *may have been* that efficiency in the agricultural sector was sacrificed to political and social tranquillity (Schön, 2009).

In more urbanised Denmark, agriculture was *the* most important sector of the economy, earning the bulk of the nation's foreign currency income up to the 1950s. Denmark specialised in the export of animal products, while much fodder was imported. Danish producers *gained* from the low world-market prices on grain, which created losses for many of their fellow farmers in the other countries. Consequently, while farmers' parties in the other three countries lobbied for governmental intervention in support of farmers, the Danish large farmers' party remained for long stubborn free traders. In the Danish case, the big problem from 1930 onward was the fall in dairy and bacon prices and the introduction of quotas in importing countries. The high proportion of exports to total production meant that the Swedish model, with butter being exported at prices below the cost of production, could not be followed. Through careful regulation of exports and production via quotas and by the depreciation of the currency, the profitable agricultural export trade had to *remain* profitable (Pedersen, 1988: 165–8). To navigate in the new environment where bilateral trade agreements set varying prices for the same product in different markets, The Ministry of Agriculture set up export boards for most products (a bacon export board, a butter export board etc.) from 1932 onwards. They were established by the Ministry of Agriculture in 1932 and similar boards were formed for other products. The boards were used to regulate supplies, distribute export quotas among exporters, and collect duties (Just, 2009). A hypothetical outcome of this regulative path, might be that, in contrast to the Swedish experience, productivity *improved* in Danish agriculture following the crisis measures[11].

Despite these differences, similarities abound: the severity of the trade crisis; the emerging strong agricultural co-operatives. There is also the appearance of political compromise between different parties in Denmark (1933), as well as in Sweden (1933) and Norway (1935), which split the non-socialist blocs and helped Social Democrats to power (Lindström, 1985; Almås, 2002: 82–8; Just, 2009)[12]. There is also a familiar argument that these agreements manifested democratic unity and had deliberate (and successful) sub-agendas of removing the ground for rural fascists (Lindström, 1985; Just, 2009).

10. Conclusion

The interwar years were an era of 'de-globalization' (Olsson, 2009). Economic interventionism and contra-cyclic policy became a dominant feature almost everywhere by the 1950s. This reflected hegemonic novelties in economics doctrines, but also a reaction on the not so remote World crisis around 1930. The crisis was, as expressed by Bordo et al. (1998), 'a defining moment' and agriculture played an important part in it (Bordo, et al., 1998; Rockoff, 1998; Libecap, 1998. The interwar years signalled the definitive fall of the pre-1914 free-trade based first food regime and the birth of the second 'mercantile-industrial' food regime (Mc Michael, 2009: 143). Thus, the narrative of the crisis as a watershed of agricultural policy, agricultural economy and the functioning of the economy in general in Scandinavia, is but a variation of a world-scale development. The ultimate forces behind the change were the same everywhere, as the crises were transferred between them via trade. National peculiarities in the pre-conditions caused stark national variations within the frames of this general development, the Nordic welfare state model (which had more complex roots than described here) was one such variation.

Notes

1 Development of land prices is treated by Bohlin & Prado, 2011.
2 For Swedish prices, see Åmark, 1942. Federico, 2005: 949-979, challenges the view of the importance of the growth of stocks.
3 Thullberg, 1977. The failure in Sweden (contrasting Denmark and Norway) to organise smallholders and middle-sized farmers separately paved the way for the formation of RLF. Cf. Just, 2009; Rydén, 1998.
4 On the similar milk regulation in Norway, see Almås, 2002: 67-71.
5 To stimulate domestic milk consumption, the dairy association introduced a sub-organisation the 'Milk propaganda' (Niskanen, 1995).
6 Gunnar Myrdal proposed 'internal dumping', i.e. discount sales of food to low-income groups (Myrdal, 1938; Morell, 1994).
7 See Morell, 2009 for a more detailed analysis, based on Hellström, 1976. Bonow, 1935: 230-242, showed that the grain regulations helped only the circa 4% of farmers who held 30 hectares or more, while regulations generally redistributed incomes from consumers to farmers.
8 Throughout the 1920s, Swedish farmers lobbied for market regulation or protection in various forms, but largely to no avail before the crisis (Hellström, 1976). There is a similar example in the USA (Libecap, 1998).
9 Even the conservatives, who otherwise stubbornly resisted state regulation of the economy, accepted it for agriculture after the crisis (Eriksson, 2004).
10 While the milk market regulation was more important, one could argue that the first step was the grain regulation, which granted similar powers to the grain association (Hellström, 1976).
11 Parcelling out of smallholdings in Denmark after the First World War, however, contributed to a farm structure in Denmark less expedient to productivity growth and may have contributed to the comparatively weak performance of the Danish economy in the 1930s (Henriksen, 2008).
12 In Norway, where smallholders voted for Social Democrats, that party enjoyed a majority. In Finland, a compromise between Agrarians and Social Democrats helped the latter to power in 1937 although crisis agreements in 1934 and 1935 left the Social Democrats out.

Bibliography

Almås, R., 2002, *Norges landbrukshistorie IV 1920–2000: Från bondesamfunn til bioindustri*, Oslo: samlaget.

Åmark, K., 1942, 'Svensk jordbrukspolitik under det senaste kvartsseklet', *Sveriges Lantbruksförbund 1917–1942*, Stockholm: LT, pp. 171–252.

Aparicio, G., Pinilla, V. and Serrano, R., 2009, 'Europe and the International Trade in Agricultural and Food Products, 1870–2000', in P. Lains P. and V. Pinilla (eds.), *Agriculture and Economic Development in Europe since 1870*, Abingdon: Routledge, pp. 52–75.

Bohlin, J. and Prado, S., 2011, 'A Market with Strings Attached: Agricultural Property Price Movements', in H. Antonsson and U. Jansson (eds.), *Agriculture and Forestry in Sweden since 1900. Geographical and Historical Studies*, Stockholm, KSLA, pp. 123–38.

Bonow, M., 1935, *Staten och jordbrukskrisen*, Stockholm: KF.

Bordo, M. et al., 1998, 'Editors' Introduction', in M. Bordo et al. (eds.), *The Defining Moment. The Great Depression and the American Economy in the 20th Century*, Chicago: University of Chicago press, pp. 1–20.

Chayanov, A.V., 1986 [1966], *The Theory of Peasant Economy*, 2nd ed. by D. Thorner et al. with a foreword by T. Shanin, Madison: The University of Wisconsin Press.

Edvinsson, R. (2005), *Growth Accumulation Crisis. With New Macroeconomic Data for Sweden 1800–2000*, Stockholm: Almqvist & Wiksell.

Eriksson, F., 2004, *Det reglerade undantaget. Högerns jordbrukspolitik 1904–2004*, Stockholm: Santérus.

Esping Andersen, G., 1992, 'The Making of a Social Democratic Welfare State', in K. Misgeld et al. (eds.), *Creating Social Democracy: A Century of the Social Democratic Labor Party in Sweden*, University Park: Pennsylvania State University Press.

Federico, G., 2005, 'Not Guilty? Agriculture in the 1920s and the Great Depression' *The Journal of Economic History*, 65(4), pp. 949–79.

Friedmann, H., 1987, 'International Regimes of Food and Agriculture Since 1870', in T. Shanin (ed.), *Peasants and peasant societies*, Oxford: Basil Blackwell, pp. 258–76.

Friedmann, H. and Mc Michael, P., 1989, 'Agriculture and the State System: The Rise and Fall of National Agricultures', *Sociologia Ruralis*, 29(2), pp. 93–117.

Hellström, G., 1976, *Jordbrukspolitik i industrisamhället - med tyngdpunkt på 1920- och 1930-talen*, Stockholm: LT.

Henriksen, I., 2008, 'The Contribution of Agriculture to Economic Growth in Denmark, 1870–1939, in P. Lains and V. Pinilla (eds.), *Agriculture and Economic Development in Europe since 1870*, London: Routledge, pp. 117-147.

Just, F., 2009, 'The Scandinavian Food System between Organization and State', in S.-O. Olsson (ed.), *Managing Crises and De-globalization. Nordic Foreign Trade and Exchange 1919–39*, London: Routledge, pp. 121–36.

Kuuse, J., 1970, *Från redskap till maskiner - Mekaniseringsspridning och kommersialisering inom svenskt jordbruk 1860–1910*, Göteborg: Göteborg University.

Libecap, G. D., 1998, 'The Great Depression and the Regulating State: Federal Government Regulation of Agriculture 1884–1970' in M. Bordo et al. (eds.), *The Defining Moment. The Great Depression and the American Economy in the 20th Century*, Chicago: University of Chicago press, pp. 181–224.

Lindström, U., 1985, *Fascism in Scandinavia 1920–1940*, Stockholm: Almqvist & Wiksell.

Magnusson, L., 2000, *An Economic History of Sweden*, London: Routledge.

Mc Michael, P., 2009, 'A Food Regime Genealogy', *The Journal of Peasant Studies*, 36(1), pp. 139–69.

Morell, M., 1994, 'Diet in Sweden during Industrialization, 1870–1939: Changing Trends and the Emergence of Food Policy', in J. Burnett and D. J. Oddy (eds.), *The Origins and Development of Food Policies in Europe*, London and New York: Leicester University Press, pp. 232–248.

Morell, M., 1998, 'Småbruken och deras jordbruksproduktion under 1910–talet och mellankrigstiden', *Bebyggelsehistorisk tidskrift*, 35, pp. 75–90.

Morell, M., 2001, *Jordbruket i industrisamhället. Det svenska jordbrukets historia IV*, Stockholm: Natur & Kultur.

Morell, M., 2009, 'Trade Crisis and Regulation of the Farm Sector. Sweden in the Interwar Years', in S.-O. Olsson (ed.), *Managing Crises and De-globalization. Nordic Foreign Trade and Exchange 1919–39*, London: Routledge, pp. 137–57.

Morell, M., 2011, 'Farmland: Ownership or Leasehold, Inheritance or Purchase', in H. Antonsson and U. Jansson (eds.), *Agriculture and Forestry in Sweden since 1900. Geographical and Historical Studies*, Stockholm, KSLA, pp. 56–73.

Morell, M., Gadd, C.-J. and Myrdal, J., 2011, 'Statistical Appendix', in J. Myrdal and M. Morell (eds.), *The Agrarian History of Sweden 4 000 BC to AD 2000*, Lund: Nordic Academic press, pp. 285–301.

Myrdal, G., 1938, *Jordbrukspolitiken under omläggning*, Stockholm: KF.

Nannesson, L., 1916–42, 'Räkenskapsresultat från svenska lantbruk', I–XXIV, *Meddelanden från Kungliga lantbruksstyrelsen*.

Nannesson, L., 1923–39, 'Räkenskapsresultat från Svenska jordbruk, X–XV, 1923/-24–1938/39', *Meddelanden från Kungl. Lantbruksstyrelsen*, Stockholm.

Nannesson, L., 1942, 'Jordbrukets driftsekonomiska förhållanden och lönsamhet under det senaste kvartsseklet', in *Sveriges Lantbruksförbund 1917–1942*, Stockholm: LT.

Niskanen, K., 1995, *Godsägare, småbrukare och jordbrukets modernisering - Södermanlands län 1875–1935*, Stockholm: Almqvist & Wiksell International.

Odhner, C-E., 1953, *Jordbruket vid full sysselsättning*, Stockholm: KF.

Olmstead, A. L, and Rhode, P. W, 1994, 'The Agricultural Mechanization Controversy in the Interwar Years', *Agricultural History* 68(3), pp. 35–53.

Olsson, H., 1945, *Jordbrukspolitiken under krisen*. Stockholm: KF.

Olsson, S. O. (ed.), 2009, *Managing Crises and De-globalization. Nordic Foreign Trade and Exchange 1919–39*, London: Routledge,

Pedersen, E.H., 1988, *Det danske landbrugs historie, IV, 1914–1988*. Odense.

Pedersen, E. H. et al., 1974, 'Nordens jordbruk under världskrisen 1929–1933', in *Kriser och Krispolitik i Norden under mellankrigstiden. Nordiska historikermötet i Uppsala 1974. Mötesrapport*, Uppsala: Almqvist & Wiksell.

Rockoff, H., 1998, 'By Way of Analogy. The Expansion of the Federal Government in the 1930s', in M. Bordo et al. (eds.), *The Defining Moment. The Great Depression and the American Economy in the 20th Century*, Chicago: University of Chicago Press, pp. 125–54.

Rothstein, B., 1992, *Den korporativa staten: intresseorganisationer och statsförvaltning i svensk politik*, Stockholm: Nordstedts juridik.

Rydén, R., 1998, *'Att åka snålskjuts är icke hederligt' De svenska jordbrukarnas organisationsprocess 1880–1947*, Göteborg: Historiska institutionen.

SCB 1937, SOS *Jordbruksräkningen* 1937 (Agricultural Census 1937). Stockholm.

SCB 1959, *Historical Statistics of Sweden* II, Örebro: SCB.

Schön, L., 2009, 'Swedish Agriculture in Economic Development, 1870–1939', in P. Lains and V. Pinilla (eds.), *Agriculture and Economic Development in Europe since 1870*, London: Routledge, pp. 148–77.

Schön, L., 2010, *Sweden's Road to Modernity. An Economic History*, Stockholm: SNS.

Schön, L. and Krantz, O., 2015, 'New Swedish Historical National Accounts since the 16th Century in Constant and Current Prices', *Lund Papers in Economic History*, 140.

SOU 1944: 65. *Jordbrukets framtida tillgång på arbetskraft*, Official investigation by H. Hyrenius, Stockholm.

Thullberg, P., 1977, *Bönder går samman - En studie i riksförbundet Landsbygdens Folk under världskrisen 1929–1933*, Stockholm: LT.

Thullberg, P., 1979, 'När odalmannen blev föreningsbonde', in T. Johansson and P. Thullberg (eds.), *Samverkan gav styrkan - Lantbrukarnas föreningsrörelse 1929–1979*, Stockholm: LT.

11 Spanish agriculture and the Great Depression

Juan Pan-Montojo and James Simpson

1. Introduction

There are surprisingly few references in the literature to the impact of the Great Depression on Spanish agriculture, either by contemporaries or in the historiography. Two explanations are usually advanced for this. In the first instance, official statistics of economic variables such as farm prices, wages, or unemployment, together with the recent reconstructions of Gross Domestic Product, suggest that Spain suffered less than most other Western European countries. This, it is argued, was because of Spain's limited international trade and having a floating currency, rather than being on the gold standard (Palafox, 1991; Martín Aceña, 2005; Comín, 2010). A second factor was that most contemporaries believed that the political reforms associated with the Second Republic (1931–6) had a greater impact on farm profitability and rural living standards than those caused by any disequilibria in international supply and demand.

Nevertheless, and as this chapter argues, the differences between Spain and other Western European nations went deeper. Although the destructive effects of the international depression were indeed probably less than those found in most other countries, so too was the state's capacity to respond to them. This was because there had been over the previous couple of decades fewer political demands and critical junctures that forced to invest in improving state capacity to regulate economic activity and carry out complex socio-economic agendas. In particular, while countries such as France or Italy had to mobilise large sections of their economies during the Great War, this was not the case in neutral Spain. Spain's natural resource endowments also created specific problems, shared though with other Mediterranean countries, as the need to use dry-farming methods limited the possibilities to introduce new labour-intensive technologies to absorb underemployed farm labour over perhaps four-fifths of the country. Indeed, the direction of technological change favoured the introduction of labour-saving mechanisation to improve farm incomes in the exceptionally large cereal sector.

Finally, the new democratic Second Republic (1931–6) radically changed the nature of political opportunities and reduced the constraints to collective

DOI: 10.4324/9781003105466-14

action by family farmers and rural wage earners. Traditional demands for structural change, and in particular a redistributive land reform in southern Spain, now coincided with calls for government to resolve low farm prices and cyclical unemployment caused by the economic downturn and adverse weather conditions, with 3 million days being lost in the province of Jaen alone because of the almost total failure of the olive harvest. However, all Republican governments found it difficult to create sufficient employment and stabilise farm markets in the short run, and resorted instead to ambitious long-term schemes and to policies that rewarded their own constituents, leading to high political polarisation in the countryside by the mid-1930s. Rural polarisation was not exceptional, in the European context in the interwar period, and a long tradition of political-scientists has underlined the relevance of rural political leanings in the transformation of political systems during the crisis of liberalism (see especially Robledo, 2019).

The chapter is divided into five sections. The first looks at the nature of Spanish agriculture on the eve of the Great Depression. Sections 2 and 3 examine the nature of the Great Depression and its impact on farming, and the limits to government intervention. Section 4 looks at popular mobilisation and social conflicts in the countryside. The last section concludes.

2. Spanish agriculture on the eve of the Great Depression

Spanish agriculture after 1900 was a relatively dynamic sector, and a highly protected one. In this sense state intervention in technical diffusion, combined with protectionism, counterbalanced allocational distortions and facilitated productivity growth between 1900 and the Civil War (see Koning, 2013). In the two decades prior to the Great Depression, the active labour force employed in the sector fell from 63 to 45% of the total according to the official statistics, and the area of cultivation rose by 14%. This helped labour productivity grow by 65%, and land output by 18% (GEHR, 1983; Simpson, 1995). Although to some degree a recovery from the late-nineteenth-century crisis, this was an exceptional performance.

The impact of the Great Depression on the farm sector, and the capacity of governments to respond to the problems it created, varied significantly across Europe. In part, this was because industrialisation was much more advanced in some countries than in others, but it was also caused by differences in land ownership and production constraints associated with diverse farming systems. In Spain, the economic impact affected farm groups very differently, and the political initiatives to resolve the problems threatened to radically change the distribution of political and economic power in the countryside. Two major characteristics in particular help define the nature of the country's 'agrarian problems', and the difficulties that these created for governments to resolve during the Second Republic.

Table 11.1 The nature of Spanish regional farming in 1929/33.

	% of Nation's agricultural area	*% of Nation's farm output by value*	*Output per hectare (pesetas)*	*Hectares/ male worker*	*Output per male worker (pesetas)*
North	7.6	18.5	797	3.4	2739
Interior	60.1	38.9	211	10.9	2315
Andalusia	19.0	16.7	288	5.7	1630
Mediterranean	12.6	23.5	607	4.3	2610
Spain	100.0	100.0	327	7.0	2303

Source: Simpson, 1995: tables 2.3 and 2.4.

Spain, even more than most countries, had highly distinctive regional farming systems, partly caused by the need to use dry-farming techniques over large areas because of the long summer droughts. A simple division of the country into four zones shows that two of them, the North and Mediterranean, accounted for a fifth of all farmland, but more than two-fifths of output in 1929/33 (Table 11.1). This can be explained by the greater possibilities of using labour-intensive techniques in areas with plentiful summer rainfall (North), or irrigation in fruit and vegetable production (Mediterranean). Elsewhere, dry-farming was needed, condition which were fine for growing extensive cereals, especially wheat, as well as wine and olive oil, but not for labour-intensive farming. However, per capita demand for the first two commodities by the 1920s was stagnant because of rising living standards, while olive oil producers were highly dependent on export markets, which suffered during the Depression. As traditional cereal production required very little labour, workers were usually employed by the task, and relatively few enjoyed annual contracts such as found over much of North-Western Europe. The dry-farming technologies of the 1930s offered few possibilities to increase yields or shift to alternative and higher value crops. By contrast, labour-saving mechanical technologies that prepared the land for sowing, and collected and threshed the cereal harvest were rapidly advancing. By the 1930s this seriously threatened workers, who had traditionally been able to earn high wages during the seasonal harvest peaks when demand greatly exceeded the village supply.

A second characteristic was the regional nature of land ownership. In Spain, as in much of Europe, the relative importance of family farmers grew significantly over the half century or so prior to the Great Depression (Carmona, Rosés and Simpson, 2019). However, in southern Spain, holdings of over 100 hectares still accounted for 52.4% of all the land, and these were worked predominately by wage labour (Malefakis, 1970: Table 3), who suffered from long periods of seasonal unemployment. At the other extreme was Galicia in the North, where holdings were frequently minuscule, and owners had to invest considerable effort and ingenuity to make them productive. In general, the structure of Spanish landownership suggests that the predominate

Table 11.2 Regional occupational distribution of active male agricultural population, 1956

	Southern Spain	*Rest of Spain*
Total active males (000s)	1,557	2,988
Labor employing entrepreneurs	18%	20%
Family operators – owners	14%	40%
TOTAL	32%	60%
Family operators – tenants	11%	17%
Hired labourers – permanent	13%	7%
Hired labourers – temporary	43%	17%
TOTAL	67%	41%

Source: Malefakis, 1970: 94.

agrarian conflicts in the south were associated with labour markets, as virtually three-fifths of the farm population were wage earners, while in the rest of the country, where almost four-fifths of the population were farmers, it revolved around questions of farm prices, land tenure, and market volatility (Table 11.2).

The economic dislocation caused by the Great Depression, and political opportunities for collective action offered by the Second Republic, are also seen with the persistence of highly localised farm contracts. This was especially true among those sub-letting plots of land on the giant estates (*dehesas*) in Extremadura, or the sharecropping *rabassa morta* contracts found in viticulture in Barcelona and Tarragona. In both cases, tenants and landowners were able to use the new political channels to pursue traditional grievances (Balcells, 1980; Domenech and Herreros, 2018; Carmona and Simpson, 2020).

3. Spanish agriculture and the crisis

The impact of the world crisis appears limited at first sight in Spain, as falls in the real GDP and GDP per capita were relatively small, and GDP had recovered its 1929 level by the outbreak of war in 1936 (Table 11.3). Investment

Table 11.3 Spanish economic indicators for the early 1930s

	GDP	*Exports*	*Capital formation*	*GDP per capita*	*Price index*	*Agric. GDP at factor costs*
1929	100	100	100	100	100	100.0
1930	97	111	98	96	100,6	86.4
1931	94	106	67	92	101,8	92.4
1932	96	113	58	94	101,0	102.5
1933	95	83	64	91	96,5	91.7
1934	98	80	64	94	98,5	102.5
1935	101	76	68	95	100,8	101.6

Source: Prados de la Escosura, 2003: A3.6, A7.4 and A5.8; Price index in Palafox, 1991: 149.

collapsed in 1931 because of the international crisis and domestic political uncertainties and exports declined steeply after 1932[1]. Agricultural production stagnated, dropping almost 13% in 1930, but then recovering in 1931 and 1932. The two massive cereal harvests of 1932 and 1934, along with the use of official prices to value output, helped them to maintain an apparent stability. Regional trends varied however, especially as export agriculture was locally concentrated, and in areas where orange or olive production had become almost a monocrop, farm revenues suffered a severe blow.

The official statistics also suggest that farm prices stagnated, rather than falling dramatically, as in other countries. Although wheat prices hardly fell at all, many farmers had problems selling their crop at the official rates, and the drop in barley prices, shown in Table 11.4, probably conveys better the real price movement of cereals (Palafox, 1991; Simpson and Carmona, 2020). The good harvests of 1932 and 1934 reduced wheat prices in 1933 and 1935, while an erroneous market forecast led the Government to permit imports in 1932, further depressing prices. The same is true with wine, as the apparent price stability in official estimates occurred at a time when producers complained of the difficulties of selling their production, and a drop in exports (Table 11.5). By contrast, olive oil showed a constant downward trend in prices, mirroring those of exports.

Export competitiveness was initially increased by the depreciation of the peseta in 1929 and 1930, but the demand for Spanish exports quickly diminished with its recovery the following year, and the protectionist turn taken by most European countries. Exports, except for sherry, were always well below their 1920s levels after 1931. Although the volume of orange exports grew, Spanish dealers had to slash prices and reduce quality to compete with South African, Palestinian, and Maghreb producers. Olive oil and table wines suffered from the protectionist and colonial preferential system adopted in France and Great Britain after 1930.

The large size of the agricultural sector made it the employer of last resort. As the economic depression increased, surplus farm labour was discouraged

Table 11.4 Prices of agricultural products
Price index 1920–29 = 100

	Wheat	*Barley*	*Wine*	*Olive oil*
1920–9	100	100	100	100
1930	95	90	87	82
1931	94	89	104	89
1932	100	100	106	89
1933	94	79	97	78
1934	102	88	104	78
1935	99	93	96	76

Source: Carlos Barciela, Jesús Giráldez, Grupos de Estudios de Historia Rural e Inmaculada López, 2005: table 4.32.

Table 11.5 Agricultural exports

	Exports in value at constant prices 1910	*Exports by quantity*			
		Wine	*Sherry*	*Olive oil*	*Oranges*
1920–29	100	100	100	100	100
1930	125	83	119	171	183
1931	109	84	155	150	145
1932	95	44	120	101	149
1933	88	61	158	69	165
1934	93	41	190	84	149
1935	96	24	211	99	118

Source: Carlos Barciela, Jesús Giráldez, Grupos de Estudios de Historia Rural e Inmaculada López, 2005: tables 4.28 and 4.31.

from moving to cities while many unemployed urban workers now returned to their old villages. This had two very different consequences given the landownership structure discussed above. First, especially in areas of latifundios in southern Spain, the supply of landless and near-landless day labourers increased just when demand was falling. By contrast, although family farmers could not by definition be unemployed, growing numbers had to be fed, straining resources at a time of low prices.

Measuring accurately the extent of this rural unemployment is therefore difficult, both because of the differences between family-run enterprises and large estates, and the seasonal nature of much of agriculture. According to official figures, there were 382,965 unemployed agricultural labourers in 1933, or more than 60% of the national total, and a third of the 1,170,000 agricultural labourers estimated by the Ministry of Labour for that year[2].

Farm structure therefore created two distinct demands for Spanish governments in the 1930s, namely the need to resolve low farm gate prices for major crops and to reduce underemployment, especially in southern Spain. To a significant extent these policies were incompatible, as higher food prices hurt both rural and urban workers, while higher harvest labour costs reduced the competitiveness of family farmers, as we shall see.

4. The limits to government intervention in agriculture during the Second Republic (1931–6)

Although the monarchical parties won the local elections of April 1931, it was clear that this was only because of widespread fraud, and that popular support for the monarchy had evaporated. The king abandoned the country, and the Second Republic was proclaimed. The Republic can be divided into three distinct phases, with centre-left or left governments during the first (1931 to November 1933), and third (spring 1936), and centre-right or right-wing governments in the second (November 1933 to February 1936). The agrarian political agenda was very different in these relatively short periods. Under the left governments, it aimed at favouring labourers, especially those belonging to the socialist union Federación Nacional de Trabajadores de la Tierra (FNTT) and poor peasants, whereas in the second period, it attempted to improve the position of employers and family farmers.

There was considerable enthusiasm initially for a land reform that promised to create not only a more equitable society considered necessary for the new democracy, but also a more dynamic agriculture that would eliminate rural unemployment, thereby winning support for the Republic from the poorer sectors of rural society. The 1932 Agrarian Reform Law has been described as a 'document of extraordinary complexity' and if 'milder' than similar legislation in Eastern Europe or Mexico, still envisaged a profound transformation of farm ownership (Malefakis, 1970: 205). It set limits to individual land ownership in each locality and for each type of crop, but all land could be expropriated in cases where it was considered to be badly cultivated; had been leased continuously for more than 12 years; or where the owner had failed to use irrigation when these facilities were available. In addition, land where seigneurial rights had been converted into full ownership during the nineteenth century was confiscated without compensation.

The initial optimism generated by the land reform quickly evaporated because of the slow results. By December 1933, only 6,000 or 7,000 families had been settled, receiving just 45,000 hectares. Settlements continued after the victory of the centre-right coalition in late 1933, with a further 6,289 families receiving 81,558 hectares between January and September 1934. However, the revised July 1935 law threatened to slow progress even further, as not only could most landowners now easily avoid having their lands expropriated, but the budget that was allocated was so small that José Antonio Primo de Rivera, the leader of the extreme-right Falange, claimed that it would take 160 years to be completed (Malefakis, 1970: 360). Although the 1935 law effectively killed-off the land reform, it contained a 'social utility' clause which permitted local authorities to settle villagers on uncultivated land when in urgent social need, a clause that would inspire massive land invasions in the spring of 1936 (see below).

There were several reasons for the limited results of the 1932 land reform. In particular, the fact that the democratically elected government respected legality, rather than arbitrarily confiscate property, gave landowners plenty of opportunities to challenge it. Indeed, Albertus argues that successful land reforms in Latin America in the twentieth century were more likely to occur under authoritarian regimes, which could ignore legal niceties, rather than democracies (Albertus, 2015).

Another problem was the new government had inherited only limited state capacity to implement it. It lacked basic statistics on crucial matters such as the numbers of landless and poor farmers; the potential area of uncultivated land that could be brought under the plough; or the capacity of local agriculture to absorb labour. The land cadastre gave limited information on farm size and the taxable income but could not be used to measure an individual's total land holdings across the country or indicate whether a low cadastre rent was the consequence of deficient cultivation, or because of the poor quality of the land. Rents were not updated and could quickly become out of date, making comparison across provinces impossible (Carrión, 1932: 98). Detailed provincial studies on local cereal and livestock production systems had been compiled in the early 1890s but there was nothing remotely similar produced during the first third of the twentieth century (Simpson and Carmona, Appendix 1). The first census of farm machinery was not published until 1932 and, as historians have shown, contained major errors (Spain. Ministerio de Agricultura, 1933: 318–26; Fernández Prieto, 1997: 139–44). Finally, except for a few newspaper reports, no detailed information existed to show how farms actually operated.

Although government agronomists were rarely critical of farming methods on the large estates they studied, considerable amounts of land were kept in pasture to feed the growing demand for meat. The massive land invasions that took place in Western Spain in 1932 and 1936 occupied some of this land, although they also infringed upon land that was already being rented to those farmers favoured by the landowners (Carmona and Simpson, 2016). Right-wing groups were quick to claim the supposed threat that the Republic posed to the private property for both large, and small, landowners.

Whereas a successful land reform might have transformed property rights and farm organisation over time, the decrees and laws affecting land and labour markets passed between 28 April and 14 July 1931 aimed at having a radical, and immediate effect, on farmers' decision-making. Tenants were now protected from eviction unless they failed to pay their rent or cultivate the land; tribunals revised, and reduced, many rents; and a preference was given to the formally constituted workers' societies for renting land, which was aimed at eliminating the problem of subletting (Malefakis, 1970: 167). Workers were to benefit from the introduction of an eight hour day, as well as arbitration boards that determined work conditions, and local workers had to be employed before 'outside' labour. Finally, and to avoid a 'lock-out', farmers were obliged to cultivate their land with the same intensity and number of workers as previously.

The centre-left government's objectives were therefore to increase wages and maintain cultivation and employment levels at a time of weak or falling farm prices. In traditional agriculture, landowners had often provided emergency employment for their workers when inclement weather or poor harvests reduced demand, and the state exceptionally offered emergency funding to municipalities for public works. This now changed as landowners had the legal obligation to employ workers chosen for them from lists drawn up by the village mayor who, before November 1933, were often Socialists. What had previously been a paternalistic system that worked to the benefit of the employer, now changed to one which benefitted other groups, and especially the Socialist FNTT syndicate. The struggle to control labour markets would prove to be even more divisive than land reform, as successful syndicate organisations in the early 1930s were able to increase agricultural wages, leading to one prominent historian to claim that 'Spain had probably been the only nation in the world in which wages had actually risen during the Depression' (Malefakis, 1970: 329). However, this reflected organised labour's control on the local commissions and, when this changed after the November 1933 elections, power switched back to the landowners, who turned once more to tenants and workers they trusted and ignore those who were members of syndicates.

As in most countries, republican governments also attempted to intervene in commodity markets, not just the home market, but also export and import markets (Chatriot, Leblanc and Lynch, 2012, introduction). Regulation was justified by the need to protect consumers and promote fair competition, as well as to help farmers, and especially the smaller ones suffering from the international crisis. The new legislation and government decrees created large numbers of new committees, commissions, and institutes, which were frequently underfunded, and lacked the necessary experienced personnel to deal with the well-informed lobbies and associations (Pan-Montojo, 2005; Robledo, 2011). To compensate, regulations were often very bureaucratic, and usually failed to pacify producers and reduce conflicts. Nevertheless, there is no reason to suppose that the new regulatory bodies would not have adapted with time, thereby expanding state capacity.

The cereal sector was the largest, and although a contemporary estimate that Spain had 2 million wheat farmers was just an exaggerated guess, cereal-legume rotations produced 28% of net farm output in 1930, more than other Western European countries (Montojo Sureda, 1945: 15; Simpson, 1995, Table 2.4; for Europe, O'Brien & Prados de la Escosura, 1992). From the late nineteenth century governments increased tariffs, and the country was virtually self-sufficient in wheat by the late 1920s. During the First World War 'maximum' prices were introduced for wheat, flour, and bread prices to protect urban consumers, but 'minimum' prices in the 1920s were used to help farmers, with governments passing numerous decrees to adapt to changing market conditions. However, governments lacked the necessary information on output and stocks, explaining the politically disastrous decision to allow imports of wheat to help depress high urban bread prices on the eve of the massive 1932 harvest, which turned out to be the country's largest to date. Politicians and economists debated the possibility of creating a vertically integrated organisation to 'manage' the wheat market but, as Rafael del Caño noted, the massive storage capacity and necessary technical and administrative systems required to operate it efficiently could not appear 'by magic' (Caño, 1933: 108). Government attempts at market intervention were widely criticised, and when they were ended in the spring of 1936, it was noted in the decree that neither the farmer had benefitted from a 'sufficiently profitable price' nor the consumer 'from cheap bread' (*Boletín del Instituto de Reforma Agraria*, abril 1936, 46: 414). It would be left to the Franco regime to implement the *Servicio Nacional del Trigo* as a state monopoly after 1937 (Barciela López, 1985).

Expanding the area irrigation was perhaps the only major policy area that was not controversial. The April 1934 law, *Obras de Puesta en Riego* aimed at extending irrigation in the Guadalquivir valley in Andalusia. The work was carried out by the state, but landowners had to pay the difference between the value of the land before and after the project was completed. Farmers who owned less than 10 hectares enjoyed special conditions for payment. The properties of those landowners who did not want to irrigate were expropriated, with compensation set at the prevailing price for dry-farming land. Small farmers received small, irrigated plots secured on a state backed mortgage. This experiment covered 64,000 hectares and was a model for much larger irrigation schemes in other parts of the country, although it was paralysed by budgetary restrictions, and by the Civil War after 1936.

5. Popular mobilisation, social coalitions, and agricultural policies

The Second Republic saw unprecedented rural mobilisation. There was a radical increase in both quantitative and qualitative terms of political expression of farmers and agricultural labourers, suggested by greater electoral participation, trade union membership number of strikes, producer associations, and other forms of collective action. Governments developed new institutions that favoured top-down mobilisation and, as Domenech has argued, this helped resolve the 'acute coordination and collective action problems of mobilizing rural labourers', benefitting especially the growth of the two great labour syndicates, the socialist FNTT and anarchist Confederación Nacional del Trabajo (CNT) (Domenech, 2013). However, spontaneous bottom-up organisations also appeared, as democratic expectations changed relations between citizens and politics. Landowners mobilised, creating new associations and collective strategies in their dealings with the unions and the left-wing parties.

The new Republican governments between 1931 and 1933 reshaped rural labour markets by increasing workers' bargaining power, by extending local authorities control over factor and commodity markets and establishing compulsory arbitration boards to review disputes. These changed the power relations between employers and the workforce, and greatly increased the number of conflicts. The arbitration boards often favoured organised labour, as the provincial representatives of the Ministry of Labour tended to appoint Socialist and republican mayors and pro-labour civil servants. However, after the centre-right won the 1933 November elections, the Ministry of Labour fell into their hands, and many Socialist local councils were suspended, and replaced by others closer to landowners and employers' interests. The gains that organised labour had achieved between 1931 and 1933 were quickly eroded, as farmers now felt free to ignore the labour legislation. Landowners feared a resurgence in trade union activities when the political pendulum moved against them once more following the victory of the Popular Front in February 1936.

Disputes were not limited to just those between the Socialist syndicates and employers. Anarchism had a long tradition in many rural districts of Andalusia and other parts of the country. They opposed the formally plural corporatist institutions in which class representatives were distributed among existing associations or unions in accordance with their membership, and instead favoured the direct election of local delegates by the working class who negotiated directly with the employers. Anarchists and their unions, grouped in the CNT, boycotted local elections, and refused to sit on the arbitration boards, rejecting their verdicts. Instead, they saw strikes and other forms of collective action as a way to prepare workers for the revolution, which would bring about the collapse of capitalism and the state. There were major disputes between anarchists and Socialists and, between anarchists and the local authorities, especially between 1931 and 1933.

Socio-political mobilisation easily triggered violence. Gil Andrés (2005: 69) suggests violence, and its threat, was the response of the voiceless, and in particular those who had little or no formal political channels to influence change. Levels of violence in Spanish society, especially in rural areas, had been relatively high even before the Republic, with violent deaths being constantly higher than 2.5 per 10.000 inhabitants in the 1920s (González Calleja, 2015). Political confrontations between 1931 and the first semester of 1936, before the beginning of the war, led to 2,629 deaths, with 44% of them occurring in municipalities with less than 10.000 inhabitants, although rural deaths were actually higher, given the large number of agro-towns with more than 10,000 inhabitants. According to González Calleja, the rural police (*Guardia Civil*) caused most deaths (51%), and among the victims whose political affiliation was known, half (50%) were socialists or anarchists. Whereas a new police force was created for the cities, the existing militarised rural police, which was unprepared to deal with the high levels of mobilisation that the new government encouraged, continued in the countryside. González Calleja (2015: 89) concludes that the security forces during the Republican period, tried to repress left-wing groups, especially anarchists, and defended employers' interests.

Violence increased tensions and exacerbated polarisation. Labour market regulation was the main source of conflicts, with waves of strikes in 1931, 1932, and 1933, coinciding with syndicates and employers bargaining over local employment conditions, especially those for the harvest. Conflicts between workers and employers were sometimes aggravated by the competition between rival syndicates to impose their hegemony. Labour market regulation raised costs for family farmers as well as for the large employers, as they often needed to hire workers at period of peak demand. Indeed, family farmers suffered doubly, as they not only had to pay higher wages to employ local workers, but they could not now find seasonal employment themselves in other villages. Even the use of unpaid family labour was theoretically forbidden if the person lived in another municipality.

The shortage of arable in areas of small tenant farmers was another source of conflict. In the areas of *dehesas* in Western Spain, especially in Extremadura, landless village farmers sublet small plots of land from large tenants who rented the estates for their winter pastures. Soil fertility was poor, implying that every few years the land was returned to pasture, and the subtenants given new contracts to cultivate different plots. The new government legislated to both reduce rents and to give priority to collectives of tenants to rent the land. Livestock producers were totally dependent on the winter pastures for their cattle and sheep, and the land invasions of 1932, and especially 1936, threated their livelihoods. Furthermore, because easily accessible land was in very short supply, conflicts arose over whether the Socialist syndicate, and the local farmers, should determine which group should have priority. While prices were stagnant or falling, wages were increasing, turning middle-sized farmers who had initially voted for the republican left or centre towards right-wing groups (Cobo, 2003).

The slowness of the land reform was the result both of the legal guarantees that allowed landowners to challenge the confiscation of their land and the lack of information, personnel and other resources in the Ministry of Agriculture. The delays caused by the legal processes inevitably produced deep resentment among the landless and near-landless. In many villages, in 1932, labourers and other small peasants occupied estates and tilled the land or worked in them and then asked to be paid. The government tried to channel collective action through a decree called of intensification, in November 1932, that enabled State technicians to declare a situation of 'severe working-class crisis' in a rural village (Malefakis, 1970; Riesco, 2006: ch. 4). If they did declare such situation, State agricultural engineers were allowed either to allocate labourers to landowners, who had to give them paid work, or to lease untilled land to unions, or to give plots in private estates to individual unemployed people. Landowners were to be compensated with rents fixed by State technicians, according to the value of the land in fiscal terms. This special solution could be applied in six Southern provinces, where unemployment was particularly serious. It ended up being an 'indirect' and provisional land reform that even a right-wing government accepted one final time in December 1934. When the left came back to power in 1936, intensification became an additional resource for the speeding up of the land reform.

6. Conclusion

The 1929 crisis was relatively mild in Spain, although exports suffered from the drop in international trade, while the use of 'official' prices hides the true extent of the weak domestic demand. For contemporaries, the wide range of economic policies that governments tried to implement were therefore identified with the reforming instincts of the Second Republic, rather than as attempts to combat the deflationary effects of the Depression. The new political elites had a vision of agriculture that had developed over the previous 30 years, and they believed that an ambitious reform programme was required to reduce land inequality, especially in the south, and rural poverty everywhere. Traditionally land inequality and poverty were considered as both social problems and the cause of technical backwardness in agriculture, but now they were also regarded as obstacles to the consolidation of democracy. To break this perverse cycle, a combination of policies that included land redistribution, the reorganisation of factor and commodity markets, and long-term planning for irrigation and technical transformation were required. As a result, the Republic created many public or quasi-public institutions to regulate markets, reorganised state-run institutions and hired more agronomists and veterinarians, and collected more and better statistical information. Had they been given more time, many of the flaws of land reform and the new regulatory institutions, which were often like those created in other Western European countries, might have been resolved better (Pan-Montojo, 2011, for the post 1939 period). Instead, a military coup d'état failed to oust the Government in July 1936. However, the Government could not put it down everywhere, and the situation gave birth to a long Civil War.

Yet there were also several important factors which hindered these reforms and contributed to the polarisation of the countryside. In the first instance, there were considerable problems associated with carrying out such complex reforms at a time when the numbers of workers were increasing, but the demand for labour was falling. Furthermore, contemporaries often failed to appreciate both the significant achievements of the sector over the previous three decades, *and* the weak state capacity that the Republic had inherited, and natural resource constraints to implement reforms. Not only had rapid economic growth before 1930 led to a rapid decline in the farm population, but agriculture productivity had increased significantly because of better farming techniques and market specialisation. In this context, the use of land reform as a short-run instrument to improve workers' living standards and respond to the problem of the international crisis must be questioned. In particular, the need to use dry-farming techniques severely limited the possibilities of raising labour productivity by creating more work through the elimination of seasonal unemployment. However, despite the desperate situation of many landless workers in the south, these had become numerically relatively small within the national economy. Spain by 1930 was a country of small farmers, who accounted for around a third of the electorate, while the latifundios contributed little more than 3% of GDP and employed only 5% of the country's labour force (Simpson and Carmona, 2020: 198).

As a result, governments had to resolve two very different, and contradictory, problems at the same time, namely market intervention to support farm prices to help the family farmers, and labour and land reforms to improve the living standards of landless workers. Higher farm prices were opposed by urban consumers and organised labour, while better work conditions hurt employers, including family farmers who needed to hire extra hands at peak periods. The attempts to resolve economic and social problems raised expectations, but the defects in their implementation led to frustration, and a polarisation of the countryside. What the agrarian reforms did achieve was to provide a focal point for farm groups to organise. Therefore, on the one hand labour syndicates, especially the socialist FNTT, provided the leadership and organisational capacity for farm workers to demand solutions to their grievances, and challenge governments over the slow speed in implementing reforms. On the other, landowners and certain groups of family farmers responded by overcoming their fragmented regional interests to provide a coherent platform to defend existing property rights, and Catholicism.

Notes

1 Almost 13% of bank deposits were withdrawn between the 1st April and the 30th of June 1931, and most probably taken abroad, and all investment indicators until 1934 showed negative tendencies (Palafox, 1991: 180-181).

2 Ministerio de Trabajo, 1934. The figures were 409,617 in 1934, 409,617, in 1935, 434,054, and 522,079 in the first semester of 1936. Almost 46.3 % of the total figure consist of 'partially unemployed' labourers, a category which is unclear.

Bibliography

Albertus, M., 2015, *Autocracy and redistribution. The politics of land reform*, Cambridge: Cambridge University Press.

Balcells, A., 1980, *El problema agrario en Cataluña. La cuestión Rabassaire.* Madrid: Ministerio de Agricultura.

Barciela, C., 1985, 'Intervencionismo y crecimiento agrario en España, 1936–1971', in P. Martín Aceña and L. Prados de la Escosura (eds), *La nueva historia económica en España*, Madrid: Editorial Tecnos.

Barciela López, C. and Giráldez, J., Grupo de Estudios de Historia Rural and López, I., 2005, 'Sector agrario y pesca', in A. Carrera and X. Tafunell (eds), *Estadísticas históricas de España*, Bilbao: Fundación BBVA, pp. 245–356.

Caño, R. del, 1933, *Producción y mercado del trigo*, Madrid: Rotativa.

Carmona, J., Rosés, J. and Simpson, J., 2019, 'The question of land access and the Spanish Land Reform of 1932', *The Economic History Review*, 72(2), pp. 669–90.

Carmona, J. and Simpson, J., 2016, 'Campesinos unidos o divididos? La acción colectiva y la revolución social de los *yunteros* durante la Segunda República en España (1931–1936)', *Historia Social*, 85, pp. 123–44.

Carmona, J. and Simpson, J., 2020, 'Cuando el rentista no es derrotado. El caso de la rabassa catalana, 1890–1936', Working Paper.

Carrión, P., 1932 (1975), *Los latifundios en España*. Madrid: Ariel.

Chatriot, A., Leblanc, E. and Lynch, E. (eds), 2012, *Organiser les marchés agricoles. Le temps des fondateurs*, París: Armand Colin.

Cobo Romero, F., 2003, *De Campesinos a Electores. Modernización agraria en Andalucía, politización campesina y derechización de los pequeños propietarios y arrendatarios. El caso de la provincia de Jaén, 1931–1936*, Madrid: Biblioteca Nueva.

Comín, F., 2010, 'La crisis internacional de 1929 y la economía española durante la Segunda República', in A. Furió (ed.), *Las crisis a lo largo de la historia*, Valladolid: Universidad de Valladolid, pp. 97–154.

Domenech, J., 2013, 'Rural labour markets and rural conflict in Spain before the Civil War (1931–36)', *Economic History Review*, 66, pp. 86–108.

Domenech, J. and Herreros, F., 2018, 'Land reform and conflict before Civil War. Landowner response to tenancy reform in 1930s Catalonia', *Economic History Review*, 71(4), pp. 1322–48.

Fernández Prieto, L., 1997, 'Selección de innovaciones en una agricultura atlántica de pequeñas explotaciones. Galicia, 1900–1936. La adopción de las trilladoras mecánicas', *Noticiario de Historia Agraria*, pp. 133–63.

GEHR, 1983, 'Notas sobre la producción agraria española, 1891–1931', *Revista de Historia Económica*, 1, pp.185–252.

Gil Andrés, C., 2005, '"A mano airada". La violencia en la protesta popular', in J. Muñoz Soro, J. L. Ledesma and J. Rodrigo (eds), *Culturas y políticas de la violencia. España, siglo XX*, Madrid: Seitemares, pp. 47–74.

González Calleja, E., 2015, *Cifras cruentas. Las victimas mortales de la violencia sociopolítica en la Segunda República española (1931–1936)*, Granada: Comares.

Koning, N., 2013, 'The evolution of farm policies: a long-term global perspective', in P. Moser and T. Varley (eds), *Integration through subordination. The politics of agricultural modernisation in industrial Europe*, Turnhout: Brepols, Rural History in Europe, 8, pp. 41–63.

Malefakis, E., 1970, *Agrarian reform and the peasant revolution in Spain: Origins of the civil war*, New Haven: Yale University Press.

Martín Aceña, P., 2005, 'La economía española en los años treinta', in S. Juliá (ed.), *República y Guerra Civil*, vol. XL of *Historia de España Menéndez Pidal*, directed by J. M. Jover Zamora, Madrid: Espasa Calpe, pp. 347–444.

Ministerio de Trabajo, 1934, *Estadísticas del paro involuntario en el segundo trimestre de 1933*, Madrid.

Montojo Sureda, J., 1945, *La política española sobre trigos y harinas (Años 1900–1945)*, Madrid: Afrodisio Aguado.

O'Brien, P. and Prados de la Escosura, L., 1992, 'Agricultural productivity and European industralization, 1890–1980', *Economic History Review*, 45, pp. 514–36.

Palafox Gámir, J., 1991, *Atraso económico y democracia: la Segunda República y la economía española, 1892–1936*, Barcelona: Editorial Crítica.

Pan-Montojo, J., 2005, *Apostolado, profesión y tecnología. Una historia de los ingenieros agrónomos en España*, Madrid: ANIA.

Pan-Montojo, J., 2011, 'Spanish agriculture, 1931–1955. Crisis, wars and new policies in the reshaping of rural society', in P. Brassley, Y. Segers and L. Van Molle (eds), *War, agriculture and food. Rural Europe from the 1930s to the 1950s*, New York: Routledge, pp. 75–95.

Prados de la Escosura, L., 2003, *El progreso económico*, Madrid: Fundación BBVA.

Riesco Roche, S., 2006, *La reforma agraria y los orígenes de la Guerra Civil (1931–1940)*, Madrid: Biblioteca Nueva.

Robledo, R., 2011, 'El Ministerio de Agricultura, 1931–1939', in R. Robledo (ed.), *Historia del Ministerio de Agricultura 1900–2008. Política agraria y pesquera de España*, Madrid: Ministerio de Medio Ambiente y Medio Rural y Marítimo, pp. 80–143.

Robledo, R., 2019, *Medio siglo del libro de Malefakis: en torno al origen de la Guerra Civil española*, DT 1914, AEHE (https://www.aehe.es/wp-content/uploads/2019/10/dt-aehe-1914.pdf).

Simpson, J., 1995, *Spanish agriculture: The long siesta, 1765–1965*, Cambridge: Cambridge University Press.
Simpson, J. and Carmona, J., 2017, 'Too many workers or not enough land? Why land reform fails in Spain during the 1930s', *Historia Agraria*, 72, pp.37–68.
Simpson, J. and Carmona, J., 2020, *Why democracy failed. The agrarian origins of the Spanish Civil War*, Cambridge: Cambridge University Press.
Spain. Ministerio de Agricultura, 1933, *Anuario estadístico de las producciones agrícolas. Año 1932*, Madrid.

12 Mexican agriculture in view of the crisis of the first globalization – Between the revolutionary crisis and the Great Depression (1914–29)

Alejandro Tortolero Villaseñor[1]

1. Introduction

Mexican agriculture, viewed by many authors as refractory to change and closed to markets after independence, underwent a number of changes in the first phase of globalization in the last third of the nineteenth century. By the end of the century, with the construction of an extensive rail network, Mexico became connected with the global economy and an internal market was taking shape. Agriculture no longer experienced the subsistence crises characterizing the eighteenth century and the classic picture of crisis, famine, epidemics, and starvation observed by Labrousse had been left behind (Labrousse, 1944). With the opening to markets, crises took on a different nature and prices became a major indicator of the situation in the countryside in hard times. My objective in this chapter is to show the changes brought about by two agricultural crises in Mexico, that of 1915 and the one ensuring from the Great Depression of 1929. In order to fully comprehend the changes stemming from the latter crisis, it is necessary to go back to the revolutionary crisis of 1915 since the agrarian reform policy then introduced would be later implemented more forcefully as a means to escape the brunt of the 1929 crisis. In short, the agrarian policy promoted in the third decade of the twentieth century cannot be understood without going back to earlier revolutionary demands.

Accordingly, I will show how strategies were adopted, ranging from increasing acreage cultivated by tenant farmers and sharecroppers, to breaking up the great estates and implementing an agrarian reform that was sometimes accompanied by strong commodity imports.

2. The revolutionary crisis

The Mexican Revolution was characterized by extreme violence. Mariano Azuela, a contemporary writer, likened the revolution to a hurricane. Numbers proved that this analogy was not literary excess on Azuela's part:

DOI: 10.4324/9781003105466-15

Mexico lost more than 2 million inhabitants. More than half of these people (65%) died because of battle, famine, and epidemics. A quarter of the people stemmed from 'lost births', and about 10% of the inhabitants who were lost inhabitants left the country because of the violence that took place (Knight, 2010: 487).

In short, what were the strategies that state leaders implemented to overcome the revolution's most critical periods between 1914 and 1915, and 1917, which people labelled 'the year of hunger'? I contend that survival for many Mexicans during the revolution cannot be attributed to happenstance. In 1978, John Womack argued that the most notable changes in farming and ranching during the revolution took place in northern Mexico, where the lizards and the buzzards retook their old pastures and where the weeds invaded growing fields. The northeast vigorously began farming commercial crops such as chickpeas and cotton. The south-central region traded in the cultivation of commercial crops for grasslands and subsistence crops like maize and beans. In 1915, harvests were poor throughout the country, with the overall volume dropping by about half. Large losses occurred in certain export crops like sugar and rice. Additionally, the number of head of cattle and other livestock such as goats and sheep also decreased. Nonetheless, the number of domestic animals increased (Womack, 1978: 33–45).

To be precise, I argue that the Mexican state instituted several then-unheard of measures to help people survive during the country's Civil War. Five of these stand out among methods of survival during the war. First, the state modified policies to facilitate imports of certain goods. Second, government officials confiscated harvests that belonged to *hacendados* in order to feed both the populace and combatants. Third, local state officials additionally implemented forced contributions, or levies to this treatment towards *hacendados*. Fourth, the state seized the holdings of landowning elites and administered their resources. And fifth, the state promoted technification and the use of fertilizers in the countryside in view of modernization to increase agricultural production (see Tortolero, 2016a).

Consequently, it can be safely stated that, despite the hurricane unleashed by the Mexican Revolution, the countryside endured and failed to collapse. There were, indeed, dark and dismal days marked by scarcity. But general depression is not the term that best portrays the Mexican countryside. If there was a one single feature that characterized rural Mexico during the decade of 1910, it was flexibility. It was this flexibility that enabled the country to withstand droughts and the violence of a catastrophic social conflict. This was largely due to the fact that much of the country remained uncultivated, with only 6% of the nation's territory under the plough. Furthermore, the hacienda, the most important form of property and agricultural exploitation in this period, was only partially engaged directly in farming. Large portions of hacienda land were rented out land to tenant farmers, farmed by sharecroppers, or simply left idle. During the most turbulent periods of the revolution, many of these idle lands were occupied and opened to cultivation.

Notwithstanding diverse forms of property in different regions, the *hacienda* represented the most common form of agricultural enterprise. Around 1910, there were about 8,431 *haciendas*, 48,635 *ranchos*, and some 7,000 indigenous communities in Mexico. The ranchos[2] are generally situated in lands that are unsuitable for larger holdings, they are small rural properties worked by the owner himself, with the aid of his family (McBride,1923: 84). The *hacendados* alone had the ability to supply domestic and foreign markets. Meanwhile, their smaller-scale cohorts engaged in farming for domestic consumption. Besides having the advantage of owning most of the land in the country, *hacendados* also held control of the most fertile land. On the eve of the revolution, 54% of the country was in the hands of large property owners, 20% owned by *rancheros*, and 6% held by *comunidades*. The remaining 20% was idle or, essentially not accounted for cultivation (Haber, Razo, and Maurer, 2003: 294).

With the exception of 1915 and 1917, this array of property types met the needs of Mexico's civil population and combatant forces during the Civil War. Furthermore, despite the absence of entirely credible data concerning the majority of Mexican agricultural products, we know that the most-commonly consumed items were maize and beans. Most of the indigenous and *ranchero* production units were for subsistence purposes, thus making it difficult to gain a clear picture from the archives (Haber, Razo and Maurer, 2003: 316). Around 1920, maize occupied 55% of the area cultivated, beans 17%, while 8% was dedicated to wheat (Zuleta, 2010: 461). The area sown in maize dropped during the Mexican Revolution, but production levels remained stable (about 2 million hectares harvested between 1912 and 1918). Production never dipped below 1 million metric tons. In fact, the 1920 harvest rose to pre-revolution levels and totalled nearly 2 million metric tons. In 1917, the worst year on record, maize consumption declined to 86.61 kilograms per capita an amount not enough to maintain a family. Previously, in 1916 the figure was 224 kilograms, and in 1914, one of worst years of the revolution, per capita consumption was 131 kilograms. During the *Porfiriato*[3], particularly in 1894, 184 kilograms of maize per capita were produced, while in 1907, this figure was 144 kilograms. With the exception of 1917, the decrease suggests that per capita maize production during the period was not below *Pax-Porfirista* levels. Evidenced by the fact that average US maize imports to Mexico did not increase significantly, it appears that this production volume was sufficient to supply both non-belligerent Mexicans and warring parties.

These statistics were telling. Between 1911 and 1920, 485,325 metric tons of maize were imported, compared to 573,975 metric tons imported in the 17 years prior to the Mexican Revolution (1894–1910). These figures indicate that an average of 33,763 metric tons were imported annually during the *Porfiriato*, while during the revolution maize imports increased to annual average 48,532 metric tons. Though a notable increase, the numbers, perhaps, do not tell the full story about the imports of the country's most important grain. The numbers appear in a different light when considering that in 1911, when maize imports grew to 41,666 tons, Porfirio Díaz was in power for almost half the year. If we assign 1911 maize imports to the Díaz regime, imports during the Mexican Revolution fall to 34,366 tons per year. It could thus be plausibly argued that Mexico imported more maize during the *Porfiriato* than during the revolution. One could also note that revolutionary-era imports mirrored *Porfiriato*-era numbers with peaks in 1916 (76,400 tons) and 1918 (66,825 tons).

The story is much the same for bean imports. The area dedicated to bean cultivation stood at more than 800,000 hectares in 1909 and five years later, during the revolution, the figure dropped to 476,315 hectares. Subsequently, there was a steady increase in acreage reaching a peak in 1918 with 721,203 hectares. A similar trend was seen in production levels: bean production rose from a high of 170,000 metric tons in 1910 to a low of 90,500 metric tons four years later. Thereafter levels gradually increased to 120,000 metric tons until the end of the Mexican Revolution. Bean production during the *Porfiriato* reached its height in 1877, with 210,068 metric tons. In 1907, 159,170 metric tons were produced. If we agree with Coatsworth's assertion that 1877 statistics are biased and that these numbers appear inflated when compared to those previously recorded, it can then be seen that, with the exception of 1914, bean production was greater during the revolution than in the Porfirio Díaz era.

The earliest statistics on bean imports from the United States date from 1905, when 3,294 metric tons arrived south of the Rio Grande. This number tripled to 9,909 metric tons in 1914 and increased nearly fourfold to 11,124 metric tons in 1915. With the exception of 1917, the '*año del hambre*' (the year of hunger), when 3,888 metric tons were imported, there are no records of other imports. Such numbers are surprising when held against Díaz-era imports. Mexico brought in about 2,360 metric tons of beans annually during the *Porfiriato*. This volume rose 18% between 1911 and 1920 when annual imports of 2,877 metric tons were reported, not a significant increase when placed in the context of the Civil War. These numbers indicate that Mexico imported beans only during the harshest years of the war, and not significant volumes outside these years.

The numbers for the peasants' major subsistence crops suggest that Mexicans found ways for making the countryside respond to wartime needs. This claim holds true if we examine sugarcane production. If we assume that sugarcane was the primary crop grown in the state of Morelos, which was home to the most definitive peasant uprising in the country, we find trends similar to those for maize and beans. For example, at the height of the Zapatista movement in 1915[4], sugarcane production reached a high of 2,424,123 metric tons, and the harvest was sufficient for exports to the United States. The Zapatistas succeeded in putting eight mills back into production. In 1916–17, however, the Carrancistas[5] closed this production and the expansion of sugar production was a product of migration to new areas of the country (Haber, Razo and Maurer, 2003: 331). Farmers maintained these high levels of production and exports through 1920. Furthermore, other states such as Veracruz and Sinaloa continued to export in later years.

Mexican agriculture, in fact, underwent serious contractions during the critical war years only. I think we can agree with those authors who have suggested that during the revolution the agricultural sector should not be described in depression-like terms. In the '*etapa armada*' (the armed stage) of the revolution agricultural output was severely affected, but this period was followed by a strong rebound. In fact, harvests of some crops, such as sugar cane, showed sufficient surpluses for export. But perhaps the more important fact is that, even with the disruptions of war and conflicts regarding land ownership and tenure that reigned throughout Mexico, export levels did not fall (Zuleta and Marino, 2010: 459). Notable increases in acreage and export levels were recorded for crops such as chickpeas, tomatoes, coffee, vanilla, and above all, sisal. The same cannot not be said about livestock – about half of domestic cattle herds were destroyed between 1910 and 1920 (Lopes, 2008: 865). Exports of leather and skins fell substantially after 1913 and did not recover until 1922.

What we are seeing in terms of Mexican agriculture during the revolution seems counterintuitive to what might be assumed. During the most critical periods of the Civil War, between 1914 and 1916, Mexican government officials mandated temporary decrees that modified certain quotas or allowed certain duty exemptions to increase the supply of basic foods, substitute the loss of certain harvests, and ease scarcity. These measures involved several basic food items – maize, butter, sugar, grains, flour, etc. – and other consumer goods such as soap, cotton, and certain fibres (Kuntz, 2010: 236–7).

If the revolution had failed to produce a collapse of the Mexican countryside, this was largely due to the fact that the main unit of production, the hacienda, continued to produce much the same as it had done during the Porfirian era. The haciendas were able to sustain population increases and even produce surpluses for export, as in the case of sisal, coffee, vanilla, and some other crops. The other important fact helping to avoid collapse was subsistence agriculture as will be explained later in this article.

In spite of the fact that the hacendados were constantly threatened by a peasant struggle that had raised the principles of the restitution of lands to the people usurped by the hacienda as in the Zapatista territory of Morelos, and even when the legislation of 1915 and the constitution of 1917 in its article 27 became powerful incentives for agrarian reform and peasant protest, in reality, except in isolated case such as Morelos or Veracruz, large farms continued to control a large part of production and Mexican territory in the years following the armed struggle.

3. The crisis of 1929

Consequently, output of the major items produce for domestic consumption did not decline in the 1920s. Nearly 3 million hectares were cropped in corn, the main item of domestic consumption, a figure that remained practically unchanged throughout the decade. Land cropped in beans, on the other hand, declined by almost a third, decreasing from 1.1 million hectares in 1920 to 709,560 in 1930. Wheat acreage also contracted, dropping from 800,320 hectares to 489,772 in the same timeframe.

Corn production remained relatively stable in the decade: 2.3 million metric tons were produced in 1920, 2.1 in 1927, 2.2 in 1928, and 1.5 in 1929. The decline in 1929 was more the result of poor weather than the world crisis, and the following year output rebounded and reached 2.1 in 1931 and 2.0 metric tons in 1932. Except for declines reported in 1924, 1929 and 1930, when output was similar to the years of the violent revolutionary crisis of 1914/15, and when less than 100,000 metric tons were produced, in the remaining years the harvest surpassed 100,000 metric tons and reached a record 185,000 metric tons in 1933. As shown in Figure 12.1, bean production always exceeded 100,000 metric tons between 1909 and 1939, except for the short periods of crisis in 1914/15 and 1929/30. Except for the crisis of 1914/1915, the wheat harvest did not experience sharp declines. The minimum recorded was 119, 000 metric tons in 1914, which more than tripled in 1929 with a production of 366,000 metric tons; throughout the 1930s output never dropped below 300,000 metric tons.

The products included in Figure 12.2 are corn, beans, rice, coffee, dried chilli peppers, wheat, chickpeas, tomatoes, cotton, sisal, sugar cane, bananas, oranges, and alfalfa. This figure shows that there were two peaks in the indices of overall agricultural production between 1893 and 1944, the four-year period between 1907 and 1910 and in 1941–4. The 1929 crisis was of very short duration. There was a notable rise in production in 1931 and by 1935 this recovery was sustained until reaching the maximum levels in 1944.

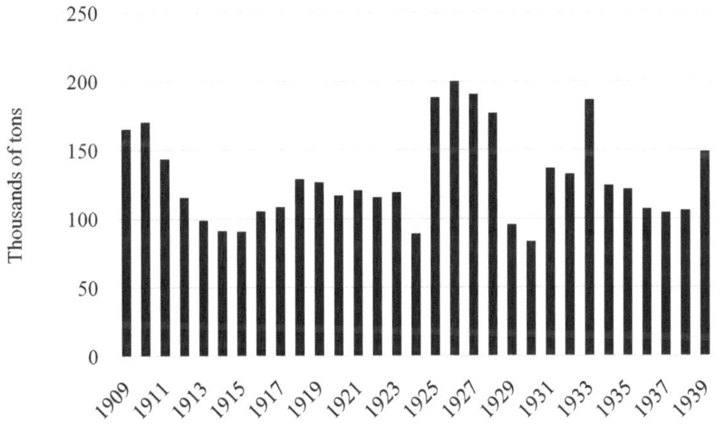

Figure 12.1 Bean production (1909–39).

Source: Estadísticas Históricas de México, México, Instituto Nacional de Estadística y Geografía (INEGI).

Figure 12.2 Overall agriculture production, 1893–1944.

Source: Estadísticas Históricas de México, México, Instituto Nacional de Estadística y Geografía (INEGI).

Another relevant fact is that output in the 1920s did not surpass figures for the Porfiriato, meaning that land distribution of the first years of the revolution had no repercussion on agricultural production.

The countryside in fact served as a sort of a sponge that absorbed unemployment and offset the decline in the urban economy and industrial exports (Knight, 2014: 283). Two thirds of the rural population resided in small communities of less than 2,500 inhabitants, lived on a diet of corn and beans, depended on subsistence agriculture and sometimes engaged in commercial agriculture for local markets. While the 1929 crisis dealt a severe blow to haciendas producing for export markets, the subsistence agriculture sector was left practically untouched. As Table 12.1 shows, the countryside, on the whole, was little affected.

Table 12.1 Indices of agricultural production value, 1928–35. *Indices 1930 = 100*

Années	*Index*
1928	121
1929	110
1930	100
1931	116
1932	112
1933	129
1934	118
1935	127

Source: Solís, L., 1973: 91 and Meyer, L., 1978: 203.

So satisfactory was the situation in the countryside that, towards the end of the 1920s, the revolutionary governments asserted that it was necessary to continue with the development plans of the victorious generals of the North who viewed entrepreneurial agriculture as the best lever to lift rural Mexico out of its relative inertia. The government began to emphasize that the ejido established by the revolution was not sufficiently productive[6]. People awarded ejidos in the modern era farm them individually in parcels and collectively maintain communal holdings with government oversight. After the Mexican Revolution, *ejidos* were created by the Mexican state to grant lands to peasant communities as a means to stem social unrest. The awarding of ejidos made peasants dependent on the government, with the creation of a bureaucracy to register and regulate them through the National Agrarian Registry (*Registro Agrario Nacional*).

According to the 1930 census figures, 57.4% of ejido land was planted and harvested, compared to 48.3% of the land in private hands. In the case of crops such as corn and sugarcane, the yield per unit was slightly higher in the ejido than in private agriculture, but the opposite occurred with beans and wheat. In short, the productivity of land had not changed much, but it was also noted that the ejido was at a disadvantage due to its lack of capital. In 1930, ejidos contributed 10.7% of the total value of agricultural production, but only possessed 1.8% of tractors, 0.4% of fixed engines, 3.4% of trucks, and 3.3% of harvesters. *Ejidatarios* were better equipped only with ploughs, accounting for 18.7% of the total. Consequently, it was the labour-intensive use of land that explained the slight competitiveness of the ejido compared to private property (Meyer, 1978: 194).

Faced with this situation, the press, the landowners, the old victorious generals of the revolution, and above all, former President Calles, the 'Jefe Máximo' who continued to wield considerable power behind the scenes during 1928–34, supported the end of the agrarian reform and the creation of new ejidos. In March 1930, a meeting of the presidential cabinet was convened, and Calles – who was present – advocated for the end of land distribution 'which was causing so much harm to the national economy' (Portes Gil, 1964: 216). In June 1930, a newspaper published the following statement by Calles,

> If we want to be honest with ourselves, we, the sons of the Revolution, have an obligation to confess that agrarianism, as we have understood and practiced it so far, is a failure. The happiness of rural men does not consist in giving them a piece of land, if they lack the preparation and the necessary means to cultivate it. So far we have been giving out land left and right, without producing more than a terrible commitment for the Nation. It is necessary to put a stop our failures.
>
> (Whetten, 1953: 101)

The leader of the revolution was seconded by the American ambassador who with great optimism viewed the new administration as having a 'healthy' point of view regarding the agrarian problem. Joining him, Jean Périer, the French ambassador in Mexico, pointed out in November 1929 that it was a pipe dream to think that agrarian reform would aid in the economic emancipation of the peasantry. In his own words:

> il est réellement chimérique de penser comme le fait ou affecte de le croire le Gouvernement mexicain que l'émancipation économique des paysans, si juste en son principe, se fera en confisquant d'une part 7 millions et demi d'hectares de terrains des grandes domaines et en donnant de l'autre à chaque 'ejidatario' 727 pesos de terres sans lui fournir en même temps ni outils agricoles, ni semences, ni animaux, ni même capital, si modeste fut-il, sans lesquels il ne pourra rien tirer de la terre qui lui a été répartie[7].

At the same time, the national press advocated a halt in land distribution. Thus, the circle seemed to be closing for the agrarian reform that had neither increased the harvested area, nor the production or yield of the country's main crops. In this context, the alternative policy of entrepreneurial agrarianism, as practised by the victorious generals of the revolutionary North, seemed to be the option.

But just when these voices were being raised, the Great Depression of 1929 entered into the picture and plans quickly changed. The crisis triggered a massive deportation of 300,000 Mexican migrant field workers from the United States. While in Mexico the countryside became a sponge that absorbed Mexican migrants expelled from the United States, other countries responded by deporting foreigners. In 1937, Cuba carried out mass expulsions of labourers from Haiti, Jamaica and the British West Indies, and in the Dominican Republic, Haitian workers were expelled or killed. The mass arrival of European immigrants in Argentina and neighbouring South American countries came to a halt (Knight, 2014: 305).

Between 1928 and 1932 the value of exports plummeted 63%. Although the export sector accounted for only 12% of Mexico's GDP, since most of its exports were to the United States the country had become increasingly dependent on the vagaries of the economy of its northern neighbour. The earthquake that shook Wall Street set off a tsunami that, to a greater or lesser extent, hit Latin America. At the same time Mexican exports fell by 63%, between 1928 and 1932, exports from Brazil dropped 44%, Argentina 40%, and Chile 83%. However, the weight of exports in GDP was higher in Argentina (27%) and Chile (30%) (Knight, 2015: 272–4). To alleviate the crisis Mexican authorities adopted two fundamental measures. The most important was to continue with an agrarian reform that only recently had been seen at the end of its rope while, at the same time, establishing trade agreements to favour exports (see Riguzi, 2003).

4. The Agrarian reform

Although many Latin American countries adopted labour reform and other measures of state intervention to allay the effects of the crisis, Mexico is unique in its agrarian reform policy. In countries such as Chile, labour reforms were fundamental in the face of the massive dismissal of workers linked to the export sector, such as the 50,000 nitrate workers dismissed in 1932 and the decline of the mining industry (Drinot and Knight, 2014: 10)[8].

In Mexico reform measures went far beyond the nationalist policies adopted by other Latin American countries and focussed on the redistribution of land that, in the view of critics of the Porfiriato, was monopolized by large landowners. While in other countries there was a perception that large foreign companies held enormous power and that it was up to the state to protect the peasants from them, in Mexico the powerful role of companies such as the United Fruit Co (UFCO) was minimal[9]. In Cuba, the 'colonos', the most Cuban of social classes, received from the state security in the possession of the land, control over the rents, and priorities in the allocation of quotas before the fall of the large American companies that go from producing the 30% of cane in 1930 to 10% in 1948. Mostly small-scale sugar cane producers, allowed to occupy land of estates, under the condition that they sell their output to the owners for processing in their sugarhouses. In the Dominican Republic, General Trujillo also favoured domestic producers over foreign firms, citing Cuba as a perverse example of antinational landlordism; 30,000 Haitians suffered from deportations and killings (Knight, 2014: 303–5). In Mexico, on the other hand, although Porfirio Diaz's vacant land legislation had left the door open to American companies at the end of the nineteenth century, the penetration of large foreign agricultural firms had been limited and large holdings were clearly rooted in Spanish colonization. Between January 1927 and October 1940, 319 individuals and North American companies, owners of about 2.5 million hectares (6.2 million acres), lost their land because of the agrarian reform in the northern states of Sonora and Baja California. This amount is similar to the properties held by Luis Terrazas, the largest landholder in Chihuahua during the Porfiriato (Dwyer, 2008: 1).

Departing from the reality of the Mexican countryside, with its varying and highly diverse agrarian structures depending on the region, a unitary view was constructed of a rural scene dominated by inefficient haciendas, with owners more interested in domination than in agriculture (Tortolero, 2016b). Agrarianism emerged as one of the fundamental pillars on which Mexican party politics was built in the twentieth century, and twentieth-century Mexico cannot be understood without the populist policies of its one-party state (Partido Revolucionario Institucional) with its peasant confederations and land redistribution policy.

This political configuration was based on the necessary assumption that the Mexican hacienda was the main cause of the country's backwardness. It was built on the idea of the lordship of the hacendado with supreme authority who governed at will, who was the owner of the life and labour of the workers, and who monopolized the land at the expense of neighbouring towns. This was the view that prepared way for the agrarian reform, first outlined by Luis Cabrera with his agrarian law of January 6, 1915, and later enshrined in Article 27 of the 1917 Constitution. It should be recalled that in 1912, Cabrera, in addition to reviving interest in the book authored by his friend Molina Enríquez, adopted his diagnosis when he wrote:

> The real agrarian problem consists of giving out land to the hundreds of thousands of dispossessed pariahs. It is necessary to distribute land, not to individuals, but to social groups. to free the villages from the economic and political pressure exerted on them by the haciendas within whose boundaries the proletarians are held as prisoners.
>
> (Cabrera, 1913: 11)

Within this institutional framework an agrarian reform was carried out with several variants appearing over the course of the twentieth century but whose basis was the constitutional principle assigning the original ownership of lands and waters to the Mexican Nation, which could transmit domain to individuals according to the dictates of the public interest.

The basic formula adopted to distribute the land, from the beginning to the end, was to restitute or endow the communities (not individuals) with land and water as a communal resource, albeit, in most cases, with individual usufruct and exploitation. Marte R. Gómez, one of the most important agronomists of the twentieth century and a public official in charge of the Ministry of Agriculture between 1940 and 1946, affirmed without hesitation that since the Ayala Plan: 'agrarian agitation and rural malaise are not to be combatted by denying lands; they are will be ended by giving land to all those demand and need them' (Gómez, 1953: 21). Prior to the 1992 reform, the communal land of the people, known as the ejido, could not be sold or mortgaged. The beneficiaries were obligated to cultivate their lands or, otherwise, face loss of their rights.

Arising from a curious blend of positivist and anarchist thought, along with the idea of restoring Mexico's pre-Hispanic past, the ejido has exerted enormous influence since 1912. When the first relevant legislation was enacted, it emerged as the key element of agrarian policy (Tortolero, 2016b: 78–80). In principle, following the law of January 6, 1915, it was assumed that the lands usurped by the hacienda would be restored to the peasants. The law's purpose was thus restitution and the distributive aspect was of secondary interest. However, either due to misplaced title deeds (or their nonexistence) of the communities or because of their inability to prove usurpations, the restitutive soon gave way to the distributive. By 1940, only 159 ejidos had recovered 1,723,321 hectares on the grounds of usurpation, and the vast majority were created through endowment of land expropriated from large landholders. Under the Agrarian Code it was established that 8 hectares of non-irrigated land or 4 hectares of land under irrigation would be allotted to each household head.

It was initially thought that land belonging to the federal government would be distributed. Small plots of communal and vacant lands would be farmed by peasants to meet their subsistence needs under a measure that was not a major break with the hacienda system. The ejido thus weakened dependence on the hacienda without abolishing it. Accordingly, the two systems coexisted until 1934 when, under Cárdenas, an offense against the hacienda was launched.

Generally speaking, hacienda lands had been safe from expropriation until at least 1930, indeed the 1930 census shows that 83% of the arable land consisted of holdings larger than 1,000 hectares. These farms were owned by 1.5% of total landholders. An additional 12% of the land was concentrated in farms ranging from 101 to 1,000 hectares (Haber, Razo and Maurer, 2003: 313). There are several reasons for this.

First, in some states, the Villista model of administering haciendas confiscated by revolutionary soldiers was put into practice. The villistas appropriated land owned by the *hacendados* and redistributed the money generated by the *haciendas* to fund military efforts and the pensions of citizens who had lost family members in the revolution. Villa also decreed that after the completion of the revolution the land would be redistributed, away from the hands of the oligarchy, to revolutionary veterans, former owners of the land from before the *hacendados* took the land, and the state itself in equal parts (Katz, 1998: 229–52). This was particularly true in Sonora under Carrancista control, as well as in Durango and Zacatecas, and to a lesser extent, in San Luis Potosi (Haber, Razo and Maurer, 2003: 301).

Second, the revolutionary generals forged an alliance with former landowners as they received large sums of money in exchange for 'protection' (Gruening, 1928: 319). This occurred only when the revolutionary generals themselves did not become owners of haciendas. Villa himself became the owner of the Hacienda de Canutillo. Alvaro Obregón became an exporter of chickpeas and a large property owner in Sonora. Plutarco Elías Calles became the owner of sugar estates in El Mante. Even lesser figures such as General Guadalupe Sánchez in Veracruz, acquired sugar estates in Córdoba, Jalapa and Orizaba.

Third, so as not to dismantle the productive apparatus in a period of instability, breaking up of large holdings was avoided. The Mexican countryside apparently responded to the demands of domestic and foreign markets during the revolutionary period, due, in large part, to the alliance between the military and former owners to prevent dismantling of the hacienda. This is the position of Haber, Razo and Maurer based on the evidence from exports of agricultural products to the United States. Mexico increased its exports of coffee, bananas, seasonal vegetables and, for the first time, it became a net exporter of sugar and cotton. Only sisal declined, not due to problems of the Yucatecan landowners, but from Asian and African competition. Corn, beans and produce for internal consumption do not seem to have undergone major changes, either. There were no massive imports of any these products from the United States and Mexico was a net exporter of beans (Haber, Razo and Maurer, 2003: 349.

Fourth, former landowners resorted to a variety of forms of resistance to preserve their properties. For example, they filed suit against legal resolutions; they formed alliances with priests, village caciques, and rural teachers to intimidate or persuade those seeking land reform to desist in their demands; they used armed force, threats, simulations, ruses, or feigned division and sales of land to small holders to delay the break-up of their property; and they colluded with governors, judges, and municipal presidents to slow down land distribution procedures (Mendoza, 2010: 45). The legal procedures were so slow-moving and complex that it became necessary for those seeking land to join movements and show loyalty to their leaders. The *agraristas* became, according to some landowners, heads of 'political cattle herds' and servants of the different agrarian committees and agencies (Martínez del Río, 1937: 58). For Semo, this is the great defeat of Mexican agrarianism: 'We must not forget that the post-revolutionary governments built their dominion and legitimacy on a corporate pact in which the peasants received land in exchange for ceding political power to the rulers' (Semo, 2012: 600).

The ulterior motive was political incorporation. Revolutionary generals first agreed to land reform, not by conviction, but to quell rebellions and agrarian agitation, and later to buy the loyalty of incipient peasant organizations in the context of considerable internal power struggles and intrigues. In this we are in agreement with Kouri (2010: 106–8).

All of this, however, was disrupted by the crisis of 1929. The massive repatriation of Mexicans from the United States and the fall of exports triggered changes in legislation. In 1931, landowners were stripped of the legal instrument of the *amparo* law and could no longer block presidential resolutions on restitution or endowment. *Amparo* literally means 'protection' in Spanish, Mexico's '*recurso de amparo*' is found in Articles 103 and 107 of the Mexican constitution – the judicial review of governmental action – to empower state courts to protect individuals against state abuses. As the corporatist policy of the regime became entrenched, the power of the landowners was transferred to the leaders and officials who emerged from the revolution. All of these factors served to accelerate land distribution.

Between 1915 and 1934, the average land area allotted by presidential resolutions was either 1.1 hectares of irrigated land or 2.2 hectares of non-irrigated acreage and benefitted 866,000 peasants, 27.8% of the total. In contrast, between 1934 and 1940, under the administration of President Cardenas, the average rose to 3.6 hectares of irrigation or 7.2 hectares of non-irrigated acreage for 729,000 recipients of land. Until 1935, the area affected by the agrarian reform was 10.8 million hectares, of which 2.8 million corresponded to cultivated land, distributed among 545,000 families, that is, an average of 5 hectares per family (Archives Historiques du Crédit Lyonnais, DEEF.73437.2, Mexico, 1934). Under Cárdenas more than

17 million hectares were distributed, allotted to 814 537 ejido farms. The agrarian reform had little effect in states such as Nayarit, Puebla, Quintana Roo, Tabasco, Tlaxcala, Colima, Chiapas, Federal District, Baja California, and Aguascalientes.

Had the 1929 crisis not occurred, agrarian policy would have looked much more like northern entrepreneurial agriculture than the distribution approach adopted under Cárdenas. The hacendados were dealt a death blow during his presidency through an agrarian policy implemented with the firm resolution on the part of the State. State participation in the economy increased throughout Latin America state in response to the crisis of 1929. In Mexico, for example, it went from 4.1% of GDP in 1920, to 6.0 in 1930 and 7.4 in 1940 (Knight, 2014: 301). It is then, in 1937, that the comparison wielded by Pablo Martínez del Río rang true. He, one of the most important *hacendados* in Porfirista Mexico, compared the sufferings of Mexican land-owners due to the carving up of their holdings to those of the victims of the punishment meted out to Chinese parricides. In his own words:

> In China a special ordeal was reserved for parricide. The guilty party was tied to a stake and the executioner stood in front of him with a large basket filled with knives. Each knife had a character designating a part of the body, nose, chest, ears, etc. The executioner took each knive at random, read the character and then proceeded to use the knife to sever the relevant body part. Soon, needless to say, the prisoner lost all human semblance. But how many times, when talking with a landowner friend about the last 'affectation' he had suffered, I recalled the terrible picture of that horrific vivisection of that hapless Chinaman!.
>
> (Martinez del Río, 1938: 10)

The result is eloquent: between 1920 and 1964 Mexico's post-revolutionary governments distributed 53 million hectares, equivalent to 26.8% of the country's total under cultivation. Previously, between 1853 and 1909, 51.1 million hectares, some 26% of the country's agricultural area had passed into the hands of private holders (Semo, 2012: 602). While in the nineteenth century the main beneficiaries of land transfer were large landowners, in the twentieth century, it was the peasants. These peasant *ejidatarios* were, accordingly, the result of the 1929 crisis.

5. Concluding remarks

GDP figures provide an indicator of this change. While between 1870 and 1895 it had grown at an annual rate of 2.1%, the annual increase was 2.7% between 1895 and 1910. Following the revolution, between 1926 and 1940, it fell to 1.2% (Haber, Razo and Maurer, 2003: 42). The share of agriculture in the GDP decreased from 24% in 1910 to 19.7% in 1926 and, finally, to 19.4% in 1940. Countries not having revolutions experienced faster growth than

Mexico. Venezuela reported annual growth at 4.9%, Colombia 4.3%, Brazil 3.6%, Peru and Chile 2.6%, Argentina 2.4%, and Uruguay 2.2% (Moreno-Brid and Ross, 2009: 92).

Thus, the share of the rural sector in economic growth had not increased as a consequence of land redistribution. Quite the contrary, while growth of Mexico's GDP during the Porfiriato was much greater than countries such as Brazil or Uruguay and almost as much as Spain's per capita rate, this trend was reversed with the revolution. In Latin America, although it fell short of Argentina's golden age, it was superior to that of Uruguay and much better than that of Brazil, as a fraction of US per capita GDP, Mexico's income per capita moved from less than 28% to 34%, and, with respect to Western Europe, relative per capita GDP increased from about 32% to 50%. Performance compared to Spain´s was particularly impressive. By 1910, Mexico's per capita GDP was nearly 90% of the Spanish level (compared to 56% in 1870) (Moreno-Brid and Ross, 2009: 59). Modernization of agriculture during the Porfiriato, with its technological packages bringing together machinery, credit, and labour, resulted in greater increases in productivity than the revolutionary agrarian reform, which was posited on the assumption that, with land redistribution, everything else would take care of itself.

This assumption was maintained, not only in Mexico but throughout Latin America, that with land redistribution, agricultural output, a necessary factor to accelerate economic growth, would improve. The reform would thus make it possible to balance income distribution, increase consumption by the peasant masses, invigorate the internal market and integrate the most excluded sectors of the social fabric by making them landowners (see Bretón, 2007: 487). Actually, following institutional economics, the fact that some accumulated at the expense of others would negatively affect society as a whole and is, according to North, one of the main reasons that explains the persisting backwardness of some societies (Gallego, 2007: 36). Accordingly, an agrarian reform would be the condition for overcoming this lag, that is, the establishment of a pact to redistribute land and wealth. However, until 1980, in the first stage of Mexico's agrarian reform, reducing social inequality was a greater priority than increasing productivity. This led to a second wave of agrarian reforms beginning in the 1980s, in which the market was held to be the only economic actor capable of efficiently allocating resources. This occurred not only in Mexico, but in all of Latin America, where, ultimately, agrarian reform had generated disparities.

Unlike in East Asia, its results were more negative than positive. Breton point out that, 'the fact is that the non-reformed sector of agriculture kept the best land and monopolized most of the services (such as credit, infrastructure or irrigation) destined for agriculture' (Bretón, 2007: 488). Elisa Botella agrees when she concludes, that in Latin America, in general, the agrarian reform processes were unsuccessful from both the economic, social, and political point of view, in different degrees, according to the countries (Botella, 2007: 51). For an agrarian reform to be positive, Simpson and

Carmona point out that the endowment of land is never enough if it is not accompanied by the promotion of research (especially in biology, high-yield technology), the price guarantees for produce grown in small farms, the adoption of agricultural extension policies, the development of public irrigation systems, the creation of credit programmes specifically aimed at small farms, and institutional policies that encourage the organization of small producers (cooperatives, rural workers' unions, agrarian associations) (Carmona and Simpson, 2007: 345).

Notwithstanding, not only in Mexico, but in other Latin American countries, agrarian reform consolidated the advancement of the family economy: some 50% of Mexican families benefitted from land distribution, a percentage in Latin American surpassed only by Bolivia[10].

Archives

Archives Historiques du Crédit Lyonnais (Historical Archives of Crédit Lyonnais)

Archives du Ministère des Affaires Etrangères, France (Archives of the Ministry of Foreign Affairs, France)

Archives de la Banque Nationale de Paris-Banque de Paribas.

Notes

1 The author would like to thank Dr. David Robichaux for the English translation.

2 The *ranchos* are agricultural farms within a *latifundium*, or a farm much smaller than a hacienda.

3 Period of Porfirio Diaz's presidency of Mexico (1876–80; 1884–1911).

4 Agrarian movement whose leader was Emiliano Zapata Salazar in the Mexican Revolution of 1910–1920.

5 The Carrancistas were followers of the Mexican president Venustiano Carranza (1917-1920) who consisted of mainly middle class urbanities, liberals, and intellectuals who desired a constitution for Mexico.

6 An *ejido* is an area of communal land used for agriculture in which community members have usufruct rights rather than ownership rights to land, which in Mexico is held by the Mexican state.

7 'It is unrealistic to think, as the Mexican government did – or would have one to believe – that the economic emancipation of the country's peasants, despite its just principle, would be achieved by confiscating seven and a half million hectares from large landowners and endowing each *ejidatario* with 727 pesos worth of land, without providing the farm implements, seed, animals, or even a modest capital, indispensable for the distributed land to bear fruit'. Archives du Ministère des Affaires, France. M. Jean Perier, Ministre de la République Française au Mexique à son excellence Monsieur Aristide Briand, Président du Conseil Ministre des Affaires Etrangères. Mexico le 6 novembre 1929.

8 Vargas in Brazil, Batista in Cuba, and even Somoza in Nicaragua, undertook labour reforms, see Knight, 2015: 298.

9 For the importance of the United Fruit Company in Central America, see Solouri, 2006.

10 Breton mentions that, up to 1970, 42.9% of families and 52.45% of domestic production units benefitted from agrarian reform. The figures for Bolivia they were 74.5% and 78.9% respectively (Breton, 2007: 489).

Bibliography

Botella, E., 2007, 'Reforma agraria, desarrollo rural y agricultura sostenible en América Latina bajo el contexto de la globalización', in R. Robledo and S. López (eds), *Interés particular, bienestar público? Grandes patrimonios y reforma agraria*, Zaragoza: Prensas Universitarias de Zaragoza, pp. 503–34.

Bretón, V., 2007, 'Mas allá de la 'nueva ruralidad': repensar la reforma agraria en América Latina', in R. Robledo and S. López (eds), *Interés particular, bienestar público? Grandes patrimonios y reforma agraria*, Zaragoza: Prensas Universitarias de Zaragoza, pp. 485–502.

Cabrera, L., 1913, *Reconstitución de los ejidos de los pueblos como medio de suprimir el esclavismo del jornalero mexicano*, México; Tip. F. Soria.

Carmona, J. and Simpson, J., 2007, 'Economías de escala, organización de patrimonios y obstáculos a una reforma agraria, Andalucía, 1880–1936', in R. Robledo and S. López (eds), *Interés particular, bienestar público? Grandes patrimonios y reforma agraria*, Zaragoza: Prensas Universitarias de Zaragoza, pp. 343–62.

Drinot, P. and Knight, A. (eds), 2014, *The Great depression in Latin America*, Durham, NC: Duke University Press.

Dwyer, J., 2008, *The agrarian dispute: The expropriation of American-owned rural land in postrevolutionary Mexico*, Durham, NC: Duke University Press.

Estadísticas Históricas de México, 1985, México: Instituto Nacional de Estadística, Geografía e Informática.

Gallego, D., 2007, 'Las empresas y los derechos de propiedad. Propuestas de la economía institucional', in R. Robledo and S. López (eds), *Interés particular, bienestar público? Grandes patrimonios y reforma agraria*, Zaragoza: Prensas Universitarias de Zaragoza, pp. 33–64.

Gómez Marte, R., 1953, *Aciertos y equivocaciones, luz y sombras de la reforma agraria mexicana*, México: Ed. Beatriz de Silva.

Gruening, E., 1928, *Mexico and its heritage*, New York: The Century Co.

Haber, S., Razo, A. and Maurer, N., 2003, *The politics of property rights. Political instability, credible commitments and economic growth in Mexico1876–1929*, Cambridge: Cambridge University Press.

Katz, F., 1998, *The life and time of Pancho Villa*, Stanford: Stanford University Press.

Knight, A., 2010, "La revolución Mexicana: su dimensión económica, 1900-1930" in S. Kuntz, *Historia Económica General de México*, México: El Colegio de México, pp. 473–502.

Knight, A., 2014, 'The character and consequences of the great depression in Mexico', in P. Drinot and A. Knight (eds), *The great depression in Latin America*, Durham, NC: Duke University Press, pp. 213–45.

Knight, A., 2015, 'Carácter y repercusiones de la gran depresión en México', in P. Drinot y A. Knight (eds), *La gran depresión en América Latina*, México: México, FCE, 2015, pp. 196–223.

Kouri, E., 2010, 'Claroscuros de la Reforma Agraria Mexicana', *Nexos*, diciembre, pp. 106–8.

Kuntz, S., 2010, *Historia Económica General de México*, México: El Colegio de México.

Labrousse, E., 1944, *La Crise de l'économie française à la fin de l'Ancien Régime et au début de la révolution*, Paris: PUF.

Lopes, M. A. de S., 2008, 'Revolución y ganadería en el norte de México', *Historia Mexicana*, LVII/3, pp. 863–910.

Martínez del Río, P., 1938, *El suplicio del hacendado y otros temas agrarios*, México: Polis.

McBride, G. McC, 1923, *The land systems of Mexico*, New York: American Geographical Society.

Mendoza García, E., 2010, 'Oposición al reparto agrario: los hacendados de Otumba y Teotihuacan, 1917–1930', *Contribuciones desde Coatepec*, 19, pp. 61–88.

Meyer, L., 1978, *Historia de la Revolución Mexicana, 1928–34: el conflicto social y los gobiernos del maximato*, México: El Colegio de México.

Moreno-Brid, J. C. and Ross, J., 2009, *Development and growth in the Mexican economy: A historical perspective*, Oxford: Oxford University Press.

Portes Gil, E., 1964, *Autobiografía de la revolución Mexicana*, México: Instituto Mexicano de Cultura.

Riguzzi, P., 2003, *Reciprocidad imposible? La política del comercio entre México y Estados Unidos, 1857–1938*, México: El Colegio Mexiquense-Instituto Mora.

Robledo, R. and López, S., 2007, *Interés particular, bienestar público? Grandes patrimonios y reforma agraria*, Zaragoza: Prensas Universitarias de Zaragoza.

Semo, E., 2012, *México, del antiguo régimen a la modernidad. Reforma y revolución*, México: UNAM.

Solis, L., 1973, *La realidad económica mexicana, retrovisión y perspectivas*, México: Siglo XXI.

Soluri, J., 2006, *Banana Cultures. Agriculture, Consumption, and Environmental Change in Honduras and the United States*, Austin: Texas University Press.

Tortolero, A., 2016a, 'State and food supply during the mexican revolution, 1911–1917: A case study in Central Mexico', (working paper presented in A. Chatriot, *State and food supply during the wars*, Paris: Sciences Po, 2016).

Tortolero, A., 2016b, 'Pionnière et discutée: la réforme agraire au Mexique depuis 1917', *Revue d'histoire moderne et contemporaine*, 64-4/4bis, pp. 66–88.

Whetten, N., 1953, 'México Rural', *Problemas agrícolas e industriales de México*, V/2, México D. F.

Womack, J., 1978, 'The Mexican economy during the revolution, 1910–1920: Historiography and analysis', *Marxist Perspectives*, I/4, pp. 80–123.

Zuleta, C. and Marino, D., 2010, 'Una visión del campo. Tierra, propiedad y tendencias de la producción, 1850–1930', in S. Kuntz (ed.), *Historia Económica General de México*, México: El Colegio de México, pp. 437–72.

13 The problem of the wheat and the political answers to the agricultural crisis in France of the 1930s

Alain Chatriot

1. Introduction

The scale of the crisis of the wheat in France of the 1930s questions the whole French economy and then mobilized public policies. It is interesting to understand in the same time the reactions of the economists, the politicians and also the representatives of the agricultural producers in the face of the crisis. The price collapse of wheat at the world level is translated in France in a cruel way at a moment when the country falls over to the surproduction. The importance of the agriculture in the French economy and the political weight maintained of rural France explains from then on the multiple legislative answers to try to contain the crisis. The debates on the liberalism, the protectionism, the planned economy and the corporatism are then embodied in concrete measures according to the variations of the parliamentary majorities.

The extent of the crisis in the wheat market in France during the interwar period and the measures taken to regulate it are fairly well known by now (Chatriot, 2016a). While these experiences are important for understanding agricultural policies on the European scale, they were also new forms of state intervention just as they marked a change in grain storage policies.

Controversies over the diagnosis of the wheat market crisis in the early 1930s show that we no longer face a crisis of the kind of crisis of the nineteenth century (Vivier, 2011). While the many laws passed reflect the mobilization of wheat producers, the failure of these mechanisms raises the question of the effectiveness of a public policy. The establishment of the 'Office du blé' (Grain Board) by the Popular Front government is understood as a response to these successive failures.

2. A controversial diagnosis

Confronted by the old problem of regulating a market that was a necessity for the population as a whole, public authorities (legislative, executive and administrative) managed crises of overproduction and the destabilization of the international market after World War I.

DOI: 10.4324/9781003105466-16

The shock of the war resulted in a desired modernization program of agriculture. A report is prepared by the Department of Agriculture that clearly states things:

> During the war, it was necessary to produce at all costs, for the security of the country. Today, after the victory, we must get to work to overproduce, to give to France, with the wealth, power and independence due to it after more than four years of glorious suffering.
>
> (Ministère de l'Agriculture et du Ravitaillement, 1919: 7)

During the 1920s and 30s, grain was consistently perceived as *the* question. It was presented as a market to protect or as prices that needed to be taxed. To the old problem of unpredictability – bad harvests necessitated imports while good years required exports – was added the shock of a world war. The equilibrium that protected French farmers through protectionist policies and tariffs introduced at the end of the nineteenth century was no longer viable (Aldenhoff-Hubinger, 2002; Chatriot, 2010).

With the war, Russia no longer exported and European production was in an upheaval. At first, there was a sharp rise in prices due to increased dependence on production from abroad. While peasants initially celebrated this situation, governments were concerned with a general decrease in buying power ['la vie chère'], and quickly, the situation changed. Farmers were suddenly confronted with the disorderly increase of supply, technical innovations and a static demand (Chatriot, 2018). This led to new crises in 1928 and again at the beginning of the 30s up to 1933 when good harvests led to the collapse of grain prices.

Gema Aparicio and Vicente Pinilla summed up one of the difficulties in the late 1920s:

> The problematic situation of the wheat market was also reflected in a progressive increase in unsold wheat stocks. The same occurred with other agricultural products. From mid 1925 onwards, the progressive accumulation of stocks of the principal foodstuffs caused a fall in international prices. [...] The simple fact of accumulating stocks also accounted for the price instability. Agents in the market were concerned because of uncertainty about both the exact quantity accumulated and the moment at which new stock would be placed on the market
>
> (Aparicio and Pinilla, 2019: 57)

Previously, the instruments of state intervention in agricultural policy were limited to protective tariffs based on subsidies, incentives for export, and quotas. However, these measures were quickly shown to be insufficient for radical market variations. Confronted with these fluctuations, new groups dealt with the question of grain in France and internationally. Until now, few historians have explored the series of conferences on grain that took place in Rome in 1927, Geneva in January 1930, in Rome in March and April 1930 and especially in London in May 1931 then in August 1933 with the creation of the International Wheat Advisory Committee (Schirmann, 2000; Graevenitz, 2009).

Certainly, the customs issues are still important around the price of wheat. French producers are still strongly opposed to the 'temporary importation' procedure, which they consider as a means of fraud for traders and millers (Chatriot, 2020). This perspective was extended with all the international debates on economic autarchy and the 'managed economy' ('économie dirigée' in French) in the 1930s (Cassez et al., 1935). However, while the issue of protectionism remains important for agriculture in the face of the crisis (Boissard, 1932; Augé-Laribé, 1933), the policy measures requested and obtained are much more diversified.

At the commentators of the agricultural current events, often the jurists or the economists, they discuss the existence of an agricultural crisis. The word 'crisis' is used regularly from the 1930s (Hallé, 1929; Laborde, 1929; Courtin, Formont, 1930; Augé-Laribé, 1931; Augé-Laribé, 1935; Romier, 1935; Maspétiol, Damougeot-Perron, 1935; Nogaro, 1936). It is sometimes replaced by that of the 'problem' (Liesse, 1930; Bertin, 1935; Liesse, 1934a; Liesse, 1934b; Sirol, 1934; Musset, 1935; Musset, 1936; Sirol, 1936). One of the notable points is that the crisis is always seen as 'world' (Delaisi, 1931; Lamor, 1931; Rivière, 1932; Delos, 1934; Hevesy, 1934; Thuriet, 1934). However, if these speeches are many, it is not simple to know if they are really received and how in the political world of the time.

To understand the political translation of these speeches obliges to follow various actors. 'It is often said that French policy is dominated by the peasants'. This quotation of an eminent American political scientist is interesting but the continuation of its text is it even more: 'This is true in the sense that the opinions of rural constituents are usually influential on parliamentary representatives; but peasants, no less than others, can be inept in shaping national affairs to their own advantage' (Tugwell, 1930: 226).

3. New collective mobilizations and new laws

Agricultural unions reemerged across France as the historical division between the unions of large property holders and the unions of republican orientation tied to mutualistic institutions were replaced by new confederations (Barral, 1968). At the same time, a specialized union developed, the General Association of Grain Producers. This association, founded in 1924, emerged out of the grain crisis (Pesche, 2000). The Association Générale des Producteurs de Blé (AGPB) developed in the mid-1920s as an alternative to the old forms of agricultural unionism (Chatriot, 2016b). The association was at the forefront of the fight against millers, traders and consumers.

Grain storage policy was understood by the actors to play an important role in responding to the crisis of wheat prices in a period of overproduction.

The AGPB emphasized the 'future scope of the storage and maintenance premium system':

> what we wanted and what we will get if the agricultural associations recognize their responsibility is *the beginning of a rational policy of market organization*. Everyone agrees that the foundation of this organization should be *the regular staggering of supply*. In the absence of a rational organization of the sale of wheat, producers, regardless of the legislative measures taken to help and protect them, will never be able to defend themselves; because they will not be able to take advantage of the measures in question. Their situation may be improved temporarily; but sooner or later, as a result of their dispersion, and their lack of cohesion, it will be their buyers, intermediaries and processors who will become the real beneficiaries; and producers will plunge once again.
>
> (Association générale des producteurs de blé, 1930: 19)

There was therefore one logical conclusion:

> Past lessons thus already made it possible to affirm that there is no solution to the problem of financing the wheat market except on collective grounds. In this respect, the last crisis will have had the fortunate result of considerably strengthening the feeling of common interests among all the producers who are equally affected [...] The stored wheat becomes an instrument of credit.
>
> (Association générale des producteurs de blé, 1930: 27)

In the summer of 1930, Minister of Agriculture Fernand David, with the support of the AGPB (Chatriot, 2019), sought the support of the Banque de France. At a meeting, the representative of the bank was reticent because with 'the bank's assistance to a particular branch of national activity, such a commitment would constitute a precedent which would not fail to be recalled by agricultural, commercial or industrial sectors'. The minister insisted, however, and concluded the interview by stating that 'the Government and the world of agriculture would not understand if the Banque de France, whose interest is in harmony with France itself, refused an effort in favor of national agriculture, which was experiencing such trying times' (Archives de la Banque de France, 1930). The following year, the same debates resumed and the archives of the Banque de France revealed the many meetings requested by André Tardieu – French Minister of Agriculture in 1931 and an influent leader of a right party – in order to move forward on this case. An agreement was reached between the bank and the credit institutions with a view to removing obstacles to the circulation of paper from cooperatives and agricultural unions. In the parliamentary debate of December 1934, when the Socialist Vincent Auriol put forth an amendment, the bank immediately prepared a reply with the firm conclusion: 'Such a transaction cannot be demanded of the Banque de France because it is contrary to the provisions and legal requirements of the laws and statutes that regulate the issuance of notes' (Archives de la Banque de France, 1934).

Above all, grain producers demanded a high price for grain as opposed to politicians who wanted to drive prices down to satisfy their constituents. The association was tied to the Chambers of Agriculture and stated in 1929:

> If our grain policy must remain subordinated to bread policy, which is itself subject to the demagogical influences of politics and the press, we might as well give up any hope of maintaining grain production or technical innovation in this area in France.
>
> (Rémond and Hallé, 1929).

According to this logic, grain producers were opposed to the increasingly modernized and well-structured millers of the interwar period.

Furthermore, beyond new specializations in agricultural production, various political movements were actively seeking support in rural France during the 1930s (Paxton, 1997; Bensoussan, 2006; Fernandez-Prieto, Pan-Montojo, Cabo, 2014).

The legal measures that followed as a result are worthy of special attention. A first law 'on the grain trade' was adopted on December 1, 1929 and was quickly completed on April 1, 1930. These laws gave *de facto* power to the Minister of Agriculture to intervene by decree on the origin and nature of grain used in mills. This was an essential measure because behind its technical appearance, it created a specific type of protectionism. On April 30, 1930, a law was proposed against the speculation on the grain trade through the creation of a permanent stock of grain and flour. This law was completed with a supplementary measure in the law of April 7, 1932 when the cost of storing grain became an essential question.

Renewed price variations quickened the rhythm of laws throughout 1933. On January 26, a law was voted to 'protect the grain market', with the aim of financial intervention to promote stock surpluses and control prices. On April 14, a law authorized the Minister of Agriculture to grant subsidies to encourage the use of indigenous grain for use other than human food and alcohol – a strong symbolic statement that was made necessary by surpluses and a collapse of prices. July 10, another important symbolic step was taken with the establishment of a minimum price for grain. While it was only in force for a brief period, the law set out all the controls that were made possible for controlling the market. The difficulties of executing the law forced the vote of December 28, 1933 reforming articles. Additional laws were passed in March and July 1934. The law of December 24, 1934 was presented as 'an attempt to clean up the grain market'. It followed a decree of October 1934 that had attempted the delicate operation of codifying all the legislation on the issue. Next, there was an attempt to return to a free-trade approach against the restrictive measures established by the law of July 1933. The consequence however was that the bottom fell out of prices. Multiple technical laws were passed in the spring of 1935 and July 13, 1935 and the use of decree-laws allowed for a first series of radical measures that were completed during the summer and through October 1935. The decree-law of October 30 returned to a certain number of previous measures by suppressing special taxes on production.

A first set of conclusions may be drawn from this quick overview. First, one must consider what a specialist of the agricultural question justly referred to as 'the soliciting of Parliament among grain producers' in 1936 (Salleron, 1936: 421). Since members of parliament were sensitive to the question of grain prices, the agrarian lobby maintained a certain influence. While some laws took years to pass, and were blocked by the Senate, they were all ultimately voted in. In the political system of the French Third Republic, the Parliament exercised certain superiority in decision-making for the economic and social policies.

The second conclusion becomes clear in the inadequacy of the successive choices. Independent of the more or less liberal, statist, or professional approaches, the principle trait of all these attempts at regulation was the incapacity to find a form of intervention adequate for the grain market. The measures were often considered illusory because there was insufficient credit to implement them and because the state did not control the wholesalers. Many were critical of this 'enormous mass of laws, decrees and acts that are successively regulating our grain trade', and that can only be explained by 'the errors of legislators in the area, the lack of an overall plan, demagogical solutions, and lack of familiarity with the most fundamental economic laws' (Touzet, 1936: 6).

Few years later, Georges Monnet, the socialist minister of Agriculture, explains:

> Our harvest in 1933 was a good one, and exceeded the home demand. In consequence, the minimum price was disregarded and a 'gangster market' made its appearance. The large flour mills, faced with numerous producers hard pressed, had no respect for the law. Supervision could not be sufficiently strict.

Monnet also comments on the choice made in 1934–5:

> The minimum price law was repealed and free-trade was re-established. It was then seen that free trade for the producer merely meant freedom to sell at starvation prices. Free trade in such a case simply means freedom for speculation. There can be no real freedom when the producer is not assured a fair return. Freedom presupposes organization, and to allow a small minority to dictate prices to their own advantage at the expense of producers and consumers alike is the reverse of freedom.
>
> (Monnet, 1937: 419–20)

4. 'L'Office du blé', a political answer to the agricultural crisis

The creation of a Grain Bureau occupied a central place in the great reforms of the Popular Front. The parliamentary debates on this entity were particularly vigorous during the summer of 1936. The institutionalization was immediately commented upon by numerous legal economists that were interested in the forms of regulation that are now referred to as a planned economy.

In his doctoral thesis of 1934, Jean Sirol saw the Grain Office as

> the proof of Parliament's will to bring forth a powerful and competent organization that is separate from itself: this is an implicit, and particularly interesting, recognition of parliament's inability, either due to the slow nature of parliamentary procedure or its incompetence, to handle countless contemporary economic problems.
>
> (Sirol, 1934: 370–1)

For this young jurist, the institution

> mark[ed] the progress of state socialism and reveals that it is not at all revolutionary, but, to the contrary, regulates and plans the national economy. Moreover, there is no doubt that among the masses, there is a new fascination for these complex organizations, nourished by considerable sums of money and whose impact on the economy is without question as long as it represents the state. This is the result of a trend that is directly opposed to liberal ideals. A trend one sees not only in France, but also in the entire world and perhaps even more so in other countries (USA, USSR, Italy, Germany, Austria and Switzerland).
>
> (Sirol, 1934: 371)

Roosevelt's New Deal can also be considered from this perspective (Patel, 2016).

The project for a national grain office had a long history among socialists (Lynch, 2002). They had proposed it to Parliament as early as January 1925 and again in October 1929 in the form of an 'institution for complete control over grain imports and a national fertilizer office'. The idea was taken up again through individual efforts in 1929 and 1934 but it appeared for many years to be too ideologically charged and the legislative and regulatory solutions were too limited.

The situation changed with the response by the President of the Council, Léon Blum, to the massive strikes that led to the Matignon Accords, and with the important social laws, published in the *Journal officiel* on June 26, 1936, on paid vacation, collective bargaining, and the 40-hour work week. The leftist government sought the creation of the Grain Office for the agricultural sector.

While the most famous laws were voted through quickly without opposition in the Senate, the agricultural questions remained problematic. The bill, allowing for the creation of a professional office controlled by the state as a response to the failures of previous legislation, was presented as early as June 18, 1936.

The text was quickly attacked however. Long debates in the two houses led to modifications to the text in July and August. Leon Blum stepped in to support the Minister of Agriculture, Georges Monnet, and the law was finally voted through in the last session of August 15, 1936. The debate focused on various elements: the status of the regulating body (the office was a public entity, a category of institution that was flexible but greatly criticized during the thirties); the problem of its leadership, given the inter-professional nature of the office; the question of how to fix grain prices annually; the creation of organizations for grain storage that were separate from the power of wholesalers; and, lastly, the organization of a monopoly for managing imports and exports.

Monnet explains one of the aims of this new institution:

> It was necessary to avoid a surplus, but there was no intention of penalizing high unit yields. He had, however, opposed those amendments in Parliament, which aimed at giving a special bonus to cultivators producing more than seventeen quintals to the hectare. Those who increased their production in years when there was a surplus were to receive a lower price for the quantity in excess, and it was only fair that the large producer should have the lower price if he exceeded his average production, and not the small producer, who perhaps grew for himself.
>
> (Monnet, 1937, 433)

Georges Monnet's other projects, including the expansion of the regulation of markets (Chatriot, Leblanc, Lynch, 2012) in the context of collective bargaining with the possibility of necessary extension by the minister, were also blocked by the Senate. The inter-professional nature of the Grain Bureau was a particularly tricky point of debate. The professional relations between producers of wheat, millers, bakers and consumers (represented by trade unions) were sometimes difficult. Another source of conflict was the suspicion that the Government wanted to establish total state control over the wheat market. Opposition to the creation of the Grain Bureau often took extreme turns in the press in the form of caricature or denunciation. Joseph-Barthélemy, a conservative jurist and editorialist for *Le Temps*, wrote on July 28, 1936: 'The well-stocked Grain Office has nothing to say... the plan is to cage off agriculture by leaving each one his niche and his reward. Such efforts are worthy of dogs'.

However, reactions to the actual creation of the institution varied. In her study of Breton peasants, the political scientist Suzanne Berger has shown that

> The Office Central [the Central Office of Mutualist Agricultural Works of the Finistère at Landerneau] protested the state role in price-fixing,

> but profited from the fact that the law required that all farmers stock their wheat in order to create a Coopérative du Blé which would provide storage facilities. [...] And the Office du Blé, creature of a Left government that Landerneau detested and feared, in fact gave the Office Central a near-monopoly of the wheat trade in Finistère.
>
> (Berger, 1972: 118)

Some figures who were opposed to the Grain Bureau had already pointed this out:

> There is no sense in burying one's head in the sand. The Grain Office has been welcomed with satisfaction throughout the peasant world. The discussions that have unfolded on the level of ideology have left them indifferent. Undoubtedly, the office appears to be an improvement to the previous situation.
>
> (Leroy, 1939: 75)

The ONIB was an inter-professional public organization, with producers, wholesalers, handlers, consumers and administrators. It is most important responsibilities were the fixing of prices, storage, and a monopoly on imports and exports. The fact that the harvests of 1936 and 1937 did not produce a surplus guaranteed the ONIB's creation. Problems did not emerge until the harvest of 1938 and functional difficulties that led to the reforms of the decree-laws of July 29, 1939.

Even though the ONIB was also applied in Algeria, it does not seem that colonial agricultural production weighed on the economic crisis. However, there are only a few studies on this subject (Swearingen, 1985; Bernard de Raymond, 2011).

5. Conclusion

As Suzanne Berger has concluded: 'The price of wheat was politically the most sensitive aspect of the agricultural depression' (Berger, 1972: 117). The important point here is the link between an economical question – low prices due to overproduction and destabilization of world market – and its political consequence. Robert Paxton emphasizes this idea and explains:

> The third dimension [of this crisis] concerned politics: it might be called a crisis of representation. There seemed to be no leader or institution in the French Third Republic with sufficient concern, comprehension, or will to devote public attention to the peasants' plight.
>
> (Paxton, 1997: 11)

Despite all the difficulties, the French parliamentary system has managed to find solutions to these agricultural difficulties without falling into the authoritarian paths of neighboring countries like fascist Italy (Mignemi, 2020). The creation of the Office du blé, in spite of its difficulties, nevertheless had to constitute finally an answer to this crisis. Answer which afterward went shown its efficiency and influenced the French and European agricultural policies (Chatriot, Conord, Lynch, 2017).

Bibliography

Aldenhoff-Hubinger, R., 2002, *Agrarpolitik und Protektionismus. Deutschland und Frankreich im Vergleich 1879–1914,* Göttingen: Vandenhoeck & Ruprecht.

Aparicio, G. and Pinilla, V., 2019, 'International trade in wheat and other cereals and the collapse of the first wave of globalization, 1900–38', *Journal of Global History,* 14(1), pp. 44–67.

Archives de la Banque de France, 1930, 1069199520 1, Crédit agricole: concours de la Banque à l'agriculture, mobilisation du stockage du blé, 1930–1932, le marché du blé 1932–1934, note sur l'intervention sollicitée de la Banque de France en faveur des producteurs de blé, août 1930.

Archives de la Banque de France, 1934, 1069199520 1, Crédit agricole: concours de la Banque à l'agriculture, mobilisation du stockage du blé, 1930–1932, le marché du blé 1932–1934, note demandée par le ministère des Finances à l'occasion d'un amendement déposé par V. Auriol, 11 décembre 1934.

Association générale des producteurs de blé, Office central du crédit agricole, 1930, *La vente rationnelle et le financement de la récolte de blé,* Paris: Imprimerie Maurice Blanchard.

Augé-Laribé, Michel, 1931, 'La crise agricole et ses effets sur la classe paysanne en France', *Revue internationale d'agriculture,* pp. 174–80.

Augé-Laribé, M., 1933, 'Nouveaux fondements du protectionnisme agricole', *Revue d'économie politique,* mars-avril, pp. 363–79.

Augé-Laribé, M., 1935, 'Nos agriculteurs devant la crise', *La Revue des Vivants,* juillet 1935, pp. 1038–46.

Barral, P., 1968, *Les agrariens français de Méline à Pisani,* Paris: Armand Colin.

Bensoussan, D., 2006, *Combats pour une Bretagne catholique et rurale. Les droites bretonnes dans l'entre-deux-guerres,* Paris: Fayard.

Berger, S., 1972, *Peasants against Politics. Rural Organization in Brittany 1911–1967,* Cambridge: Harvard University Press.

Bernard de Raymond, A., 2011, 'Une 'Algérie californienne'? L'économie politique de la standardisation dans l'agriculture coloniale (1930–1962)', *Politix,* 95, pp. 23–46.

Bertin, M., 1935, *L'économie dirigée et le problème agricole français,* Paris: Presses universitaires de France.

Boissard, A., 1932, *Les échanges internationaux et la politique douanière française au cours de la crise économique,* rapport présenté devant le Conseil national économique, Paris: Imprimerie nationale.

Cassez, E. et al., 1935, *L'économie dirigée et l'agriculture,* Paris: Librairie de l'Institut international agronomique.

Chatriot, A., 2010, 'Jaurès et les débats sur le protectionnisme agricole', *Cahiers Jaurès,* 195–6, janvier-juin, pp. 21–48.

Chatriot, A., 2016a, *La politique du blé. Crises et régulations d'un marché dans la France de l'entre-deux-guerres,* Paris: IGPDE/CHEFF.

Chatriot, A., 2016b, 'Le rôle des organisations agricoles françaises dans la politique économique au XXe siècle. L'exemple de l'AGPB (1924–1940)', in D. Fraboulet, M. Margairaz and P. Vernus (eds.), *Réguler l'économie. L'apport des organisations patronales. Europe XIXe-XXe siècles*, Rennes: Presses universitaires de Rennes, pp. 281–91.

Chatriot, A., 2018, 'La taxation du pain. L'Etat et l'organisation du ravitaillement durant la Première Guerre mondiale en France', in F. Descamps and L. Quenouëlle-Corre (eds.), *Une fiscalité de guerre? Contraintes, innovations, résistances*, Paris: CHEFF/IGPDE, pp. 289–305.

Chatriot, A., 2019, 'Storage and financing of the French wheat market in the interwar period', in W. Ronsijn, N. Mignemi and L. Herment (eds.), *Stocks, seasons and sales: Food supply, storage and markets in Europe and the New World, c. 1600–2000*, Turnhout: Brepols, CORN Series, 17, pp. 211–24.

Chatriot, A., 2020, 'Les fraudes à l'admission temporaire: une question politique face aux crises agricoles dans la France de la IIIe République', in Béatrice Touchelay (ed.), *Fraudes, frontières et territoires XIIIe–XXIe siècles*, Paris: IGPDE/CHEFF, pp. 277–300.

Chatriot, A., Conord, F. and Lynch, E. (eds.), 2017, *Orienter et réguler les marchés agricoles: entre pilotage national et politique agricole commune*, Montreuil-sous-bois: FranceAgriMer.

Chatriot, A., Leblanc, E. and Lynch, E. (eds.), 2012, *Organiser les marchés agricoles. Le temps des fondateurs, des années 1930 aux années 1950*, Paris: Armand Colin.

Courtin, R. and Formont, P., 1930, 'Essai sur la crise agricole: production et population', *Revue d'économie politique*, juillet, pp. 1084–123.

Delaisi, F., 1931, 'Le problème international du blé', *Revue économique internationale*, avril, pp. 47–62.

Delos, A., 1934, 'Le problème du blé', *Revue économique internationale*, décembre, pp. 499–549.

Fernandez-Prieto, L., Pan-Montojo, J. and Cabo, M. (eds.), 2014, *Agriculture in the age of fascism. Authoritarian technocracy and rural modernization, 1922–1945*, 'Rural History in Europe' 13, Turnhout: Brepols, Rural History in Europe, 13.

Graevenitz, F. G. von, 2009, 'From kaleidoscope to architecture. Interdependence and integration in wheat policies (1927–1957)', in K. K. Patel (ed.), *Fertile ground for Europe? The history of European integration and the common agricultural policy since 1945*, Baden-Baden: Nomos Verlag, pp. 27–45.

Hallé, P., 1929, 'La crise actuelle du blé', *Le Redressement français*, 1er-15 octobre, 4(16), pp. 10–13.

Hevesy, P. de, 1934, *Le problème mondial du blé. Projet de solution*, Paris: Librairie Félix Alcan.

Laborde, F., 1929, 'La crise du blé en France', *Revue Politique et Parlementaire*, 421, 10 octobre, pp. 418–27.

Lamor, H., 1931, *Le problème national et international du blé*, Paris: Les Presses modernes.

Leroy, L., 1939, *Les paysans et l'Office du blé*, Paris: Flammarion.

Liesse, A., 1930, 'Le problème du Blé en France. Remèdes empiriques - remèdes normaux', *L'Economiste français*, samedi 16 août, pp. 193–95.

Liesse, A., 1934a, 'Le problème du Blé', *L'Economiste français*, samedi 16 juin, pp. 737–9.

Liesse, A., 1934b, 'Le problème du Blé en France et dans le monde', *L'Economiste français*, samedi 1er septembre, pp. 257–9.

Lynch, E., 2002, *Moissons rouges. Les socialistes français et la société paysanne durant l'entre-deux-guerres (1918–1940)*, Villeneuve d'Ascq: Presses universitaires du Septentrion.

Maspétiol, R. and Damougeot-Perron, G., 1935, *La crise du blé en France et dans le monde,* Paris: Pedone.
Mignemi, N., 2020, 'The battle of wheat and other fascist battles in Italian agriculture (1920s–1930s)', in G. Béaur (ed.), *Alternative agriculture in Europe (sixteenth-twentieth centuries),* Turnhout: Brepols, 'Rural History in Europe', 16, pp. 167–91.
Ministère de l'Agriculture et du Ravitaillement, 1919, *Avant-projet de programme agricole tendant à l'intensification de la production et à la réforme des méthodes administratives,* Paris: Imprimerie nationale.
Monnet, G., 1937, 'The place of agriculture in the economic policy of the French government', *International Affairs (Royal Institute of International Affairs 1931–1939),* 16(3), May-June, pp. 418–39.
Musset, R., 1935, 'Problèmes du blé', *Annales de Géographie,* 44 (248), pp. 113–26.
Musset, R., 1936, 'Le problèmes du blé en France', *Annales de Géographie,* 45(257), pp. 528–9.
Nogaro, B., 1936, *Les prix agricoles mondiaux et la crise,* Paris: Librairie générale de droit et de jurisprudence.
Patel, K. K., 2016, *The new deal. A global history,* Princeton: Princeton University Press, coll. 'America in the World'.
Paxton, R. O., 1997, *French peasant fascism. Henry Dorgères's greenshirts and the crises of French agriculture, 1929–1939,* New York, Oxford: Oxford University Press.
Pesche, D., 2000, *Le syndicalisme agricole spécialisé en France. Entre la spécificité des intérêts et le besoin d'alliance,* Paris: L'Harmattan.
Rémond, G. and Hallé, P., 1929, *La politique du blé,* Rapport présenté à l'Assemblée des présidents des chambres d'agriculture de France, extrait du *Compte rendu des travaux de l'Assemblée des présidents des chambres d'agriculture de France,* Paris, pp. 19–20 mars.
Rivière, P., 1932, *L'Aspect agricole de la Crise mondiale de surproduction de 1929–1931,* Paris: Jouve et Cie.
Romier, M., 1935, 'La crise du blé', *Cahiers du bolchévisme,* 1er janvier 1935, pp. 49–60.
Salleron, L., 1936, 'L'Office du blé', *Revue Politique et Parlementaire,* 501, 10 septembre, pp. 421–35.
Schirmann, S., 2000, *Crise, cooperation économique et financière entre États européens 1929–1933,* Paris: CHEFF.
Sirol, J., 1934, *Les problèmes français du blé,* Paris: Librairie du Recueil Sirey.
Sirol, J., 1936, 'Les caractères actuels de la crise agricole et, en particulier, la crise du blé en France', *Revue d'économie politique,* janvier–février, pp. 146–88.
Swearingen, W. D., 1985, 'In pursuit of the Granary of Rome: France's wheat policy in Morocco, 1915–1931', *International Journal of Middle East Studies,* 17(3), août, pp. 347–63.
Thuriet, G., 1934, *la crise mondiale et les produits agricoles,* Paris: Jouve et Cie.
Touzet, M., 1936, *Le problème du blé en France et sa solution législative actuelle, avec le commentaire des décrets-lois du 30 Octobre 1935,* Bordeaux: Imprimerie René Samie.
Tugwell, R. G., 1930, 'The agricultural policy of France', I, II, III, *Political Science Quarterly,* June, September, and December, pp. 214–30, pp. 405–28 and pp. 527–47.
Vivier, N., 2011, 'Pour un réexamen des crises économiques du XIXe siècle en France', *Histoire & mesure,* XXVI-1, pp.135–56.

14 Agriculture in Switzerland and the crises of the 1920s and 1930s

Anne-Lise Head-König

1. Introduction

After the First World War Swiss agriculture was confronted with similar problems to those which arose in several other countries. High prices prevalent during the war fell drastically and exports declined. It obliged the agricultural sector to reorient its production, a slow and lengthy process, made all the more difficult by periodical crises characterised by falling prices and a huge drop in exports, mainly in the dairy and animal sectors. Swiss agriculture in the interwar years was in constant difficulty (Baumann and Moser, 1999: 76 ff.) with crises of varying length and intensity, regularly necessitating the intervention of the State with protectionist measures. The general crisis of the years 1921–1922 was relatively short and abrupt with widespread unemployment throughout the economy. The 1926–1927 crisis in the milk and dairy sector (with a decline in the milk price paid to the producer of –18.9% in 1927 compared to 1925 due to an overproduction of milk and difficulties in exporting) paved the way for the first major steps in reorienting production and reducing the debts in the farming sector. But these measures had only moderate results, and the situation scarcely improved before the World Crisis which impacted the agricultural sector in Switzerland later than in other countries. The delayed impact was probably due to the fact that it first hit the cereal sector, which in Switzerland was highly protected. In Switzerland the crisis became acute as from 1931 to 1932.

Lasting for several years, it necessitated drastic measures to protect the indebted farming sector suffering from reduced profitability consequent to overproduction and high prices. Losses of market shares to competitors in foreign countries were aggravated until the devaluation of the Swiss franc decided on September 1936. Despite the State's policy and farm lobby interventions, the policy of debt relief could not prevent the demise of numerous small unprofitable farms. In fact, the numerous State interventions decided in the 1930s until the Second World War had long-lasting effects: they impacted the agricultural sector significantly both in terms of production and structural change up to the end of the twentieth century.

DOI: 10.4324/9781003105466-17

2. The diversification of agricultural production and the arguments in favour of increasing cereal production at the expense of milk production

After the First World War, like some other small countries, Switzerland was confronted with the choice made in previous decades of the one-sided specialisation in dairy and animal products – with its very strong emphasis on cheese production for export, but hardly any butter production – and cattle breeding (Baumann and Moser, 1999). This specialisation was due to a greater profitability derived from cheese making rather than butter making, a fact which can be observed in Switzerland since the seventeenth century. Up to the First World War, the cultivation of cereals for bread making was considered of very secondary importance, since they could be imported cheaply and the cultivated area regressed considerably as from the last third of the nineteenth century. According to the Government's statistics, the domestic production provided about one eighth of the cereals necessary to feed the population in 1914. The experience of this scarcity during the First World War had a double impact on post-war agricultural policy: first, the realisation that the country could not rely heavily on imports in times of crisis, hence the necessity to grow more indigenous grain and to constitute more reserves and second, that in order to achieve this, the emphasis on dairy products had to be reduced all the more since these exports encountered major obstacles in the immediate after-war years.

This double objective remained a constant until after the Second World War. It was to be achieved by encouraging farmers to become more efficient, and to grow more cereals – the indigenous production having to be protected by a policy of subsidies – and for them to diversify their production, a leitmotiv of the policy of the Union of Swiss Farmers running through all the interwar years. The general view, but especially of those with a conservative outlook, both Catholics and Protestants, despite their lasting deep antagonism (Emil Savoy, the representative of Canton Fribourg in the Swiss Council of States, versus Ernst Laur, the Secretary of the Union of Swiss Farmers), was that it was important to retain as many farms as possible for both ideological and economic reasons. Nevertheless, it was agreed that only those farms – whatever their size, small- or medium-sized – should be maintained as functioning entities that could attain a minimum of profitability. This point of view was in evidence in the 1927–1928 Parliamentary debates following the difficulties encountered by milk producers, which were a consequence of the price decline in the early months of 1926. Yet in the years before the 1930s to resort to any kind of political or economic pressure to produce all that was needed and effectively consumed in the country was out of question due to the wide variety of production conditions in different regions. In the mountainous areas especially, the production of cereals and vegetables was more at risk than milk production and the income it produced.

Since the early 1920s, the Government and the Union of Farmers considered that, apart from securing supplies in the case of an import crisis, to encourage the cultivation of cereals and to subsidise this with a price guarantee, tariff protection, and later the payment of a premium to the milling industry, fulfilled additional socio-economic and ideological purposes. This point of view was constant during the whole interwar time, and never ceased to be propagated. This was for four main reasons.

First, according to the Federal Government it was necessary to increase the range of agricultural products and it was its conviction when the new incitements to increase cereal production were first implemented during the 1921–1922 crisis, that these would also benefit the labour market situation since they offered more work opportunities. Cereal production often associated with potato and vegetable growing required more labour input than fodder crops for cattle breeding and dairy production. According to data published by the Government referring to statistics established in 1922 30 working days per ha were needed to produce fodder crop on light soil, 52 working days per ha for cereals and as much as 151 working days for one ha of potatoes. And if these agricultural workers were to remain in the countryside, as was the official argument, they would not increase the already huge number of the unemployed (nearly 140,000 in August 1921 and as many as about 150,000 in February 1922, all economic sectors included). This argument was repeated periodically in the 1930s, too. And it would appear to me that this argument together with the fragile political international situation in the 1930s also explains the continuous acceptance by a majority of Parliament members of the decision to subsidise a guaranteed minimal price for bread making cereals. With increased unemployment any measure to keep more people from moving from poor rural areas to wealthier urban centres in order to benefit from better unemployment benefits was welcome. This was at a time when larger towns such as Basle and Zurich introduced strict measures to restrict the immigration of the poor, even of Swiss nationals, a problem exacerbated in the years 1934 and 1935 but to which historians have given scarcely any consideration.

Second, an increased cereal production would help to reduce the overproduction of milk, a leitmotiv constantly repeated during the interwar period. At the same time this would reduce the economic risk for farmers relying exclusively on fodder crops and cattle breeding, since they were much more vulnerable than those with a multi-purpose production. But within the farming community itself, these views were strongly disputed (Baumann and Moser, 1999: 161–168), especially in the upland regions where cereal production was not appropriate, whereas cattle-breeding and milk production were less subject to short-term climatic fluctuations. The guaranteed price for bread making cereals could be an incentive for those farmers able to produce cereals efficiently, and especially after 1933 (Figure 14.1) when the milk price was at its lowest (Ritzmann, 1996: 484).

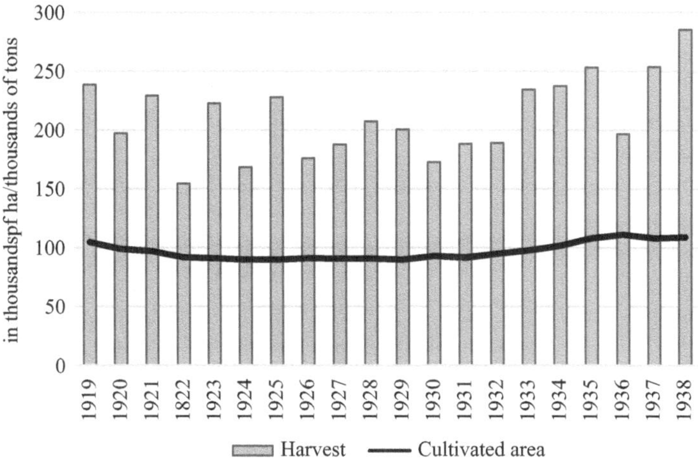

Figure 14.1 Cereal for bread making.
Source: Brugger, 1968: 106, 126, 128.

Third, according to the Government, if the farmers in the lowland (*'dans la plaine'*) were to diversify their agricultural production, this would help the farmers in upland regions to sell them their young livestock more easily.

Fourth, for both the Government and the Swiss Farmers' Union, there was in addition the ideological component that agricultural workers remaining in a rural context would further maintain traditional family values, a core feature of the peasant mentality and thus not be influenced by urban values, many of which were then considered to be harmful.

3. Protectionism up to the World Crisis: First incentives to prompt diversification in the agricultural sector

Throughout the repeated crises during the interwar years the State had to intervene in order to protect the main sectors of agriculture so that they could survive despite foreign competition. The sectors supplying the home market, such as wine growing, the production of sugar beet and of cereals were helped either by the restriction of imports, the payment of premiums or the fixing of minimum prices as in the case of cereals. With regard to cereals, there were some ferocious political controversies in Parliament among the supporters of industry, opposed to any measure susceptible to increase the price of food on the domestic market, then the consumers, finally the farmers. The stumbling block was the level of the minimum price guaranteed for indigenous cereals compared to the much lower price for imported cereals, the additional costs this entailed and the funding of the subsidies. For those sectors also producing for foreign markets, such as the dairy sector, there was a combination of measures to protect them: a minimum price guarantee for the milk, a number of customs tariff increases to prevent cheaper products from being imported and subsidies covering part of the transport costs to the borders for exported cattle, among others.

In the management of the 1921–1922 crisis a number of factors can be discerned which will reoccur a decade later in destabilising the agricultural sector and in leading to the measures implemented. Apart from being a turning point away from a rather liberal to protectionist agriculture, most measures introduced in the early twenties were still applied in the 1930s and sometimes even more strictly. This is why it is important to consider also the crises of the early twenties and not just the World Crisis beginning at the end of the twenties.

In the years 1921–1922 the price of the main agricultural products plummeted. Within one year, the price paid to Swiss cheese producers fell by 37%, to those of fat oxen by 31% and to those of pigs by 35%. This fall in prices was not specific to Switzerland. It was the result of considerable changes occurring in production conditions and in the indebtedness and impoverishment of several economies which disrupted trade flows between European countries and between Europe and overseas countries such as Argentina. Neither Switzerland nor other small countries involved in the First World War were prepared for the rapid changes which occurred in their foreign trade. All sectors, both industrial and agricultural, were hit hard by the international economic crisis, not only because of devaluation and the reduced purchasing power of their trading partners, but also because some of these began to recover and required fewer imports. This state of affairs deeply impacted exports, especially of small but much specialised countries such as Switzerland, the Netherlands or Denmark. In this first, violent, but relatively short-lived, post-war crisis, the Swiss Government countered its effects with the usual tools. These were a provisional customs tariff to restrict imports, which gave a certain protection to various agricultural sectors considered important, such as cereal production, dairy production, livestock breeding and wine growing – wine growers in the French-speaking part of Switzerland were especially insistent in this matter. Additionally there were incitements to revive trade, especially with neighbouring countries and Great Britain. Such sectors also benefitted from specific measures such as 'an extraordinary financial help' which permitted their partial recovery.

From 1922 until the Second World War, indigenous cereal production benefitted from a guaranteed price with the objective of encouraging domestic production and relieving the pressure on the market for dairy products. In 1924, the Government even proposed revising the Constitution in order to give the State a monopoly on cereals to ensure a sufficient supply, but this plan was rejected by popular vote. A less monopolistic text was adopted in 1929 and in 1932 it was decided to reaffirm the policy already adopted of buying up the national production at fixed prices. Regarding cattle breeding and the disrupted market after the First World War, it was decided to allocate a subsidy for each exported head of cattle in order to make the cattle price competitive abroad. But cattle breeders were not only affected by the near collapse of their exports abroad (Brugger, 1968: 274–276). Especially those in upland regions were doubly hit since the crisis also disrupted the domestic market, the lowland cash-poor farmers being unable to buy young cattle from the highland breeders. The reorganisation of the dairy sector brought together most milk producers and exporters: the Union of Milk Producers (UCPL) and the Union of Cheese Sellers and Trade (USCF) and gave them an enormous influence in political and Parliamentary life. The guaranteed price for cheese was fixed twice a year with the requirement to maintain the price of milk at the highest level possible while taking into account the market situation. Despite the fact that these different measures helped to alleviate the effects of this crisis, the improved situation was short-lived and in the years 1926–1927 early signs of the coming Great Depression, such as over indebtedness in the farming sector, were already making themselves felt. This led the Parliament to provide temporary relief in 1928 in order to alleviate the crisis and to help heavily indebted farmers, mostly smallholders.

Since the early 1920s, both the Swiss Government and the Swiss Farmers' Union advocated a structural change in the dairy sector considered as being too dependent on the world market. Butter was an important object of intense discussions since a significant proportion had to be imported for national consumption. Between 1922 and 1927, these imports represented between 33.9% and 42.8% of domestic consumption. As early as 1924 the milk associations (the fédérations laitières) were persuaded to offer a guaranteed price for butter to promote an increase in production (Hürlimann, 1944: 71). But as the milk price paid for butter production was less attractive for producers than that paid for cheese, the level of domestic butter production hardly changed even in the 1926–1927 milk crisis and the demand for imported butter remained high. It was only at the beginning of the 1930s with the overproduction of milk and the impossibility of increasing the traditional exports of cheese that radical changes occurred. Domestic butter production increased due to customs duties helping to reduce imports of butter and with measures to support the price.

4. The reorientation of the dairy sector and the related chain reactions during and after the World Crisis

At the beginning of the 1930s new difficulties arose in the Swiss animal production and dairy industry and for two reasons. In the home market there was a sharp increase in the overall production of milk to be processed, all the more so since the consumption of drinking milk was tending to decline, especially in towns (Moser and Brodbeck, 2007: 113), and this despite a slight increase in population (Figure 14.2).

In addition, the consumption of cheese did not increase significantly since the retail price was not adapted to the increased output of cheese. Abroad,

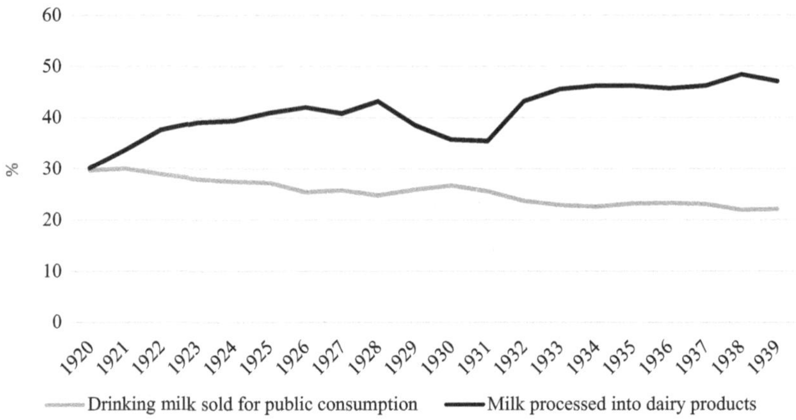

Figure 14.2 Changes in the milk uses
Source. Statistiques laitières de la Suisse, 1923: 6; 1927: 397; 1938: 17; 1940: 9; FF:88/1; 1936: 385.

increasing difficulties limited the exports of animal and dairy products such as the institution of quotas in several countries, but also monetary devaluation and the competition from new entrants in these sectors. With the crisis and the slump prevailing on the international market for cereals, several European and overseas countries had been prompted to reorient their own agricultural production which was to generate, in turn, a worldwide surplus in animal and dairy products. Some new entrants to the market, especially those from the Southern Hemisphere (Argentina, Australia), managed to increase their exports, but in a context of declining consumption, whereas traditional European exporters of dairy and animal products were confronted with a diminishing demand. The situation was the same for Swiss exports. But the Swiss dairy farming community suffered from foreign competition even in its home market when imported cheese was cheaper. This was the case in 1931 when in that year, cheese imports practically doubled compared to those in 1930 (Brugger, 1968: 287).

Since such imports threatened the domestic sale of the more expensive Swiss cheeses, it was decided in 1932, to adjust the customs tariff to partially protect the domestic market. In fact, the adjustment was a compromise and took into account one important factor: it should not prevent the import of soft cheeses produced in countries which were some of the best customers for Swiss hard cheese. The decline in exports necessitated a reorientation of the uses of milk, all the more so since the farmers' response in order to compensate the declining milk price was to produce more and more milk for maintaining their income. The specific situation of local and regional producers in various upland regions, such as in the Grisons and the Bernese Oberland or in the Jura, added to the increase of the amount of milk to be processed. On the one hand they were confronted with a huge decline in cattle sales which implied a decrease in milk use – fewer calves to be fed with milk – and simultaneously they were seriously affected by the tourist crisis with a decrease in the number of guests, hence a lower consumption of milk. As a result, their milk surplus was processed into cheese and butter which had to be sold in the lowlands, but this, in turn, prevented the lowland producers from selling part of their production to the mountain regions during the tourist season as was the custom.

The increase in butter production resulted in the creation, in 1932, of the Butyra (*Centrale Suisse de ravitaillement en beurre*), the central organisation for the butter supply, both to take charge of the Swiss butter which was not sold directly to consumers and to regulate imports of butter. In fact, butter production at the national level increased much more quickly than expected, creating an overproduction on a scale 'having never been seen hitherto' according to the Swiss Government in 1935 (Table 14.1).

The problem with the butter was that its price should not be too high for consumers in order to prevent a switch from animal fat to cheaper vegetable fats and oils. This risk was referred to several times by Ernst Laur, the Swiss representative in many international agricultural Congresses in the 1930s, since the dairy and animal sectors were among the most price sensitive ones when the income of the population tended to decline (see Laur, 1934). It must be noted that consumers' preference was an additional important factor influencing domestic consumption. As was noted in 1932 'in Geneva, the population is accustomed to consuming Danish butter and doesn't want any other sort'. In fact, switching to a generally satisfactory quality of butter at national level required nearly a decade.

The dilemma of the Swiss authorities in the matter of overproduction and price regulations which would help the butter producers was also the result of a typical Swiss financial compromise: customs duties on imported butter were to finance the so-called price-guarantee which had been introduced as an incentive for more butter production and less cheese production. But with

Table 14.1 Butter production and butter imports *(in tons)*

Year	*Domestic production*	*Imports*
1929	15,700	7,551
1930	16,000	8,520
1931	16,132	10,591
1932	22,911	3,697
1933	25,500	520
1934	29,000	296
1935	28,550	137
1936	27,000	1,460
1937	26,000	2,550

Source: Statistiques laitières de la Suisse, 1931: 714; 1938: 29.

the increase in domestic production though, there were fewer imports and fewer customs duties could be levied.

Faced with a striking imbalance between supply and demand, the Government took a number of steps to address it. Apart from tariff increases on foreign butter, it implemented some major measures to limit the domestic production of milk. Additional taxes were introduced on the import of concentrates from September 1932, increased in 1933 and then quotas were applied. These measures were effective and the imported quantities of concentrates declined from 734.7 tons in 1932 – a record-year of imports – to 495.7 tons in 1934. For Swiss milk producers milk quotas became the rule as from 1933. All their milk had still to be delivered to processing centres, but with a guaranteed price being paid only for a limited quantity of milk which was to be fixed annually, the surplus of delivered milk being paid for at the market price. Adjustments to the quotas according to altitude (alpine character of the production and type of fodder, etc.) were also made.

However, a new element had not been taken into account: the fact that the increased milk output was not only the result of the increasing use of imported concentrates and fertilisers, but also of an increased drive to modernisation.

5. The near demise of condensed milk exports and collateral damage for cattle breeders and the meat market

The sector of the milk and animal products industry was significantly impacted by changes occurring in specific branches of their production due to the difficulties encountered by the export industry. This was particularly the case for the condensed milk sector. Swiss exports represented 7.7% of the world-wide exports of condensed milk in 1929, but only 1.7% in 1935. The exports to the Strait Settlements, by far the biggest purchasers of Swiss condensed milk in 1929, in decreasing by 94.6% between 1929 and 1934 reflect this collapse. In terms of total quantities, Swiss exports regressed by 85% between 1929 and 1936 (Figure 14.3) at a time when some European competitors managed to limit the impact of the crisis in this sector. Dutch exports declined by 13% in these years but managed to recover in 1936, Danish exports declined by 33%, French exports were more critically affected (–60.5%). At world-wide level though, there was a general decrease in the condensed milk trade between 1929 and 1935 (–28.1%).

However, the changes occurring in the Swiss condensed milk sector were due to some specific reasons which had further repercussions for the entire agricultural sector dependent on animal products. The main factor explaining the decrease in the production of condensed milk and its export was the production costs due to a relatively high milk price paid to Swiss farmers for this type of production. Compared to the price received by foreign competitors on the world market it was much too high despite the sharp decrease in the milk price paid to the Swiss producers between 1929 and 1936. Added to

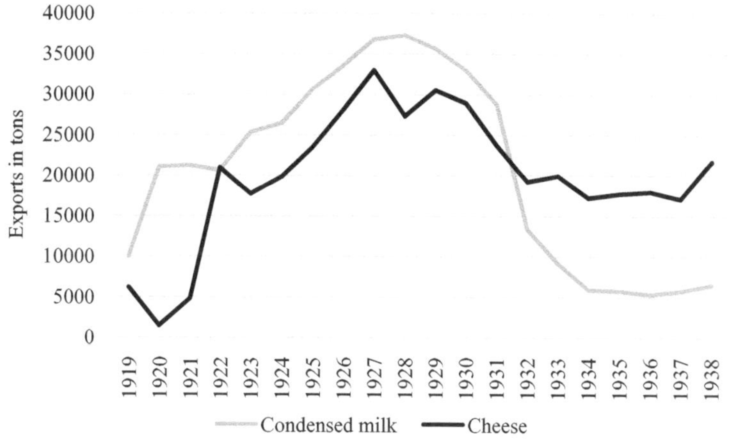

Figure 14.3 Condensed milk and cheese exports
Source. Statistiques laitières de la Suisse, 1936: 33, 42; 1939: 31.

this the raw materials necessary for the packaging of the condensed milk did not exist at all in Switzerland but had to be imported. This was a supplementary burden on the cost of production. As a result of too high an end price for the foreign buyers, the two main companies specialising in this sector, Nestlé and Berna Milk Co. decided to close their production facilities and relocate abroad, a process which began after the First World War, but accelerated in the early 1930s, and contributed to the near total demise of this sector.

On the domestic market the decline of exports in this sector had a bigger impact than is apparent at first glance. Not only did it increase the pressure on the milk farmers' incomes and force the Federal Government to continue its interventionist policy and to extend its support for the milk sector, it also increased the available milk which from condensed milk was switched to the production of other dairy products such as cheese and butter. Apart from contributing to the increase in the overproduction in these two branches, this new orientation had an unwelcome side-effect for the other branches of the milk and animal sectors. One of the advantages of the condensed milk production had been that the milk was used in its entirety and thus did not produce any by-products such as whey and skimmed milk. With the shift towards cheese and butter production, the amount of milk residues increased and was recycled in the production of pork. However, at the same time, imports of feed concentrates surged since their price had declined significantly. So, together with the increased milk residues they contributed to a large increase in the pig population. It was so huge that the Government ordered an 'extraordinary' Census based on the data of 300 communes which took place in November 1933 and was renewed the following year. Compared to 1931, the number of pigs had increased by 34%.

The overproduction of pork was accompanied by a sharp drop in price. Between 1926 and 1933, the price for pork dropped by 46%, but never to the even lower Dutch or Danish level. With the price decrease in pork, consumption increased which, in turn, had some unexpected negative consequences for the beef and veal meat markets. This was further detrimental to the cattle breeding regions which lost parts of their domestic market and contributed to worsen the situation of farmers in mountain area at a time when many of them were already affected directly or indirectly by the tourist crisis. As noted before, it also impacted the amount of milk to be processed in upland regions.

6. Declining hard cheese exports: Higher prices and lower quality, a dilemma partly made in Switzerland

6.1 Cheese quality

With the decline in cheese exports, controversy over its causes increased, all the more so since this rendered the existence of large sections of the farming population still more precarious. Specialists agreed that there was a worldwide decline in demand which was also being felt in countries such as Denmark and the Netherlands also specialising in cheese production. However, the origins were to be found partly at home, due to a growing discrepancy between the quality of the cheese ('un avilissement de la qualité': Käppeli and Rubattel: 1931) and its price on foreign markets. After being stocked for more than three months many a Swiss cheese was no longer up to standard, as was especially the case for Emmental cheese. This view is borne out by the fact that at the beginning of the 1930s an increasing quantity of cheese was classified as being of second-rate quality and then having to be discarded on receipt by the USF (Union Suisse du commerce *de* fromage)[1]. Still worse, some cheese was classified as third-rate (Table 14.2)[2]. According to the Government, despite a higher price than that of foreign competitors the demand for Swiss cheese would not have decreased so significantly had the cheese been of better quality. In addition, consumers had also become much more demanding than in previous decades, but they were only prepared to pay a higher price if the quality was satisfactory both with regard to the texture and the storage qualities of the cheese.

In Parliamentary discussions in the early 1930s numerous negative factors were quoted to explain the deterioration in quality and they varied according to the political affiliation of the speaker in question. Either the price guarantee system established since the 1921–1922 crisis was too rigid and offered no incitement for producers to improve the quality of their dairy products, or it was the quality of the fodder and too many cheaply imported concentrates and fertilisers, or there were not enough regulations to ensure that farmers were not spreading purine on their meadows the whole year round, or controls for the cleanliness and the quality of the milk in the dairies were neither

Table 14.2 The quality of Swiss hard cheese

Year of production	*First-rate cheese* %	*Second-rate cheese* %	*Third-rate cheese 'fromage de rebut'* %
1928–29	77.2	18.5	4.3
1929–30	74.4	21.0	4.6
1930–31	73.9	21.9	4.2
1931–32	75.9	21.2	2.3
1932–33	69.1	29.2	1.7
1933–34	69.5	28.6	1.9
1934–35	65.5	33.3	1,2
1935–36	69.7	29.2	1.1
1936–37	76.1	22.6	1.9
1937–38	75.3	23.9	0.8
1938–39	72,7	26.5	0.8

Source: Statistiques laitières de la Suisse, 1931: 718; 1935: 24; 1939: 15.

rigorous nor sufficiently frequent according to the USF in 1935 (Bericht, 1935: 44–45). This would appear to be in contrast with the Danish and Dutch policies on hygiene (Bull. officiel, 1935: 22–23). But it must also be stressed that these two competitors on the world market had significant natural advantages in comparison to Switzerland, among others a much longer period of green feeding.

6.2 Uncompetitive export prices

Export prices in many countries were determined not only by the state of the domestic market, and the price paid to producers, but also by the policy with regard to State subsidies. Butter was a case in point here. As the Swiss Government insisted in 1932 regarding butter it was difficult to compete with Denmark, which had been the main supplier of butter to Switzerland for many years and 'which no other [country] has surpassed in the making of quality butter'. The price paid to Swiss producers for milk to be used for butter-, cheese making and condensed milk was in stark contrast to that paid to their foreign competitors, for instance, being 133% higher than that paid to Dutch producers in 1932, or 248% higher in the case of Danish producers in 1934 (Table 14.3). Never before had the price discrepancy been so great.

In the interwar period the price differences were due to the fact that several countries competing with the Swiss pursued a different price policy for their exports: prices were set according to the use of the milk, a much lower price being paid for milk used in the dairy industry and a higher one for drinking milk. Thus, in contrast to the price paid for cheese-making, the differences in the prices paid for drinking milk abroad or in Switzerland were much less marked. It is quite obvious from the data shown on Tables 14.3 and 14.4 that Swiss cheese exports decreased due to the combination of the various factors mentioned above.

Table 14.3 Comparisons of milk prices for cheese-making paid to the producers in three competing markets

Year	*Milk price for cheese-making (in ct./liter)*		
	Switzerland	*Netherlands*	*Denmark*
1929	24.6	19.9	18.6
1930	22.6	15.4	14.4
1931	21.8	12.1	11.1
1932	20.3	8.7	7.6
1933	19.0	8.8	6.3
1934	18.8	8.9	6.4
1935	18.5	9.0	6.5
1936	18.5	10.6	7.3

Source: Statistique laitière de la Suisse, 1936: 69.

Table 14.4 Cheese exports
(in tons)

Year	*Switzerland*	*Netherlands*	*Denmark*
1929	30,509	95,815	6,583
1930	28,970	93,775	5,727
1931	23,724	86,390	4,256
1932	19,222	77,138	6,593
1933	19,967	63,912	10,079
1934	17,248	61,186	6,381
1935	17,777	61,052	6,663
1936	17,997	56,840	9,529

Source: Statistique laitière de la Suisse, 1936: 68.

7. Production costs and domestic prices

In Switzerland, the high cost of agricultural products had been a problem long before the World Crisis. However, the problem became especially acute since this crisis affected all economic sectors and also contributed to a general decline in exports. The option of domestic consumption serving to substitute the lack of foreign demand, at least with regard to agricultural products, was not feasible with the then existing prices. In addition, the State's decision in 1932 to reduce the wages of its own employees as a consequence of changed economic conditions could hardly help to stimulate home demand. Attempts were made to reduce the cost of the end products, but to no avail, since, apart that of the guaranteed price for milk producers, the two fundamental factors which had a significant impact on the price formation mechanism – the level of interest rates to be paid by producers together with the margins of the intermediaries and distributors – were outside the State's competence. The State could only exert 'a moral pressure' (Muller, 2010: 203). But as shown in Figure 14.4, when as from 1931 most food prices began to decline, this

Figure 14.4 Food prices

(retail prices in kg or liter)

Source. Annuaire statistique de la Suisse, 1938: 293–294.

was also because of a lower demand due to the increase in widespread unemployment. The prices of products depending on a price guarantee fell more slowly, while the bread price declined to yet a greater degree since it reflected the massive price collapse of wheat on international markets.

As already mentioned, interest rates resulting in a high level of indebtedness among producers were one of the major reason for the high cost of production and the high prices paid by consumers. Such interest rates decreased between 1929 and 1932, but only slowly, the banks fearing a reduction in their profit margins (Muller, 2010: 564–565) and the lower rates applied to farming mostly concerned new mortgages only. After 1933, however, the issue of the level of agricultural interest rates became less acute due to the fact that the indebtedness of parts of the farming community had reached such a high level that the Government was forced to implement a systematic policy of debt relief for 'deserving' farmers. The second major element affecting the cost of consumers' purchases was the increasing margins practised in the distribution sector which concerned not only domestic production but also that of imported products. The Government's suggestion that the intermediaries 'should be more accommodating and reduce their prices' had little effect. Both producers of meat and producers of dairy products, for instance, were confronted with the problem of the increased margins that intermediaries required for selling their products and which negatively impacted a potential increase in consumption, particularly in animal products. This can be seen in the retail prices and margins of butchers and milkmen. In the first case, countermeasures were sometimes successful on a local basis, but scarcely in the second case.

Among others, the Bally shoe manufacturer decided to bypass butchers and to keep its own pig farms. In the early 1930s it raised up to 8,000 pigs to supply its workers with meat at an affordable price, that is to say at cost price (Bull. officiel, 1935: 31). With regard to drinking milk, as shown in Figure 14.2, total demand did not increase for several reasons. One factor was increasing urbanisation and this brought about a change in the social structure of the population. With increasing income the urban population drank less milk, but consumed more cheese and meat. Even within towns a similar trend existed: the more people's income increased, the less milk they drank. In Zurich, families of the upper class drank 0.49 litre milk per person daily and those of the lower class as much as 0.64 litter. For many observers, however, the main factor behind the declining global consumption of drinking milk was to be found essentially in the high margin existing between the price paid to the producer and the price paid by the consumer. The margin increased over the years, from 28% on average in the years 1923–1925, to 34% in 1926–1928 and even to 43% in 1931–1933. It varied only slightly according to the town. In the view of the well-organised milk associations (the fédérations laitières) this high margin was justified by the necessity for them to cover their increased costs, compared to those which had existed before the war: there were increased costs of transport, distribution, personal, refrigeration, hygienic measures, and quality control. Nevertheless it is clear that milk traders were well organised when it came to defend their own interests.

8. The World Crisis: Indebted farmers and State interventions

Among the factors contributing to the deteriorating financial situation of the farming population in the first interwar years and even more so during the World Crisis itself, apart from the decline in demand, mortgage debts played a major role as well as the frequent recourse to joint guarantees which increased the risk of over-indebtedness spreading still further. This was the case in 1922 and even to a greater extent in 1926–1927, when the first signs of hardship emerged in parts of the farming sector, some five years before the turmoil of the World Crisis would seriously affect the income of all farms (Ritzmann-Blickenstorfer, 1996: 558). But during the World Crisis all sections of the farming community did not suffer equally. According to a Government report published in 1935 (FF, 87/2, 1935: 267), there were as many as 14 different types of land use and the degree of over-indebtedness of producers varied from the lowest proportion affected at 5% (wine-growers, fruit-growers and vegetable producers), to the most affected at 26.7% (dairy producers) and 33% (cattle breeders), with the remaining categories of over-indebted producers varying between 8% and 20%. These huge differences are to be ascribed to structural factors (climate, altitude and soils), as well as to socio-economic ones, such as the possibility of additional income coming from outside agriculture, for instance, from still functioning sectors of industry or even newly developing industry such as in canton Valais (Lorenzetti, 2010), to the family structure. for instance, grown-up children working outside the farming sector and contributing to the running costs of the family farm, as was still the case in the 1930s and 1940s in the grassland regions of canton Lucerne (Head-König, 2012: 304–305) or to declining income from poor farming management.

Nevertheless, the principal reason for over-indebtedness by far was the high debt incurred by young farmers who had acquired a farm during or just after the war without possessing sufficient capital of their own. Both ways of acquiring a farm, either through inheritance – with the concomitant problem of siblings' compensation – or outright purchase, were to blame for the financial plight of many younger farmers, the degree of over-indebtedness invariably being higher in the case of purchase. With the deterioration of the economic situation in the agricultural sector in 1926–1927[3] the Government increased its current subsidies and, then in 1928, created a special relief fund to provide temporary financial relief for over-indebted farmers, especially smallholders. A total of 16,109 farmers benefitted from these measures, which were the main instruments applied in an attempt to reduce and limit indebtedness. When the crisis became acute from 1932, these measures were reactivated together with the creation of cantonal Caisses de secours pour les paysans. Thus, for milk producers alone the total subsidies increased from 10.2 million francs in 1927–28 to 42.5 million in 1935–1936 and decreased slowly afterwards (Baumgartner-Girardot, 1982: 277). In addition to these interventions there were lengthy and arduous Parliamentary negotiations which lasted until 1940 before a more comprehensive debt relief policy could be implemented. It included a limitation to the seizures of assets, a ban on increasing mortgages and on the taking out of new loans, as well as introducing constraints on the transfer and the sale of farm assets (Lorenzetti, 2017: 198–200).

In future siblings' compensation should be based on the yearly return of the farm (*valeur de rendement*) with a possible addition of 25% on the value calculated, a clause which, in fact, did not prevent speculation on farmland since investors from outside farming could conclude land transactions at the market price, with certain restrictions. Hence, between 1929 and 1939, the number of tenant farms increased by 32.3% (Brugger, 1968: 28).

The debt relief policy in the 1930s was aimed only at part of the 238,000 farms mentioned in the 1929 Federal Census. Only 151,000 would be eligible depending on various stipulations such as adequate size, potential profitability, and the viable possibility to feed a family. In the event only 20,350 over-indebted farmers could benefit from debt relief through being able to fulfil the very stringent requirements imposed by the decision-makers (FF, 88/2, 1936: 266–267). Three factors had to be taken into account for a farmer to qualify. First, there was the farm itself. (The level of its indebtedness should make its survival possible, which eliminated all part-time farmers, since their farms were too small.) Second, there was the farmer himself. (A full-time farmer had to be of good morals, be capable of managing the farm by applying efficient and rational methods, who agreed to introduce farm bookkeeping, who was able to repay his debts according to plan and who was willing to be supervised by the competent authority.) Third, there was the farmer's family itself. (Their lifestyle had to be appropriate, otherwise the 'supervision could be extended to the whole family if the household expenses were in excess of gross income'.) For instance, between 1933 and 1940, although 15.1% of all farms of canton St. Gallen wished to be assisted, ultimately only 6.7% of all farms received help.

9. Conclusion and outlook: The long-term effects of interwar measures both on agricultural output and on the legal situation in the farming world

The interwar period was a decisive phase for the development of State intervention. In the long run it significantly impacted the agricultural sector with regard to production, structural change and ownership. But the implementation of a permanent policy in place of various temporary measures, which was aimed at protecting and diversifying national food production and keeping as many viable family farms as possible, necessitated a number of legal adaptations. First, there was the enactment of legal constraints in the Civil Code and the Code of Obligations to hamper speculation on farmland. This meant restricting disposal, changing the method of calculation for access to ownership by way of family transfer and succession, protecting tenants and putting a cap on indebtedness. Second, this also implied a change in the so called economic articles (les articles dits économiques) of the Federal Constitution regarding production control and regulation of production and guaranteed prices. These measures were the result of laborious and lengthy Parliamentary discussions but were duly adopted in several distinct steps as from the 1940s. The cap on indebtedness was successful: from 15 to 20% of farms' gross return farms in the 1930s, the debt service burden decreased to about 8% in the 1950s–1960s and to 3–4% in the beginning of the 1980s. In contrast, the protectionist policy of fixed price and market guarantees was a failure. In less than a generation after the war, it had to be abandoned completely in the face of growing 'butter mountains, cheese mountains and milk lakes'. It was replaced by a policy of individual farm quotas which, in turn, also had to be abandoned.

Sources

The main documents consulted are: *Annuaire international de statistique agricole*, Rome; *Annuaire statistique de la Suisse; Annuaire agricole de la Suisse; Statistiques laitières de la Suisse; Statistique du commerce de la Suisse.* Rapports annuels; Recueil des lois fédérales (RO); Feuille fédérale (FF) with its Messages du Conseil fédéral à l'Assemblée fédérale in the years 1928, 1932, 1935, 1936, 1938, 1940.

Notes

1 On the cartel-like organisation of the USF and its relationship with the Swiss State, see Ryser 2015.
2 Nevertheless, part of the second-rate cheese could still be exported once it was recycled as processed cheese (Gallati 1943: 16, 119).
3 In Parliament in 1928 it was stated that in the three previous years the indebtedness in farming had increased between 17 % and 25%.

Bibliography

Baumann, W. and Moser, P., 1999, *Bauern im Industriestaat: agrarpolitische Konzeptionen und bäuerliche Bewegungen in der Schweiz 1918–1968*, Zürich: Orell Füssli.

Baumgartner-Girardot, H.-U., 1982, *Agrargeschichte und Agrarpolitik der Schweiz in der Zwischenkriegszeit von1920–1940*, unpublished M.A. thesis Zurich, University of Zurich.

Bericht über die Verhältnisse der Schweizerischen Käseunion, 1935, Erstatter von Spychiger, A. et al. zu Handen von Bundesrat H. Obrecht.

Brugger, H., 1968, *Manuel statistique de l'agriculture Suisse/Statistisches Handbuch der schweizerischen Landwirtschaft*, Berne: Impr. Federative.

Brugger, H., 1985, *Die schweizerische Landwirtschaft 1914 bis 1980. Agrarverfassung, Pflanzenbau, Tierhaltung*, Aussenhandel, Frauenfeld: Huber.

Bulletin officiel de l'Assemblée fédérale, 1935, *Producteurs de lait. Prolongation de l'aide*. Conseil des Etats, Session de printemps, 1935, vol. 1, séances du 26.03.1935 (pp. 21–25) et du 27.03.1935 (pp. 25–39).

Gallati, W., 1943, *Die schweizerische Schachtelkäseindustrie und der Verband Schweizerischer Emmentaler Schachtelkäsefabrikanten (SESK)*, Bern-LeipzIg: Haupt.

Head-König, A. L., 2012, 'Farm transfer, marriage, household and parental power in rural Switzerland, 1860–1960', in A. L. Head-König (ed.), *Practices, Marriage Strategies and Household Formation in European Rural Societies*, Turnhout, Brepols Publishers, Rural history in Europe, 7, pp. 283–309.

Hürlimann, J., 1944, *Staatliche Preis- und Absatzsicherungspolitik in der schweizerischen Landwirtschaft seit Ende der 20er Jahre bis zum Kriegsausbruch 1939*, Zürich: Kommerzdruck und Verlags AG.

Käppeli, J. and Rubattel, R., 1931, 'Amélioration de la production de qualité dans l'industrie laitière suisse', offprint of the *Annuaire agricole suisse*, 1931, 36 p.

Kaufmann, O. K., 1946, *Das neue ländliche Bodenrecht der Schweiz*, St. Gallen: Fehr.

Laur, E., 1934, *L'organisation de la production et de la vente des graisses alimentaires*, Conférence à l'Assemblée annuelle de la Commission internationale d'Agriculture, à Budapest, le 18 juin 1934, Berne: Impr. Federative.

Lorenzetti, L., 2010, *Destini periferici: modernizzazione, risorse e mercati in Ticino, Valtellina e Vallese, 1850–1930*, Udine: Forum.

Lorenzetti, L., 2017, 'Agrarian debt in rural Switzerland. Economic causes and poltical responses (1890–1940)', *Rural History*, 28/1, pp. 189–204.

Moser, P. and Brodbeck, B., 2007, *Milch für alle: Bilder, Dokumente und Analysen zur Milchwirtschaft und Milchpolitik in der Schweiz im 20. Jahrhundert*, Baden: hier + jetzt.

Müller, P., 2010, *La Suisse en crise (1929–1936): les politiques monétaire, financière, économique et sociale de la Confédération helvétique*, Lausanne: Ed. Antipodes.

Ritzmann-Blickenstorfer, H., 1996, *Historische Statistik der Schweiz*, Zürich: Chronos.
Ryser, D., 2015, 'Bundesanstalt oder Kartell? Die Aushandlung des Verhältnisses zwischen Staat und Schweizerischer Käseunion, 1933–1939', *Schweizerisches Jahrbuch für Wirtschafts- und Sozialgeschichte/Annuaire Suisse d'histoire économique et sociale*, 30, pp. 125–142.

15 Conclusion – Agricultural crises and government responses during the interwar period in the Atlantic trading network

Price V. Fishback

1. Introduction

Prior to World War I the markets for farm products had become increasingly global with declines in transport and trade costs (Jacks, 2010; Pinilla in this volume, Chapter 3). The War greatly hindered agriculture in the areas where it was fought, and prices of farm goods rose enormously. Farmers in the United States, Canada, Argentina, Australia, and Sweden therefore benefited from the high prices being paid for farm goods during the War and in the immediate aftermath when the combatants were working to return to normal times. When normal production levels in the combatant economies were reached and farm prices fell to reflect the renewed supply, farm prices fell. Farmers in the countries that benefited from the war boom fared poorly, particularly if they had overestimated the length of the boom when they were borrowing to expand. The farmers in the combatant countries fared better in the sense that they were returning to a more normal setting.

Problems developed again when the worldwide Depression caused incomes and demand to fall between 1929 and 1934–5. Figure 2.1 in the chapter by Ernst Langthaler (Chapter 2) shows that an index of world agricultural trade volume (basically export output) fell from 100 to around 88 in 1934 before recovering to around 96 in 1937. The situation for prices was much worse with the index of value per unit in Langthaler's Figure 2.1 falling from 100 in 1929 to around 38 in 1935 and recovering only to around 45 in 1937. Langthaler's Table 2.1 shows that between 1929 and 1930–7, trade volume fell most for sugar, silk, wheat, and tobacco from 100 in 1929 to 77–83 in the later years, while the volume of coffee, rice, butter and corn (maize) traded rose. Indexes of values per unit in 1930–7 were substantially lower for all crops, falling from 100 in 1929 to below 50 for cotton, wheat, wool, coffee, silk, rubber, rice, and butter. Sugar and tobacco values fared better, falling to only 53 and 64 respectively (Langthaler, Chapter 2, Table 2.1). Farmers in nearly every country faced significant problems. Farm workers, in particular, also faced severe problems because they now had to compete for work with an influx of unemployed industrial workers who returned to rural areas. The farmers in many of the countries successfully lobbied for government policies

DOI: 10.4324/9781003105466-18

designed to protect their incomes and established the precursors of many government agricultural programs in the modern era.

When the markets for agriculture goods had been local, fluctuations in harvests led to countervailing price responses that served to limit fluctuations in income from the crop. Bad harvests reduced supply and raised farm prices, and good harvests increased supply and led to lower farm prices. Thus, farm income fluctuated less than the fluctuation in output. When transport and transactions costs fell and the farms became connected to the world market, the farmers' income opportunities expanded. They could sell locally but had the option to export at even higher prices when world prices were rising but they face greater risk of fluctuations in farm prices that were unconnected to their own harvests. The good news was that a significant number of bad harvests in other countries could push world prices higher during good local harvests and local farm incomes rose more than before. The bad news came when boom harvests in the rest of the world led world prices to fall and farmers facing a bad local harvest saw their incomes fall more than the decline in output. During the boom even farmers with good harvests might see prices fall more than they would have when the farmer was disconnected from the world economy.

Farmers responded to the problems in the 1920s and 1930s by lobbying their governments to limit the impact of the drops in prices. One way was through international trade policies. Some countries added tariffs that taxed imported goods and increase the gap between the local price and the world price. Some adopted import quotas that insured that most of the goods consumed were produced locally. A similar result came through import licensing. Some countries limited trading by controlling the amount of currency that could be exchanged. The policies had substantial impact. Paul Brassley (Chapter 4) reports that protectionism reduced continental European imports by half for wheat and a third for beef and butter, while German, French, and Italian domestic agricultural prices were more than twice the domestic price in the United Kingdom by 1933.

Another came through internal regulations. A number of governments instituted debt relief programs. Several adopted programs that had a mercantilist beggar-thy-neighbor flavor. The programs were designed to buy output from farmers at prices higher than the world price. Such purchase programs often led to surpluses in production and governments set up organizations that would then sell the surplus into the world market. Other countries achieved a similar goal with nonrecourse loans that set a target price. When the market price exceeds the target price the farmer just sold the crop, but when the market price was lower the farmer gave the crop to the lender.

The farmers' demands for protection faced opposition within the countries. After all, low farm prices meant lower prices for consumer goods. The political economic process often led to disputes over policy that in some countries led to policy reversals when different parties gained control of the government. Some countries pressed for deeper long-term changes with land reform meant to increase the share of land holders among farmers. In many cases large landholders maintained significant political clout and as a result were the primary beneficiaries of the protection programs.

This chapter is a summary chapter that compares and contrasts the experiences in the United States with what happened in the countries discussed in the rest of the chapters in the volume. It discusses the heterogeneity of the experiences, the problems faced when unemployed labor flooded the countries during the Great Depression, the various international trade policies followed in the 1920s and 30s, provision of debt relief, efforts at land reform in countries that political turmoil, and the sea of internal regulations established. Between the end of World War II and the early 2010s world trade has expanded and barriers to trade for most goods have been reduced. However, the interwar internal regulations set the precedents for modern policies protecting farm incomes in high-income countries today. Arguably, these policies have propped up domestic farmers at the expense of world markets and impeded the growth of less developed agricultural countries around the world.

2. Heterogeneity across countries and within countries

Even as the world market fell apart during the Great Depression, remember that there were both demanders and sellers in these markets and they had different attitudes towards price changes. There was also a great deal of heterogeneity based on whether the battles in World War I were fought in the country, the types of crops exported and imported, the share of the working population in agriculture, and the depth of the Great Depression. Table 15.1 shows the extent of the Great Depression in the 1930s and the agricultural share of the workforce around 1920 for countries prominently mentioned in the volume. The United Kingdom had the lowest agricultural share at about 7%. Because the share was so low, farmers were unable to get the government to impose much in the way of tariffs because the government worried that their manufacturing exports would be harmed (Brassley, Chapter 4). Other countries with relatively low agricultural labor force shares between 19 and 30% were Argentina, the United States, Switzerland, and Germany. On the high side above 60% were Bulgaria, Mexico, Poland, Turkey, and the Union of Soviet Socialist Republics.

The extent of the Great Depression shown in Table 15.1 varied greatly across the economies. How the economies reacted to the problems in the farm sector was strongly influenced by what was happening in the rest of the economy. If the industrial sector fell apart as well, the countryside ended up being flooded with migrants from urban areas seeking work or moving back to farm areas with relatives to seek subsistence. The United States, Canada, and Mexico faced the deepest troughs during the Great Contraction from 1929 to 1933 with real GDP per capita falling to 67% of their 1929 levels in 1933 and not reaching the 1929 level again until 1940. Spain fared reasonably well through 1935 as real GDP per capita fell only 12% between 1929 and

Table 15.1 Real GDP per capita in the interwar era and farm shares of working population

	Information on real GDP per capita (1929=100)					*Agriculture, forestry, and fishing*	
Country	*1920 level*	*1930s minimum*	*Year of minimum*	*Reached 1929 level before 1941*	*Value in 1940*	*Share of working population*	*In year*
Argentina	80	81	1932	no	95	20	1914
Bulgaria	81	96	1934	1935	137	73	1920
Canada	76	67	1933	1940	106	35	1921
Denmark	79	100	1929	1929	101	42	1921
France	69	84	1932	1939	86	43	1921
Germany	69	83	1932	1935	133	24	1925
Greece	61	91	1931	1933	95	50	1920
Hungary	69	89	1932	1935	106	58	1920
Italy	78	91	1934	1937	104	55	1921
Mexico	105	78	1932	1936	106	63	1921
Poland	89	75	1933–5	1938	Invaded	77	1921
Spain	78	63	1938	No	76	56	1920
Sweden	74	98	1932	1934	120	41	1920
Switzerland	74	94	1936	1937	99	26	1920
Turkey	64*	67	1932	1933	138	82	1935
United Kingdom	80	93	1931	1934	125	7	1921
United States	85	67	1933	1940	100	28	1920
USSR	42	100	1929	1930	155	88	1926

*Value in 1923.
Source: Real GDP per Capita is from the Maddison Project Database (2020). Agriculture, Forestry, Fishing Share of Working Population is from Palgrave MacMillan Ltd (2013).

1933, but a Civil War beginning in 1936 caused a fall to 63% of the 1929 level in 1938. The countries that fared well in the early 1930s were Bulgaria, Denmark, Sweden, Switzerland, Turkey, the United Kingdom, and the Union of Soviet Socialist Republics. Their GDP per capita troughs were at most 7% below the 1929 level, and all recovered to well above the 1929 level by the end of the decade. Germany's GDP fell to 83% of the 1929 level in 1932 and then recovered to 33% above the 1929 level by the end of the decade, but its GDP figures were inflated by the large military buildup leading into World War II.

The extent to which countries relied on different types of exports strongly influenced their stances. The United States, for example, was a large net exporter of wheat and several other crops; therefore, farmers producing those crops gained relatively little from tariff protections (Irwin, 2017). Denmark's dairy and animal producers remained free traders on grains and other imports that they used to feed their animals (Morell, Chapter 10).

The political situation situations also varied. The major combatants of World War I had to make the costly transitions from war-time economies to normal peace-time activities. Germany was saddled with high reparations payments and went through periods of hyperinflation. Hungary lost its place in the Austro-Hungarian Empire. Immediately after the war, it went through transitions from a monarchy to a Bolshevik state before the counterrevolutionaries took over and established a limited parliamentary state with strong elements of authoritarianism (Varga, Chapter 8). Poland regained its independence, fought a series of border wars from 1919 to 1921, faced hyperinflation, and had to establish new trade relationships once its borders were set (Janicki, Chapter 9). Greece, Turkey, and Bulgaria had engaged with each other in a series of bloody wars between 1911 and 1922 with forced shifts of refugee populations (GTB). Rules set by the League of Nations left all three with financial problems (Petmezas, Chapter 7). Mexico experienced a Revolution during the 1910s with several changes in the factions in control (Tortolero, Chapter 12). The Bolshevik revolution led to the formation of Soviet Russia and a dramatic change in the organization of the overall economy (Langthaler, Chapter 2).

There was also a great deal of diversity in the experiences within countries. In Italy the districts that were not harmed much or performed well during the Depression included the Piedmont rice growers, the Asti wine makers, and the districts supported by the Fascist governments, including Low Lombardy, Ferrara, and the Po Delta. The areas that performed poorly included Liguria and Upper Tuscany, which specialized in olives and specialty crops; the subsistence economies of the Southern Apennines and Northern Clusters; the export-oriented Naples, central and southern Apulia, Calabria, and north-eastern Sicily; and the large arable estates of the South (Rome) and Sardinia (Chiapparino and Morettini, in this volume, Chapter 5). In Spain the North and Mediterranean areas accounted for 20% of the land and 40% of the output because they were blessed with plentiful summer rain or had healthy irrigation of fruit and vegetable production. Elsewhere, farmers relied on dry farming methods to produce cereals, wine, or olive oil (Pan-Montojo and Simpson, Chapter 11). Different regions of the United States specialized in different crops, cotton in the South, tobacco in the upper South, sugar in Louisiana and Colorado, corn in the Midwest, wheat in the Great Plains, and citrus fruits in Florida and California. During Mexico's revolution the northeast established commercial crops like chickpeas and cotton, while the south-central areas began commercial marketing of grassland crops, corn, and beans (Tortolero, Chapter 12).

3. Problems with unemployed labor

The problems in the agricultural sector were worsened by unemployment problems. In the United States the unemployment rate was over 20% for four years and over 10% for an entire decade. The problems in American cities touched off a return to rural areas, and unemployment in a number of rural areas was worsened by the decline in labor demand caused by the Agricultural Adjustment Administration (AAA) reductions in land cultivated (Fishback, 2017). The situation appears to have been worse in Poland, where Tadeusz Janicki (Chapter 9) reports that there were about 4.5 million "superfluous" people in 1935, which led consumption in villages to be cut in half, while consumption in cities fell only 8–13%.

World War I and American immigration restrictions greatly limited Italian outmigration to the United States, creating more problems with unemployment. Francesco Chiapparino and Gabriele Morettini (Chapter 5) show that in most of Italy, agriculture was a sort of sponge-sector, capable of absorbing unemployment by compressing incomes and the standard of living, even to the very limits of subsistence. However, unemployment problems worsened in the Ferrara and Po Delta regions because large number of landless laborers depending entirely on their wages for subsistence. To resolve some of these problems the Fascist regime actively sought to relocate at least some of the workers on newly reclaimed lands in other areas. They found that once the emigration opportunities were cut, the agricultural areas in Italy that were most successful were the ones where agricultural workers had the highest mobility in domestic migrations.

Meanwhile, in Argentina Julio Djenderedjian and Juan Luis Martirén (Chapter 6) find that labor productivity in agriculture bounced around along a trend from around 3 to 3.4 in 1902 to 3.8–4 in 1936. But this growth was much slower than in industry during the same time period. They find that a key sector that played an intermediary role was the construction sector, which was able to absorb large amounts of labor during boom times and release them again during busts.

Spain's unemployment problems were worsened by the fact that demand for agricultural labor fell just as the supply of agricultural day workers rose. Juan Pan-Montojo and James Simpson (this volume, Chapter 11) show that in many parts of Spain small family farms dominated and the family farmers would not become unemployed but typically had to feed more people and per capita consumption fell. In southern Spain the unemployment problems were more severe. Dry-farming methods limited opportunities to use new labor-intensive technologies to absorb underemployed farm labor. In fact, labor-saving mechanization was the direction of technological change in the large cereal sector in southern Spain where farms with over 100 hectares accounted for 52.4% of land and were worked by wage labor and roughly 60% were wage workers. By 1933 about one-third of agricultural laborers were unemployed and the unemployed agricultural laborers account for about 60% of the total unemployed in the country.

4. Trade policy

To reduce the competition for their farmers when world prices fell, the nations established a variety of trade policies, including tariffs, import quotas, import licensing, bilateral, or multi-lateral agreements with other nations, and currency exchange controls.

Aside from tariffs on wool and sugar, the United States probably had the least success in using tariffs to protect their farmers. US exports of all kinds boomed during and immediately after World War I, as the war hampered production among the combatants and a couple of post-war years were needed to return to normal production. Faced with dropping prices and declining export opportunities in 1921 and 1922, the United States increased tariffs on a broad range of goods, including agriculture goods in 1921 and 1922. Abraham Berglund (1922: 29) considered the tariffs in 1922 to be among the highest in history to that time. The argument made for the US increase in the agricultural tariffs was to help farm prices keep up with the changes in nonfarm prices. Doug Irwin (2017) describes this as a futile goal for most farm good, however, because the United States was a net exporter of most agricultural goods. US farmers exported roughly half of their cotton, one-third of their tobacco, and one-fifth of wheat and flour in the 1920s. In fact, the overall tariff legislation harmed most farmers by increasing the ratio of nonfarm to farm prices (Irwin, 2017).

The situation in wheat provides an example of the path of followed by tariffs of quite a few agricultural goods during the period. Table 2.4 from the chapter by Langthaler (Chapter 2) provides a comparison of wheat tariffs across countries that shows the progression of rates over time. The US tariff on wheat was set at 5.71 gold francs per quintal in the early 1920s. By 1927 it had been surpassed, as France raised its rate in several steps from 2.68 in 1926 to 7.11 in 1927 to 16.24 in 1929, Germany raised its rates from 4.32 in 1926 to 6.17 in 1927 to 8.03 in 1928 with a drop to 3.89 in 1929. Switzerland also adopted cereal tariffs and Spain increased them in the early 1920s (Head-König and Pan-Montojo and Simpson, both in this volume, Chapters 14 and 11). Meanwhile, the United Kingdom, the Netherlands, Belgium, and Denmark had no wheat tariffs (Langthaler, Chapter 2).

In 1930 the United States increased most of its tariffs again with the infamous Smoot-Hawley Tariff Act. Doug Irwin (2017) finds that the average absolute increase in the tariff was small relative to a number of earlier tariff acts, but a strong deflation in the United States from 1929 to 1933 sharply increased the tariff as a percentage of US domestic prices. Irwin (2017) argues that the Smoot-Hawley Act likely had only a small direct impact on farmers and overall GDP in the United States, but it contributed to an international trade climate that encouraged protectionism throughout the world. Table 2.4 in the Langthaler chapter (Chapter 2) chapter shows that the US wheat tariff rose to 8 in 1929 through 1931 and then was lowered to 5 and below afterward. France retained its 16.24 rate through 1934, Germany raised its rate above 13.8 from 1930 to 1932 before allowing it to drop to 4.32 in 1933. Italy raised its rates above 19.6 from 1930 to 1933 and then let it drop slightly to 18.4 in 1934. The United Kingdom at 0.8 in 1931, the Netherlands at 3.12 in 1932, Belgium at 1.45 in 1933, and Denmark at 0.31 in 1934 established token rates.

A wide range of countries followed protectionist policies for other products during the 1920s and expanded them in the 1930s. Here are just a few of many examples. France relied on tariffs, import quotas, and subsidies, particularly for wine (Chatriot, Chapter 13). Italy increased its protections against wheat, rice, and sugar (Chiapparino and Morettini, Chapter 5). The Swiss imposed tariffs for cereal, dairy, livestock breeding, and wine, while providing subsidies to defray transport costs for exported cattle to the border (Morell, Chapter 10). Switzerland 1932 imposed tariffs on cheese and butter and the import of concentrates, while also adopting milk import quotas (Head-König, Chapter 14).

Other countries eschewed protectionism when it made economic sense. Denmark adopted only a very small wheat tariff as late as 1934 because cereals provided fodder for their large dairy and animal sectors. This allowed Danish farmers to avoid having to raise the price when selling those goods internationally (Morell, Chapter 10). The United Kingdom adopted only a token tariff because it imported large amounts of food and feared that imposing agricultural tariffs to protect farmers, who accounted for less than 8% of the population, would harm their markets for manufacturing exports, which accounted for 77% of exports (Brassley, Chapter 4). In efforts to promote its industry, the Polish government launched a "cheap bread" policy in which it gathered grain reserves, imposed export duties on cereals and dropped its tariffs on wheat and rye in 1929 (Janicki, Chapter 9). During the Mexican Revolution, the governments in power eliminated import duties in years with bad harvests to ensure enough food for the population (Tortolero, Chapter 12).

A number of countries lowered their barriers to imports with favored trading partners using bilateral and multi-lateral trade agreements in the 1920s and 1930s. The United States had negotiated a variety of Most Favored Nations clauses during the 1920s. Doug Irwin (2017) suggests that these clauses helped limit retaliatory tariffs against the United States in a number of countries after the Smoot-Hawley Act passed in 1930. One exception was Canada, which immediately raised tariffs on 16 key imports from the United States that cut the value of US exports to Canada by 78% and reduced the Canadian share of US exports from 18% in 1929 to 12.6% in 1933.

Instead of relying on tariffs, Britain diverted many of its imports to the British Commonwealth countries by eliminating tariffs on their goods and negotiated bilateral agreements with Argentina and the Scandinavian countries, which were important both as agricultural suppliers and recipients of UK manufactures (Brassley, Chapter 4). France signed a bilateral trade agreement with Greece in July 1933. Germany signed bilateral agreements with Greece in August 1932, Bulgaria in June 1932, and Turkey in 1934. Between 1933 and 1939 Germany absorbed 52% of Bulgarian, 48% of Greek, and 38% of Turkish tobacco. The three countries exported to Germany more than they imported, while German demand stabilized prices and rural incomes in all three (Petmezas, in this volume, Chapter 7). Meanwhile, a supplement to a 1931 trade agreement with Germany opened its market to Hungarian wheat, rye, barley, and corn. Subsequently, Germany accounted for about 50 to 60% of Hungarian exports. In 1934 Hungary joined a tripartite agreement with Austria and Italy, and Italy imported about 12 to 20% of Hungary's exports (Varga, Chapter 8).

In the wheat market there was some relief from a "gentlemen's agreement" between 22 countries, including most of the ones in this volume, that was negotiated at the Conference of Wheat Exporting and Importing Countries in August 1933. It was helped by the US adoption earlier in the year of the Agricultural Adjustment Act with its focus on limiting output (Langthaler, Chapter 2). Unfortunately for the United States, the agreement did little to increase wheat exports, which were still as high as 168 million 60-pound bushels in 1928 but fell to an average of 36.3 million from 1934 to 1940 (Béaur and Chiapparino, Introduction of this volume, and series Ee574 in Carter et.al. 2004).

After the United States passed the Reciprocal Trade Agreement Act of 1934, the United States negotiated bilateral trade agreements in 1934 with Cuba, in 1935 with Brazil, Belgium, Haiti, and Sweden, in 1936 with Colombia, Canada, Honduras, Netherlands, Switzerland, Nicaragua, Guatemala, and France, in 1937 with Finland and Costa Rica, in 1938 with Czechoslovakia and Ecuador, and in 1939 with the United Kingdom, a second agreement with Canada, Turkey, and Venezuela (Irwin, 2017: 366–433).

5. Government efforts to provide debt relief

When international prices fell, a large number of farmers faced problems in repaying their loans, including mortgages on land and equipment, intermediate term loans for tools and seeds, and short-term consumption loans until the harvest was finished. The situation often worsened when there was general deflation in the country, as the farmers were forced to repay amounts in their currency in real terms that were higher than the amounts they borrowed. A substantial number of countries reacted by adopting policies to improve access to credit or provide debt relief for troubled farmers.

5.1 Credit policies in the United States

In the US federal loan support for farmers began in 1917 after the Federal Farm Loan Board was created to provide seed money for 12 Federal Land Banks (FLB). Each of the 12 banks was originally endowed with $750,000, which it then loaned to groups of farmers seeking mortgages who formed national farm loan associations on a cooperative basis to provide mortgages to the members of the association. By 1929 the original endowments had almost fully been repaid and approximately 4,600 national farm loan associations owned nearly all of the capital stock in the FLBs. The government also provided for the creation of federal joint-stock banks that were privately financed. The FLB loans to associations and joint-stock land bank loans had interest rates capped at one percentage point higher than the interest rate on their most recent bond issues up to a maximum of 6%. As a result, farm mortgage interest rates on the FLB and joint-stock mortgages were substantially lower than rates charged by other lenders outside the Northeast in 1928. In addition, the loans were amortized for equal annual payments over a time horizon of over 30 years at a time when most farm mortgages were 3–5-year loans with repayments of interest until the full principal was due at the end of the loan (Snowden, 2013: 47, 67; Glock, 2016). By 1927 the Federal Farm Loan Board (1929: 32, 35) claimed that the Federal Land Banks and joint-stock banks held approximately one-fifth of all US farm mortgage debt. In 1923 Federal Intermediate Credit Banks (FICBs) were organized to provide loans to cooperative marketing associations and provide discounts of agricultural paper endorsed by a variety of lenders. By 1929 these activities had aided about a million farmers (Federal Farm Loan Board (1929: 78–9). At various times, on an ad hoc basis, Congress also authorized emergency crop and feed loans in the 1920s to offset disastrous crop years (Federal Farm Loan Board, various years; Halcrow, 1953; Glock, 2016).

As farm prices fell after 1929, a sharp rise in farm foreclosure rates contributed to the demise of the joint-stock mortgage banks (Glock, 2016). Meanwhile, more than half of the states passed mortgage moratoria laws designed to make it more difficult to foreclose on delinquent borrowers. This came at a future cost, however, as private lenders anticipated the risk of future moratoria and increased mortgage interest rates and made fewer loans in the years that followed (Alston, 1984; Rucker and Alston, 1987).

Under Roosevelt's New Deal, the Farm Credit Administration was created to take over the role played by the FLBs, set up 12 regional banks to provide both short- and intermediate-term credit to thousands of local production credit associations and other lenders serving agriculture, and to set up 12 regional banks to provide credit for farm cooperatives (https://www.fca.gov/about/history-of-fca downloaded on 1/25/2022). The expansion in New Deal mortgage lending helped reduce the foreclosure rate with an elasticity of -0.49 (Rucker and Alston, 1987). It also created new programs for production loans and emergency crop and feed loans and ultimately accounted for about 30% of all New Deal era loans. In an attempt to guarantee higher farm prices, the Commodity Credit Corporation distributed 12% of the loans in a price support program in which the farmer took out a nonrecourse loan with a base output price. If the market price fell below the base price, the farmer repaid the loan by giving the crop to the lender; otherwise, he sold the crop and repaid the loan in cash. The Farm Security Administration targeted a relatively small share of the New Deal loans at low-income farmers to help them become farm owners (Fishback, 2017).

The Rural Electrification Administration handed out about 1% of the New Deal loans to rural electricity cooperatives to provide access to electricity for rural farms and households that previously had not had access to the grid. These electrification loans were associated with increases in farm output per acre, increases in the use of machinery, reductions in the amount of time the farmer worked off of his farm, and decreases in infant mortality rates (Kitchens and Fishback, 2015).

5.2 Examples of debt relief in other countries

Debt relief was offered to farmers in a number of countries, and in many it was targeted at larger land holders. In Hungary debt relief was offered to farmers in 1933 and 1935. Estates with debt above a threshold were able to obtain protection from the government from being sold by auctions. The state spent nearly 110 million pengos on debt relief between 1933 and 1937 to protect about 1.1 million hectares of land, of which about 61% aided land holders in farms with more than 60 hectares (Varga, Chapter 8). In Germany estate owners in 1929 began receiving state subsidies for debt relief but little relief was offered to small farmers (Langthaler, Chapter 2). Turkey also established a state Agricultural Bank but offered few funds to small owner-farmers (Petmezas, Chapter 7). The Swiss government established a 1928 special relief fund for over-indebted farmers, and then in 1933 provided systematic debt relief for "deserving" farmers with 5% of the relief going to wine, fruit and vegetable producers, 26.7% to dairy producers, and 33% for cattle farms (Head-König, Chapter 14).

Bulgaria operated one of the largest debt relief efforts. Under the 1930 National Debt Relief Act the state covered a debt of 6.6 million out of 10 million nonperforming agricultural credits (a quarter of GDP) for 1.2 million rural households (Petmezas, Chapter 7). In Greece the government suspended all taxation on all agricultural production except for taxes and tariffs on tobacco and currants. Then in May 1937 Greece wrote off a large portion of the 1936 total agricultural debt owed to private and public creditors in equal shares. That debt was valued at about half of the value of the average annual output (Petmezas, Chapter 7).

6. Internal attempts to control prices and output

In response to the problems faced by farmers, a large number of countries sought to "stabilize" their agricultural markets by setting fixed prices for domestic farmers above the world price. This often led to increased production that government entities often purchased from farmers. Some countries tried to limit these surpluses with production controls. Most of the countries discovered that the policies did not work well and tried various fixes. Yet, these policies became the precedents for many policies followed by high-income countries today.

6.1 Domestic farm policies in the United States

Between 1924 and 1928 the US Congress considered the adoption of various forms of the McNary-Haugen bill, which would have had major international trade implications for the crops involved. The bill was designed to prop up domestic farm prices. It would create an export corporation that would buy up surplus output above domestic consumption at a target price based on the pre-War ratio of farm prices to nonfarm prices and in some cases the current tariffs on the commodity. The surplus was then to be sold in the world market, probably at a lower price. The losses on the resale of the commodities were to be recouped by required an equalization fee to be covered by the domestic price of the good. Versions of the bill passed both houses of Congress in 1927 and 1928 but were vetoed by President Calvin Coolidge (Kelley, 1940; Black, 1928; Halcrow, 1953: 242–8). The Hoover administration actually followed an alternative route in 1929 by setting up the Federal Farm Board, which created national corporations that would provide loans to cooperatives to make marketing advances on a fixed-price basis. The Federal Farm Board worked through government corporations that used loans and purchases to obtain surplus wheat and cotton and prop up their prices. The actions appeared to have propped up prices in 1930, but the Farm Board ended up obtaining and having to store large stocks of both crops. It stopped lending before the 1931 harvest and was closed down in 1933 (Halcrow, 1953: 258–62).

The central program of the New Deal efforts that began in 1933 was the Agricultural Adjustment Administration (AAA) grants designed to control production. The supporters of the McNary-Haugen and Federal Farm Board programs all agreed that control of production was needed to make those programs work. The AAA offered rental and benefit payments to farmers to take land out of production for specific crops and accounted for roughly 10% of all New Deal grants awarded. The 1933 program was financed mostly through a tax on the processing of the agricultural product supported. After the processing tax was declared unconstitutional in 1936, the agricultural lobby succeeded in obtaining a new Soil and Domestic Allotment Act that continued the AAA payments out of the general fund while the rhetoric emphasized soil conservation and improvements to the land (Alexander and Libecap, 2000).

A series of studies show that the AAA tended to benefit large farmers at the expense of farm workers, croppers, and tenants. The two factors that most strongly influenced the distribution of AAA grants and farm loans were the average size of farms and representation on the House Agricultural Committee (Fishback, Kantor, and Wallis, 2003). Econometric estimates of the impact of AAA payments on per capita personal income and consumption mostly found slightly negative effects (Fishback and Kachanovskaya, 2015; Fishback, Horrace, and Kantor, 2005). The AAA was also associated with declines in the overall farm population, the number of white and black sharecroppers, and the number of black tenants in the cotton-producing counties (Fishback, Haines, and Rhode, 2012; Depew, Fishback, and Rhode, 2013; Whatley, 1983). Both the AAA grants and loan programs (described below) contributed to an increase in the use of farm machinery, particularly tractors in some parts of the country.[1]

In an unpublished analysis of the impact of the AAA grants and farm loans on cotton agriculture in the 1930s, the AAA grants and farm loans tended to work cross purposes. The AAA contributed to sharp reductions in the cotton acreage harvested, as it was designed to do, but the farm loans provided resources to farmers that offset about one-third of that drop. While the AAA contributed to a rise in cotton output per cotton acre harvested, the farm loans served to reduce that measure largely because it contributed to a rise in cotton acreage harvested. The AAA also had positive effects and the farm loans negative effects on the real value of farm machinery. The AAA contributed to declines in the use of mules and horses, while the farm loans partially offset the decline. Neither program appears to have had much effect on farm incomes. This combination of results suggest that the farm loans brought less productive land and animal-based technologies into production in ways that partially offset the changes wrought by the AAA program (Depew, Fishback, Kantor, Rhode, and Sorensen, 2018).

When the AAA shifted its emphasis towards soil conservation after 1935, it contributed to an increase in farm size and the use of anti-erosion methods in the Plains states that helped eliminate another Dust Bowl problem in the 1970s. The 1970s and 1930s shared the same weather patterns that had created the Dust Bowl in the 1930s, but the use of the anti-erosion methods prevented large dust storms from forming (Hansen and Libecap, 2004).

6.2 Internal controls in Sweden

Before the Great Depression in 1928, Sweden appointed an agricultural committee to regulate supply and market relations, sought to unify cooperatives under the leadership of the general agricultural society, SAL and encouraged a Farmers Union to organize all farmers. The union and the SAL reinforced each other. Sweden in 1930 set an import quota for grain and stipulated minimum prices that large mills were to pay to farmers. Soon thereafter, they established a Swedish grain association that guaranteed it would buy all bread grain good enough to grind at fixed prices and then sell the grain to the mills. The association could also charge fees when grain products imported (Morell, Chapter 10).

Similarly, the national association of Swedish dairies (SMR) was given the right to collect a price equalization fee on all milk used for butter, cheese, or cream in Sweden, even from producers not engaged in SMR dairies. The fees financed a price subsidy for butter exporters. Butter was subsidized further by a consumption tax on margarine. By 1938 91% of Swedish dairy milk came through SMR dairies. Similar regulations with fees on domestic sales on exports were set up for beef, pork, and eggs (Morell, Chapter 10).

Mats Morell (here in Chapter 10) shows that the start of regulation led to outcomes that encouraged further regulation. When land in wheat rose at the expense of land for fodder grain, wheat prices were regulated but fodder grain prices were not. Guaranteed sales of wheat at fixed prices led to increased wheat surpluses, causing the government to impose a wheat fee. Part of the surplus was stored but much was sold at a discount as fodder. Meanwhile, fees on domestically consumed milk were supposed to subsidize butter exports, but the guaranteed butter price and falling fodder prices led to increased butter production that needed to be exported. This led the government to introduce new taxes on fodder. After pork prices were stabilized, the government sought to limit pork production by restricting the import of corn (maize). In general, productivity in farming rose while employment in farming did not fall very fast. The growth in food consumption did not match the large amounts produced in response to the fixed prices, which raised the cost to the government of dumping the surplus in export markets (Morell, Chapter 7).

In 1939 Sweden began determining agricultural prices while viewing the entire farm sector as one single company. The model used to compute the farmgate prices was based on wage rates (and shadow wages, for farm family members), input prices, and income goals. Representatives of the state, the RLF and the cooperative movement, later joined by a consumer delegation, were involved in the discussions. The prices chosen were guaranteed by the state with a goal to equalize the incomes of medium-sized family farmers and industrial workers (Morell, Chapter 7).

6.3 Internal controls in the rest of Europe

Spain tried to intervene in commodity markets at home and to control exports and imports at various times. During World War I the government set maximum prices for wheat, flour, and bread. In the 1920s it set minimum prices for farmers. But these efforts were criticized by both farmers and consumers. Spain also offered state-backed mortgages. A more popular policy was the expansion of irrigation works, funded by payments by landowners based on the change in land value associated with the introduction of irrigation and special deals for small farmers (Pan-Montojo and Simpson, Chapter 11).

In Italy the Fascists in 1925 sought strategic self-sufficiency in wheat with the *Battaglia del Grano,* which administered the internal wheat trade through a system of mandatory storage. To upgrade yields, the government introduced new selected varieties, relaunched a reclamation campaign, and heavily promoted food cultivation and yield improvements. They redoubled their efforts again in 1935 when faced with the sanctions introduced by the League of Nations following the invasion of Ethiopia (Chiapparino and Morettini, Chapter 5).

Switzerland operated a variety of internal policies. During the 1920s they began guaranteeing prices for cereal and cheese. All milk was delivered to processing centers at a guaranteed price for a fixed amount of milk, and market prices were paid for the surplus. The guarantees were one reason why Swiss exports of condensed milk fell heavily in the early 1930s. The Swiss also tried price guarantees for butter, but the Swiss still imported butter extensively until the 1930s when overproduction of milk and tariffs on butter and the price guarantees led to a shift to butter. In 1932 they created a central organization named Butyra to take charge of butter not sold to consumers and regulated butter imports. This led to a large domestic butter surplus in part because consumers were slow to switch from the Danish butter that they had long been consuming. Swiss subsidies to milk producers also quadrupled between 1927–8 and 1935–6. Anne-Lise Head-König (Chapter 14) reports that these fixed price and market guarantees generally failed. After World War II they eventually led to "growing butter mountains, cheese mountains and milk lakes" and were abandoned. A switch to individual farm quotas also was later abandoned.

Between 1929 and 1939 Alain Chatriot (Chapter 13) reports that the French government tried a variety of policies to address problems with dropping prices but found many to be unsatisfactory. A 1929 law gave *de facto* power to the Minister of Agriculture to regulate the origin and nature of grain used in mills. In 1930 a law was proposed to create a permanent stock of grain and flour to protect against price speculation, and the policy was fully established by 1932. In January 1933 financial intervention was allowed to control prices through holding of stock surpluses. To make use of the surplus stocks, an April 1933 law allowed the Minister of Agriculture to provide subsidies for non-food and non-alcohol uses of the grain. In July 1933 a minimum price of grain was established and multiple laws in 1933 and 1934 were enacted to deal with the difficulties that arose. In 1935 France tried a return to free trade but the experiment ended when prices dropped sharply. The government then tried several policies to offset the fall in prices. In 1936 France established a Grain Bureau program designed to fix prices, purchase, and store surplus production, and create a monopoly on the imports and exports of grain. The proponents of the Grain Bureau were able to set up the policy due to an absence of grain surpluses in 1936 and 1937. The large harvest of 1938, however, created difficulties with the program that led to additional reforms in 1939 (Chatriot, Chapter 13).

Hungary's Boletta System of 1930 granted a price supplement over sales price of wheat and rye for 4 fiscal years largely to the benefit of large estates. The government also set up a bonus system in which farmers were paid a price in Hungarian pengos for exports that exceeded the value that would have been paid at the official exchange rate. In 1934, to handle wheat exchanges under Hungary's agreements with German, Italy, and Austria, Hungary set up the Futura, a monopoly agricultural corporation that established minimum wheat prices based on the high wheat purchase price ensured in the agreement. Large landowners were the primary beneficiaries of the Futura's activities because they were the primary exporters and received higher prices on several commodities sold to the Futura (Varga, Chapter 8).

Britain's internal controls included policies following from the Agricultural Marketing Act of 1933, which allowed the regulation of both imports and home production and eventually led to Marketing Boards for milk, potatoes, hops, and pigs. At a time when UK agricultural output was value at £215 million, Brassley (Chapter 4) reports estimates that the higher prices associated with the marketing acts increased farm incomes by £40 million and subsidies and tax relief to farmers were worth £33 million. Meanwhile, the Agricultural Wages Board increased farm workers' wages by about £16 million.

In Germany in 1933 the Nazi regime established the New Order of German agriculture. Producers, processors, and traders were required to join the Reich Food Estate (RFE), which channeled basic farm products from producer to consumer at fixed prices. Agricultural prices improved from 1934 to 36 but then stagnated, which meant that farm prices declined relative to industrial prices. The RFE promoted production competition in a manner similar to Italy's Battaglia del Grano with mixed results. Nazi ideology idealized medium-sized farms that were community-oriented and tried to protect them with a new law for inheriting farms in 1933. The 1936 Four-Year Plan helped prepare for war by establishing well-equipped peasant farms throughout and resettling small landholders to East Europe to provide them with land taken from the indigenous population (Langthaler, Chapter 2) In 1930 in Poland, nine years before it was invaded by Germany, the government sought to raise farm prices in 1930 by introducing state purchases of cereals and sought to aid farmers by reducing industry prices with new policies against cartels in 1933 (Janicki, Chapter 9).

7. Land reform

Several countries experienced revolutions and/or Civil Wars between 1910 and 1940, and land reform became a central goal. In Mexico the revolution lasted from 1910 to 1920 with reverberations felt through 1940. During the revolution the various sides sought to ensure that the populace was fed. For most of the period domestic production was adequate, but during bad harvests, those in charge encouraged food imports from the United States. Legislation in 1915 and the Constitution of 1917 provided mechanisms that threatened the owners of large estates with demands for restitution of lands to peasants and legislation. The goal was to create *ejidos*, in which community members had usufruct rights that allowed them to use and derive income from use of the land but not sell the land. Despite these efforts, except in the states of Morelos and Veracruz, large farms remained primarily in control in years after the armed struggle. In the 1930 census 83% of the arable land consisted of holdings larger than 1,000 hectares and was held by 1.5% of total landholders. An additional 12% of the land was concentrated in farms ranging from 101 to 1,000 hectares (Tortolero, Chapter 12).

Even though some leaders were calling for the end of ejido creation in the late 1920s and early 1930s, the problems in export markets and the sudden repatriation of 300,000 Mexicans from the United States diminished their power. In 1931 landowners were stripped of their ability to go to court to block state demands for restitution or endowment of their lands. When President Cardenas came to power, the reform process sped up. Until 1935 agrarian reform involved distributing 10.8 million hectares among 545,000 families. Under Cárdenas from 1934 to 1940 more than 17 million hectares were distributed to over 814,000 ejido farms. The agrarian reform varied by region and had little effect on about one-third of the Mexican states (Tortolero, Chapter 12).

Hungary passed a Land Reform Act in 1920 in the midst of the turmoil followed the demise of the Austro-Hungarian Empire. The reform involved about 8.5% of its agricultural land, as 400,000 applicants each received roughly one hectare (2.47105 acres) of land. In 1935 when Hungary embarked on some additional land reforms, 29% of the land was in large estates with more than 570 hectares and 48% of the land was in farms with land more than 57 hectares. At the other end of the distribution, 10% of the land was in plots of less than 2.8 hectares and 32% in lands with less than 11.4 hectares. The land reform efforts included an act on settlement in 1935 that would subdivide about 240,000 hectares of land for settlement within 25 years. In addition, a 1935 Decree was designed to make it easier for landowners with separate plots around the village to consolidate the land into one tract. Between 1935 and 1941 a total of 98 villages from 1935 to 41 consolidated about 180,000 hectares. The process was estimated to raise productivity by 20% with a consequent rise in the value of land (Varga, Chapter 8)

In the Union of Soviet Socialist Republics its 1921 New Economic Policy tried to liberalize domestic markets, while the state controlled foreign trade by fostering grain, timber, and oil exports. The government ran into losses in hard currency due to falling export prices combined with bad harvests that raised domestic prices for grain. The 1928 Five-Year plan called for increased grain exports to finance technology imports for industry. To eliminate the backwardness of peasant farms and holdouts by larger landowners, the government established technology-intense state farms, forced conversions of peasant villages into collective farms, and displaced large landowners. Peasant rebellions led them to call off the campaign in 1930, but it was restarted in 1931. Crop failures due to drought in 1931 and wet weather in 1932 caused the Great Famine. The program was reorganized again through technology transfer, fixed delivery quotas and plots for family use (Langthaler, Chapter 2).

Spanish agriculture was not hit as hard by the Depression. Figure 11.4 in the Pan-Montojo and Simpson chapter (Chapter 11) shows that farm prices in Spain did not fall nearly as far as the price declines in the Figures in the Langthaler contribution (Chapter 2). Real GDP per capita fell only 12% between 1929 and 1933 and began recovering in 1934. The Spanish government focused more on long-term land reform. A Labor and Socialist government gained government control in from 1931 until November 1933. This leftist government sought to weaken the power of estate owners with land market decrees in April and July 1931 by protecting tenants from eviction unless they had not paid rent or not cultivated the land. They established tribunals that lowered many rents and gave preference to workers' syndicates for renting the land. Farmers were required to cultivate land with same intensity and number of workers as before. When a center-right to right government returned to power late in 1933 the estate owners returned to working with the tenants and workers they trusted and ignored the syndicate members (Pan-Montojo and Simpson, Chapter 11).

The Labor/Socialist government in Spain also embarked on land reform with the 1932 Agrarian Reform Law. It set limits to individual land ownership in each place and for each crop; allowed for the expropriation of land if it was badly cultivated, had been leased continuously for more than 12 years, or the owner failed to use available irrigation; and land where seigneurial rights had been converted to full ownership in the nineteenth century was to be confiscated without compensation. Fewer than 14,000 farmers received land under the Act by September 1934 and the revisions to the law in July 1935 slowed the process further. The new government did allow for a social utility clause to settle villagers on uncultivated land when in urgent social need, which inspired massive land invasions in 1936. The land invasions were soon followed by the destructive Spanish Civil War, which drove Spain's GDP per capita to 63% of the 1929 level by 1938 (Pan-Montojo and Simpson, Chapter 11).

8. Conclusions

The chapters in the volume document the experiences in the agricultural sector in several countries in Europe and three countries in the Americas that were involved in the Atlantic trading network during the interwar period. The nature of trade automatically led to heterogeneity as buyers praise lower prices and producers dislike them. There was also heterogeneity in the experiences of farmers across countries and within countries with respect to the crops they produced, the political settings, their experience with price changes in the 1920s, and the extent to which the entire economy experienced a downturn during the Great Depression. Thus, the chapters document a rich range of experiences within the larger backdrop of the Atlantic agricultural network.

Following a period of increasing globalization of agricultural markets, World War I sharply limited the agricultural activities of the main combatants, which led to sharp increases in agricultural prices and farm incomes in countries where the fighting was not located. In consequence, during the 1920s the combatants experienced more of a return to normalcy while farmers in the countries that expanded production during the war went through hard times. In the 1920s some countries began to limit trading by increasing tariffs and establishing quotas, while some experimented with aiding farmers by offering them price guarantees when purchasing the products. When the Great Depression hit, the farm regions in many of countries faced a flood of unemployed workers that put more downward pressure on farm incomes and opportunities. In the early 1930s, nearly every country sought to protect at least some of their farmers, usually large farmers, against price declines in the international markets. Many countries raised their tariffs and some set quotas for imports of goods produced by their farmers. By 1932 a number of countries began reestablishing trade with key trading partners through bilateral and multilateral agreements. Many governments offered subsidized loans or debt relief to their farmers. Nearly every country regulated agriculture in some form, through subsidies, by setting minimum prices, by purchasing surpluses, or by limiting output. Often the regulations led to problems that led to new regulatory fixes while setting the precedents for the domestic farm programs that continue to protect farmers in the modern era.

Note

1 See Sorensen, Fishback, Kantor, and Rhode (2011), Clarke (1994), and Whatley (1983, 1985).

Bibliography

Alexander, B. and Libecap, G., 2000, "The Effect of Cost Heterogeneity in the Success and Failure of the New Deal's Agricultural and Industrial Programs", *Explorations in Economic History*, 37 (October), pp. 370–400.

Alston, L., 1984, "Farm Foreclosure Moratorium Legislation: A Lesson from the Past", *American Economic Review,* 74(3) (June), pp. 445–57.

Berglund, A., "Tariff Act of 1922", *American Economic Review,* 13 (March 1923), pp. 14–33.

Black, J. D., 1928, "The McNary-Haugen Movement", *American Economic Review* 18(3) (September), pp. 406–27.

Carter, S., Gartner, S. S., Haines, M. R., Olmstead, A. L., Sutch, R., and Wright, G. (eds.), 2004, *Millennial Edition of the Historical Statistics of the United States,* New York: Cambridge University Press.

Clarke, S., 1994, *Regulation and the Revolution in United States Farm Productivity,* New York: Cambridge University Press.

Depew, B., Fishback, P., Kantor, S., Rhode, P. and Sorensen, T., 2018, "The New Deal and Cotton Agriculture During the Great Depression", Working Paper at University of Arizona.

Depew, B., Fishback, P. and Rhode, P., 2013, "New Deal or No Deal in the Cotton South: The Effect of the AAA on the Agriculture Labor Structure", *Explorations in Economic History,* 50 (October), pp. 466–86.

Farm Credit Administration, 1935, *Financing Agriculture in 1934,* Washington, DC: GPO.

Farm Credit Administration, 1936, *Farm Credit Quarterly,* June 1936, Washington, DC: GPO.

Federal Farm Loan Board, 1930, *Thirteenth Annual Report of the Federal Farm Loan Board for the Year Ended December 31, 1929,* Washington, DC: Government Printing Office.

Fishback, P., 2017, "How Successful Was the New Deal? The Microeconomic Impact of New Deal Spending and Lending Policies", *Journal of Economic Literature,* 55(4) (December), pp. 1435–85.

Fishback, P., Horrace, W. and Kantor, S., 2005, "Did New Deal grant Programs Stimulate Local Economies? A Study of Federal Grants and Retail Sales during the Great Depression", *The Journal of Economic History,* 65 (March), pp. 36–71.

Fishback, P., Horrace, W. and Kantor, S., 2006, "The Impact of New Deal Expenditures on Mobility During the Great Depression", *Explorations in Economic History,* 43 (April), pp. 179–222.

Fishback, P. and Kachanovskaya, V., 2015, "The Multiplier for the States in the Great Depression.' With Valentina Kachanovskaya", *Journal of Economic History,* 75 (March), pp. 125–62.

Fishback, P., Kantor, S. and Wallis, J., 2003, "Can the New Deal's Three R's Be Rehabilitated? A Program-by-Program, County-by-County Analysis", *Explorations in Economic History* (October), pp. 278–307.

Glock, J., 2016, "The Rise and Fall of the First Government-Sponsored Enterprise: The Federal Land Banks, 1916–1932", *Business History Review,* 90 (Winter), pp. 623–45.

Halcrow, H. G., 1953, *Agricultural Policy of the United States,* New York: Prentice-Hall.

Hansen, Z. and Libecap, G., 2004, "Small Farms, Externalities, and the Dust Bowl of the 1930s", *Journal of Political Economy,* 112 (June), pp. 665–94.

Irwin, D., 2017, *Clashing Over Commerce: A History of U.S. Trade Policy* Chicago: University of Chicago Press,.

Jacks, D., 2010, "Trade Costs in the First Wave of Globalization", *Explorations in Economic History,* 47(2) (April), pp. 127–41.

Kelley, D., 1940, "The McNary-Haugen Bills, 1924–1928: An Attempt to Make the Tariff Effective for Farm Products", *Agricultural History,* 14(4) (October), pp. 170–80.

Kitchens, C. and Fishback, P., 2015, "Flip the Switch: The Spatial Impact of the Rural Electrification Administration, 1935–1940", *Journal of Economic History,* 75 (December), pp. 1161–95.

Maddison Project Database 2020, Downloaded on January 27, 2022 from https://www.rug.nl/ggdc/historicaldevelopment/maddison/releases/maddison-project-database-2020?lang=en

Palgrave Macmillan Ltd (eds)., 2013, *International Historical Statistics,* "B1 Economically Active Population by Major Industrial Groups (in thousands)", London: Palgrave Macmillan. https://doi-org.ezproxy4.library.arizona.edu/10.1057/978-1-137-30568-8_397

Rucker, R. and Alston, L., 1987, "Farm Failures and Government Intervention: A Case Study of the 1930s", *American Economic Review,* 77, pp. 724–30.

Snowden, K., 2013, *Mortgage Banking in the United States, 1870–1940* Research Institute for Housing America. Special Report.

Sorensen, T., Fishback, P., Kantor, S. and Rhode, P., 2011, "The New Deal and the Diffusion of Tractors in the 1930s", Working paper, University of Arizona.

Whatley, W. C., 1983, "Labor for the Picking: The New Deal in the South", *The Journal of Economic History,*45(4) (December), pp. 905–29.

Whatley, W. C., 1985, "A History of Mechanization in the Cotton South: The Institutional Hypothesis", *The Quarterly Journal of Economics,* 100(4) (November), pp. 1191–215.

Index

Note: **Bold** page numbers refer to tables; *italic* page numbers refer to figures and page numbers followed by "n" denote endnotes.

agrarian reform: 1932 Agrarian Reform Law 196, 272; crisis in 1930s 46–8; Mexican agriculture 9, 206, 210, 213–21, 271; in Spanish case 42–4, 48, 203

Agricultural Adjustment Act (AAA) 31–2, 40, 260, 263, 266–7

Agricultural Marketing Act 31, 68, 69, 269

agricultural trade 22–3, *23*, *25*; composition of leading commodities, 1929–37 **24**

Ancien Régime: agricultural crisis of 42–3; outbreak of war and French invasion 43

Aparicio, G. 61, 225

Argentine agriculture, 1930s crisis 97–8; agricultural GDP 99, *99*, 106, *107*, 109, *109*; annual growth rates 103, **103**; 'Belle Epoque' 97; cultivated area and cereal production 101, *102*; economic expansion 98–101; European immigration 108, *108*; First Globalization 99; investment and export growth 100, **100**; labor productivity 104–6, *105*; 'optimistic' stance 97; professions declared by adults 107, **108**; reallocation 106–10; role of primary sector 98; Total Factor Productivity (TFP) 98, 101–4

Association Generale des Producteurs de Ble (AGPB) 226–7

Astor, P. 66

Atlantic trading network: credit policies in United States 263–5; domestic farm policies in United States 265–7; examples of debt relief in other countries 265; government efforts to provide debt relief 263–5; heterogeneity across countries and within countries 257–9, **258**; internal attempts to control prices and output 265–70; internal controls in rest of Europe 268–70; internal controls in Sweden 267–8; land reform 270–2; problems with unemployed labor 259–60; trade policy 260–3

Austro-Hungarian Customs Union 140

banking sector: in Austria and Germany 121; bankruptcies 6, 10, 127; crisis of 1929 1–2; crisis of 1930 130; in France 227; in Greek 133; in Hungary 141; peasantry 119; in Poland 157, 160, 162; in Sweden 173, 176, **177**; in Switzerland 249; in Turkey 117, 124; in US 263–5

Barrett, H. 71

Barthelemy, Joseph 231

'battle for grain' (*battaglia del grano*) 3, 7, 77, 84, 88, 93, 94, 268, 270; *see also* wheat

beef: European imports 73, 256; in Sweden 180, 267; in Switzerland 246; in UK 60, **60,** 62, 64, 66; in US 4

Bell, A. 71

Berger, S. 231, 232

Berglund, A. 261

Blum, Leon 230, 231

Boletta System 148, 269

Bolshevik revolution 30, 259

Bordo, M. 186

Brassley, P. 256, 270
Bretton Woods System 22, 34
British abolition of the Corn Laws 44
British-centered/'extensive' food regime 22
Bulgaria: annual rates of change of main agricultural indexes **126,** 126; foreign trade of 123, *124*; price index in *125,* 125
butter 179; in 1929–30 and 1930–1 175; European imports 73, 256; as leading commodities, 1929–37 23, **24**; in Mexican government 210; in Netherlands 63; in Sweden 63, 174, 180–1, 185, 267–9; in Swiss Government 237, 241, **243,** 243–5, 247, 249, 252, 262; in UK **60,** 60–2, **61, 63,** 66; *see also* milk
Butyra 243, 269

Calles, Plutarco Elias 213, 217
Cárdenas (President) 9, 217–19, 271
Carmona, J. 47, 221
cattle breeders 237–8, 240–1, 244–6, *245,* 250
Chatriot, A. 9, 269
'cheap bread policy' 158, 262
cheese: in Canada 63; exports 246–8; in New Zealand 63; in Sweden 174, 179–80, 267; Swiss 237, 240–3, *245,* 245–7, **247, 248,** *249,* 250, 252, 253n2, 262, 268–9; in UK 60–2, **61, 62, 63,** 66; *see also* milk
Cherrington, J. 71
Chiapparino, F. 260
Civil War 3, 29
coffee 255; as leading commodities, 1929–37 23, **24**; in Mexico 210–11, 217; in UK 60
collectivization 29–30, 35
Commodity Credit Corporation 264
Conference of Wheat Exporting and Importing Countries 28, 263
consumption: declining revenue 1; fertilizer 143; food consumption 59, 128, 181, 268; in France 5; low-income section 115; market 165, *165,* **165**; in Mexico 208, 210–11, 217, 220; Milanese urban market 86; in Spain 260; in Sweden 173–4, 179–81, 267–8; in Switzerland 241–3, *242,* 246, 248–50; in UK 59; in US 7, 22, 24, 266
'contrary trends,' existence of 13
Coolidge, Calvin 31, 266
corn: in Argentina 97, 101, *102,* 106; British abolition of the Corn Laws 44; cotton-wheat-corn coalition 32, 35; in Hungary 143–4, 150, 262–3; as leading commodities, 1929–37 23, **24**; in Mexico 210–13, 217; in Midwest 259; in Sweden 268; in US 30; *see also* maize
cotton: cotton-wheat-corn coalition 32, 35; in Greece 127, 131–2; as leading commodities, 1929–37 23, **24**; in Mexico 207, 210–11, 217; in Turkey 126, 131–2; in United States 4–5, 7, 30, 32, 259, 261–2, 267
counter-revolutionary governments 142
Court, A. 71
Crash of 1929 *see* Great Depression

dekulakization 30, 35
Delli Gatti, D. 85
Diaz Alejandro, C. F. 97
Diaz, Porfirio 209, 215
Djenderedjian, J. 260
Dust Bowl problem 267

Economic Committee of the League of Nations 23
ejido 213, 216, 217, 219, 221n6, 270
Enfield, R. R. 72
Europe: Argentine agriculture, 1930s crisis 108, *108*; beef 73, 256; butter 73, 256; European Community 11; European Rural History Conference 2; European War 115; immigration 108, *108*; internal controls in 268–70; wheat in 256, 268

Farm Security Administration 264
Fascism 3, 9; activism of 77; German 21
Federal Intermediate Credit Banks (FICBs) 264
Federal Land Banks (FLB) 263–4
Federico, G. 6, 8, 11, 61
fertilizers 25, 143, 160–1, 163, 207, 230
Firbank, R. 71
First World War 1, 3–4, 6, 11, 29, 59, 61, 73, 97, 139, 155, 157, 172, 198, 236–7, 240, 245
Five-Year plan (1928) 21, 30, 271
food regime crisis: commodity flows 22–7; and (inter-)national transition pathways, 1925–39 22–34; regulatory institutions 27–34; theory 21–2
Four-Year Plan (1936) 33

France, 1930s crisis: controversial diagnosis 224–6; 'L'Office du blé' 230–2; new collective mobilizations and new laws 226–9; problem of wheat 224, 227, 261
Franciosa, L. 83
Franco regime: autarchy, black market and technological backwardness 48–50; exception of Spain 39
French Wars 13
Friedmann, H. 8

General Agreement of Tariffs and Trade 22, 34
Geneva Conference 129, 130
German agriculture: Fascism 21; importer of wheat and rye 60; markets 131, **131**; National Socialist Revolution 21; New Order 33–4, 270; unprocessed tobacco imports 131, **131**; wheat trade, 1924–38 *34*
Gömbös, Gyula 148–50
Gomez Marte, R. 216
Gonzalez Calleja, E. 200
grain: 'battle for grain' *(battaglia del grano)* 77, 84, 88, 93, 94, 268, 270; in Bulgaria 118; 1928 First Five-Year Plan 30, 271; in France 224–6, 228–32, 269; Greek farmers 128; in Hungary 141, 144, 147, 148; international grain prices 29, 47; in Italy 88–9; in Poland 157–60, 164, 262; in Sweden 171, 174–5, 180–1, 185, 267; in Switzerland 237; in UK 60, 64; in US 3–7, 22, 31, 122, 258
Grain Bureau program 269
The Grapes of Wrath (Steinbeck) 1
Great Depression 9–12; in 1929 1–2, 22–3, 59; on Argentine economy 98, 100–2, 105–6, 110–11; crisis of global food regime 21–2; in Hungary 144, 151; of late nineteenth century 89; in Mexico 206, 214; in South-eastern Europe 115, 120, 121–5, 132 (*see also* tobacco); in Spain 190–3; in Switzerland 241; of thirties 10, 48; 'wheat problem' (*see* wheat); *see also individual countries*
'Great Discontinuity' 24
The Great Transformation 21
Greece: banking sector in 133; cotton in 127, 131–2; foreign trade of 123, *124*; grain 128; indexes of agricultural acreage and production 128, **129**; price index in *125*, 125; tobacco 8, 123, *124*, 125, *125*, 262, 265; wheat in **129**
'Green Revolution' in 1930s 36
Gross Domestic Product (GDP) 115

Hitler, Adolf 21, 33, 150
Horthy, Miklós 141, 148
Hungary's dual agriculture, 1929 crisis: agricultural land area by land use categories 144, *144*; average yield of main cereals 143, *143*; changing crisis management 147–51; duality of farm structure 138; evolution of day labour wages in Pengős 145, *145*; land distribution 138, *140*; majority of peasant society 146–7; origin of dual structure 140–2; population and number of employees in agriculture 138, *138*; population per 100 active agricultural employees 138, *139*; production of main cereals 143, *143*; share of agricultural employees 138, *139*; survival and adaptation strategies 142–7
hunger supply 160

Imperial Economic Conference *see* Ottawa Agreements Act
Import Duties Act 67
inorganic/chemical fertilisers 42
International Wheat Agreement 29
Irwin, D. 261, 262
Italian agriculture, 1930s recession: agrarian and forestry area (Afa) 83, **84**; agricultural capitalism of the Low Po Valley 80–1; agricultural production per groups of crops and macro-areas 86, **87**; agricultural zones 95n1; clusters 80–2, *82*; disaggregation of 80; GDP and added value 78, *78*; general considerations 93–5; 'high farming' 77; marked heterogeneity of 77; markets and policies 86–9; national and international (import) wheat prices 83, *83*; 1931 Population Census 80; population growth, mobility, and efficiency 90, **91**; Principal Component Analysis 80; relevance of mobility 89–93; in 1930s recession 78–82; variation in agricultural output of Afa 91, *92*; wheat yields and cultivated areas 1929 and 1938 88, *89*; wholesale price index 78, *79*; winners and losers in recession 82–5; workers per sector 78, *79*

Janicki, Tadeusz 9, 260

Karolyi, Gyula 148
Kopsidis, M. 132, 141
Kouri, E. 218

land reclamation: in Argentina 98–9, 103–4; Atlantic trading network 270–2; in Hungary 138, *140,* 140–7, *144,* 149–50, 265; in Italy 80, 84, 91; in Mexico 207–8, 210, 212–21; in Poland 155–6, 160, 162; in South-eastern Europe 117, 119, 126–9, 132–3; in Spain 45, 47–50, 191–3, 196–202, 259–60; in Sweden 173, 183, 267; in Switzerland 250–1; in UK 59, 71; in US 6, 25, 263–4
Land Reform Act 271
Langthaler, E. 8, 255, 261, 271
League of Nations Economic Committee 67
Leith Ross, Frederick 72
Leuven: European Rural History Conference 2
London World Economic Conference 28, 130
Long Depression of 1873–96 *see* Great Depression

maize: in Hungary *143*; in Mexico 207–10; in Sweden 181, 268; in UK 61, **61,** 62, **63,** 64; in US 4, 7; *see also* corn
Martiren, J. L. 260
McDougall, F. L. 73
McMichael, P. 8
McNary-Haugen bill 265–6
Meat/mutton 60, **60,** 62, 64: in Poland 160; in Spain 49, 51; in Sweden 173–4, 197; in Switzerland 244–6, 249–50; in UK 60–5, **61, 62, 63,** 67–8; in US 22
Mexican agriculture: agrarian reform 215–19; bean production 211, *211*; crisis of 1929 210–14; indices of agricultural production value 212, **212**; overall agriculture production 211, *212*; revolutionary crisis 3, 206–10, 213, 262
MidWest 4, 259
Miguez, E. 97
milk: 'Milk propaganda' 186n5; in Norway 186n4; in Poland 158, 162; in Sweden 174–5, 179–83, 186n10, 267–8; in Switzerland 236–8, 240–7, *242, 245,* **248,** *249,* 250–2, 262, 268–70; in UK 68–71
Monnet, G. 229, 231
Morell, M. 9, 267
Morettini, G. 260

National Debt Relief Act 126, 265
Nazi regime 33–6, 130, 270; *see also* German agriculture
New Economic Policy (1921) 29, 271

Odhner, C.- E. 178
Old Regime, crisis of *see Ancien Régime*
Orwin, C. S. 59, 60, 66, 72
Ottawa Agreements Act 68

Pan-Montojo, Juan 9, 260
Paterson, Rex 71
Paxton, R. O. 232
Perier, Jean 214
Perren, R. 73
pigmeat/pork: in Sweden 175, 180–1, 267–8; in Switzerland 245–6; in UK 60, **60,** 62
Pinilla, V. 8, 46, 225
Polanyi, K. 8, 21, 36; Polanyian perspective 21
Polish agriculture, 1929–35 crisis: agriculture in interwar Poland 155–7; causes of agricultural crisis 158; changes in structure and agricultural production 162–4; decline in income and financial problems 158–60, **159**; decline in purchases of industrial products and autarkization of rural economy 160–2, *161*; farm animals 163, **163**; market consumption index 165, *165,* **165**; peasant workshops in farm 166n3; social problems 164–5; 'superfluous people' 164; yield of major field crops 163, **163**
Popular Front: creation of Grain Bureau 230; in France 3; *Office national interprofessionnel du ble* in 1936 7, 224; victory of 200
prices: Bulgaria *125,* 125; formation processes 44; in Greece *125,* 125; of imported unprocessed tobacco leaves in US 120, *121*; internal attempts to control prices and output 265–70; international grain prices 29, 47; Italian agriculture, 1930s recession 78, *79,* 83, *83*; price-guarantee 243; Switzerland,

1920s and 1930s crises 247–50, **248,** *249*; in Turkey *125,* 125; in UK 61, **61**; in US 120, *121*; wheat *27*

real inheritance system 140
Reciprocal Trade Agreement Act 263
reclamation campaign 88, 268
Reich Food Estate (RFE) 270
residual 111n4
rice: in Italy 81, 84, 88, 90, 262; as leading commodities, 1929–37 23, **24**; in Mexico 207, 211
Riksforbundet landsbygdens folk (RLF) 179
Roosevelt, Franklin D. 21, 31, 32, 35, 40, 129, 230, 264
Rooth, T. 66
Rothstein, B. 183
Rowntree, B. 66
rubber 23, **24,** 255
Rural Electrification Administration 264
ruralism 88
'rural Italies' *see* Italian agriculture, 1930s recession
Russian Revolution 29
rye 60, **60,** *143,* 148, 150, 158, 262–3, 269

Saltsjobadsavtalet agreement (1938) 184
Sanchez, Guadalupe 217
Second Republic 3, 190–1, 193, 195, 199, 202
Second World War 9, 11, 41, 60, 61, 73, 133, 237, 240
silk 23, **24,** 81, 255
Simpson, J. 9, 47, 220, 260, 271
Sirol, J. 230
'smallholders debts' 149
Smoot-Hawley Tariff Act 261–2
Snowdon, H. N. 71
Soil Conservation and Domestic Allotment Act (1936) 32, 266
Soviet Great Break 29–30
Soviet Socialism 21
Spanish agriculture: Agrarian crisis in 1930s 46–8; agricultural crisis of Ancien Régime 42–3; agricultural exports 194, **194, 195**; autarchy, black market and technological backwardness of Franco regime 48–50; and crisis 193–5; Civil War 272; crisis of 1847 44; end-of-the-century depression 44–6; on eve of Great Depression 191–3; final crisis of traditional agriculture 50–1; integration of world agricultural product markets 44–6; limits to government intervention during Second Republic (1931–6) 190–1, 195–9; nature of regional farming 193, **193**; persistence of food crises 43–4; popular mobilisation, social coalitions, and agricultural policies 199–201; technological change 41
Steinbeck, John: *The Grapes of Wrath* 1
Stiglitz, J. E. 2, 8, 11, 59
stock market 1–2, 10, 121
Street, A. G. 68, 70, 71
'structural deflation' 25
sugar: in Hungary 140, 146; in Italy 81, 86, 88, 262; as leading commodities, 1929–37 23, **24**; in Mexico 207, 209–11, 215, 217; in Poland 161; in Sweden 171, 175; in UK 60, 62; in US 259, 261
Swedish agriculture, 1930s crisis: agricultural crisis and recovery 175–8; comparisons with Scandinavia and beyond 184–5; creation of agricultural regulations 180–1; crisis policy and crisis agreement of 1933 181–2; crisis, regulated market and corporatist welfare state 182–4; in early twentieth century 172–3; economic and agricultural development in 1920s 173–5; internal controls in 267–8; 'Milk propaganda' 186n5; organisational efforts in 1920s 178–80
Swedish dairies (SMR) 267
Switzerland, 1920s and 1930s crises: arguments in favour of increasing cereal production at expense of milk production 237–9, *239*; butter production and imports 243, **243**; collateral damage for cattle breeders and meat market 244–6, *245*; declining hard cheese exports 246–8, **247, 248**; demise of condensed milk exports 244–6, *245*; diversification of agricultural production 237–9; food prices 248, *249*; indebted farmers and state interventions 250–2; long-term effects of interwar measures 252; production costs and domestic prices 248–50; Protectionism up to World Crisis 239–41; reorientation of dairy sector and related chain reactions 241–4, *242*

Tardieu, Andre 227
'Third World' 22
tobacco: agricultural-export economies 118; economies before crisis 119–21; export of oriental tobacco 118, *118, 120*; export reorientation and introverted growth in late 1930s 130–2; fundamental policy regime shift 133; in German markets 131, **131**; imports in US 131, **131,** 259, 261; initial negative effects of the world crisis 125–9; in Italy 81, 92; as leading commodities 23, **24**; long-term financial and demo-economic constraints 115–18; in Poland 161; policy reactions to Great Depression 121–5; price of imported unprocessed tobacco leaves in US 120, *121*; shock transmission mechanisms 121–5; tax revenues 118; trade of Greece, Bulgaria and Turkey 8, 123, *124,* 125, *125,* 262, 265; in UK 60; value of imports and exports 122, **123**
Tortolero, A. 9
Total Factor Productivity (TFP) 98, 102–4, 106, 110
Tracy, M. 61
transition theory 21–2
Trianon peace treaty 148–9
Turkey: agricultural production and acreage 127, **128**; basic indexes of agricultural acreage and production 133, **134**; deaths and widespread material destruction 116; foreign trade of 123, *124*; indexes of per capita GDP growth in interwar period 116, *116*; League of Nations 117; price index in *125,* 125

Union of Cheese Sellers and Trade (USCF) 241
Union of Milk Producers (UCPL) 241
Union of Soviet Socialist Republics 6, 8, 257–8, 271
Union of Swiss Farmers 237–9
United Kingdom (UK), 1929 crisis: changing agricultural policies 67–9; crop areas and outputs in Great Britain 69, **69**; explaining changes in trade 65–6; Germany, importer of wheat and rye 60; grass area and livestock population in Great Britain 70, **70**; impact on agriculture 69–71; imports as percentage of total world exports 60, **60**; as major world agricultural importer 59–65; physical quantities of UK imports 62, **63**; sources of imports 62, **63**; 'state-led agricultural revolution' 36; UK import costs 62, **62**; USA – production and exports 64, **64**; World and UK product price indices 61, **61**
United States (US): banking sector 263–5; beef 4; consumption in 7, 22, 24, 266; corn in 30; credit policies in 263–5; domestic farm policies 265–7; grain in US 3–7, 22, 31, 122, 258; land reclamation 6, 25, 263–4; maize 4, 7; meat 22; New Deal 30–2; price of imported unprocessed tobacco leaves 120, *121*; prices 120, *121*; sugar in US 259, 261; tobacco 131, **131,** 259, 261; unprocessed tobacco imports 131, **131**
USF (Union Suisse du commerce *de* fromage) 246, 247, 253n1

Valenti, G. 77
valorisation schemes 11
Varga, Z. 9

wheat: acreage, production, stocks and prices, 1923–32 *27*; in Argentine 97, 101, *102,* 106; Battle of 3, 7, 268; in Bulgaria 126; cotton-wheat-corn coalition 32, 35; in Denmark 262; in Europe 256, 268; exports by selected countries, 1924–38 **26**; in France 224–7, 231–2; "gentlemen's agreement" 263; in Germany, 1924–38 33, *34*; in Greece **129**; in Hungary *143,* 143–6, 148, 150, 262, 269; imports by selected countries, 1924–38 **26, 28**; international cooperation 27–9; in Italy 80, *83,* 85, 88–9, *89,* 92, 94, 262; as leading commodities, 1929–37 23, **24**; in Mexico 208, 211, 213; in Poland 158, **163,** 262; price formation processes 44; problem 24–5, 28, 29; in Soviet Union, 1924–38 *31*; in Spain 45, 47, 192, 194, **194,** 198; in Sweden 174, 180, 267–8; in Switzerland 249; in Turkey 127, **128, 134**; in UK **60,** 60–2, **61, 62, 63,** 64–9, **69,** 73–4; in United States 4–6, 9, 10, 30–2, *31, 32,* 258–9, 261, 263, 266; 1932 Wheat Act 67, 69; World trade, 1929–37 *25*
Womack, J. 207
wool 23, **24,** 60, 67, 106, 255, 261
'the world crisis' *see* Great Depression